National Audubon Society
Field Guide to
North American Mammals

A Chanticleer Press Edition

National Audubon Society
Field Guide to
North American Mammals

John O. Whitaker, Jr.,
Professor of Life Sciences,
Indiana State University

Robert Elman, text consultant

Visual key by Carol Nehring

Alfred A. Knopf, New York

This is a Borzoi Book
Published by Alfred A. Knopf, Inc.
Copyright © 1980 by Chanticleer Press,
Inc. All rights reserved under
International and Pan-American
Copyright Conventions. Published in the
United States by Alfred A. Knopf, Inc.,
New York, and simultaneously in Canada
by Random House of Canada Limited,
Toronto. Distributed by Random House,
Inc., New York.

Prepared and produced by
Chanticleer Press, Inc., New York.

Color reproductions by Cliche + Litho,
AG, Zurich, Switzerland.
Type set in Garamond by Dix Type Inc.,
Syracuse, New York.
Printed and bound in Japan.

Published December 1980
Tenth Printing, July 1994

Library of Congress Catalog Card
Number 79-3525
ISBN 0-394-50762-2

CONTENTS

Contents

John O. Whitaker, Jr., is Professor of
Life Sciences at Indiana State
University, where he teaches courses in
animal ecology, vertebrate zoology,
mammalogy, and herpetology. Over
the past 20 years he has written over
100 technical and popular articles on
the food, habits, reproduction, and
parasites of our native North American
fauna. He is co-author, with W. J.
Hamilton, Jr., of *Mammals of the
Eastern United States* (2nd Ed.) and
co-author, with R. E. Mumford, of
Mammals of Indiana, soon to be
published by Indiana University Press.

ACKNOWLEDGEMENTS

This book would not have been possible without the many research papers and books on North American mammals. Particular thanks is due Chris Maser for allowing use of his unpublished "Mammals of Western Oregon." Robert Elman served as text consultant and was especially helpful with the carnivore accounts. Angus Cameron also made valuable contributions. Sydney Anderson reviewed the photographs and helped develop the thumb tab guide. My wife Royce read and greatly improved many of the species accounts. Laura Bakken typed drafts of the text and contributed helpful suggestions.

I also owe a great debt to William J. Hamilton, Jr., for his advice and encouragement throughout graduate school and the ensuing years as well as to my parents and my family for their help, support, and patience throughout.

The personnel of Chanticleer Press have been a pleasure to work with. I would like to thank Paul Steiner, the publisher, and Gudrun Buettner and Milton Rugoff for their creative support and guidance. I am particularly grateful to Anne Knight, Richard Christopher, Susan Rayfield, and Susan Linder. I also want to credit Carol Nehring, Helga

Lose, Ray Patient, and Dean Gibson for their special efforts in the production of this book. Finally, I would like to thank the photographers whose pictures make this guide to North American mammals not only unique, but a thing of beauty.

John O. Whitaker, Jr.

INTRODUCTION

The mammals of North America make up one of the most diverse and fascinating groups of wildlife in the world. However, one cannot go mammal-watching as one goes bird-watching—for the simple reason that most mammals are nocturnal, secretive, and make few sounds audible to our ears. In a morning's walk on our 40-acre tract of woods at Brazil, Indiana, we can expect to see perhaps five species of wild mammals—Fox Squirrels, Eastern Chipmunks, Eastern Cottontails, Woodchucks, and, on the pond, Muskrats. If we are very lucky we will see a deer. But we may see or hear as many as 30 species of birds and 10 species of amphibians and reptiles. Nevertheless, many kinds of mammals are present on the 40 acres. If we pound with a stick on the bases of enough dead upright stumps containing woodpecker holes we are likely to drive out a Southern Flying Squirrel. Raccoon tracks are abundant in the mud around small streams and pools and in depressions that have recently contained water. In the dusty road along the edge, Opossum tracks are often discernible. Droppings of rabbits are common and those of deer may occasionally be seen. Ridges of earth pushed up by the Eastern Mole cross

GREENLAND
BAFFIN BAY
HUDSON BAY
MB
NF
ON
QU
NB
NS
ME
MN
WI
VT
NH
MA
NY
MI
CT
RI
IA
PA
NJ
IN
OH
IL
MD
DE
ATLANTIC OCEAN
WV
VA
MO
KY
NC
K
TN
AR
SC
MS
AL
GA
LA
FL
GULF OF MEXICO
CARIBBEAN SEA

lawns, flower beds, and sometimes woodland clearings. If one looks closely, one may find discarded black cherry pits, caches of stored food, or burrows under tree roots—all made by the White-footed Mouse. In wooded areas, poking one's finger into leaf mold may disclose the round burrows of Woodland Voles. Often near moist logs are found burrows of the Short-tailed Shrew, and under the lips of banks along streams or roadways are tiny pathways made by other shrews. Seeing a small mammal that is rare can give one as much pleasure as sighting a new species of bird.

We have designed this guide to help you learn the ways of mammals—their behavior, breeding habits and range, as well as tracks and other evidence that mark their presence when they cannot be seen. If you are patient and learn to be alert for these signs, you will soon get to know the species found in your area.

It is our hope that the many color photographs, drawings, and our unique range charts, as well as the descriptive text for each species, will stimulate a lifelong interest in mammal-watching.

Geographical Scope

Since this guide is intended primarily for field use, we have included in it all the land-dwelling or land-breeding species of wild mammals found in North America north of Mexico. Whales and their kin are mammals, too, but they are ocean-dwelling species and therefore beyond the scope of this guide.

Photographs as a Guide to Identification

This is the first field guide to present mammals in full-color photographs rather than in paintings. These photographs are not only beautiful and true to nature but also show mammals in their natural setting and often engaged in characteristic behavior. We believe that these photographs contribute a new and exciting dimension to identification in the field. In a few instances, when a good photograph was unobtainable, a drawing accompanies the species description.

Organization of the Color Plates Unlike other field guides, in which mammals are arranged in scientific order by families, we have arranged them according to size, shape, and color—the features one notices in the field. Thus, the group called Shrews includes the Shrew-mole, a mole that more resembles shrews. Similarly, the group called Tree Squirrels contains the Bushy-tailed Woodrat, which has the characteristic fluffy tail of tree squirrels. Armored Mammals includes the unrelated Porcupine and the Nine-banded Armadillo because of their unique adaptations for defense against predators. Similarly, we have placed the skunks and the Raccoon with the Coati, Ringtail, Opossum, Wolverine, and Badger because all are of medium size and have distinctive body markings.

The color plates are arranged as follows:

Chipmunks, Ground Squirrels, and Prairie Dogs
Pocket Gophers and Moles
Shrews
Voles, Lemmings, and Pikas
Rats and Mice
Bats
Tree Squirrels
Skunks, the Raccoon, and the Badger
Weasel-like Mammals
Armored Mammals
Muskrats, Marmots, and Beavers
Hares and Rabbits
Foxes, Wolves, and the Coyote
Cats
Pig-like Mammals
Hoofed Mammals
Bears
Sea Lions, Seals, and the Walrus

Silhouette and Thumb Tab Guide
The organization of the color plates is explained in a table preceding them. A silhouette of one of the most typical members of a group appears on the left. Silhouettes of the mammals within that group are shown on the right. For example, the group Voles, Lemmings, and Pikas is represented by a silhouette of a Brown Lemming. This representative silhouette is repeated in a thumb tab on the left edge of each double page of color plates devoted to that group of mammals.

Captions
The captions under the photographs give the plate number, common name of each species (or subspecies), total body length from tip of nose to tip of tail, and page number of the text description. For larger animals, height at the shoulder may also be included. The animal's sex is given for those species in which it can be determined visually.

Track Guide
A unique guide to mammal tracks follows the Silhouette and Thumb Tab Guide. Tracks are arranged according to shape in the following groups:

Hand- and Foot-like
Bird-like
Hand-like
Pads with 5 Toes
Pads with 4 Toes
Foot-like
Hoofed

The group of Hand- and Foot-like tracks is divided into those with 4-toed foreprints and 5-toed hindprints, such as the Norway Rat's, and those with fore and hind prints both having 5 toes, such as the Muskrat's. Tracks of Pads with 4 Toes are divided into those with and without claw marks; canids, or dog-like mammals, leave tracks with claw marks while cats do not. Foot-like tracks are made by such diverse animals

How to Measure Mammals

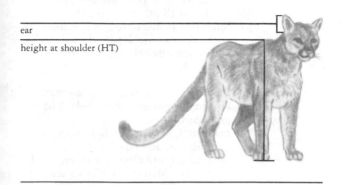

ear

height at shoulder (HT)

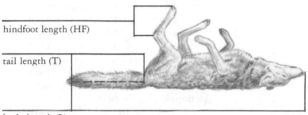

hindfoot length (HF)

tail length (T)

body length (L)

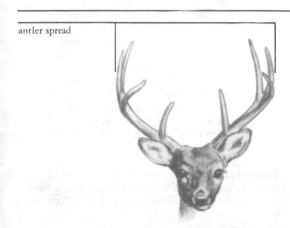

antler spread

as the Gray Squirrel and the Grizzly Bear. In the group Hand- and Foot-like tracks we show both fore and hind prints. In all other groups, the hindprint is illustrated. A familiarity with the basic track patterns will enable you to identify the sign of many mammals.

Classification of Mammals
Biologists divide plants and animals into major groups called phyla. The phylum Chordata includes all mammals, as well as fishes, birds, amphibians, and reptiles. Phyla are divided into classes, with mammals in the class Mammalia. Classes are subdivided into orders, orders into families, families into genera (singular: genus), and genera into species (singular: species). The species is the basic unit of our classification system and is generally what people have in mind when they talk about a "kind" of animal. A species is a population of animals that possesses common characteristics and freely interbreeds in nature to produce fertile offspring. Although species occasionally crossbreed, the hybrid offspring are often sterile or partially so.
The scientific name of a species consists of two Latin or Latinized words. The first word, the generic name, is capitalized; the second, the specific name, is not. Thus, in the name of the Meadow Jumping Mouse, *Zapus hudsonius, Zapus* is the genus and *hudsonius* the species.
The classification of mammals in this guide is based on the *Revised Checklist of North American Mammals North of Mexico,* 1979, by Jones, Carter, and Genoways, published by Texas Tech University.

Types of Mammals
In the class Mammalia there are 19 orders that contain living species. Nine of these orders occur in North America north of Mexico:

Order	Number of Species
Marsupials	1
Shrews and Moles	37
Bats	40
Edentates	1
Lagomorphs	19
Rodents	200
Carnivores	54
Sea Cows	1
Ungulates	15
Total Species	368

Organization of the Text The text describes mammals in taxonomic order, according to their scientific classification. Within each order, the families, genera, and species are arranged in phylogenetic sequence, beginning with the most primitive mammals and ending with the most advanced. The one exception is the group sea lions, seals, and the Walrus, which until recently were classed in the separate order Pinnipedia, but are now placed within the order Carnivora. In our text these aquatic carnivores are grouped together following the land-dwelling carnivores.

Each species description includes the following information:

Names Listed first is the common name as given in the Texas Tech University checklist (1979). However, for *Ovis canadensis* we have retained the familiar name Bighorn Sheep rather than Mountain Sheep, and for *Ovis dalli* the more common form Dall Sheep rather than Dall's Sheep. If a species has alternate common names, the most familiar are also given, within quotation marks. The scientific name of a species, shown below the common name, is italicized.

Related Species Following the species name we occasionally give the names of other species (or subspecies) that are closely related to it but not sufficiently different to warrant a separate account. In many cases they are the subject of dispute as to whether they merit the status of species or subspecies.

Description This paragraph describes the mammal, including color, distinctive markings, and anatomical features. In bats, these features include the interfemoral membrane, calcar (a spur on the wing), and tragus (a projection at the base of the external opening of the ear). Key identification characteristics are italicized. For some of the smaller mammals, such as shrews and rodents, species are identified on the basis of dental patterns. Measurements (given in both English and metric systems) include length from tip of nose to end of tail (L), length of tail (T), length of hindfoot from heel to tip of longest toenail (HF), and weight (Wt). Ear measurement, when given, is from notch to tip. For bats, the length of the forearm (FA) is given and, occasionally, the length of the tragus.

Similar Species Here we briefly identify other species that may be confused with the one being described. (Those that can be distinguished by geographic range are not included.) Unlike related species, each similar species is described in full elsewhere in the book.

Sign The evidence that a particular animal is or has been in a particular area is called "sign." Sign can take many forms, including tracks in mud or snow, scat (fecal matter), burrows and burrow openings, food remnants and caches, mud slides, houses and nests. Description of sign, especially of the larger carnivores and the hoofed mammals, may include the following information:
Scat: Color, shape, consistency, contents, and where most likely to be found.

Dental Patterns

Shrews

side view

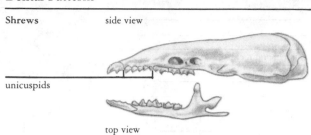

unicuspids

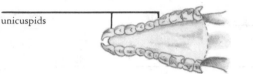

top view

unicuspids

Microtine Rodents

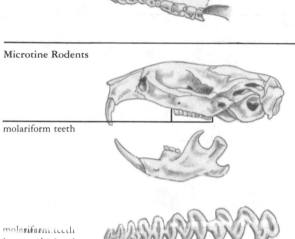

molariform teeth

molariform teeth
loops and triangles

Cricetine Rodents

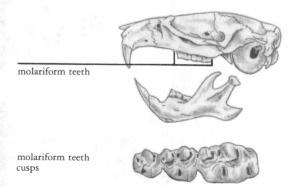

molariform teeth

molariform teeth
cusps

Parts of a Bat

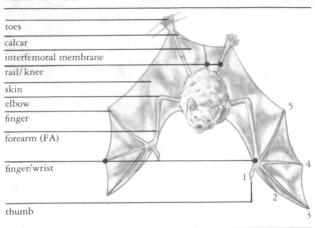

toes
calcar
interfemoral membrane
tail/ knee
skin
elbow
finger
forearm (FA)

finger/wrist

thumb

5

4

1

2

3

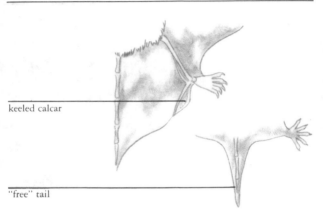

keeled calcar

"free" tail

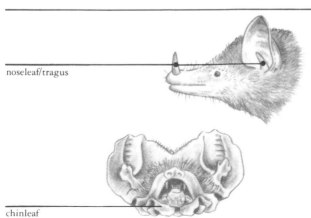

noseleaf/tragus

chinleaf

Tracks: Fore and hind print size and shape; straddle (width between prints); walking or running stride (distance between sets of prints); and distinguishing marks, such as claw impressions or tail drag. Accompanying this description are drawings of foreprint (at left), hindprint (at right), and typical walking track. Unless otherwise indicated, tracks represent impressions made in firm mud.

Breeding When breeding habits apply to all species in a family, they are described in the family introduction. When breeding information is unique to a particular mammal, it is included in the species account.

Habitat All mammals are restricted to certain natural areas—called habitats—depending on the type of vegetation, soil, air, rainfall, light intensity, and food they favor. An animal with a specialized diet can live only where the food it eats is found. Some species, such as the Deer Mouse, have adapted to many habitats; others, such as the Water Shrew, are confined to a narrow range. Where habitats grade into one another, mammalian communities also tend to merge. The following are the major North American habitats and some of the mammals found in them.

Woodlands: There are essentially two major types of forests in North America. The coniferous forest, composed of fir, spruce and pine, is home to Moose, Mule Deer, and Snowshoe Hares, which browse the needles; squirrels, Martens, and Fishers live in the trees. Lynx, wolves, and Wolverines are major predators. Maple, oak, beech, and other trees that shed their leaves in fall are common trees of the deciduous woods. Many mammals thrive in this habitat, where more varied food is available and the winters are less severe. Among them are Black Bears, Bobcats, foxes, Raccoons, skunks, chipmunks, and many kinds of mice, which occupy a labyrinth of tunnels in the leaf mold of the forest floor.

Grasslands: This habitat covers the center of the continent, where rainfall is too scarce for trees to grow but sufficient to prevent deserts from forming. Grasses provide the basic food for many mammals, ranging from pocket gophers and jack rabbits to the larger grazing animals, such as Pronghorn and Bison.

Arid Areas: Although one might expect the great arid areas—the shortgrass prairies and deserts of the West—to harbor few mammals, a variety have adapted to conditions of limited vegetation and little free water. Many store food and obtain water from vegetation either directly or by metabolizing it. Many mammals have light colors that blend with the landscape and fringes on their toes that help them move through the loose sand. Most are nocturnal, preferring to be about when the air is cooler and when there may be dew on the ground. Kangaroo mice and pocket mice live here, as well as jack rabbits and ground squirrels. The major predators include the Badger, Coyote, and Black-footed Ferret, a rare marauder in prairie dog towns. Deer and Pronghorn inhabit the moister edges of this habitat.

Wetlands: Ponds, marshes, and swamps support a variety of aquatic mammals, including the Beaver, Muskrat, Nutria, and rice rats. Most eat the leaves and roots of wetland vegetation as well as crayfish, clams, snails, and small fish. The most common predator is the Mink, but foxes, Raccoons, and Coyotes stalk the edges. In the Northeast, the Star-nosed Mole can be found in mucky areas.

Streams and Lakes: Beavers build their dams along small streams and may live in the banks of larger ones. Water Shrews live along tumbling mountain

brooks in the North and Northwest.
Oceans: The ocean supports billions of planktonic organisms, which feed both fish and larger ocean-dwelling mammals such as seals, whales, and the Walrus. Through the eons, these mammals have evolved streamlined shapes and flippers that enable them to swim swiftly through the water in pursuit of fish and other food. Their chief predator in arctic waters is the Polar Bear.
Tundra: This vast, treeless plain stretches from timberline north to the polar icecap. Vegetation is limited to lichens and other low-growing plants, which form the principal food of such mammals as Caribou, Muskoxen, lemmings, shrews, and Arctic Hares. These, in turn, are preyed upon by wolves and the Arctic Fox.
Other North American Habitats: These include talus slopes, where long-tailed shrews and pikas live; mountains, where Bighorn Sheep and Mountain Goats make their home; and cultivated areas, where many rodent species, such as the Deer Mouse and House Mouse, forage among corn, wheat, and soybean crops

Range Each species account includes a geographical range. A range map is also provided except for a few species that have an extremely limited range north of Mexico. Within its range a species will not be evenly distributed, and the various areas it occupies may be separated by many miles. As an additional aid, unique range charts in the appendices give range by state or province for many genera of the smaller mammals that are difficult to identify by sight alone.

Comment The account concludes with information on the mammal's behavior and life history. We also mention any closely related species that are similar in appearance to the animal described but which occupy only a limited range.

How to Find Mammals

Because most mammals are extremely secretive, the best way to find them and learn about them is by looking for and examining their sign.

1. Observe their tracks in snow, sand, or mud. Follow the tracks and attempt to determine which mammal made them and what it was doing. Discovering that it climbed a tree or entered a burrow will help you to identify it.

2. Look for runways among vegetation, especially in thick grass. See if there are associated burrow entrances, piles of fecal pellets, or plant cuttings, such as cut grass. Type of burrow entrance, scat, and cuttings can aid in identifying many small mammals such as voles and harvest mice.

3. Search for food remnants and caches. Grass or twig cuttings, parts of seeds or nuts, pieces of cattail or other aquatic plants, partially eaten mammals, and food caches, such as piles of black cherry pits or other seeds, pine cones, or snails, will help in identification.

4. Set a grid pattern of live traps; capture, mark with a non-harmful substance, and then release small mammals. Be sure to supply plenty of food and nesting material in traps and check them every few hours so that captured animals do not starve or die from exposure. Live traps can be purchased or cheaply made from ordinary snap-back mousetraps and tin cans. Remove one end of the can and wire the trap to the inside so that the treadle and half the trap protrudes. Wire a piece of hardware cloth to the metal wire so that if an animal steps on the treadle it will spring up and close the can without injuring the animal. Tin cans may also be sunk into the ground to serve as pitfalls. Put them under logs or in thick vegetation, but be sure to cover them in rainstorms and keep them free of accumulated water to

prevent animals from drowning. These devices make it possible to determine the area an animal frequents and the habitat it prefers. Animals can be kept for a time and their behavior studied, although one cannot assume that they will behave in captivity as they do in the field.

Conservation Status Some species of North American mammals are listed by the U.S. and Canadian governments as "endangered" (in danger of becoming extinct) or "threatened" (close to becoming endangered). Both federal and state governments give full protection to these species (see the list following this introduction).

Range Charts and Glossary Unique range charts prepared for this guide help identify many of the smaller mammals that are similar in appearance. Since most of them occupy specific geographic areas, the charts often make it possible to verify an identification based on where the mammal was seen. A glossary and abbreviations of states and provinces are also located in the appendices.

LIST OF ENDANGERED AND THREATENED MAMMALS

The following list of endangered and threatened mammals of North America north of Mexico is based on official lists compiled by federal agencies of the United States and Canada.

An endangered species is one whose existence in North America is threatened with imminent extinction through all or a significant portion of its range. A threatened species is one that is likely to become endangered if the factors affecting its vulnerability are not reversed.

Endangered: Gray Myotis (*Myotis grisescens*), central and southeastern U.S.

Indiana or Social Myotis (*Myotis sodalis*), eastern and midwestern U.S.

Hawaiian Hoary Bat (*Lasiurus cinereus semotus*), Hawaii

Virginia Big-eared Bat (*Plecotus townsendii virginianus*), Kentucky, West Virginia, Virginia

Vancouver Marmot (*Marmota vancouverensis*), Canada

Utah Prairie Dog (*Cynomys parvidens*), Utah

Delmarva Peninsula Fox Squirrel (*Sciurus niger cinereus*), Maryland, Pennsylvania, Virginia

Morro Bay Kangaroo Rat (*Dipodomys heermanni morroensis*), California

Salt-marsh Harvest Mouse
(*Reithrodontomys raviventris*), California
Red Wolf (*Canis rufus*), southeastern
U.S.
Gray Wolf (*Canis lupus*), Arizona,
Indiana, Michigan, Montana, New
Mexico, North Dakota, Oregon, Texas,
Washington, Wisconsin, Wyoming
San Joaquin Kit Fox (*Vulpes macrotis
mutica*), California
Northern Swift Fox (*Vulpes velox hebes*),
northern plains of U.S., Canada
Brown or Grizzly Bear (*Ursos arctos
horriblis*), western Canada, Alaska,
Idaho, Montana, Wyoming
Black-footed Ferret (*Mustela nigripes*),
western U.S., western Canada
Sea Otter (*Enhydra lutris*), Canada
Jaguar (*Felis onca*), southwestern U.S.
Eastern Cougar (*Felix concolor couguar*)
eastern U.S. and Canada
Mountain Lion (*Felis concolor*), western
U.S., Canada
Florida Panther (*Felis concolor coryi*),
southeastern U.S.
Ocelot (*Felis pardalis*), Arizona, Texas
Jaguarundi (*Felis yagouaroundi*),
Arizona, Texas
Margay (*Felis wiedii*), southwestern
Texas
Manatee (*Trichechus manatus*),
southeastern U.S.
Columbian White-tailed Deer
(*Odocoileus virginianus leucurus*),
Washington, Oregon
Key Deer (*Odocoileus virginianus
clavium*), Florida
Sonoran Pronghorn (*Antilocapra
americana sonoriensis*), Arizona
Wood Bison (*Bison bison anthabascae*),
Canada

Threatened: Gray Wolf (*Canis lupus*), northern
Minnesota
Southern Sea Otter (*Enhydra lutris
nereis*), California
Peary Caribou (*Rangifer tarandus pearyi*),
northern Canada

HOW TO USE THIS GUIDE

Example 1 In a damp wooded area in the
Gray shrewlike southeastern part of Virginia, you
mammal with observe a uniformly gray shrewlike
short tail in mammal with a short tail foraging on
damp woods the forest floor.

1. Turn to the Silhouette and Thumb Tab
   Guide preceding the color plates.
   Among the silhouettes for shrews, you
   see that the one for Short-tailed Shrews
   (color plates 48, 56–57, 60) most
   closely resembles the specimen you
   observed.
2. Turning to the color plates, you find
   that plate 60—the Short-tailed Shrew
   —seems to match your specimen. The
   caption gives you the species length and
   the page number of the species
   description.
3. Reading the species description, you
   note that a closely related species—the
   Swamp Short-tailed Shrew—occupies
   the same range and habitat.
4. Referring to the Range Charts in the
   back of the book, you discover that the
   only shrew occurring in this part of
   Virginia is the Swamp Short-tailed
   Shrew.

Example 2 In an open wooded area in the
Tan-colored Deer northeastern U.S. you observe a tan-
with Antlers colored deer grazing in a meadow. As it
in Open Woods darts away into the woods, you note

that its antlers have a forward main
beam, and you see a flash of white as
the tail is raised.

1. In the Silhouette and Thumb Tab
   Guide you turn to the section labeled
   Hoofed Mammals. Scanning the
   silhouettes for antler patterns, you find
   that the White-tailed Deer, plate 285,
   most closely resembles what you saw.
2. Turning to the color plates, you see
   that the male White-tailed indeed
   matches the deer you observed.
3. Reading the species description
   confirms your identification.

Part I
Color Plates

Key to the Color Plates

The color plates on the following pages are divided into 18 groups:

Chipmunks, Ground Squirrels, and Prairie Dogs
Pocket Gophers and Moles
Shrews
Voles, Lemmings, and Pikas
Rats and Mice
Bats
Tree Squirrels
Skunks, the Raccoon, and the Badger
Weasel-like Mammals
Armored Mammals
Muskrats, Marmots, and Beavers
Hares and Rabbits
Foxes, Wolves, and the Coyote
Cats
Pig-like Mammals
Hoofed Mammals
Bears
Sea Lions, Seals, and the Walrus

uette and umb Tab Guide To help you learn to recognize mammals by their general shape, silhouettes of the different types of mammals within each group appear on the following pages. The silhouette that best typifies its particular group has been inset as a thumb tab at the left-hand edge of each double page of plates, thus providing a quick and convenient index to the color section.

ck Guide Since most mammals are nocturnal and reclusive, a knowledge of animal signs —that is, tracks, scat, or similar evidence—is one of the most valuable aids to identifying mammal species. The Track Guide, which follows the Silhouette and Thumb Tab Guide, will familiarize you with various types of animal tracks and the mammals that made them.

Thumb Tab	Group
	Chipmunks, Ground Squirrels, and Prairie Dogs
	Pocket Gophers and Moles
	Shrews
	Voles, Lemmings, and Pikas

Mammals		Plate Numbers
	chipmunks	1–8, 13, 14
	ground and antelope squirrels	9–12, 15–19, 22, 25–30
	prairie dogs	20, 21, 23, 24
	pocket gophers	31–36
	moles	37–42
	long-tailed shrews	43–47, 49–52, 54, 55, 58, 59
	short-tailed shrews	48, 56, 57, 60
	shrew-mole	53
	voles	61, 62, 64, 66–77

Thumb Tab	Group
	Voles, Lemmings, and Pikas
	Rats and Mice

Mammals		Plate Numbers
	lemmings	63, 65, 78
	pikas	79–81
	kangaroo rats and pocket mice	82–90, 95–97, 100–111, 115
	jumping mice	91–94
	grasshopper mice and woodrats	98, 99, 119, 131, 134, 135, 138, 139
	white-footed and pygmy mice	112, 114, 120, 124–130, 132, 133
	harvest mice	113, 116, 118, 122
	black rat and Norway rat	117, 137, 140
	rice and cotton rats	121, 136, 141
	house mouse	123

Bats

Tree Squirrels

Mammals		Plate Numbers
	big-eared bats	142–146
	leaf-nosed and ghost-faced bats	147, 154, 164, 174, 180
	free-tailed bats	148–153
	evening and myotis bats	155–163, 165–173, 175–179
	flying squirrels	181, 183, 184
	tree squirrels	182, 185–188, 191–195
	bushy-tailed woodrat	189
	rock squirrel	190, 196

Skunks, the Raccoon, and the Badger

Weasel-like Mammals

Mammals		Plate Numbers
	skunks	197–200
	ringtail, raccoon, coati, wolverine	201, 202 205, 206
	opossum	203
	badger	204
	weasels	207–210, 212, 214
	marten and fisher	211, 213
	river otter	215
	sea otter	216

Thumb Tab	Group
	Armored Mammals
	Muskrats, Marmots, and Beavers
	Hares and Rabbits

Mammals		Plate Numbers
	nine-banded armadillo	217, 218
	porcupine	219, 220
	muskrats	221, 222
	nutria	223
	beaver	224
	marmots	225–228, 230
	mountain beaver	229
	hares and jack rabbits	231–236, 239–241, 243
	cottontails and rabbits	237, 238, 242, 244–248

Thumb Tab	Group
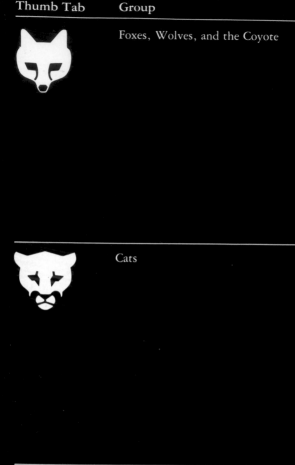	Foxes, Wolves, and the Coyote
	Cats
	Pig-like Mammals

Mammals		Plate Numbers
	foxes	249, 251–255, 257–260, 265
	wolves and coyote	250, 256, 261–264, 266
	bobcat and lynx	267–269
	mountain lion, jaguarundi, ocelot, jaguar	270–274
	wild boar	275
	peccary	276

Hoofed Mammals
(with horns)

Mammals	Plate Numbers
muskox	277
bison	278
barbary sheep	279
mountain goat	280
dall sheep	281, 282
bighorn sheep	283
pronghorn	284

Thumb Tab	Group

Hoofed Mammals
(with antlers)

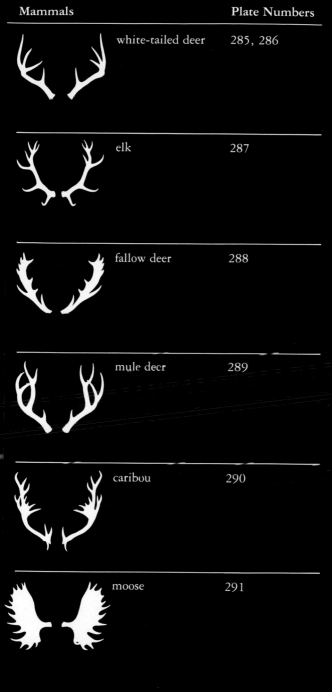

Mammals	Plate Numbers
white-tailed deer	285, 286
elk	287
fallow deer	288
mule deer	289
caribou	290
moose	291

Thumb Tab	Group
	Bears
	Sea Lions, Seals, and the Walrus

Mammals		Plate Numbers
	bears	292–296
	walrus	297
	eared seals	298–303
	elephant seal	304, 305
	hooded seal	306, 307
	hair seals	308–313

Hand- and Foot-like
(4-toed foreprints, 5-toed hindprints)

Hand- and Foot-like
(5-toed fore and hind prints)

White-footed Mouse,
p. 471

Norway Rat, *p. 518*

Round-tailed Muskrat,
p. 507

Gray Squirrel, *p. 413*

Eastern Chipmunk,
p. 372

Long-tailed Weasel,
p. 574

Muskrat, *p. 509*

Raccoon, *p. 562*

Striped Skunk, *p. 585*

Black-footed Ferret,
p. 576

Beaver, *p. 457*

Nutria, *p. 530*

Bird-like

Hand-like

Pads with 5 Toes

Meadow Vole, *p. 495*

Red Squirrel, *p. 419*

Marsh Rice Rat, *p. 464*

Northern Grasshopper Mouse, *p. 480*

White-throated Woodrat, *p. 486*

Hispid Cotton Rat, *p. 482*

Virginia Opossum, *p. 275*

Black-tailed Prairie Dog, *p. 408*

Nine-banded Armadillo, *p. 339*

River Otter, *p. 589*

Badger, *p. 581*

Coati, *p. 565*

Fisher, *p. 570*

Wolverine, *p. 579*

Eastern Spotted Skunk, *p. 583*

Mink, *p. 578*

Ringtail, *p. 560*

Marten, *p. 569*

Pads with 4 Toes
(without claws)

Pads with 4 Toes
(with claws)

Foot-like

Ocelot, *p. 599*	Lynx, *p. 602*	Jaguar, *p. 595*

Jaguarundi, *p. 601*	Bobcat, *p. 603*	Mountain Lion, *p. 596*

Gray Wolf, *p. 539*	Coyote, *p. 535*	Red Wolf, *p. 538*

Gray Fox, *p. 540*	Swift Fox, *p. 547*	Arctic Fox, *p. 542*

Polar Bear, *p. 557*	Black Bear, *p. 552*	Porcupine, *p. 527*

Hoofed

Bison, *p. 665*

Muskox, *p. 670*

Collared Peccary, *p. 643*

Bighorn Sheep, *p. 672*

Mountain Goat, *p. 668*

Pronghorn, *p. 661*

Mule Deer, *p. 651*

Wild Boar, *p. 639*

Elk, *p. 647*

White-tailed Deer, *p. 654*

Moose, *p. 656*

Caribou, *p. 658*

The color plates on the following pages are numbered to correspond with the description of each species in the text. The caption under each color plate gives the mammal's common name, size, and the number of the page on which it is described. In the instances where a mammal's gender can be determined visually, the sex of the species is also included in the caption.

Chipmunks, Ground Squirrels, and Prairie Dogs

These small to medium-size rodents have moderately bushy tails and are often brightly colored. All are active by day and most of them hibernate. Chipmunks sport light and dark stripes on face and body; their chattering helps one spot them as they scurry over the forest floor and up trees. Most ground squirrels are uniformly colored, spotted, or finely speckled; a few are striped but never on the face. All are burrowers and many live in colonies. The largest members of this group, the chunky-bodied prairie dogs, are also colonial burrowers. Unlike chipmunks, ground squirrels and prairie dogs do not climb; they are most easily observed sitting bolt upright near burrow entrances.

1   Uinta Chipmunk, 7¾–9⅝″, *p. 383*

2   Townsend's Chipmunk, 8⅞–12½″, *p. 376*

3   Lodgepole Chipmunk, 7¾–9½″, *p. 382*

4 Least Chipmunk, 6⅝–8⅞″, *p. 373*

5 Colorado Chipmunk, 7¾–9⅝″, *p. 383*

6 Yellow-pine Chipmunk, 7⅛–9⅝″, *p. 374*

7 Cliff Chipmunk, 7¾–10⅞″, *p. 379*

8 Eastern Chipmunk, 8½–11¾″, *p. 372*

9 Golden-mantled Ground Squirrel, 9⅛–12⅛″, *p. 406*

10   White-tailed Antelope Squirrel, 7⅝–9⅜″, *p. 389*

11   Harris' Antelope Squirrel, 8¼–9¼″, *p. 388*

12   Texas Antelope Squirrel, 7⅝–9⅜″, *p. 389*

13 Alpine Chipmunk, 6½–7⅞", *p. 373*

14 Merriam's Chipmunk, 8¼–11", *p. 378*

15 Thirteen-lined Ground Squirrel, 6¾–11¾", *p. 399*

16 Mexican Ground Squirrel, 11–15″, *p. 400*

17 California Ground Squirrel, 14⅛–19¾″, *p. 404*

19 Round-tailed Ground Squirrel, 8–10½", *p. 406*

20 Gunnison's Prairie Dog, 13⅜–14⅝", *p. 411*

21 White-tailed Prairie Dog, 13⅜–14⅝", *p. 411*

22 Richardson's Ground Squirrel, 9¾–14″, *p. 393*

23 Black-tailed Prairie Dog, 14–16¼″, *p. 408*

24 Utah Prairie Dog, 13⅜–14⅝″, *p. 411*

25   Townsend's Ground Squirrel, 6⅝–10¾", *p. 390*

26   Franklin's Ground Squirrel, 15–15⅝", *p. 402*

27   Belding's Ground Squirrel, 10–11¾", *p. 395*

28 Uinta Ground Squirrel, 11–11⅞″, *p. 394*

29 Columbian Ground Squirrel, 12⅞–16⅛″, *p. 397*

30 Arctic Ground Squirrel, 11¾–15¾″, *p. 398*

Pocket Gophers and Moles

Adapted for burrowing, these animals have well-developed foreclaws, small eyes and ears, and soft fur that can lie either backward or forward. Pocket gophers have thick-set bodies; characteristic rodent incisors, which are yellow and always visible; and external, fur-lined cheek "pockets," which they cram with vegetation. Moles have more streamlined bodies and eat mainly earthworms. Both are active by day and night and throughout the year but spend most of their time underground.

31 Camas Pocket Gopher, 11¾″, p. 430

32 Plains Pocket Gopher, 7⅜–14⅛″, p. 431

33 Yellow-faced Pocket Gopher, 8⅞–12⅝″, p. 433

34   Botta's Pocket Gopher, 6⅝–10¾″, p. 427

35   Northern Pocket Gopher, 6½–9¼″, p. 428

36   Southeastern Pocket Gopher, 9–13¼″, p. 433

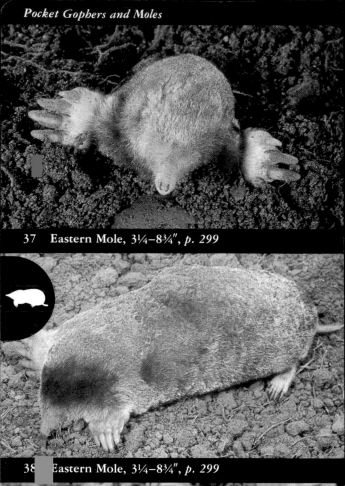

37 Eastern Mole, 3¼–8¾″, *p. 299*

38 Eastern Mole, 3¼–8¾″, *p. 299*

39 Hairy-tailed Mole, 5½–6¾″, *p. 298*

40　Broad-footed Mole, 5¼–7½″, *p. 297*

4　tar-nosed Mole, 5⅞–8¼″, *p. 300*

42　Coast Mole, 5¾–6⅞″, *p. 297*

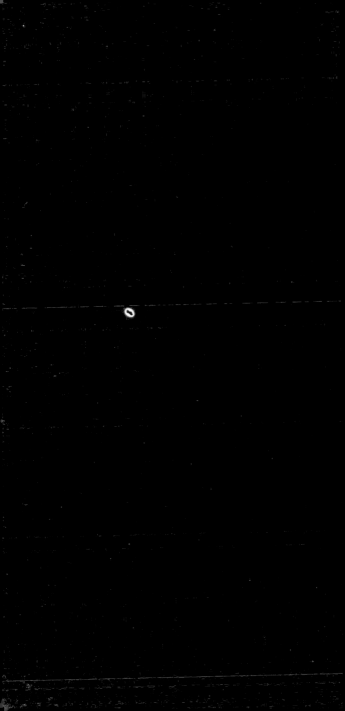

Shrews

These exceedingly active animals are
seldom seen by man and still less often
recognized. North American shrews
look so similar that they are difficult to
tell apart. All 30 North American
species are small and have soft brownish
or grayish fur, 5 clawed toes, pointed
snouts, tiny eyes, and sharp teeth with
chestnut-colored tips. Many can be
distinguished only on the basis of their
unicuspid teeth. They live in a variety
of habitats, but most species prefer
moist areas. The Shrew-mole, which
looks like a shrew and so is grouped
here with them, has white teeth and
somewhat developed forelimbs.

43 Pygmy Shrew, 3⅛–3⅞″, *p. 291*

44 Smoky Shrew, 4¼–5″, *p. 287*

45 Arctic Shrew, 4–5″, *p. 288*

46 Masked Shrew, 2¾–4⅜", *p. 280*

47 Pacific Shrew, 5⅛–6¼", *p. 283*

48 Short-tailed Shrew, 3¾–5" *brownish form*, *p. 291*

49   Ornate Shrew, 3⅜–4¼″, *p. 284*

50   Pacific Water Shrew, 5⅞–6⅞″, *p. 286*

51   Southeastern Shrew, 2⅞–4¼″, *p. 281*

52 Trowbridge's Shrew, 4⅜–5¼", *p. 289*

53 Shrew-mole, 4⅛–5", *p. 296*

54 Water Shrew, 5⅝–6¼", *p. 285*

55 Vagrant Shrew, 3¾–4¾″, *p. 282*

56 Least Shrew, 2¾–3½″, *p. 293*

57 Southern Short-tailed Shrew, 3½–5⅞″, *p. 293*

58 Long-tailed Shrew, 4⅛–5½″, p. 288

59 Desert Shrew, 3–3¾″, p. 294

60 Short-tailed Shrew, 3¾–5″, p. 291

Voles, Lemmings, and Pikas

 Voles and lemmings have small pudgy bodies; blunt faces with beady eyes; tiny, often inconspicuous ears; and short legs and tails. These rodents live in open grassy areas, although some voles prefer woodland and some lemmings seek out tundra bog. Pikas, akin to rabbits and hares, are small and stout but have rounded ears and no visible tail. These highly social creatures inhabit rocky mountain slopes, where they can be seen cutting grasses, which they dry and cure like hay.

61 Northern Red-backed Vole, 4¾–6¼", *p. 491*

62 Southern Red-backed Vole, 4¾–6¼", *p. 491*

63 Brown Lemming, 4¾–6⅝", *p. 512*

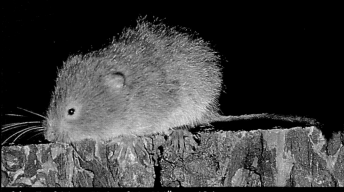

64   Red Tree Vole, 6¼–8⅛″, *p. 494*

65   Southern Bog Lemming, 4⅜–6⅛″, *p. 513*

66   Dusky Tree Vole, 6¼–8⅛″, *p. 494*

67 Woodland Vole, 4⅛–5¾", *p. 505*

68 Rock Vole, 5⅜–7¼", *p. 501*

69 Yellow-cheeked Vole, 7¼–8⅞", *p. 501*

70 California Vole, 6¼–8⅜″, *p. 498*

71 Long-tailed Vole, 6¼–10⅜″, *p. 500*

72 Creeping Vole, 4¾–6⅛″, *p. 502*

73   Water Vole, 7¾–10¼″, *p. 506*

74   Tundra Vole, 6–8⅞″, *p. 499*

75   Montane Vole, 5½–7½″, *p. 497*

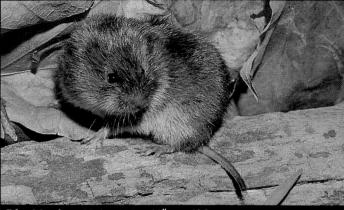

76 Meadow Vole, 5½–7¾″, *p. 495*

77 Prairie Vole, 5⅛–6¾″, *p. 504*

78 Collared Lemming, 5¼–6⅜″, *p. 515*

79   Collared Pika, 7–7¾″, *barking*, p. 343

80   Collared Pika, 7–7¾″, p. 343

81   Pika, 6⅜–8½″, p. 343

Rats and Mice

This huge assemblage of small rodents, many of which are quite common, shows numerous variations in form and habits. Most have large ears, moderately large eyes, and long tails. Primarily omnivorous and nocturnal, they live in nearly all habitats; most use burrows and only a few hibernate.

82 Agile Kangaroo Rat, 10⅜–12⅝″, *p. 450*

83 Banner-tailed Kangaroo Rat, 12¼–14⅜″, *p. 453*

84 Chisel-toothed Kangaroo Rat, 9⅝–11¾″, *p. 450*

85   Fresno Kangaroo Rat, 8¾–10¼", *p. 455*

86   Ord's Kangaroo Rat, 8⅛–11⅛", *p. 448*

87   Giant Kangaroo Rat, 12¼–13¾", *p. 452*

88   Merriam's Kangaroo Rat, 8¾–10¼", *p. 455*

89   Desert Kangaroo Rat, 12–14¾", *p. 455*

90   Panamint Kangaroo Rat, 11¼–13⅛", *p. 453*

91 Pacific Jumping Mouse, 8½–10¼", *p. 523*

92 Woodland Jumping Mouse, 8–10", *p. 525*

93 Meadow Jumping Mouse, 7¼–10", *p. 522*

94 Western Jumping Mouse, 8½–10¼", *p. 523*

95 Arizona Pocket Mouse, 4¼–5⅞", *p. 439*

96 San Joaquin Pocket Mouse, 5–6⅜", *p. 439*

97 Silky Pocket Mouse, 3⅞–4¾″, *p. 438*

98 Southern Grasshopper Mouse, 4¾–6½″, *p. 481*

99 Northern Grasshopper Mouse, 5⅛–7½″, *p. 480*

100   Long-tailed Pocket Mouse, 6¾–8¼″, *p. 441*

101   Great Basin Pocket Mouse, 5¾–7¾″, *p. 440*

102   Dark Kangaroo Mouse, 5¾–7″, *p. 447*

103 Pale Kangaroo Mouse, 5⅞–6¾″, *p. 447*

104 Desert Pocket Mouse, 6⅜–8½″, *p. 443*

105 Bailey's Pocket Mouse, 7⅞–9⅛″, *p. 442*

106 Spiny Pocket Mouse, 6½–8⅞″, *p. 446*

107 Little Pocket Mouse, 4¼–5⅞″, *p. 439*

108 Plains Pocket Mouse, 4⅜–5⅛″, *p. 437*

109   Heermann's Kangaroo Rat, 9¾–13⅜″, *p. 451*

110   California Pocket Mouse, 7½–9⅜″, *p. 445*

111   San Diego Pocket Mouse, 6⅞–7⅞″, *p. 445*

112   Oldfield Mouse, 4¾–6″, *p.* 471

113   Eastern Harvest Mouse, 4¼–5⅞″, *p.* 466

114   Northern Pygmy Mouse, 3⅜–4⅞″, *p.* 479

115 Mexican Spiny Pocket Mouse, 8–11⅝″, *p. 456*

116 Fulvous Harvest Mouse, 5¼–7⅞″, *p. 467*

117 Black Rat, 12¾–17⅞″, *p. 516*

118   Western Harvest Mouse, 4½–6¾", *p. 466*

119   Mexican Woodrat, 11⅜–16⅝", *p. 488*

120   California Mouse, 8⅞–11⅛", *p. 469*

121   Marsh Rice Rat, 7⅜–12″, *p. 464*

122   Salt-marsh Harvest Mouse, 4¾–6⅜″, *p. 467*

123   House Mouse, 5⅛–7¾″, *p. 520*

124   Deer Mouse, 4¾–8¾″, *juvenile, p.* 470

125   Brush Mouse, 7⅛–9⅜″, *p.* 474

126   Cotton Mouse, 6–8⅛″, *p.* 473

127 White-footed Mouse, 6⅛–8⅛″, *p. 471*

128 Deer Mouse, 4¾–8¾″, *p. 470*

129 Golden Mouse, 5⅞–7½″, *p. 479*

130 Piñon Mouse, 6¾–9⅛″, *p. 476*

131 Eastern Woodrat, 12¼–17⅜″, *p. 484*

132 Florida Mouse, 7¼–8¾″, *p. 478*

133   Cactus Mouse, 6¾–8⅝″, p. 468

134   Desert Woodrat, 8¾–15⅛″, p. 487

135   Southern Plains Woodrat, 11¾–15″, p. 485

136　Hispid Cotton Rat, 8¼–14⅜″, *p. 482*

137　Norway Rat, 18⅛″, *grayish-black form, p. 518*

138　Dusky-footed Woodrat, 13¼–18¾″, *p. 489*

139   White-throated Woodrat, 11⅛–15¾″, p. 486

140   Norway Rat, 12⅜–18⅛″, brownish form, p. 518

141   Yellow-nosed Cotton Rat, 9¼–10¼″, p. 484

Bats

The only mammals that fly, bats "swim" through the night air on wings —their most distinctive feature— which consist of a double membrane thinly stretched across enlarged arm bones and greatly enlongated fingers. Most bats have small eyes and poor vision and use echolocation to navigate and locate prey. Nearly all North American species are insectivorous; in winter, when few insects are available, most hibernate hanging upside down, often in vast numbers. Some migrate to warmer climates.

142　Allen's Big-eared Bat, 4⅛–4⅝″, *p. 329*

143　Spotted Bat, 4¼–4½″, *p. 327*

144　Rafinesque's Big-eared Bat, 3⅝–4¼″, *p. 328*

145 Townsend's Big-eared Bat, 3½–4⅜″, *p.* 327

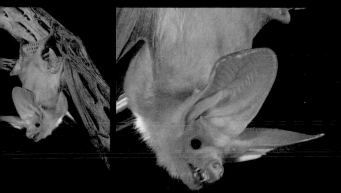

146 Pallid Bat, 4¼–5⅛″, *p.* 330

147 California Leaf-nosed Bat, 3¾–3⅝″, *p.* 306

148   Underwood's Mastiff Bat, 6⅜–6⅝″, *p. 335*

149   Pocketed Free-tailed Bat, 3⅞–4⅝″, *p. 333*

150   Western Mastiff Bat, 5½–7½″, *p. 334*

151　Big Free-tailed Bat, 5⅛–5¾″, *p. 334*

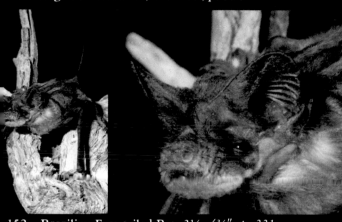

152　Brazilian Free-tailed Bat, 3½–4⅜″, *p. 331*

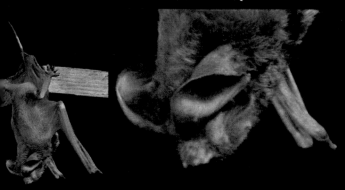

153　Wagner's Mastiff Bat, 3¼″, *p. 336*

154 Ghost-faced Bat, 2⅜–2⅝″, *p. 305*

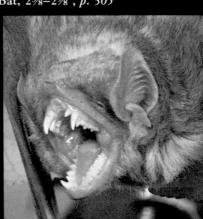

155 Northern Yellow Bat, av. 4½″, *p. 325*

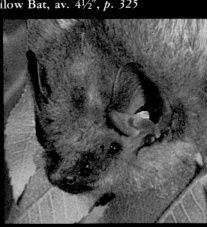

156 Southern Yellow Bat, 4¼–5″, *p. 326*

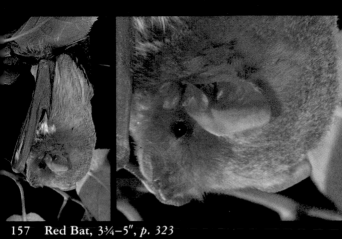

157 Red Bat, 3¾–5″, *p. 323*

158 Seminole Bat, 4⅛–4⅜″, *p. 324*

159 Eastern Pipistrelle, 3¼–3½″, *p. 321*

160   California Myotis, 2⅞–3⅜", *p. 318*

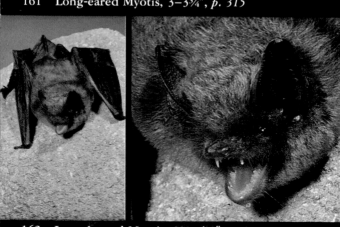

161   Long-eared Myotis, 3–3¾", *p. 315*

162   Long-legged Myotis, 3⅜–4⅛", *p. 317*

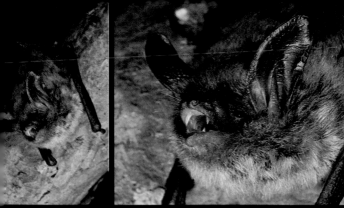

163   Keen's Myotis 3⅛–3½", *p. 314*

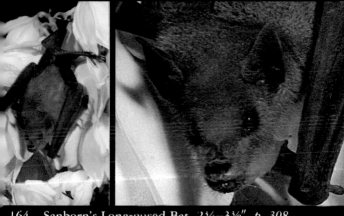

164   Sanborn's Long-nosed Bat, 2¾–3⅜", *p. 308*

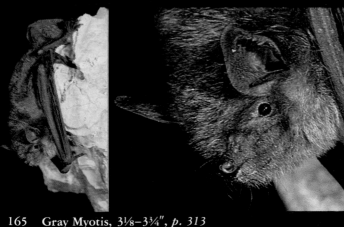

165   Gray Myotis, 3⅛–3¾", *p. 313*

166 Big Brown Bat, 4⅛–5″, *p. 322*

167 Small-footed Myotis, 2¾–3¼″, *p. 319*

168 Evening Bat, 3⅛–3¾″, *p. 326*

169   Little Brown Myotis, 3⅛–3¾″, *p. 310*

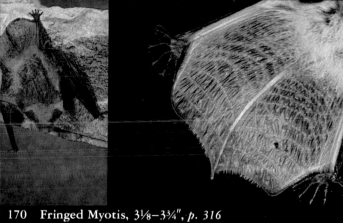

170   Fringed Myotis, 3⅛–3¾″, *p. 316*

171   Cave Myotis, 3½–4½″, *p. 314*

172   Yuma Myotis, 3⅜–3⅞″, *p. 311*

173   Southwestern Myotis, 3⅛–3½″, *p. 316*

174   Mexican Long-nosed Bat, 3–3½″, *p. 307*

175 Western Pipistrelle, 2⅜–3⅜″, *p. 320*

176 Indiana Myotis, 2¾–3⅝″, *p. 317*

177 Southeastern Myotis, 3⅜–3⅞″, *p. 312*

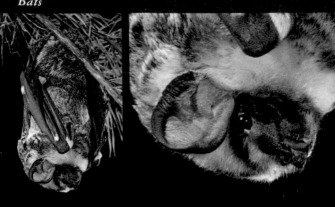

178 Hoary Bat, 4–6″, *p. 324*

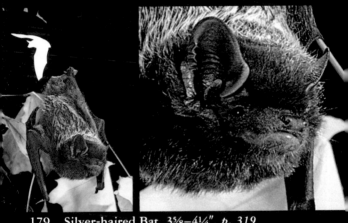

179 Silver-haired Bat, 3⅝–4¼″, *p. 319*

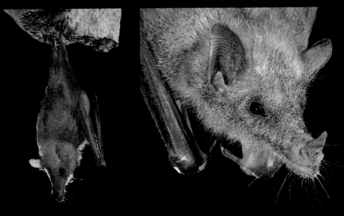

180 Long-tongued Bat, 2¼–3⅛″, *p. 307*

Tree Squirrels

Tree squirrels have long bushy tails and prominent eyes and ears. Most are diurnal, active all year, and live in forests, where they nest in a tree crotch or cavity. Flying squirrels, the only nocturnal members of this group, have furred folds of skin along their sides; these are spread open like wings when they glide through the air. The Bushy-tailed Woodrat, a rodent included here because it resembles tree squirrels, is also nocturnal and can survive in almost any type of habitat within its primarily northwestern range.

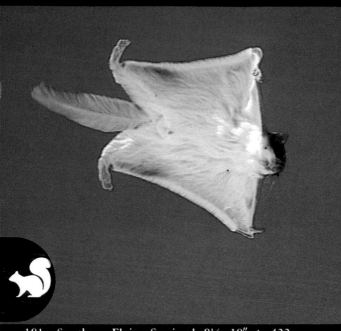

181   Southern Flying Squirrel, 8¼–10", *p. 422*

182   Gray Squirrel, 16⅞–19¾", *albino form, p. 413*

183 Southern Flying Squirrel, 8¼–10″, *p. 422*

184 Northern Flying Squirrel, 10⅜–14½″, *p. 423*

185 Douglas' Squirrel, 10⅝–14″, *p. 421*

186 Fox Squirrel, 17⅞–27½″, *p. 417*

187   Red Squirrel, 10⅝–15¼″, *p. 419*

188   Gray Squirrel, 16⅞–19¾″, *p. 413*

189   Bushy-tailed Woodrat, 11½–18½″, *p. 490*

190   Rock Squirrel, 16⅞–20¾″, *p. 403*

191 Western Gray Squirrel, 17½–23¼″, *p. 415*

192 Arizona Gray Squirrel, 20¼–22⅜″, *p. 419*

193   Abert's Squirrel, 18¼–23″, *p. 416*

194   Kaibab Squirrel, 18¼–23″, *p. 416*

195 Gray Squirrel, 16⅞–19¾", *black phase, p. 413*

196 Rock Squirrel, 16⅞–20¾", *black form, p. 403*

Skunks, the Raccoon, and the Badger

Among the most familiar North American mammals, the medium-size animals in this group all bear distinctive markings. Skunk species are easily identified by the white stripes or spots on their black fur. Their mustelid relative, the Badger, has a white stripe extending from between the shoulders up over the head and into a blaze, or "badge," upon its dark snout. The Raccoon and its relatives, the Ringtail and the Coati, have ringed tails. The Opossum's small black ears and dark eyes contrast with its white face; it is unique among North American mammals in having a long, naked prehensile tail.

197 Eastern Spotted Skunk, 13½–22¼", *p. 583*

198 Striped Skunk, 20½–31½", *p. 585*

199 Hog-nosed Skunk, 20¼–35¾″, *p. 588*

200 Hooded Skunk, 22–31⅛″, *p. 587*

201   Ringtail, 24¼–31⅞″, *p.* 560

202   Raccoon, 23¾–37⅜″, *p.* 562

203   Virginia Opossum, 25⅜–40″, p. 275

204   Badger, 20½–34¼″, p. 581

205   Coati, 33⅜–52¾", *p.* 565

206   Wolverine, 31½–44¼", *p.* 579

Weasel-like Mammals

A slim, elongated body, low-slung and sleekly furred, short legs, and a long tail characterize weasels and the fellow mustelids that resemble them—the Marten, the Fisher, the Mink, the Ermine, the Black-footed Ferret, and otters. All are a shade of brown, many are white below, and some turn white in winter. Their habitats are varied: the Marten spends much time in trees; weasels, the Mink, and the Ermine prefer the forest floor; and otters are at home in streams or at sea.

207 Least Weasel, 6¾–8⅛", *p. 573*

208 Ermine, 7½–13½", *winter, p. 571*

209 Long-tailed Weasel, 11–21¾", *p. 574*

210 Ermine, 7½–13½", *with jumping mouse, p. 571*

211 Marten, 19¼–26⅞″, *p.* 569

212 Black-footed Ferret, 19¾–22⅝″, *p.* 576

213   Fisher, 31⅛–40¾", *p. 570*

214   Mink, 19¼–28¼", *p. 578*

215 River Otter, 35–51⅝″, *p. 589*

216 Sea Otter, 30–71¼″, *female with pup, p. 591*

Armored Mammals

 Although the Armadillo and the Porcupine belong to separate orders, each is uniquely armored against would-be predators. The Armadillo is clad in bony plates, while the Porcupine has a rump and tail covered with sharp quills, which bristle when the animal feels threatened, usually discouraging a predator.

217 Nine-banded Armadillo, 24¼–31½", *p. 339*

218 Nine-banded Armadillo, *defense posture, p. 339*

219 Porcupine, 25½–36½", *yellow phase*, p. 527

220 Porcupine, 25½–36½", *female with young*, p. 527

Muskrats, Marmots, and Beavers

This group of medium-size rodents includes both aquatic species and burrowers. The Muskrat, with a long, vertically flattened scaly tail; the Nutria, with a long, round, scantily-haired tail; and the paddle-tailed Beaver favor lakes, ponds, streams, or marshes. The burrowing marmots and the Woodchuck look like big ground squirrels and have moderately long, bushy tails. Another burrower, the virtually tailless Mountain Beaver, is often found near streams in its Pacific Northwest range.

221   Round-tailed Muskrat, 11¼–15″, *p. 507*

222   Muskrat, 16⅛–24⅜″, *p. 509*

223 Nutria, 26⅜–55⅛″, *p. 530*

224 Beaver, 35½–46″, *p. 457*

225   Olympic Marmot, 17¾–32¼″, *p. 387*

226   Hoary Marmot, 17¾–32¼″, *p. 387*

227 Woodchuck, 16½–32¼", *adult with young, p. 384*

228 Yellow-bellied Marmot, 18½–27⅝", *p. 386*

229 Mountain Beaver, 9⅜–18½", *p.* 367

230 Vancouver Marmot, 17¾–32¼", *p.* 387

Hares and Rabbits

Hares and Rabbits have large eyes; small, often cottony tails; long ears; and long hindlegs with large feet. Hares generally have longer ears and longer hindlegs than rabbits and are better adapted for jumping. Relying on their ability to make a speedy getaway, hares occupy open country, resting on the ground or in shallow depressions. Rabbits seek concealing shelter in dense vegetation and, especially in winter, may hide in burrows, particularly those abandoned by Woodchucks.

231 Snowshoe Hare, 15–20½″, *winter, P. 356*

232 White-tailed Jack Rabbit, 22¼–25¾″, *p. 359*

233   Arctic Hare, 18⅞–26¾″, *winter, p. 358*

234   Northern Hare, 22¼–27¼″, *blue phase, p. 358*

235   Snowshoe Hare, 15–20½″, *p. 356*

236   Arctic Hare, 18⅞–26¾″, *p. 358*

237   Nuttall's Cottontail, 13¾–15⅜″, *p. 352*

239   Antelope Jack Rabbit, 21⅝–26⅛″, *p. 362*

240   Black-tailed Jack Rabbit, 18¼–24¾″, *p. 360*

241   White-tailed Jack Rabbit, 22¼–25¾", p. 359

242   Desert Cottontail, 13¾–16½", p. 352

243 Cape Hare, 25¼–27⅝″, *p. 363*

244 European Rabbit, 18–24″, *p. 354*

245 New England Cottontail, 14¼–19″, *p. 351*

246 Brush Rabbit, 11⅛–14¾″, *p. 348*

247   Swamp Rabbit, 20⅞–21¼″, *p. 353*

248   Marsh Rabbit, 14⅛–18″, *p. 349*

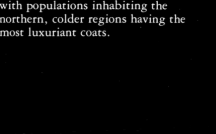

with populations inhabiting the
northern, colder regions having the
most luxuriant coats.

249 Red Fox, 35⅜–40⅜", *silver phase, p. 544*

250 Gray Wolf, 39½–80⅝", *ht.* 26–38", *p. 539*

251   Arctic Fox, 29½–35⅞″, *blue phase*, p. 542

252   Arctic Fox, 29½–35⅞″, *ht.* 10–12″, *p.* 542

253   Red Fox, 35⅜–40⅜″, *ht.* 15–16″, *p. 544*

254   Red Fox, 35⅜–40⅜″, *pouncing, p. 544*

255   Red Fox, 35⅜–40⅜″, *cross phase, p. 544*

256   Red Wolf, 55¼–65″, *ht. 15–16″, p. 538*

257 Gray Fox, 31½–44¼", *ht.* 14–15", *p. 548*

258 Swift Fox, *young, p. 547*

259   Kit Fox, 23⅝–31½", *ht.* 12", *p. 547*

260   Swift Fox, 23⅝–31½", *ht.* 12", *p. 547*

261   Gray Wolf, 39½–80⅝″, *ht.* 26–38″, *p.* 539

262   Gray Wolf, 39½–80⅝″, *ht.* 26–38″, *p.* 539

263 Coyote, 41⅜–52″, *ht.* 23–26″, *p.* 535

264 Coyote, 41⅜–52″, *ht.* 23–26″, *p.* 535

265   Arctic Fox, 29½–35⅞", *ht.* 10–12", *winter, p. 542*

266   Gray Wolf, 39½–80⅝", *white phase, p. 539*

Cats

Differing in size and color, North American wild cats all have lithe, powerful bodies, short heads with prominent ears, eyes that are vertically slit and face forward, whiskers, and fleshy paws with retractile claws. The fur may be plain, mottled, or spotted, and the tail long or short.

267   Bobcat, 28–49⅜″, *p. 603*

268   Lynx, 29⅛–41⅞″, *p. 602*

269   Bobcat, 28–49⅜″, *with Snowshoe Hare, p. 603*

270   Mountain Lion, 59⅛–108″, *p. 596*

271 Mountain Lion, 59⅛–108″, *p. 596*

272 Jaguarundi, 35–54″, *p. 601*

273   Ocelot, 36¼–53⅞″, *p. 599*

274   Jaguar, 62–95¼″, *p. 595*

Pig-like Mammals

Related to the domestic pig, the Wild Boar and the Peccary have stocky bodies covered with grizzled dark hair, long heads with a cartilaginous disk-shaped snout, and short legs with hooved feet. The Wild Boar has a moderately long, uncoiled tail and upper tusks that curl up, while the much smaller Peccary is virtually tailless with upper tusks pointing down.

275 Wild Boar, 4½–6', *ht.* to 3', *p.* 639

276 Collared Peccary, 34½–40", *ht.* 20–22", *p.* 643

Hoofed Mammals

These animals walk on two-part hooves formed by the third and fourth toes. All males and many females bear head ornamentation in the form of antlers or horns. Their size ranges from medium to large and color from white to dark brown. Hair may be short, as in deer, or very long, as in the Muskox.

277   Muskox, 6¼–8′, *ht.* 3–5′, *p.* 670

278 Bison, 10–12½′, *ht. to 6′, male, p. 665*

279   Barbary Sheep, 4¼–6¼′, *ht.* 3–3½′, *male, p.* 676

280 Mountain Goat, 4–5¾′, *ht.* 3–3½′, *p.* 668

281 Dall Sheep, 52¾–60¼″, *ht.* 33–42″, *male, p.* 674

282   Dall Sheep, 52¾–60¼″, *ht.* 33–42″, *male,*

black phase, p. 674

283   Bighorn Sheep, 5¼–6′, *ht.* 3–3½′, *males (left);*

4¼–5¼′, *ht.* 2½–3′, *female (right), p. 672*

284   Pronghorn, 49¼–57⅛″, *ht.* 35–41″, *male with*

harem, p. 661

285 White-tailed Deer, 4½–6¾′, *ht.* 3–3½′, *male,*

286   Key Deer 32–40″ ht. 18–24″ ♂ 654

287   Elk, 6¾–9¾′, *ht.* 4½–5′, *male with harem, p.* 647

Fallow Deer, 55–71″, *ht. about* 39″, *female (left)*,

males (right), p. 650

289   Mule Deer, 3¾–6½′, *ht.* 3–3½′, *male with antlers*

in velvet, p. 651

290   Caribou, 4½–6¾', *ht.* 3–3½', *male, p. 658*

291 Moose, 6¾–9′, *ht.* 6½–7½′, *male with antlers*

Bears

The largest terrestrial carnivores, bears have massive, densely furred bodies; moderate-size heads with small, rounded ears; small, close-set eyes; and tiny tails. Their coloration varies: Polar Bears are white; Grizzlies may be tawny to blackish-brown; and Black Bears range from black through brown to nearly white, and in Alaska there is even a "blue" phase.

292 Black Bear, 4½–6¼′, *ht.* 3–3½′, *blue phase, p.* 55.

293   Black Bear, 4½–6¼′, *ht.* 3–3½′, *black and*

294   Grizzly Bear, 6–7′, *ht.* 4¼′, *p.* 555

305   *Grizzly Bear (to 7', ht. 4½', with salmon, p. 555*

296 Polar Bear, 7–11′, *ht. about* 4′, *p. 557*

Sea Lions, Seals, and the Walrus

Adaptations to their aquatic life include large, streamlined bodies, flippers for limbs, and vestigial ears and tails. Coloration varies and a few have distinctive markings; whiskers are often present. The Walrus has large ivory tusks.

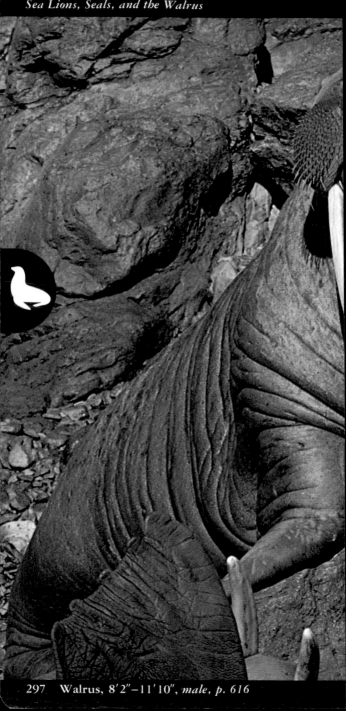

297 Walrus, 8′2″–11′10″, *male, p. 616*

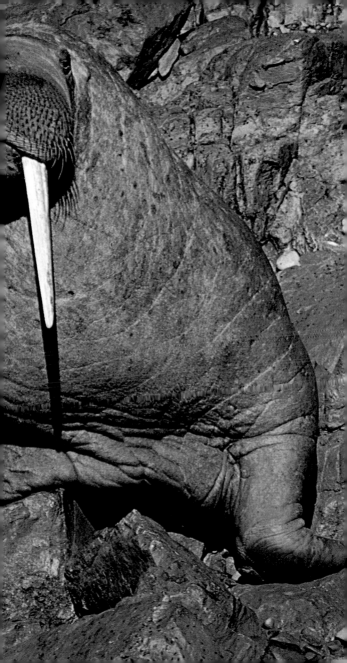

298   Northern Sea Lion, 8'10"–10'6", *male, p. 613*

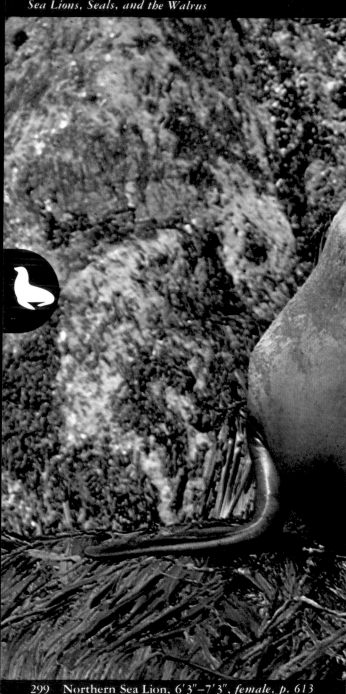

299 Northern Sea Lion, 6′3″–7′3″, *female, p.* 613

300   Northern Fur Seal, 6' 3"–7' 3", *male;*

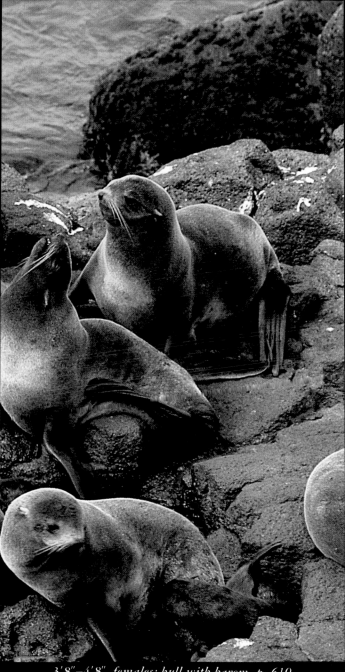

3' 8" – 4' 8", *females: bull with harem, p. 610*

391   California Sea Lion, 6'6"–8'3", male, p. 614

302   California Sea Lion, 5′–6′6″, *female, p. 614*

303   Guadalupe Fur Seal, 6′3″, *male, p. 612*

304   Northern Elephant Seal, 14'9"–21'4", *male, p. 629*

305 Northern Elephant Seal 9'10"–11'6" *female*

nursing pup, p. 629

306   Hooded Seal, 6′7″–8′2″, *male, p. 628*

307   Hooded Seal, 6–7', *female, p. 628*

308   Harbor Seal, 4'–5'7", *female nursing pup, p. 619*

309   Ringed Seal, 4′3″–5′3″, *p. 622*

310   Ribbon Seals (*cont.*) with pups to 63 l-

311 Harp Seal, 4'7"–6'7", *female with pup, p. 623*

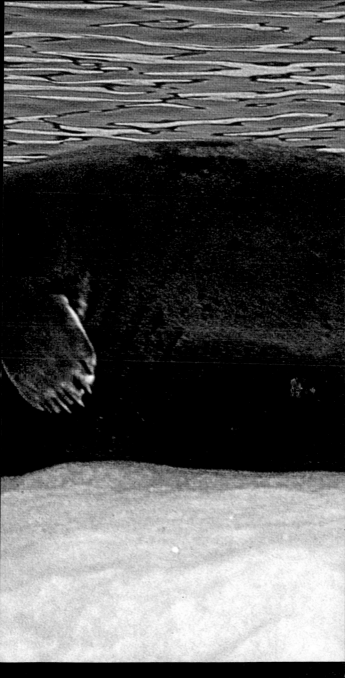

313   Gray Seal, 9'10", *male, p.* 626

Part II
Text Descriptions

The numerals preceding the species descriptions in the following pages correspond to the plate numbers in the color section. If the description has no plate number, it is illustrated by a drawing that accompanies the text.

Pouched Mammals
(Order Marsupialia)

Marsupials are nonplacental mammals that generally have a pouch, or "marsupium," on the belly in which the female carries her young, although in a few species the pouch is reduced or absent. After a gestation period of 1–2 weeks, young are born when still in a very undeveloped, or "embryonic," state. The tiny newborn, about the size of a dime in most species, must make its way from the base of the mother's tail to the pouch, where it attaches itself to a nipple. In higher animals the placenta provides continued nourishment to the fetus, which allows for a longer gestation period and greater development of the young. Marsupials are often thought to be primarily Australian. The 250 species that occur there have adapted to many niches filled by higher mammals in other parts of the world. There are marsupial flying squirrels, moles, mice, cats, rabbitlike animals (the bandicoots), as well as woodchuck-like animals (the wombats), a dog (the Tasmanian wolf), and an anteater. In addition, several species of marsupials (constituting 2 families) are found in South America; and one species, Virginia Opossum (*Didelphis virginiana*), is found in North America.

203 Virginia Opossum
(*Didelphis virginiana*)

Description: House cat size. Grizzled white above; long white hairs cover black-tipped fur below. In some areas, individuals may appear brownish or blackish. *Long, naked prehensile tail.* Head, throat, and cheeks whitish; *ears large, naked, black with pinkish tips.* Legs short; *first toe of hindfoot opposable* (thumblike) and *lacks nail.* Females with fur-lined abdominal pouch. L 25⅜–40″ (645–1,017 mm); T 10–21″ (255–535 mm); HF 1⅞–3⅛″ (48–80 mm); Wt 4–14 lb. (1.8–6.3 kg).

Sign: *Tracks:* In mud, hindprint approximately 2″ wide, with 5 toes printing: large thumblike toe slanted inward, or backward, 3 middle toes close together, and remaining toe separate; foreprint slightly smaller, with 5 toes printing in starlike fashion. Hind and fore prints parallel and close together; straddle 4″; walking stride 7″.

Habitat: Open woods, brushy wastelands, farmlands.

Range: Most of e U.S., except Maine, n Michigan, and n Minnesota. Extends southwest to Colorado and most of Texas. Also se Arizona and the coastal areas of California, Oregon, Washington, and s British Columbia.

Nocturnal and solitary. When threatened, it sometimes rolls over, shuts its eyes, and allows its tongue to loll, feigning death, or "playing possum," for some time. More often, it tries to bluff its attacker by hissing, salivating, and opening its mouth wide to show all of its 50 teeth. The opossum does not hibernate. During very cold weather, it may "den up" for several days at a time, but when hungry it risks frostbite on its naked ears and tail to seek food. Many are killed on highways while attempting to feed on roadkills. Carrion forms much of its diet, which also includes insects, frogs, birds, snakes, mammals, earthworms, fruits, and berries (persimmons are consumed heavily in season, and apples and corn are particularly favored). It makes a leaf nest in a hollow log, fallen tree, abandoned burrow, crevice, or shelter. After a gestation period of only 12–13 days, the 1–14 "living embryos," each as tiny as a navy bean, climb up through the hair of the female and enter the vertical opening of her pouch. Each takes one of the 11–13 nipples in its mouth and remains thus attached to the mother for 2 months. Those who do not obtain a nipple perish. Two, sometimes 3, litters are born a year. Because of the male's forked penis, there is a myth that mating is through the female's nose. It is hunted with hounds for its fur, which, although not particularly valuable, is used for trimming; and for its meat, which many consider a delicacy. The average life span is about 7 years.

Shrews and Moles
(Order Insectivora)

Insectivores are small mammals with short, dense fur, 5 clawed toes on fore and hind feet, and small eyes and ears. The ears are usually hidden beneath the fur, yet in many species hearing is quite acute. As the name of the order implies, shrews and moles eat many insects and their larvae. But they also eat many other invertebrates and, in fact, are not even the most exclusively insectivorous of North American mammals; bats, for example, feed almost entirely on insects. The order includes land-dwellers, burrowers, and some that spend much of their life in water. Two families are represented in North America: shrews (Soricidae) and moles (Talpidae).

SHREWS
(Family Soricidae)

Shrews look somewhat like mice, but
have a long and slender pointed snout,
a continuous row of needle-sharp teeth,
tiny eyes, and 5 clawed toes on both
fore and hind feet (mice have 4 toes on
forefeet). As in moles, their fur can lie
forward or backward, facilitating
movement in the burrows. Shrews
range in size from less than 1½″
(35 mm) to 7½″ (180 mm); the world's
smallest mammal, weighing less than
1/16 oz. (2 g), is Savi's Pygmy Shrew
(*Suncus etruscus*), found in the
Mediterranean region and Africa. All
North American shrews have teeth with
chestnut-colored tips. Many species are
similar and can be distinguished only
by the size of their unicuspid teeth,
5 in most species.

Exceedingly active and nervous, shrews
dart about constantly. Because of their
high metabolism, they feed every 3
hours, both day and night, resting
during intervals between meals. A
shrew's energy output surpasses that of
any other mammal, compelling it to eat
up to twice its own weight per day. It
eats mainly invertebrates but also
plants, fungi, and small mammals,
alive or dead. Many shrews have high-
pitched, squeaky voices; and some
employ supersonic sounds in
echolocation like bats.

Generally solitary, shrews fight to
defend their nest areas and viciously
battle any animal they perceive as an
attacker, including their own kind.
They must engage in complex courtship
behavior to progress from aversion to
copulation. Musk glands on their flanks
exude an odor thought to be repellent
to some carnivores, such as cats, which
often kill shrews but won't eat them.
However, shrews are consumed by
owls, snakes, and some mammals; the
glands are probably more important for

territorial marking and sexual
recognition than for discouraging
predators.

There are 1 to several litters per year,
with 2–10 young born blind, pink,
and hairless. An unusual habit,
probably unique to shrews, is the
chain-formation reaction of the
unweaned young to danger. At the
slightest disturbance, even the sound of
rain or a change in temperature, each
juvenile grasps with its mouth the base
of the tail of its closest neighbor,
forming a caravan with the mother in
the lead. From a distance, the moving
chain might be mistaken for a small
snake. The shrew's life span is 1–2
years, but most shrews probably live
less than a year. If a shrew is excited or
frightened, its heart may beat 1,200
times per minute, and sometimes it is
literally frightened to death by capture
or a loud noise.

Tracks and sign are of limited
usefulness in identifying species, as
both are tiny and not distinctive. Prints
are often blurred dots, and burrows so
small as to be mistaken for tunnels of
large earthworms.

---

46 Masked Shrew or Cinereous Shrew
(*Sorex cinereus*)
Related species: Mt. Lyell, Preble's

Description: *Very small. Brownish above; belly silvery or
grayish. Long tail* brown above, buff
below. Third unicuspid usually smaller
than fourth. L 2¾–4⅜″ (71–111 mm);
T 1–2″ (25–50 mm); HF ½″ (10–
14 mm); Wt ⅛–⅜ oz. (2.4–7.8 g).

Similar Species: In East, Southeastern Shrew smaller
with shorter, less hairy tail and shorter
snout. In West, Vagrant and Dusky
shrews have third unicuspid usually
smaller than fourth.

Habitat: Various; most common in moist fields,
bogs, marshes, moist or dry woods.

Range: Throughout n North America south to Washington, Idaho, s central Utah, n central New Mexico, Nebraska, Iowa, Indiana, extreme n Kentucky, Maryland, and south throughout the Appalachians.

Although one of the most widely distributed mammals in North America, this small secretive shrew is primarily nocturnal and rarely seen. Although all shrews are noted for their voracious appetites, the Masked Shrew's is particularly large; its daily consumption often equals or exceeds its own weight. It feeds mostly on moth and beetle larvae, slugs, snails, and spiders. It makes a nest of leaves or grass under a log, in a stump or clump of vegetation.

Now recognized as separate species, but closely related, are Mt. Lyell Shrew (*Sorex lyelli*), found only in Tuolumne and Mono counties, California; and Preble's Shrew (*Sorex preblei*) in eastern Oregon.

51 Southeastern Shrew
"Bachman's Shrew"
(*Sorex longirostris*)

Description: *Brownish above;* buff below. *Long tail.* L 2⅞–4¼" (72–108 mm); T 1–1⅝" (26–40 mm); HF ⅜–½" (9–13 mm); Wt ¹⁄₁₆–⅛ oz. (2–4 g).

Similar Species: Masked Shrew has longer snout, longer and hairier tail.

Sign: Pencil-size burrows, especially in mossy areas.

Habitat: Moist areas but also fields, brushy areas, and woods.

Range: Southeastern U.S. (except in the Appalachians) from s Maryland to n Florida, west through s Indiana and Illinois to the Mississippi River; west of the Mississippi only in Arkansas and Louisiana.

Little is known of the Southeastern's habits, although they are thought to be similar to those of the Masked Shrew. It eats spiders, moth larvae, slugs and snails, centipedes, and vegetation. This species is sometimes called Bachman's Shrew, after naturalist John Bachman, who discovered it in 1837. One of the first two specimens was retrieved from the gullet of a hooded merganser, a duck which preys on a wide variety of small aquatic wildlife.

55 Vagrant Shrew
"Wandering Shrew"
(*Sorex vagrans*)

Description: In summer: *brownish to grayish above;* grayish tinged with brown or red below. In winter: all parts grayish or blackish. Long tail one color or grading to lighter below. *Fourth unicuspid larger than third.* L 3¾–4¾" (95–119 mm); T 1¼–2" (34–51 mm); HF ⅜–⅝" (11–14 mm); Wt ⅛–⅜ oz. (3–8.5 g).

Similar Species: Pacific and Dusky shrews have longer tails.

Habitat: Mixed forests.

Range: Southern British Columbia south to n California, n Nevada, Arizona, e New Mexico.

This tiny creature spends much of its time in the runways of voles where it finds such foods as insect larvae, slugs and snails, spiders, and other invertebrates, as well as the subterranean fungus *Endogone.* Its common and scientific names allude to its extraordinary activity in pursuit of food, rather than its wanderings, which are no greater than those of other shrews.

Dusky Shrew
(*Sorex monticolus*)

Description: In summer: fur short and *rust-brown above;* slightly lighter and less reddish below. In winter: fur longer and darker above and below. *Tail indistinctly bicolored.* L 4⅛–4⅞" (105–125 mm); T 1¾–2¼" (43–55 mm); HF ⅜–⅝" (11–14 mm).

Similar Species: Pacific Shrew brownish below with a longer tail; Vagrant Shrew has shorter tail.

Habitat: Forests near streams; wet meadows with sedges or willows.

Range: Western North America from Alaska south to n and central Oregon, most of Idaho, Utah and New Mexico, with isolated population in ne and s California.

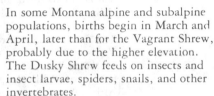

In some Montana alpine and subalpine populations, births begin in March and April, later than for the Vagrant Shrew, probably due to the higher elevation. The Dusky Shrew feeds on insects and insect larvae, spiders, snails, and other invertebrates.

---

47 Pacific Shrew
(*Sorex pacificus*)

Description: In summer: dark reddish-brown to dark brown. In winter: cinnamon above; slightly lighter below. *Long tail usually tan or brown above and below,* but sometimes indistinctly bicolored. *Fourth unicuspid larger than third.* L 5⅛–6¼" (129–160 mm); T 2⅛–2¾" (54–68 mm); HF ⅝–¾" (15–19 mm).

Similar Species: Dusky and Vagrant shrews smaller with shorter tails.

Habitat: Spruce and redwood forests; stands of alder-skunk cabbage along stream edges.

Range: Pacific coast, n California, and s Oregon.

Unlike most North American shrews, the Pacific Shrew is nocturnal. It feeds on slugs and snails, centipedes, amphibians, insect larvae, and other invertebrates.

49 Ornate Shrew
(Sorex ornatus)
Related species: Inyo, Ashland, Suisun

Description: *Grayish-brown above;* slightly lighter below. *Tail dark brown above and below, darkest at tip. Fourth unicuspid larger than third.* L 3⅜–4¼″ (86–110 mm); T 1¼–1¾″ (30–44 mm); HF ⅜–⅝″ (10–14 mm).

Habitat: Along streams; in brushy areas of valleys, foothills; yellow pine forests.

Range: Southern two thirds of coastal California; also central California.

This species may interbreed with the Vagrant Shrew where their populations overlap at Tolay Creek, on the north side of San Pablo Bay, California. Although the 2 species may be combined eventually, the Ornate's incisor pattern is closer to that of the Dusky Shrew. Its habits are probably similar to those of the other small long-tailed shrews.

Closely related species include the slightly smaller Inyo Shrew (*Sorex tenellus*), found in southwest Nevada and adjacent Mono and Inyo counties, California; the Ashland Shrew (*Sorex trigonirostris*) on the west slope of Grizzly Mountains, Ashland, Oregon, which differs only in minor skull characteristics; and the nearly black Suisun Shrew (*Sorex sinuosus*) on Grizzly Island and adjacent tidal marshes in Solano County, California.

Dwarf Shrew
(Sorex nanus)

Description: *Tiny. Grayish-brown above; gray below.*
Long tail slightly darker above than
below. L 3¼–4⅛″ (82–105 mm);
T 1½–1¾″ (38–42 mm); HF ⅜″ (10–
11 mm).

Similar Species: Masked and Merriam's shrews have
distinctly bicolored tails and third
unicuspids usually smaller than
fourth.

Habitat: Spruce forests in the Grand Canyon
area; Douglas fir and white fir forests at
7,000–9,000′ (2,100–2,700 m)
elevation in New Mexico; on the
Beartooth Plateau, Montana, where
rocky gutters alternate with patches of
alpine tundra vegetation.

Range: Restricted to Wyoming, Montana, and
sw South Dakota south to n central
Arizona and n New Mexico.

The habits of this rare shrew are
presumably similar to those of other
long-tailed shrews. It feeds on soft-
bodied insects and spiders.

---

54 **Water Shrew**
(Sorex palustris)
Related species: Glacier Bay Water

Description: Very dark or black above; belly grayish-
white. *Long tail. Hindfeet have fringe of
stiff hairs.* L 5⅝–6¼″ (144–158 mm);
T 2½–3⅛″ (63–78 mm); HF ¾″ (18–
21 mm); Wt ⅜–⅝ oz. (12–17 g).

Similar Species: Most other shrews much smaller.
Among western shrews, Pacific Water
Shrew dark below with fringe of hair on
hindfoot poorly developed.

Habitat: Among boulders along mountain
streams or in sphagnum moss along
mountain lakes.

Range: Most of Canada south throughout ne
California, through Utah, with an
isolated population in the White

Mountains of e Arizona; the central states to ne South Dakota, n Minnesota, Wisconsin, and Michigan; and New England south through the Appalachians to the Nantahala Mountains of North Carolina.

At home in and around water, it can dive to the bottom, but when it stops swimming, air entrapped in the fur pops it back to the surface like a cork. Owing to the fringe of hairs on the hindfoot, which increases the foot's surface area and traps air bubbles, the shrew can actually run on the water surface. Its velvety fur is water resistant, but if it does become wet, the shrew takes to shore and dries itself thoroughly with rapid strokes of the hindleg; its hair fringe then functions as a comb. It eats aquatic food, such as mayfly and stonefly nymphs, as well as terrestrial invertebrates. Enemies include weasels, mink, pickerels, pikes, bass, and large trout.

A closely related species, differing in minor skull characteristics, is the Glacier Bay Water Shrew (*Sorex alaskanus*), known only from Point Gustavus, Glacier Bay, Alaska.

50 Pacific Water Shrew
(*Sorex bendirii*)

Description: *Large. Dark brown above and below.* Long tail. *Hindtoes slightly fringed.* L 5⅛–6⅛" (147–174 mm); T 2⅜–3⅛" (61–80 mm); HF ¾"–⅞" (18.5–21 mm); Wt aver. ½ oz. (16.1 g).

Similar Species: Water Shrew white below with well-developed fringe on hind toes.

Habitat: Marshes, along streams, sometimes in moist forests.

Range: Coastal n California north to extreme se British Columbia.

This shrew is the largest member of its genus in North America. On land it eats earthworms, sow bugs, spiders, centipedes, and other invertebrates, and it readily enters water to take aquatic arthropods. It can run on top of the water for several seconds, gaining buoyancy from the air trapped in its partially fringed toes; it can also dive to the bottom.

44 Smoky Shrew
(Sorex fumeus)

Description: *Brownish in summer; grayish in winter.* Long tail dark brown above and lighter, sometimes yellowish, below. L 4¼–5″ (110–127 mm); T 1½–2″ (37–52 mm); HF ½″ (12–15 mm); Wt ¼–⅓ oz. (6–9 g).

Similar Species: Masked Shrew usually smaller, browner, paler below.

Sign: Dime-size burrow openings along stream of road banks, under logs, or at bases of large trees.

Habitat: Various types of moist wooded areas, but also in deep woods, swamps, and along streams where woods and fields meet.

Range: Northeastern U.S. south through the mountains to e Tennessee, n Georgia, and n South Carolina, and north through s Ontario, Quebec, New Brunswick, and Nova Scotia.

Active in even the coldest weather, the Smoky Shrew commonly lives in extensive burrows in the leaf mold of the forest floor. It makes a leaf nest in a hollow log or stump, or under rocks. Small invertebrates, such as insects and their larvae, earthworms, sow bugs, and centipedes, form its diet.

45 Arctic Shrew
"Saddle-backed Shrew"
(*Sorex arcticus*)
Related species: Pribilof, St. Lawrence
Island

Description: Tricolored fur: *dark brown back, light
brown sides,* and *grayish belly* tinged with
buff; pattern more distinct in winter.
Long tail. L 4–5" (101–126 mm); T
1¼–1¾" (30–46 mm); HF ½" (12–
15 mm); Wt ¼–⅜ oz. (6–11 g).

Habitat: Swamps, bogs, marshes, grass-sedge
meadows.

Range: Across much of Canada and Alaska
south to North Dakota, extreme ne
South Dakota, Minnesota, Wisconsin,
and Michigan's upper peninsula.

The unique tricolored pattern of the
Arctic Shrew's fur has given rise to its
other common name, Saddle-backed
Shrew. Unlike other shrews, these are
quite docile, can be handled, and
seldom attempt to bite. They have a
low rapid chatter. Caterpillars,
centipedes, beetles, and their larvae are
chief foods.
Closely related species, also with
tricolored coats, include the Pribilof
Shrew (*Sorex pribilofensis*), bicolored in
winter and known only from the
Pribilof Islands, west of Alaska; and the
slightly smaller St. Lawrence Island
Shrew (*Sorex jacksoni*), known only from
St. Lawrence Island in northwest
Alaska.

58 Long-tailed Shrew or Rock Shrew
(*Sorex dispar*)
Related species: Gaspé

Description: *Long and slender. Dark gray. Long tail*
uniformly dark above and below.
L 4⅛–5½" (103–139 mm); T 1⅞–
2⅝" (48–66 mm); HF ⅝" (13–
16 mm); Wt ¼ oz. (5–6 g).

Similar Species: Smoky Shrew smaller, lighter, with a shorter tail, paler below. Water Shrew larger, with fringe of stiff hairs along sides of feet; occurs along mountain streams.

Habitat: Usually in deep, dark, cool, moist recesses among boulders or talus slopes.

Range: Mountainous areas from Maine through the Smoky Mountains of North Carolina and Tennessee.

This shrew is rare, and only a few living specimens have been observed. It eats small invertebrates, especially spiders, centipedes, and beetles. A closely related species is the slightly smaller Gaspé Shrew (*Sorex gaspensis*), known only in the Gaspé Peninsula of Quebec, Mt. Carleton in New Brunswick, and Cape Breton Island in Nova Scotia. It is usually found near streams in coniferous mountain forests.

52 Trowbridge's Shrew
(*Sorex trowbridgii*)

Description: Grayish to brownish above; slightly paler below. *Long, distinctly bicolored tail*, dark above; nearly white below. *Third unicuspid smaller than fourth.* L 4⅜–5¼" (110–132 mm); T 1⅞–2⅜" (48–62 mm); HF ½" (12–15 mm); Wt ¼–⅓ oz. (6–9) g.

Sign: Tiny burrows in leaf mold.

Habitat: Mature forests of West Coast.

Range: Extreme sw British Columbia south through w Washington, w Oregon, much of California.

This small shrew feeds upon various insects and other invertebrates as well as seeds, especially those of the Douglas fir. Maturation is in February, just before breeding, which occurs through May. Most individuals probably live no more than 1½ years.

Merriam's Shrew
(*Sorex merriami*)

Description: *Pale grayish above* with paler flanks;
*whitish below. Long distinctly bicolored
tail.* L 3½–4¼" (88–107 mm); T 1⅜–
1¾" (33–42 mm); HF ½" (11–
13 mm); Wt ⅛–¼ oz. (4.4–6.5 g).

Habitat: Much drier than that of most shrews;
sagebrush, but also grasslands and
woodlands.

Range: Western U.S. in isolated colonies west
from w North Dakota to New Mexico.

Little is known about the habits of this
shrew, which often is found in deserts
with the Sagebrush Vole. Its diet
includes caterpillars, adult and larval
beetles, cave crickets, and ichneumonid
wasps. Glands on the flanks of males,
prominent from April through June,
give the animal a strong odor, most
likely to attract females, but also
believed to repel predators.

Arizona Shrew
(*Sorex arizonae*)

Description: Small. Brown above; slightly lighter
below. *Long tail indistinctly bicolored:*
brownish above, lighter below.
Distinguished from other shrews in its
range by *first incisors with tines on inner
side.* L 3¾–4½" (93–114 mm); T 1½–
1¾" (37–46 mm); HF ½" (11–
13 mm).

Habitat: Dry, mountainous regions.

Range: Huachuca, Santa Rita, and Chiricahua
mountains of se Arizona; Animas
Mountains, Hidalgo County, in sw
New Mexico.

First described in 1977, the habits of
this species are unknown but are
probably similar to those of other long-
tailed shrews.

43 Pygmy Shrew
(*Microsorex hoyi*)

Description: *Tiniest mammal in North America,* weighing no more than a dime. Brownish to grayish above; pale or silvery below. *Third and fifth unicuspids tiny.* L 3⅛–3⅞" (78–98 mm); T 1⅛–1⅜" (27–35 mm); HF ⅜–½" (9–12 mm); Wt ⅛ oz. (2.2–3.8 g).

Similar Species: Other long-tailed shrews larger with only the fifth unicuspid reduced.

Habitat: Deep woods, open and brushy fields; moist sphagnum moss bogs.

Range: Alaska and most of Canada south to ne Washington, nw Montana, and east to ne North Dakota, n Iowa, Wisconsin, the upper peninsula of Michigan, n New England and n New York, ne Pennsylvania, and nc Ohio. Southern Appalachians from Maryland to sw North Carolina.

The Pygmy Shrew is one of the rarest North American mammals, and little is known of its behavior in the field. It forages among dead plant matter, probably feeding on insects and insect larvae, small earthworms, centipedes, spiders, and other invertebrates. It has been proposed that the Pygmy Shrews found in the southern Appalachians be classed as a separate species, *M. winnemana*.

48, 60 Short-tailed Shrew
(*Blarina brevicauda*)
Related species: Swamp Short-tailed

Description: *Largest shrew in North America.* Solid gray above and below. *Short tail.* L 3¾–5" (96–127 mm); T ¾–1" (20–25 mm); HF ½–¾" (12–20 cm); Wt ½–1 oz. (14–29 g).

Similar Species: Southern Short-tailed Shrew smaller; previously considered the same species, the two remain distinct where both

occur together in Nebraska. Least
Shrew brownish.

Sign: Burrows less than 1″ across, wider than
high. Piles of snail shells under logs.

Habitat: Woods and wet areas in warmer and
drier parts of range.

Range: Southeastern Canada and ne U.S. south
to Nebraska, Missouri, Kentucky, and
in the mountains to Alabama. Isolated
populations in ne North Carolina and
the w central part of Florida.

One of the most common North
American mammals, this shrew is also
one of the most ferocious. It bites its
victim in the throat and face,
paralyzing it almost instantly with a
poison in its saliva. The shrew then
drags the victim into its nest,
sometimes eating it while it is still
alive. The venomous saliva is not
dangerous to man, but a bite may be
painful for several days. A voracious
eater of from half to more than its own
weight per day, it devours earthworms,
snails, centipedes, beetles, and other
invertebrates, quantities of the tiny
subterranean fungus *Endogone,* and
sometimes even mice and smaller
shrews. Using its sturdy snout as well
as its powerful forefeet, it excavates
underground runways which it
patrols for prey mainly in early
morning and late afternoon. Males
mark their burrows with secretions
from well-developed glands on hip and
belly, and other males hunting mates
will not enter burrows so marked. This
system of territorial marking is
fortunate, since meetings between
members of this species often result in
fierce combat. However, fights usually
end when one shrew assumes the
submissive posture of lying on its back,
allowing the other to flee. Mates,
however, may form unions that are
more or less permanent. Young are
born in spring or summer in bulky
nests of shredded grass or leaves, 6–8″

wide, beneath a log or stump.
Closely related is the Swamp Short-
tailed Shrew (*Blarina telmalestes*), known
only from Dismal Swamp, Virginia.

57 Southern Short-tailed Shrew
(*Blarina carolinensis*)

Description: *Gray above and below. Short tail.* Total
length seldom over 4" (100 mm).
L 3½–5⅞" (88–151 mm); T ¾–1⅛"
(19–28 mm); HF ⅜–¾" (11–20 mm);
Wt ¼–¾ oz. (5.5–22 g).

Sign: Small burrows wider than high; snail
shells piled under logs.

Habitat: Primarily woodlands.

Range: Southeastern U.S. north to s Nebraska,
s Illinois, south of the Appalachians,
and north to Maryland.

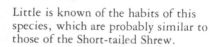

Little is known of the habits of this
species, which are probably similar to
those of the Short-tailed Shrew.

56 Least Shrew
(*Cryptotis parva*)

Description: Grayish-brown or brownish above; *paler
below. Short tail. Only 3 unicuspids visible*
(the fourth is behind the third). L 2¾–
3½" (69–89 mm); T ½–⅞" (12–22
mm); HF ½" (9–12 mm); Wt ⅛–¼
oz. (4–6.5 g).

Similar Species: The only other North American short-
tailed shrews, the Short-tailed and the
Southern Short-tailed, are gray with
5 unicuspids.

Habitat: Grassy or weedy fields, sometimes in
marshy areas or wet woods.

Range: Throughout se U.S. north to se central
New York and s Minnesota, west to
South Dakota, ne Oklahoma, e Texas.

Most active at night but sometimes
moving about by day, the Least Shrew

has a metabolism that demands voracious, almost constant feeding; it eats moth and beetle larvae, earthworms, spiders, and internal organs of large grasshoppers and crickets. It probes loose soil and leaf litter for prey, which it detects chiefly with the stiff hairs around its mouth. It is sometimes called a "bee mole" after its habit of entering beehives to feed on the brood. While most shrews tend to be solitary, this species may be fairly social: 25 were found in a leaf nest under a log in Virginia, and in Texas 2 nests contained 12 and 31 individuals, respectively. In a laboratory, 2 were observed cooperating in excavating a burrow, with one digging and the other removing dirt from the burrow and packing the tunnel walls.

---

59 Desert Shrew
(*Notiosorex crawfordi*)

Description: Grayish, washed with brown above; pale gray below. Long grayish tail, lighter below. The only North American shrew with 3 *unicuspids*. Ears more noticeable than in most shrews. L 3–3¾" (77–93 mm); T ⅞–1¼" (22–32 mm); HF ⅜" (9–11.5 mm); Wt. ⅛ oz. (2.9–5 g).

Habitat: Arid regions, especially in sagebrush and prickly pear. Sometimes found in woodrat nests or in large masses of vegetation at the base of agave cactus or other plants in desert areas.

Range: Southern California east through Arizona, New Mexico, s Colorado to w Arkansas, w Texas.

Like many desert animals, the Desert Shrew can exist solely on the water obtained from its food, usually the soft inner parts of larger insects.

MOLES
(Family Talpidae)

Moles are larger than shrews, with
proportionally shorter tails. They are
among the most subterranean of
mammals. Their bodies are
streamlined, head and body merging
together with almost no indentation at
the neck. The pelvis is narrow,
enabling them to change direction
easily in burrows, often by
somersaulting. Fur is velvety and
grainless, allowing moles to move as
easily backward as forward in tight
burrows. Earholes are concealed within
the fur, which keeps them from
becoming clogged with dirt; hearing is
well developed. Eyes are light-sensitive
pinhead-size dots, and vision is poor.
The most important sensory organ is
the flexible and often naked snout; the
mole finds food chiefly through its keen
senses of scent and touch and the
vibrations picked up by its whiskers.
The enormously enlarged, long-clawed
forefeet, turned outward, execute a
kind of breaststroke, enabling a mole to
virtually swim through porous soil at
about a foot per minute. The tunnels
are of two types: subsurface, which
appear as ridges; and deep, which are
generally marked by cone-shaped
molehills, usually 6–8″ high, and most
common in wet weather. Moles are
active day and night and throughout
the year. Most are solitary except
during the mating season, when a male
will seek out a female in her burrow.
Owing to their underground habitat,
moles have a low predation rate, which
allows them to maintain populations by
producing only 1 annual litter of 2–6
young, born in early spring in a nest
chamber supplied with a maternity
cradle of dry vegetation. Moles eat
several kinds of invertebrates and small
amounts of vegetable matter, but

earthworms are their major food. Their tunneling activity, while a nuisance in lawns, is beneficial because it aerates soil, allowing rain to penetrate, thereby reducing erosion.

53   Shrew-mole
(*Neurotrichus gibbsii*)

Description: *Smallest mole in North America* and the only one with *no major development of digging forelegs.* Gray. Long, hairy tail about half its total length. Nine teeth on each side of upper jaw. L 4⅛–5″ (103–126 mm); T 1¼–1¾″ (32–43 mm); HF ⅝–¾″ (14–18 mm); Wt ¼–⅜ oz. (9–11 g).
Habitat: Deep, soft soil. Coniferous and deciduous rain forests; sometimes brushy areas or moist weedy ones.
Range: West Coast, from nw California to sw British Columbia.

This creature is aptly named, for it is characterized by the size and forefeet of a shrew and the large head and dental structure of a mole. It is unique among moles in being able to climb low bushes, which it explores for insects. Earthworms, sow bugs, beetles, insect larvae, and some vegetation form its diet.

Townsend's Mole
(*Scapanus townsendii*)

Description: *Large. Black.* Short, thick, *nearly naked tail,* and nearly naked snout. Eleven upper teeth on each side, with unicuspids crowded and uneven. Eyes tiny but visible. L 7¾–9¼″ (195–237 mm); T 1¼–2″ (34–51 mm); HF ⅞–1⅛″ (24–28 mm).
Similar Species: Other western moles smaller: Coast Mole has evenly spaced, uncrowded

unicuspids; Broad-footed Mole
brownish or grayish.

Habitat: Meadows, fields, lawns.
Range: West Coast, from extreme n California
to extreme s British Columbia.

It eats earthworms but also snails,
slugs, centipedes, insects, and
vegetation. Named for John Townsend,
who first described it, this is one of 8
North American mammals whose
scientific name honors the nineteenth-
century naturalist.

42 Coast Mole
(*Scapanus orarius*)

Description: Velvety black fur. *Nearly naked tail* and
naked pink snout. Unicuspid teeth
evenly spaced and uncrowded. Eyes tiny
but visible. L 5¾–6⅞″ (147–175
mm); T 1–1¾″ (26–43 mm); HF ¾″
(19–23 mm).
Similar Species: Townsend's Mole much larger, with
unevenly spaced, crowded unicuspids.
Broad-footed Mole brownish or grayish.
Habitat: Deciduous woods.
Range: Northern California north through
coastal Oregon, Washington, sw
British Columbia. Also n Oregon, se
Washington, and w central Idaho.

This mole's inky fur is a good example
of the frequent correlation in mammals
between moist habitat and dark
coloration. Earthworms are its main
food, but it also eats insects, centipedes,
snails and slugs, and some vegetation.

40 Broad-footed Mole
(*Scapanus latimanus*)

Description: Usually *brownish or grayish,* seldom
black. *Short, hairy tail,* short hairs at
base of snout. Unicuspids unevenly

spaced and usually crowded. L 5¼–
7½" (132–190 mm); T ¾–1¾" (21–
45 mm); HF ¾–1" (18–25 mm).

Similar Species: In the West, Townsend's and Coast
moles have nearly naked tails.

Habitat: Moist soil in various habitats from
valleys to mountains.

Range: Southern central Oregon south through
most of California.

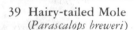

Its forefeet are wide but no broader
than those of most other moles.
It eats mainly earthworms but also
snails, slugs, insects, and some
vegetation.

39 Hairy-tailed Mole
(*Parascalops breweri*)

Description: Dark gray or nearly black above;
slightly lighter below. *Only eastern mole
with a short, hairy tail.* Older
individuals may have white snout, tail,
and feet. L 5½–6¾" (139–170 mm);
T ⅞–1⅜" (23–36 mm); HF ¾" (17–
21 mm); Wt 1⅜–2⅜ oz. (40–64 g).

Similar Species: Eastern Mole often larger, with short,
nearly naked tail.

Sign: Typical mole runs of rounded ridges in
dry woodland soils of northeastern U.S.
are likely to have been made by this
species.

Habitat: Woods with well-drained light soil;
also brushy areas; occasionally lawns or
golf courses adjacent to woods.

Range: Extreme se Canada southwest through
mountains of North Carolina and
Tennessee, west through e Ohio.

Tunneling beneath the surface by day,
the Hairy-tailed Mole often emerges at
night to feed. If abroad by day, it may
be so oblivious to human presence that
it can be caught by hand; it is
occasionally captured by cats and other
predators. Like most other moles, it
eats earthworms but also grubs,

beetles, ants, and other invertebrates in daily quantities up to 3 times its own weight. Like other moles, it is active all winter but frequents deeper, hence better insulated, tunnels. It may live in the wild for 4–5 years, but its legacy of extensive tunnels may be used by succeeding generations.

37, 38 Eastern Mole
"Common Mole"
(*Scalopus aquaticus*)

Description: Short, velvety fur; gray in northern parts of range, brownish or tan in southern and western parts. *Forefeet broader than long,* with palms turned out; *toes slightly webbed.* Tail very short and nearly naked. Snout long, flexible, and naked. No visible eyes. L 3¼–8¾" (82–223 mm); T ¾–1½" (18–38 mm); HF ½–1⅛" (15–29 mm); Wt 3–5 oz. (82–140 g).

Similar Species: Hairy-tailed Mole has short, hairy tail.

Habitat: Open fields, waste areas, lawns, gardens, and sometimes woods, in well-drained loose soil.

Range: Most of e U.S. from Gulf Coast north to extreme se Wyoming, s Minnesota, lower peninsula of Michigan, most of Ohio, e West Virginia, central Pennsylvania, and Massachusetts.

This mole spends nearly all of its time underground, becoming most active at dawn or dusk. In winter it prefers deeper burrows. It feeds mainly on earthworms but also eats larvae and adults of many kinds of insects and other invertebrates. The Latin species name *aquaticus* alludes to its webbed toes; it is the least likely of North American moles to occur in moist soil. Forefeet spade alternately, shoving earth under the body, which the hindfeet then shove behind into the tunnel. Nests are underground, usually beneath a log, stump, or boulder; Florida individuals do not build nests.

41 **Star-nosed Mole**
(*Condylura cristata*)

Description: Black. Long hairy tail. Large digging forelegs. *22 pink fleshy projections on nose.* L 5⅛–8¼″ (152–211 mm); T 2⅛–3¼″ (53–84 mm); HF 1–1¼″ (26–30 mm); Wt 1–2⅜ oz. (30–75 g).

Sign: Burrows with 1½″ openings into streams, lakes, or ponds. Openings surrounded by mounds of excess dirt.

Habitat: Wet woods, fields, or swamps; sometimes relatively dry areas, lawns.

Range: The Northeast from se Labrador south through much of Minnesota, ne Indiana, n Ohio, south through the Appalachians, and along coastal Virginia. Isolated populations along Georgia coast.

This mole's tentacle-like nose projections are mobile and very sensitive, apparently helping it to find its way about the burrow and locate food. When the Star-nosed Mole forages, its tentacles are constantly in motion; however, when it eats, they are clamped together out of the way. It searches about in the muck near its main burrows, presumably after earthworms, its favorite food. It also eats many aquatic items, including fish. An adept diver and swimmer, it propels itself along, even under ice, by moving feet and tail in unison. It is more dependant on water during winter, when the frozen ground makes it difficult for the Star to obtain its usual foods. Nests are constructed of leaves, grass, or other vegetation, usually in a hummock or other raised area above the moist habitat. The young develop rapidly and by 3 weeks leave the nest and hunt for themselves.

Bats
(Order Chiroptera)

Members of this order inhabit most of the temperate and tropical regions of the world, except a few remote islands. Although precise numbers are not known, bats are probably exceeded only by rodents as the most numerous mammals. Four families of 39 known species occur within our range.

Bats are the only mammals that truly fly. They probably evolved from primitive shrewlike creatures that lived in trees and whose forelimbs eventually evolved to become wings (the order name means "flying hand"). In bats, arm bones and muscles are enlarged: 4 greatly elongated fingers spread wing membranes when in flight and draw them together when at rest, folding the wing along the forearm (FA); a claw "thumb" projects from the end of the forearm; and a small bone (the calcar) juts back from the ankle bone to help support a membrane between the legs (the interfemoral membrane). The calcar is said to be "keeled" when there is a flat projection of bone protruding from the calcar into the interfemoral membrane. Bat bodies are generally well furred, but wing membranes are often naked and transparent. Unlike birds, which flap their wings up and down, bats "swim" through the air. Some species fly with the agility of swifts and occasionally hunt with such birds at dusk. Wing beats may be as rapid as 20 per second. With wings folded, bats can walk or climb, and some can swing from branch to branch. At rest, they hang head downward, sometimes by 1 hindfoot, using the other to groom their fur and clean their teeth.

Most North American bats have small eyes and relatively poor vision; hence "blind as a bat." However, they do not bump into things and can zero in on the tiniest insects by means of echolocation, similar to sonar. While flying, the bat emits through its nose or slightly opened mouth a continuous series of supersonic sounds (about 30 to 60 squeaks per second, ranging in pitch from about 30,000 to 100,000 cycles) that bounce off objects and are picked up by the bat's complex ears. In many bats, a projection from the ear's inner base, the tragus, is a useful feature for species identification and is thought to enhance hearing. Muscles in the ears contract and relax in synchronization with the vocalization, blocking emitted sounds and receiving the echoes. From the way the sound waves are interpreted, the bat determines size, location, density, and movement, if any, of the object it approaches. In addition to supersonic sounds, bats make harsh, shrill chirpings and screechings within the range of human hearing when upset or during mating season.

Nocturnal mammals, bats leave daytime roosts about dusk and usually fly to a stream, pond, or lake where they dip their lower jaws into the water to drink. They then catch insects in their mouths, or scoop them into their wings or interfemoral membrane. Bats may feed as they fly, turning a somersault as they extract food from the wing membrane, or, if their meal is too large, alight to dine.

The legend that bats fly into people's hair is based on the fact that they often fly very close to animals, including humans, seeking the insects that sometimes swarm about their heads. Since nearly all North American bats are insectivorous and many live in northern parts of the continent, where few insects are active in winter, most bats hibernate; others migrate to warmer climates, up to 1,000 miles away.

Solitary bats tend to live among the leaves of trees; social bats cluster in caves, hollow trees, buildings, or other protected places. Hibernating bats die if the temperature drops below freezing, and a too-warm cave can speed up their metabolism to the point that all stored body fat is burned up and they starve to death. Unlike other hibernators, they awaken very rapidly, a protection against danger.

Most bats mate in fall. In many hibernating species, sperm is stored in the female over the winter and fertilization is delayed until the spring. This adaptation prevents birth during the unfavorable winter months. The stirring of one bat awakens others, resulting in closely synchronized behavior. Ovulation occurs nearly simultaneously in all members of the colony, and most give birth at the same time. Most bats give birth to 1, or sometimes 2, offspring annually. Young are born feet first, a presentation probably unique in mammals. Some bats live up to 20 years or more. Bats consume hundreds of thousands of tons of destructive insects annually. They are susceptible to rabies, though they may recover from the disease, but rarely attack humans or other animals.

LEAF-CHINNED BATS
(Family Mormoopidae)

Of the 8 species primarily restricted to tropical habitats of the New World, only 1 is found in our range. The bizarre faces of Mormoopid bats have flaps and grooves on the chin that are believed to enhance echolocation. The tragus has a horizontal pocket-like fold of skin.

154 Ghost-faced Bat
(*Mormoops megalophylla*)

Description: Reddish-brown to dark brown. Short tail projects from upper side of interfemoral membrane. *Folds of skin across chin* from ear to ear make it unique in North America. L 2⅜–2⅝" (59–66 mm); FA 1⅞–2¼" (46–56 mm).

Habitat: Desert or scrub, usually in caves or mines often very hot and with high humidity; seldom in buildings.

Range: Only in s Texas and s Arizona.

Strong, swift flyers, they emerge late in the evening to hunt just above the ground. These bats roost in loose colonies, about 6" apart. While colony size varies, up to 500,000 bats have been found in one roost. They apparently do not hibernate.

LEAF-NOSED BATS
(Family Phyllostomatidae)

There are 140 species in tropical regions of the New World; only 5 species reach their northern limit in the sw United States. Except for the Hairy-legged Vampire Bat, recently reclassified in this family, the noses of these bats are ornamented with a vertical projecting flap, which plays a part in the emission of ultrasonic sounds. Fairly large eyes enable them to see quite well. They can hover in flight.

---

147 California Leaf-nosed Bat
(Macrotus californicus)

Description: Grayish to dark brownish above, with fur nearly white at base; paler below. Large ears. *Erect triangular flap on nose.* L 3⅜–3⅝″ (84–93 mm); FA 1⅞–2¼″ (47–55 mm).

Habitat: Desert scrub. By day, abandoned mine tunnels.

Range: Southern California, extreme s Nevada, and w Arizona.

The only bat in our area with large ears and a leaf nose. It roosts by day, usually fairly close to the entrance of a mine tunnel, in small groups of up to 100 bats, which do not touch each other. After dark, it drops from its perch into flight. Leaf-nosed Bats eat various insects, including some flightless forms, which they probably detect as they hover and then swoop to seize from the ground. After feeding for about an hour, they retreat to their night roosts in a sheltered area. They often dangle by one leg from a mine tunnel's ceiling, which they can cross in a swinging stride, using their hindlegs alternately. They do not hibernate.

180 Long-tongued Bat
(*Choeronycteris mexicana*)

Description: Gray or brownish above; paler below.
Large eyes. *Long, slender nose has an erect
arrowhead-shape flap of skin.* Tiny tail
extends less than halfway to end of
interfemoral membrane. L 2¼–3⅛"
(55–78 mm); FA 1⅝" (43–44 mm).

Similar Species: Sanborn's and Mexican Long-nosed bats
lack tail.

Habitat: Canyons in mountain ranges rising
from the desert. By day, usually caves
and mines, sometimes in buildings,
where they tend to hang near the
entrance.

Range: Extreme sw California, se Arizona, and
extreme sw New Mexico.

The long tongue, tipped by a brush of
tiny nipple-like projections, and the
lack of lower incisors make it easy for
this bat to lap up flower nectar and
fruit juices. It also eats insects and
pollen and may serve to pollinate
certain plants. Bats in Arizona probably
migrate to Mexico for the winter.

174 Mexican Long-nosed Bat
(*Leptonycteris nivalis*)

Description: Grayish-brown above; paler on
shoulders and underparts. *Long nose has
a leaflike projection. No tail.* Medium-size
ears, averaging about ⅝" (15 mm). L
3–3½" (76–88 mm). FA 2⅛–2⅜"
(55–60 mm); Wt ¾ oz. (21 g).

Similar Species: Sanborn's Long-nosed Bat sometimes
smaller, with shorter forearm.

Habitat: Colonies in caves, particularly in pine-
oak habitat.

Range: In the U.S. only at Emory Peak, in Big
Bend National Park, Texas.

It emerges late from its daytime
roosting cave, apparently moving to
lower levels to feed on nectar and

pollen. This is facilitated by its elongated nose and long, flexible tongue, which can be extended as far as 3".

164 Sanborn's Long-nosed Bat
(*Leptonycteris sanborni*)

Description: Reddish-brown on back; brownish on belly. *No visible tail. Long nose has erect leaf-shaped projection on tip.* Large eyes. L 2¾–3⅜" (69–84 mm); HF ½–¾" (13–17 mm); FA 2–2⅛" (51–56 mm).

Similar Species: Mexican Long-nosed Bat usually larger, less reddish, with smaller forearm; Long-tongued Bat has small tail.

Habitat: Caves and mines where mountains rise from the desert.

Range: Southern Arizona and extreme sw New Mexico.

This bat emerges late to feed on nectar and pollen as well as insects. It inserts its long snout into flowers; the hairlike projections on the long tongue help sweep food into its mouth. It either alights on vegetation while feeding or hovers somewhat like a hummingbird. During late pregnancy, females congregate in large maternity colonies. In the fall it apparently migrates to Mexico, where it spends the winter.

Hairy-legged Vampire
(*Diphylla ecaudata*)

Description: Dark brown or reddish-brown above; paler below. Interfemoral membrane well furred. *No tail.* Short, rounded ears; small tragus. Large eyes. *Outside lower incisor has 7 fan-shaped lobes* (unique among bats). Cheek teeth reduced. L 2⅝–3⅜" (65–87 mm); FA 2–2¼" (50–56 mm).

Habitat: Usually in caves but also mines and hollow trees.

Range: Normally, central Mexico south into South America. The 1 North American record is for a bat taken from an abandoned railroad tunnel near Comstock, Val Verde County, Texas.

Vampire bats feed entirely upon blood and occur only in the New World. They were discovered in Mexico in the sixteenth century by the Spanish conquistadores who named them after the blood-sucking creatures of eastern European legend. Sleeping by day in caves or other dark protected places, these bats feed at night chiefly on the blood of birds, such as chickens, turkeys, guinea fowl, ducks, and geese, but also mammals, including pigs, cattle, and horses. They bite chickens on the lower legs or near the cloaca, where there are few feathers. The Vampire is one of the few bats that uses its wings for walking. After locating its prey, it often lands nearby, then scuttles over to it, and may climb up its leg (if large) or jump on it. Perching lightly on its sleeping or motionless prey, it uses sharp upper incisors to quickly inflict a wound so shallow that the victim rarely notices. Curling its tongue into a tube which fits a V-shaped notch in its lower lip, the bat laps the blood, which flows freely, due to an anticoagulant in the bat's saliva. Unless the victim is very small, the amount of blood taken by the bat is not harmful; more serious, after the bat has flown away, are the potential for blood loss owing to slowed clotting, the vulnerability of the open wound to infection, and the transmission of rabies. These large-eyed bats have fairly good vision but a poorly developed system of echolocation. They usually congregate in small groups of only 1–3 per cave, rarely more than 12, though in 1 cave 35 were found.

EVENING BATS
(Family Vespertilionidae)

Most North American bats are
members of this family, which is found
in temperate and tropical regions
throughout the world. Evening Bats
have plain noses, earlobes that form a
tragus, and tails that extend only
slightly beyond the back edge of the
interfemoral membrane. These "vesper
bats," seen chiefly in the evening, are
insectivorous. Most have a well-
developed sense of echolocation,
sending out ultrasonic vibrations
through their mouths. During winter,
a few migrate to southern regions, but
most hibernate; many exhibit delayed
fertilization. On late summer evenings
they often swarm at cave entrances. The
significance of this swarming is not yet
known, although it is speculated that
they may be exploring possible
hibernation sites.

---

169 Little Brown Myotis
(*Myotis lucifugus*)

Description: Variable shades of glossy brown above;
buff below. Ears, ⅝" (14–16 mm);
*tragus short and rounded. Calcar without
keel,* or sometimes with weak keel.
L 3⅛–3¾" (79–93 mm); T 1¼–1⅝"
(31–40 mm); HF ¼–⅜" (8½–10
mm); FA 1⅜–1¾" (34–42 mm); Wt
⅛–½ oz. (3.1–14.4 g).

Similar Species: In the East, Southeastern Myotis often
has white belly; Indiana Myotis has
prominent keel on calcar; Keen's
Myotis has longer ears and longer,
thinner tragus. In the West, Long-
legged Myotis has keeled calcar; Long-
eared Myotis and Southwestern Myotis
usually have longer ears and longer,
thinner tragus; Yuma Myotis generally
smaller.

Habitat: In summer, forms nursery colonies in

buildings. In winter, hibernates in caves and mines in the East.

Range: Much of North America north to middle Alaska, south throughout most states except Florida, Texas, and s California.

One of the most common bats in the U.S. Nursery colonies begin forming in April or May and disperse from late July through August. The first 2–3 days after the young are born, their mothers suckle them constantly, except while foraging. If disturbed, the mother may take the young in flight by carrying it crosswise with the infant's mouth grasping one teat and its hindlegs tucked under the opposite armpit. Then, until they are ready to fly on their own, the young remain in the roost while the mother hunts for small insects, especially flies and moths. In the fall these bats may fly several hundred miles to a hibernating site; they can often be seen swarming at cave entrances. From September or October through March or April they hibernate in irregular clusters, some tight, some loose. Their nitrate-rich guano was sold as fertilizer in the first half of this century.

---

172 Yuma Myotis
(Myotis yumanensis)

Description: *Short, dull fur.* Variable shades of brown above; lighter below, with throat sometimes whitish. *Calcar not keeled.* L 3⅜–3⅞″ (84–99 mm); T 1⅜–1⅞″ (32–45 mm); HF ⅜″ (9–11 mm); FA 1⅜–1½″ (33–37 mm); Wt ¼ oz. (5–7 g).

Similar Species: Little Brown Myotis and Cave Myotis larger; California, Small-footed, and Long-legged myotises have keeled calcar.

Habitat: Always near ponds, streams, or lakes. By day, under sidings or shingles.

Night roosts often in buildings; nursery colonies in caves, mines, buildings, or under bridges.

Range: Western North America: California to British Columbia, east to w Montana, Idaho, w Nevada, Utah, Colorado, New Mexico.

Closely associated with water, it feeds by flying very low over the surface. Principal foods are midges, moths, termites, and other small insects. During breeding season the males usually remain alone.

177 Southeastern Myotis
(*Myotis austroriparius*)

Description: Dull brown, with *short, thick, woolly fur; underparts buff;* in Indiana, populations white. L 3⅜–3⅞″ (84–99 mm); T 1⅜–1¾″ (36–45 mm); HF ⅜–½″ (10–12 mm); FA 1⅜–1¾″ (35–42 mm); Wt ¼–⅜ oz. (7–12 g).

Similar Species: Little Brown Myotis has longer woolly fur with burnished tips; Keen's Myotis has longer ears and longer, thinner tragus; Indiana Myotis has keeled calcar; Small-footed Myotis has smaller foot and keeled calcar.

Habitat: In the North, caves; in the South, buildings or hollow trees, as well as caves in Florida.

Range: Southeastern U.S.: n Florida, much of Georgia, s Alabama, Mississippi, Louisiana, Arkansas, w Tennessee, w Kentucky; separate population in s Illinois, s Indiana.

Nursery colonies begin forming in March in caves where water is plentiful. Florida caves have some of the largest colonies, with up to 90,000 bats packed 150 per sq. ft. In winter, most of these bats leave the maternity caves to seek shelter in other protected places, such as culverts, bridge beams, or buildings, where they gather in small numbers. Predators include corn and rat snakes.

165 Gray Myotis
(*Myotis grisescens*)

Description: Medium-sized. Grayish or brownish. Unlike most myotises, *fur uniform in color from base to tip.* Calcar not keeled. Ears relatively short; tragus relatively short and rounded. L 3⅛–3¾″ (80–96 mm); T 1⅜–1¾″ (32–44 mm); HF ¼–⅜″ (8–11 mm); FA 1⅝–1¾″ (41–46 mm); Wt ¼ oz. (6–9 g).

Sign: In caves, rocks and water covered with stinking feces may indicate active summer colonies.

Habitat: Caves, usually containing much water.

Range: Alabama and w Georgia north to s Indiana and s Illinois, west to Missouri and nw Oklahoma.

This true cave species feeds on various insects but is partial to mayflies. Females and young congregate apart from the males and disband in late July or August after the young are weaned. These bats move in large flocks between summer and winter caves, with hibernating colonies forming in October. Most bats that summer in Tennessee, Kentucky, and Illinois hibernate in one large cave complex, the Coach-James Cave in Kentucky. Owing to disturbances from cave exploration, opening caves to the public, and the flooding of caves through dam building, bat populations have declined considerably, and this species is now considered endangered.

171 Cave Myotis
(*Myotis velifer*)

Description: Large. Light brown in eastern part of range to black in western part. *Calcar not keeled.* Ears, ⅝–¾" (15–17 mm), reach tip of nose when extended forward. L 3½–4½" (90–115 mm); T 1⅝–1⅞" (41–49 mm); HF ⅜–½" (10–12 mm). FA 1½–1⅞" (37–47 mm).

Similar Species: Yuma, California, and Small-footed myotises smaller; Southwestern, Long-eared, and Fringed myotises have longer ears; Long-legged Myotis have keeled calcar.

Habitat: Arid Southwest; in summer, caves, mines, sometimes buildings; in winter, caves.

Range: West Texas north to s central Kansas, west through s New Mexico, s Arizona, extreme se California.

The Cave Myotis sometimes forms very large colonies, estimated at 15,000–20,000 in Kansas nurseries. In winter, tight clusters of these bats hibernate in caves, sometimes on walls or ceilings, sometimes in crevices. Except for those in Kansas, these bats migrate between summer and winter quarters. Nursery colonies may form either in the hibernating or summer caves.

163 Keen's Myotis
(*Myotis keenii*)

Description: Variable shades of brown; paler below, belly slightly yellowish. *Long ears,* ⅞" (17–19 mm), which when laid forward protrude about 4 mm beyond nose. *Tragus thin and long,* ⅜" (9–10 mm). Calcar not keeled. L 3⅛–3½" (79–88 mm); T 1⅜–1¾" (36–45 mm); HF ¼–⅜" (7–9 mm); FA 1⅜–1½" (34–39 mm); Wt ⅛–⅜ oz. (5–10 g).

Similar Species: In the East, Little Brown,

Southeastern, and Indiana myotises have shorter ears and a shorter, more rounded tragus; Little Brown Myotis have glossier back fur. In the West, Long-eared Myotis has longer ears; Fringed Myotis has rear edge of interfemoral membrane fringed.

Habitat: In the West, dense forests. In the East, hibernates in caves and mines in winter; roosts under loose bark, shutters, shingles in summer.

Range: West Coast in Washington and British Columbia. In East, from Newfoundland, Virginia, and w Georgia west to Arkansas, Nebraska, and Saskatchewan.

This bat hibernates singly or in clusters of 4–6, often wedged into tiny crevices. In summer, a few small maternity colonies have been found, including 30 bats under the bark of an elm tree. Sometimes hundreds of these bats may be seen swarming at cave entrances in the fall. They feed on small insects, particularly flies.

161 Long-eared Myotis
(Myotis evotis)

Description: Long glossy fur, light brown to brown. *Ears dark, usually black,* and *longer than in any other myotis,* 1″ (22–25 mm); when laid forward *extending ¼″ (7 mm) beyond nose.* L 3–3¾″ (75–97 mm); T 1⅜–1¾″ (36–46 mm); HF ¼–⅜″ (7–10 mm); FA 1⅜–1⅝″ (35–41 mm).

Habitat: Coniferous forests of high mountains; sometimes in buildings.

Range: Western North America, from s British Columbia and Saskatchewan south through California and w New Mexico.

By day, this bat roosts singly or in small clusters in buildings and perhaps under tree bark; night roosts are sometimes in caves. Small nursery colonies of 10–30 bats form in buildings. It feeds heavily on small moths and also eats flies, beetles, and other insects.

173 Southwestern Myotis
(*Myotis auriculus*)

Description: Dull brownish fur. *Large brown ears,* ¾″ (14–20 mm) long, and a long, thin tragus. *Calcar not keeled.* L 3⅛–3½″ (78–88 mm); T 1⅜–1¾″ (36–45 mm); HF ¼–⅜″ (7–9 mm); FA 1⅜–1⅝″ (38–40 mm).

Similar Species: Long-eared Myotis has longer ears; Fringed Myotis has fringe of hair along edge of interfemoral membrane.

Habitat: Deserts, mesquite or chaparral to forests, especially in areas of rocky outcroppings.

Range: Southeastern Arizona and sw New Mexico.

Little is known of this species except that it roosts at night in buildings and caves; its day roosts have not been found.

170 Fringed Myotis
(*Myotis thysanodes*)

Description: Reddish-brown or brown above; slightly lighter below. Unique among myotises in having a *fringe of hairs on back edge of interfemoral membrane.* Ears ¾″ (16–20 mm) long. L 3⅛–3¾″ (80–95 mm); T 1½–1¾″ (37–42 mm); HF ¼–⅜″ (8–11 mm); FA 1½–1¾″ (39–46 mm).

Habitat: Roost in caves, mines, buildings, and other protected locations; oak, piñons, and juniper forests; desert scrub.

Range: Scattered west from w South Dakota, Colorado, and Big Bend area of Texas, to California and British Columbia.

This colonial bat, found in much of the Southwest, roosts by day in protected spots and may rest in night roosts between foraging bouts. Its diet includes moths, crickets, and harvestmen ("daddy longlegs"). Nursery colonies, from which males are usually absent, sometimes number in the low hundreds. Its winter habits are unknown.

176 Indiana Myotis or Social Myotis
(Myotis sodalis)

Description: Uniformly *pinkish-brown. Calcar keeled.* Ears moderate in size; tragus relatively short and rounded. Lips and nose pinkish. L 2¾–3⅝″ (71–91 mm); T 1⅛–1¾″ (27–44 mm); HF ¼–⅜″ (7–9 mm); FA 1⅜–1⅝″ (35–41 mm); Wt ¼ oz. (5–8 g).

Similar Species: Little Brown Myotis lacks keeled calcar.

Habitat: Wooded or semiwooded areas along streams in summer; caves in winter.

Range: Midwestern U.S. from extreme ne Oklahoma, n Arkansas and Missouri north to s Michigan; east to New England south to Alabama.

In October, these bats congregate for hibernation in a few large caves with high humidity, where they mate. They sleep in tightly packed clusters, usually only one row deep and so neatly aligned that lips and noses appear as bands of pink. In spring, they leave their caves and spread into wooded areas over their range, where they feed on a variety of small insects.

162 Long-legged Myotis
(Myotis volans)

Description: *Large.* Tawny or reddish to nearly black above; grayish to pale buffy below.

Unique in the West in having *calcar with well-developed keel. Underarm and interfemoral membrane furred to elbow and knee.* Ears short. L 3⅜–4⅛″ (87–103 mm); T 1½–1⅞″ (37–49 mm); HF ¼–⅜″ (8–10½ mm); FA 1⅜–1¾″ (35–42 mm).

Similar Species: Other large western myotises lack well-developed keel on calcar.

Habitat: In summer, trees, crevices, and buildings, particularly in forested areas.

Range: Western North America north through much of British Columbia, east to s Alberta, w Montana, sw South Dakota, w Nebraska, w Colorado, w New Mexico, Big Bend area of Texas. An isolated population in w North Dakota.

These bats form nursery colonies of up to several hundred members that disperse in fall. Winter behavior is unknown. They feed primarily on small moths but also eat other small insects.

160 California Myotis
(*Myotis californicus*)

Description: Dull fur, light to dark brown with yellowish or orangish cast above; paler below. Ears, wings, and interfemoral membrane dark. *Tiny foot,* ¼″ (5–7 mm) long. *Calcar keeled.* L 2⅞–3⅜″ (74–85 mm); T 1⅜–1¾″ (36–42 mm); FA 2⅞–3⅜″ (74–85 mm).

Similar Species: Small-footed Myotis has glossy fur.

Habitat: Desert to semidesert areas; in Southwest, especially rocky canyons. By day, in buildings, under bridges, under bark, in hollow trees; by night, buildings.

Range: Western North America north to sw British Columbia, east to Idaho, Colorado, and New Mexico.

In winter, some of these bats hibernate in mines, while others remain active. They feed on small flies, moths, and a

few other insects. An ability to veer suddenly sideways, up, or down makes their flight conspicuously erratic.

---

167 Small-footed Myotis
(*Myotis leibii*)

Description: Glossy fur, light tan to golden brown above; buff to nearly white below. Wings and interfemoral membrane dark brown. *Calcar keeled.* Black ears and a black mask. L 2¾–3¼″ (71–82 mm); T 1¼–1½″ (30–38 mm); HF ¼–⅜″ (6–8 mm); FA 1¼–1⅜″ (30–36 mm); Wt ¼ oz. (6–9 g).

Similar Species: Pipistrelles have tricolored red fur; California Myotis has duller fur; Little Brown Myotis lacks keel on calcar.

Habitat: Little is known; has been found beneath rock slabs, a sliding door, wallpaper, and in crevices.

Range: Much of w U.S. In the East, from New York and Maine south through the Appalachians. Isolated populations in Kentucky, Missouri, Arkansas, and Oklahoma

Its hindfoot, for which it is named, is usually slightly smaller than that of other members of its genus. It hibernates in small numbers in caves, often wedged into crevices, sometimes under rocks on the cave floor.

---

179 Silver-haired Bat
(*Lasionycteris noctivagans*)

Description: Medium-size. *Nearly black,* with *silvery-tipped hairs on back,* giving frosted appearance. Interfemoral membrane lightly furred above. Short, rounded, naked ears. L 3⅜–4¼″ (92–108 mm); T 1½–1¾″ (37–45 mm); FA 1½–1¾″ (37–44 mm); HF ⅜″ (9–10 mm); Wt ¼–½ oz. (9–15 g).

Similar Species: Some members of *Lasiurus* also have whitish-tipped fur, but they are much lighter colored overall. They also have much more fur on upper part of interfemoral membrane.

Habitat: In summer, north woods in protected spots (under bark; in dead trees, woodpecker holes, bird nests). In winter, hibernates in trees, crevices, buildings, and other protected places.

Range: Most of U.S. and s Canada.

This beautiful, solitary bat emerges in early evening, flying very slowly to feed on a variety of insects but especially favoring moths and flies. Generally migrating south for the winter, it possesses a well-developed homing instinct; one bat traveled 107 miles to its home roost. In southern Illinois, it occasionally hibernates in silica mines but very rarely enters caves. Over major parts of its range it can be found only during the spring and fall migration.

175   Western Pipistrelle
(*Pipistrellus hesperus*)

Description: *Smallest bat in U.S.* Light yellow or grayish to reddish-brown above; belly whitish. Wings, interfemoral membrane, ears, nose, and feet blackish. *Calcar keeled. One tiny premolar behind canine.* L 2⅜–3⅜″ (60–86 mm); T 1⅛–1⅜″ (27–32 mm); HF ¼″ (6–7 mm); FA 1⅛–1⅜″ (27–33 mm); Wt ⅛–¼ oz. (5–6 g).

Similar Species: California and Small-footed myotises usually larger, with two tiny premolars behind the canine.

Habitat: Caves, deserts, rocky areas, scrub, buildings.

Range: Southwestern U.S. from n central and Big Bend areas of Texas, w New Mexico, Utah north to e Oregon, se Washington.

Usually the first bat to appear in the evening, it often flies before dark and is even seen in broad daylight. Its flight is erratic and slow, less than 6 mph. These bats drink while skimming a pond or stream, dipping their lower jaws to sip while flying. In colder areas, they hibernate in caves, mines, and crevices; some migrate. The jerky flight of the closely related Common Pipistrelle, (*Pipistrellus pipistrellus*), the "common bat" of Great Britain and Europe, inspired the name of "flittermouse" for bats in general ("*Fledermaus*" in German).

159 Eastern Pipistrelle
(*Pipistrellus subflavus*)

Description: *Smallest bat in the East.* Reddish to light brown. *Hairs tricolored:* dark at base, light in middle, dark at tip. Calcar not keeled. Tragus blunt. *One tiny premolar behind canine.* L 3¼–3½" (81–89 mm); T 1⅜–1¾" (36–45 mm); FA 1¼–1⅜" (31–35 mm); Wt 16 14 oz. (3.3–6 g).

Similar Species: Most myotises have longer, thinner tragus and two tiny premolars behind the canine; all lack distinctly tricolored hairs.

Habitat: By day, usually hangs in vegetation. Some maternity colonies found in buildings. Hibernates in caves, mines, or crevices.

Range: Eastern U.S. west to Texas, Oklahoma, s Kansas, Iowa, se Minnesota.

Emerging early from its daytime hiding place, it feeds on tiny insects, especially leafhoppers, planthoppers, beetles, and flies. In the fall, it migrates to a small mine or cave to hibernate. During hibernation it is often covered with water droplets, which sparkle like diamonds and give it a whitish appearance.

166 Big Brown Bat
(*Eptesicus fuscus*)

Description: *Large. Brown* above, varying from light
(deserts) to dark (forests), usually
glossy; belly paler, with hairs dark at
base; wings and interfemoral membrane
black. Calcar keeled. *No reduced premolar
behind canine.* No fur on wings or
interfemoral membrane. L 4⅛–5″
(106–127 mm); T 1¾–2″ (42–
52 mm); HF ⅜–½″ (10–11.5 mm);
FA 1¾–2″ (42–51 mm); Wt ½–
⅝ oz. (13–18 g.)

Similar Species: Evening Bat much smaller; myotis bats
usually smaller with 2 (sometimes 1)
tiny premolars behind the canine.

Sign: Droppings on floor; dirty markings on
building exteriors at entry points.

Habitat: In summer, buildings and sometimes
hollow trees. In winter, caves, mines,
buildings, storm sewers, other
protected places.

Range: Throughout U.S. and s Canada, except
s Florida and s central Texas; very
common through much of range.

In Canada, this is the most common
bat to hibernate in buildings. However,
some retreat to caves and mines, where
they hang near the entrance either
singly or in small groups usually of not
more than 5 or 6. Babies often fall to
the floor, but many are retrieved by
their mothers, who find them by their
continual squeaking. Diet consists
mostly of large beetles but also wasps,
ants, planthoppers, leafhoppers, flies, a
few moths, and many other kinds of
insects. It does not feed in winter but
depends for energy on fat reserves,
which constitute one third of its body
weight. Its flying speed of 40 mph is
the fastest reported for any bat.

157 Red Bat
(*Lasiurus borealis*)

Description: *Males bright red* or orange-red; *females dull red,* brick, or chestnut; *both sexes frosted white on back and breast,* with a whitish patch on each shoulder. Ears small and rounded; tragus small. Interfemoral membrane furred above. L 3¾–5″ (95–126 mm); T 1¾–2⅜″ (45–62 mm); HF ⅜″ (8.5–10 mm); FA 1½–1¾″ (37–42 mm); Wt ⅜–½ oz. (9.5–15 g).

Similar Species: Hoary Bat larger, browner, more frosted; Seminole Bat deep mahogany brown; Yellow Bats yellowish with fur only on basal half of interfemoral membrane, none on back half.

Habitat: In summer, among foliage, usually in trees, along hedgerows, or at forest edge.

Range: Extreme s Canada and much of U.S. west through North Dakota, e Colorado, and Texas; in the Southwest: California, sw Nevada, sw Utah, most of Arizona.

One of the few few mammals in which coloration differs between male and female, this solitary bat by day hangs 4–10′ above ground, among dense foliage that provides shade from above and at sides but is open below, allowing a downward fall into flight. Females with young usually roost at 10–20′. Emerging early in the evening, these fast flyers often use the same route each night in foraging for many kinds of insects, especially moths, beetles, planthoppers, leafhoppers, ants, and flies. Occasionally they alight on vegetation to pluck off insects. The Red Bat commonly has 3–4 offspring at a time, and it is the only bat with 4 nipples. While all evidence indicates that the young are not carried about during flight, females with young attached are often found on the ground; they may have been blown down or scared out of a tree by a predator and could not take off due to the weight of the young. It migrates to the southern parts of its range for the winter, or may hibernate, sometimes emerging on warm days to feed.

---

158 Seminole Bat
(*Lasiurus seminolus*)

Description: *Mahogany brown,* with *slight silver "frosting." Interfemoral membrane furred above.* Ears short and rounded; tragus very short. L 4⅛–4⅜" (108–114 mm); T 1¾–2" (44–52 mm); HF ¼–⅜" (8–9 mm); FA 1⅜–1¾" (35–45 mm); Wt ¼–½ oz. (7–14 g).

Similar Species: Among other members of this genus, Red Bat lighter; yellow bats yellowish; Hoary Bat much larger, light brown with much frosting.

Habitat: Clumps of Spanish moss.

Range: Abundant in se U.S. from e North Carolina to e Texas, wherever Spanish moss occurs.

As its name implies, this bat is frequent in the homelands of the Seminole Indians. By day, it generally hangs 3½–5' above ground in clumps of Spanish moss that have clear areas beneath, permitting a downward fall into flight. Unlike most bats, it usually gives birth to 3–4 young, born late May–early June.

---

178 Hoary Bat
(*Lasiurus cinereus*)

Description: *Largest bat in the East. Light brown above* with tips of *fur heavily frosted white;* throat buff. Ears short and rounded, with black, naked rims. *Interfemoral membranes well-furred above.* L 4–6"

(102–152 mm); T 1¾–2⅝" (44–65 mm); HF ¼–⅝" (6–14 mm); FA 1¾–2¼" (42–59 mm); Wt ¾–1¼ oz. (20–35 g).

Similar Species: Silver-haired Bat blackish with light frosting.

Habitat: Hangs from evergreen branches.

Range: Throughout continental U.S. except for peninsular Florida; also found in s Canada.

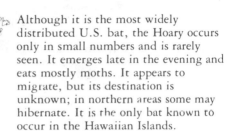

Although it is the most widely distributed U.S. bat, the Hoary occurs only in small numbers and is rarely seen. It emerges late in the evening and eats mostly moths. It appears to migrate, but its destination is unknown; in northern areas some may hibernate. It is the only bat known to occur in the Hawaiian Islands.

155 Northern Yellow Bat
(*Lasiurus intermedius*)

Description: Large. *Yellowish-brown, washed with black above. Long, silky fur. Dorsal half of interfemoral membrane well-furred above.* Ears broad and rounded; tragus broad below, tapering near tip. L av. 4½" (115 mm); T 2" (51 mm); HF ⅜" (10¼ mm); FA 1¾–2¼" (45–56 mm).

Similar Species: Southern Yellow Bat smaller where the two occur together, only in s Texas.

Habitat: By day, clumps of Spanish moss in areas of longleaf pine and turkey oak. In the Rio Grande Valley, palm trees.

Range: Southeastern U.S., primarily from coastal North Carolina to e Texas.

This tree-loving species congregates to feed, and females form loose colonies during breeding season; otherwise it is solitary. It forages about 15–20' above the ground.

156 Southern Yellow Bat
(*Lasiurus ega*)

Description: *Large. Yellowish-buff. Basal half of interfemoral membrane furred above.* Ears, ¾" (17 mm) long, rather large for a bat of this genus, higher than wide, pointed, partially furred outside, and reaching end of nose when laid forward. L 4⅜–5" (109–126 mm); T 1⅞–2⅛" (47–53 mm); HF ⅜" (10 mm); FA 1¾–1⅞" (45–48 mm); Wt ⅜–¾ oz. (9.2–22.5 g).

Similar Species: Northern Yellow Bat larger where the two occur together in s Texas; Red Bat more reddish; Western Pipistrelle much smaller.

Habitat: By day, hangs among vegetation.

Range: Extreme s California, s Arizona, extreme sw New Mexico.

Little is known about this beautiful bat except that it emerges early from its day roost in leafy vegetation and feeds on insects.

---

168 Evening Bat
(*Nycticeius humeralis*)

Description: *Reddish-brown* to dark brown above; tawny below. No fur on wings or interfemoral membrane. Calcar not keeled. Tragus short and curved. Only *1 upper incisor and no reduced premolar* behind canine. L 3⅛–3¾" (78–93 mm); T 1⅜–1½" (35–37 mm); HF ¼–⅜" (7–10 mm); FA 1¼–1½" (33–39 mm); Wt ¼ oz. (5–9 g).

Similar Species: Big Brown Bat much larger; myotises usually have two tiny premolars behind canine.

Habitat: In summer, buildings and hollow trees; winter residence not known.

Range: Southeastern U.S. west to Texas and se Nebraska and north to s Iowa, s Michigan, and s Pennsylvania, but not in the Allegheny Mountains.

This low-flying species tends to soar higher in the evening, lower at night. Maternity colonies sometimes number in the hundreds; they disperse by fall. Although sometimes seen among those bats swarming at cave entrances, the Evening Bat almost never enters caves.

143 Spotted Bat
"Death's Head Bat" "Jackass Bat"
(*Euderma maculatum*)

Description: Black above with *three large white spots on back* (one on each shoulder and at base of tail); white below. *Huge ears,* almost 2" (51 mm) long. L 4¼–4½" (107–115 mm); T 1⅞–2" (46–50 mm); FA 1⅞–2" (48–51 mm).

Habitat: Apparently lives primarily in crevices in rocky cliffs and canyons.

Range: Southern California and s Nevada through sw Colorado, Arizona, w New Mexico, with scattered records north to Montana.

One of the rarest North American bats, it emerges late, carrying its huge ears forward during flight and giving a loud, high-pitched call. It feeds almost entirely on moths. The ears are held erect when the bat is alert or just before taking flight and are curled and lie backward when the bat rests. It appears to be relatively solitary but sometimes hibernates in small clusters. It is called the Death's Head Bat because of its striking coloration.

145 Townsend's Big-eared Bat
(*Plecotus townsendii*)

Description: Pale gray or brown above; *buff underparts.* Wings and interfemoral membrane naked. *Enormous ears,* 1¼–1½" (31–37 mm) long, extending to middle of body when laid back; 2 large glandular lumps on nose. L 3½–4⅜" (89–110 mm); T 1⅜–2⅛" (35–54 mm); HF ⅜–½" (10–13 mm); FA 1½–1⅞" (39–47 mm); Wt ¼–⅜ oz. (9–12 g).

Similar Species: In the East, Rafinesque's Big-eared Bat has white underparts. In the West, Allen's Big-eared Bat has pair of leaflike flaps projecting forward from base of ears.

Habitat: Usually in caves; sometimes in buildings, especially on West Coast. In the West, scrub deserts, pine and piñon-juniper forests. In the East, generally oak-hickory forests.

Range: Western U.S. north to s British Columbia, east through Idaho, Wyoming, Colorado, New Mexico, Oklahoma, Texas; scattered populations in Arkansas, Missouri, Kentucky, Virginia, West Virginia.

This bat emerges late to feed almost entirely on moths. In summer, females form nursery colonies of up to about 200 bats in the West and 1,000 in the East; males are solitary. During winter, when they hibernate in caves, the great ears are folded on the back like a ram's horns; if the bats are disturbed, the ears unfold and move in circles like antennae. Even in the coldest weather, these bats often move between caves.

144 Rafinesque's Big-eared Bat
(*Plecotus rafinesquii*)

Description: Brown, with *white-tipped fur on belly.* Wings and interfemoral membrane naked. *Large ears,* 1¼" (32–36 mm) long, extending to middle of back when laid back; 2 large glandular lumps on nose. L 3⅝–4¼" (92–106 mm); T 1⅝–2⅛" (41–54 mm); HF ¼–½" (8–12 mm); FA 1⅝–1¾" (40–46 mm); Wt ⅜ oz. (9–12 g).

Similar Species: Townsend's Big-eared Bat has buff fur on belly.

Habitat: Usually buildings in forested regions in the South. Caves or mines in the North.

Range: Southeastern U.S. west to Louisiana and Arkansas and north to Kentucky, s Indiana, and North Carolina.

Upon being disturbed, these bats unfold their large ears; when the bats are resting, ears are coiled against the side of the head rather like a ram's horns. This reduces the ear's surface area, minimizing water loss. They roost singly, and they hibernate. The ability to hover like a butterfly enables them to pluck insects from foliage.

142 Allen's Big-eared Bat
(*Idionycteris phyllotis*)

Description: *Tawny above* with hairs dark brown at base; underparts slightly lighter. No fur on wings or membranes. Tragus, ½" (16 mm) long; white patches behind ears. *Enormous ears, 1½" (40 mm) long, with two flaps projecting forward from bases* (the only big-eared bat with such flaps). L 4⅛–4⅝" (103–118 mm); T 1¾–2¼" (46–55 mm); HF ⅜–½" (10–11 mm); Wt ⅜–½ oz. (10.4–13.2 g).

Habitat: Caves and mines in forested mountains.

Range: Arizona and w New Mexico.

Like other big-eared bats, it emerges late in the evening. Its ears lie back when it is resting, becoming erect if it is disturbed. Maternity colonies form in protected places in rocks or mines.

146 Pallid Bat
(*Antrozous pallidus*)

Description: *Large.* Creamy to beige above; nearly white below. *Big ears,* 1–1⅜″ (25–35 mm) long, separated at base. Wings and interfemoral membrane essentially naked. L 4¼–5⅛″ (107–130 mm); T 1⅜–1⅞″ (35–49 mm); HF ⅜–⅝″ (11–16 mm); FA 1⅞–2⅜″ (48–60 mm); Wt 1–1¼ oz. (28–37 g).

Similar Species: All other big-eared bats much darker.

Sign: Droppings (guano) on hay in barn or floor of buildings; somewhat resembling mouse droppings but segmented and consisting chiefly of insect fragments.

Habitat: Deserts; daytime roosts in buildings and crevices, less often caves, mines, hollow trees, and other shelters.

Range: Deserts from n central British Columbia and e Washington to s California, s Kansas, w Texas.

Emerging late at night and beating its wings more slowly than many bats (only 10–11 beats per sec.), this stately bat is unique in feeding primarily on the ground; several have been caught in mousetraps. Its food consists of many large insects, including flightless beetles, crickets, scorpions, and grasshoppers; in captivity, it has captured and consumed lizards. Its several calls include an insect-like buzz; high-pitched dry, rasping, thin double notes; single, clear, resonant high-pitched notes; and clicks. The first two are generally given when the colony is disturbed, the latter two at night in flight. The summer colonies of from 30–100 bats are unusual in that they include members of both sexes and young. A skunklike odor given off by glands on the muzzle is most pronounced when the bat is disturbed.

FREE-TAILED BATS
(Family Molossidae)

Some 80 species are distributed throughout the warmer parts of the world; 6 species occur in our region. Free-tailed bats have naked tails extending well beyond the edge of the interfemoral membrane; usually at least half the tail is free. Wings are narrow and flight swift and straight. Since their faces somewhat resemble those of mastiff-type dogs (molossids), these snub-nosed, thickset species are also known as mastiff bats. They groom themselves with spoon-shaped bristles on the hind toe of their broad feet. Thumb and toe claws have double talons.

152 Brazilian Free-tailed Bat
(*Tadarida brasiliensis*)

Description: *Smallest free-tailed bat.* Dark brown or dark gray above, with hairs whitish at base. *Ears separated at base.* Calcar pointed backward, extending the short interfemoral membrane more than half the length of tail. L 3½–4⅜″ (90–110 mm); T 1⅜–1¾″ (33–44 mm); FA 1⅜–1¾″ (36–46 mm); Wt ⅜–½ oz. (11–14 g).

Habitat: Buildings in the Southeast and on West Coast; caves from Texas to Arizona.

Range: Throughout s U.S., in the West, north to s Oregon and s Nebraska; in the East, north to n Louisiana, Alabama, and South Carolina; a few scattered further north.

The Brazilian Free-tailed Bat is by far the most common bat in the Southwest; a U.S. population of at least 100 million also makes it one of the most numerous mammals in the country. In the East and on the West Coast, it hibernates but does not migrate. From

Texas through the Southwest, it lives in huge colonies in caves, packed 250 per sq. ft. While a few hibernate, most migrate to Mexico for the winter, usually toward the end of October, and return in March to mate. The young hang by themselves in a nursery; mothers returning to the cave nurse any baby. Many young lose their grip on the ceiling and perish on the cave floor, as females make no attempt to save them. At least 1 million of these bats live in the largest colony, in Frio Cave, Texas. The Carlsbad Caverns in New Mexico were first discovered as a result of the bats' emergence from them. Although the cavern population has declined from an estimated 8–9 million in the 1930's to several hundred thousand, the bats' daily emergence is a major tourist attraction.

At sunset, bats begin flitting about inside the cave, causing a slight rise in temperature and humidity. After circling for several minutes they begin to emerge in a counterclockwise spiral, ascending 150–180' from the depths of the cave into the night air. Emergence may be either continuous, split into 2 groups with an interval of half an hour, or "puffy," beginning with many bursts of from several hundred to several thousand bats at a time, giving way after 15–20 minutes to a continuous stream. They make a great roar and form a dark cloud visible miles away; when flight is at its heaviest, 5,000–10,000 bats emerge each minute. Generally they fly throughout the night, at 10–15 mph, feeding on a variety of small insects, especially moths, ants, beetles, and leafhoppers captured in the interfemoral membrane. Each night, a bat eats up to one third its own weight; 250,000 bats can consume half a ton of insect pests. While they may roam up to 150 miles, most Carlsbad bats feed within a 50-mile radius. The return to the caves is

even more spectacular than the
emergence: most bats appear just at
sunrise and from heights of 600–
1000′ plummet straight down at speeds
of more than 25 mph. The life span of
these bats is 13–18 years; hawks and
owls are their only predators. Bat
droppings, called guano, were used
during the Civil War as a source of
sodium nitrate for gunpowder and
mined as fertilizer from the turn of the
century through the 1940's. Droppings
in the Carlsbad Caverns over the past
17,000 years have formed guano
deposits covering several thousand sq.
ft. to a depth of almost 50′. A few
small-scale guano mines are still in
operation. A hazard of entering bat
caves is the danger of rabies,
transmitted by a bat bite or, much
more likely, by the airborne virus.

149 Pocketed Free-tailed Bat
(*Tadarida femorosacca*)

Description: Dark gray or brown above and below;
lower half of hairs nearly white. Wings
long and narrow. Tail free about half its
length. *Ears joined at base.* L 3⅞–4⅛″
(98–118 mm); T 1¼–1¾″ (30–
42 mm); FA 1¾–2″ (44–51 mm).

Similar Species: Brazilian Free-tailed Bat's ears not
joined; other free-tailed bats have larger
forearms.

Habitat: Rock outcrops in desert.

Range: Southern California, s Arizona, small
area in se New Mexico, Big Bend area
of Texas.

By day, it roosts in rock crevices or
other shelters in rocky areas, in small
colonies usually composed of less than
100 members. As it drops from its
perch into the air at night it gives a
loud, high-pitched call. It feeds on
moths, ants, wasps, leafhoppers, and
other insects. The femoral "pocket,"

which gives this bat its common and species names, is inconspicuous.

151 Big Free-tailed Bat
(*Tadarida macrotis*)

Description: *Large.* Reddish-brown, dark brown, or black, with *hairs white at base. Tail free for an inch or more.* Ears joined at base and extending beyond tip of nose when laid forward. L 5⅛–5¾″ (129–144 mm); T 1¾–2″ (43–50 mm); FA 2¼–2⅜″ (58–64 mm).

Similar Species: Other free-tailed bats smaller; Underwood's Mastiff and Western Mastiff bats larger.

Habitat: Rocky areas; day roosts in rocky cliffs.

Range: Widespread but usually uncommon; sometimes locally abundant in parts of California and Nevada east to Kansas and Texas. Scattered autumn records far from normal range in British Columbia and Iowa.

This colonial bat emerges late to feed primarily on moths but also on crickets, grasshoppers, ants, and other insects. It sometimes chatters loudly when feeding.

150 Western Mastiff Bat
"Bonnet Bat"
(*Eumops perotis*)

Description: *Largest bat in North America.* Body sparsely furred, with dark brown hairs white at base. *Enormous ears,* 1–1½″ (25–40 mm) long, joined at base and protruding over forehead. L 5½–7½″ (140–185 mm); T 1½–3¼″ (35–80 mm); FA 2¾–3¼″ (72–82 mm).

Similar Species: Underwood's Mastiff Bat smaller, with smaller ears.

Sign: Day roost crevices can often be spotted by the yellowish urine stains on rocks below and by the large size of the droppings.

Habitat: Rocky cliffs and canyons; also buildings.

Range: Southern California, extreme s Nevada, s Arizona, extreme sw New Mexico, Big Bend area of Texas.

By day these bats form small colonies, usually with fewer than 100 members. Because of their large size and long wings, they require considerable space to launch themselves into flight, so roosting sites are usually situated to permit a free downward fall for at least 10'. To enter roost crevices, bats sweep into long vertical slits at least 2" wide, then climb rapidly to wedge themselves into a narrow spot. Roosts are alternated throughout the year. As night approaches, loud squeaks may be heard near the entrance. During flight, cries are frequent and can be heard more than 1,000' away. Foraging high and at great distances from roosting sites, the bats feed primarily on moths, which constitute 80% of their diet, but also eat ground-living crickets and long-horned grasshoppers. When they crawl on all fours, as they often do, the tail sticks straight up and perhaps serves as a tactile organ. From the way its large ears cover its head, the creature gets the nickname "Bonnet Bat."

---

148 Underwood's Mastiff Bat
(*Eumops underwoodi*)

Description: *Large,* free-tailed bat. Dark brown above; grayish below. Body hairs lighter at base. *Large ears,* 1⅛–1⅜" (29–33 mm) long, joined at base and projecting over forehead. L 6⅜– 6⅝" (160–167 mm); T 2–2⅜" (52– 60 mm); HF ¾" (15–20 mm); FA 2⅝– 2⅞" (67–70 mm); Wt 1⅞–2⅛ oz. (53–61 g).

Similar Species: Brazilian Free-tailed and Big Free-tailed bats much smaller; Western Mastiff Bat larger, with bigger ears.

Habitat: Deserts.

Range: Pima County, Arizona.

This little-known bat makes frequent ear-piercing calls during flight. Its range extends south to northern Central America.

153 Wagner's Mastiff Bat
(*Eumops glaucinus*)

Description: Large. *Gray or nearly black;* slightly lighter below. Free tail extends far beyond interfemoral membrane. Ears joined at base. Wings long and narrow. L 3¼" (80 mm); FA 2¼–2⅜" (57–66 mm).

Similar Species: Brazilian Free-tailed Bat, the only other eastern free-tailed bat, much smaller (forearm less than 50 mm), with ears not joined at base.

Habitat: Of the specimens taken, many were found under "Cuban tile," often used as roofing material in Coral Gables, Fla.

Range: Extreme se Florida near Miami and Ft. Lauderdale.

Although considered a rare bat, it flies about over the city of Miami, making a high, piercing noise that can be heard even over downtown traffic.

Edentates
(Order Edentata)

Edentata (Latin for "without teeth") is a misleading name for members of this order, which includes armadillos, sloths, and anteaters. The name of the order originated in the eighteenth century, when they were classified with such truly toothless creatures as the pangolin and the duck-billed platypus. In fact, only the anteaters are toothless, and the giant armadillo, with up to 100 teeth, is among the most toothy of mammals. What distinguishes the edentates from other living mammals is their unique feature of extra articulations between some of the vertebrae. Members of this diverse group are found primarily in South and Central America, where they developed when those areas were separated from the rest of the New World; the only North American representative is the Nine-banded Armadillo (*Dasypus novemcinctus*); its teeth are simple pegs.

217, 218 Nine-banded Armadillo
(*Dasypus novemcinctus*)

Description: The only North American mammal armored with *heavy, bony plates*. Scaly-looking plates cover head, body, and tail. Between wide front and back plates, a midsection of 9 (sometimes fewer) narrow, jointed armor bands permit the body to curl. Head small. Underparts and upright ears are soft. Sparsely haired body is brown, tan, or sometimes yellowish but, depending on where it burrows, may be stained dark, even black, by earth or mud. L 24¼–31½" (615–800 mm); T 9⅝–14⅜" (245–370 mm). HF 3–4" (75–100 mm).

Sign: Burrows, often along creek banks, with entrance holes about 6–8" across.
Scat: Like clay marbles, and, in fact, consisting chiefly of clay, for an armadillo consumes much dirt as it feeds on insects.
Tracks: Foreprint about 1¾" long, 1½" wide; hindprint over 2" long, 1½" wide. In sand or dust, blurred and appear almost hooflike. In soft earth or mud, occasionally all the long toes show more or less clearly; forefoot has 4 toes, the middle ones closely spaced, the outer spread wide and much shorter; hindfoot has 5 toes more evenly spread, the 3 middle ones long, the outer ones short, with no separation from heel pad. Trail sometimes shows only occasional footprints, for some are obliterated by the drag marks of the armor shell.

Habitat: Abundant in sandy soils; in clay, where digging is more difficult; along streams where soil is moist and flaky, for during the dry season it must dig its insect foods from the earth. The relative ease with which it can burrow has much bearing on whether it will be abundant in a region.

Range: Southeastern U.S., where in recent years it has rapidly expanded its range:

most of Florida and parts of Georgia west to se Kansas, Oklahoma, Texas.

The Spanish conquistadores first encountered this strange creature and named it the "little man in armor." It spends most waking hours digging for food and building burrows, grunting almost constantly. The breeding burrows contain a nest of leaves or grass; mating occurs in the fall. There is a delay of 14 weeks before the embryo is implanted in the uterine wall. A single egg divides into 4 identical quadruplets, often used in experiments requiring 4 identical animals. Well-formed at birth and with eyes open, they can walk about within hours. Their skin, however, is soft during infancy, becoming hard slowly; they resemble miniature piglets as they trail after their mother. There is one litter per year. The Nine-banded Armadillo does not hibernate and cannot survive prolonged below-freezing weather. It roots for insects and snuffs about in vegetation for ants and invertebrates. It also eats crayfish, amphibians, reptile and bird eggs, and carrion. For such a clumsy-looking animal it is surprisingly swift. It can swim short distances, gulping air to inflate its intestines for increased buoyancy, and can cross small streams by walking underwater on the stream bed. It goes about its business with a steady, stiff-legged jog, but when approached, escapes by running away or rolling into a ball to protect its vulnerable belly; it can also burrow underground with amazing speed. Its meat tastes somewhat like pork, and its decorative shell is used to make bowls or baskets.

Pikas, Rabbits, and Hares
(Order Lagomorpha)

Lagomorphs, or "hare-shaped" animals
(from the Greek, *lagos* "hare" and
morpha "form"), possess two pairs of
upper incisors, the first enlarged and
chisel-like, the second small, directly
behind the first, and lacking cutting
edges. As in some other animals, the
incisors continue to grow throughout
life but are constantly worn down by
use. Lagomorphs are characterized not
only by the tandem upper incisors but
by the location of the scrotum in front
of the penis rather than behind it.
Except for marsupials, no other
mammals have this genital structure.
On account of the prominent gnawing
teeth and their eating habits, for many
years these animals were incorrectly
classed as rodents. In our area the order
is represented by two families: the
rabbits and hares (Leporidae) have long
ears and long, jumping hindlegs; the
pikas (Ochotonidae) have small,
rounded ears and nonjumping hindlegs
only slightly longer than forelegs. Strict
vegetarians, they make the most of
their meals by eating their food twice
(reingestion). Vulnerable to predators,
they evolved a protective mechanism of
quickly filling the stomach, then
hurrying to a hiding place, where they
defecate pellets of soft, green,
undigested material, which they then
eat and digest normally to obtain
maximum nutrition.

PIKAS
(Family Ochotonidae)

Pikas, similar in shape to guinea pigs, have prominent ears evenly rounded into semicircles, furred soles of the feet, and no visible tail. They are active by day and, unlike rabbits and hares, are highly vocal and social, living in large colonies and constantly communicating with their fellows in shrill nasal bleats and barking chatters. The name "pika" comes from the Tunga people, a Mongoloid race from northeastern Siberia; it was originally pronounced *peeka* but has been Americanized to *pie-ka*.

79, 80 **Collared Pika**
(*Ochotona collaris*)

Description: Brown above, gray on sides, with *pale gray collar* on neck and shoulders; belly light. Ears dark, edged with buff. L 7–7¾" (178–198 mm); HF 1⅛–1¼" (29–31 mm).
Similar Species: Pika is brownish, lacks collar.
Breeding: 2–6 young born in spring.
Habitat: Talus slopes.
Range: Southeastern Alaska to sw Mackenzie Territory.

Like the Pika to the south, this animal piles summer plant cuttings into haystacks to serve as its winter food.

---

81 **Pika**
"Cony" "Whistling Hare" "Piping Hare"
(*Ochotona princeps*)

Description: Brownish. *Small rounded ears. No visible tail.* L 6⅜–8½" (162–216 mm); HF 1¼–1⅜" (30–36 mm); Wt 3¾–4½ oz. (108–128 g).

Similar Species: Collared Pika has dusky collar.

Sign: *Scat:* Black and sticky, likened to "round pellets of black tapioca." *Tracks:* Seldom visible except in patches of snow or mud; complete cluster, showing all 4 feet, no more than 3" wide, less than 4" from hind to fore prints. Front feet have 5 toes, but often the reduced fifth toe does not print; hindfeet, with 4 toes, slightly larger than forefeet but not greatly elongated, so there is no mistaking track for a rabbit's.

Breeding: 2–6 young born blind and naked May–June; a second litter may be produced in late summer.

Habitat: Talus slides; rocky banks; steep, boulder-covered hillsides; usually at elevations of 8,000–13,500'.

Range: Western North America from central California and n New Mexico north to middle British Columbia.

The Pika feeds on many species of green plants, eating some on the spot and, in late summer, when foraging may continue into evening, scurrying back and forth carrying cuttings to boulders near its home. It spreads them to dry in the sun, curing its "hay" as a farmer does; haystacks are not high but may contain up to a bushel of vegetation, primarily grasses and sedges but including fireweed, dryad, stonecrop, sweetgrass, and thistles. Even when large, piles are frequently moved for better drying or to shelter them from rain. Later, the dried vegetation is stores in the Pika's den deep among the rocks. In winter, it does not hibernate but, kept warm by its long, thick fur, remains active, feeding on stored hay and lichen. A Pika characteristically jerks its body upward and forward with each call, which perhaps explains why calls tend to be ventriloquial, sometimes seeming to come from far off when, in fact, echoing from sources almost underfoot. The naturalist

Thomas Nuttall described the call as "a slender, but very distinct bleat, so like that of a young kid or goat," that he was astonished when "the mountains brought forth nothing much larger than a mouse." On one occasion of a weasel's attempt to capture a Pika by chasing it among the rocks, when the Pika began to tire, another Pika ran between it and the weasel, which then pursued the intruder until this time the weasel tired and withdrew to easier prey. While it is not known if such behavior is widespread, it is easy to see how it could have evolved as a defensive response beneficial to the entire community.

RABBITS AND HARES
(Family Leporidae)

Rabbits and hares, both small grazing mammals, have long ears, long hindlegs, and bulging eyes on the sides of the head, which enable them to watch for danger over a wide arc. Does (females) are larger than bucks (males), the reverse of the case in most mammals.

Primarily nocturnal, they can scent enemies, thump the ground with a hindleg when alarmed, and, in turn, sense the ground vibrations caused by the thumps of other rabbits or hares nearby. They "freeze" when threatened and instantly switch direction when running. Most rest in "forms," or shallow depressions in the ground. They give a piercing distress call (the hare's is louder and deeper than the rabbit's), the young squeal almost inaudibly, does may grunt or purr while nursing, but rabbits and hares are generally silent. Their astonishing reproductive powers help compensate for their high rate of predation. Hares (*Lepus*) are generally larger than rabbits and have longer ears and longer, more powerful hindlegs; they usually live in a more open habitat than rabbits and attempt to outrun predators. Rabbits, less proficient runners, try to elude enemies by hiding in dense cover.

Hares make no maternity nests—their young are born well developed, fully furred, and with eyes open. They are able to move about within hours and fend for themselves; they require little protection. Cottontail rabbits (*Sylvilagus*) do make nests, because their young, born naked and with eyes closed, need an extended period of maternal care. About a week before giving birth, the pregnant cottontail finds a suitable spot, usually where tangled brush or high grass provides a screen, and makes a saucer-like depression in the ground, about 3–4" deep and 8" across. She then bites off downy fur from her breast and belly, mixes it with soft, dead grasses and leaves, and uses this to line the nest and make a second layer to cover the young while she is away foraging. This soft coverlet not only helps to keep them dry and conceal the nest, but the removal of the mother's fur exposes her nipples, facilitating nursing.

The signs, including tracks, of all members of this family are similar and are presented for the most common species, the Eastern Cottontail (*Sylvilagus floridanus*).

Pygmy Rabbit
(*Sylvilagus idahoensis*)

Description: *Smallest rabbit in North America.* Buffy-grayish or blackish above. *Tail gray above and below. Whitish spots at sides of nostrils.* Ears 1⅜–1⅞" (36–48 mm) long; L 9¾–11⅜" (250–290 mm), T ¾–1¼" (20–30 mm); HF 2¼–2¾" (58–72 mm); Wt 8⅜–16 oz. (246–458 g).

Similar Species: Cottontails larger, with tail white below.

Sign: Burrows with 3" opening and 3 or more entrances; scattered quantities of tiny fecal pellets slightly over ¼" in diameter.

Habitat: Sagebrush, especially stands of tall sage (*Artemisia tridentata*).

Range: Southeast Washington, s Idaho, and extreme sw Montana south to w Utah, Nevada, and small section of central California.

The Pygmy Rabbit differs from all other native North American rabbits by digging its own burrow system. It mates in spring and summer and has about 6 young per litter. These rabbits are seldom eaten because of the strong sage flavor of their flesh.

246 Brush Rabbit
(*Sylvilagus bachmani*)

Description: Small. Reddish-brown mottled with black; lighter in winter but still mottled. *Short legs. Small tail. Short dark ears,* 1⅞–2½" (50–64 mm) long. L 11⅛–14¾" (280–375 mm); T ¾–1¼" (20–43 mm); HF 2⅝–3¼" (67–85 mm); Wt 15⅞–34 oz. (450–965 g).

Similar Species: Desert Cottontail, the only cottontail that shares its range (in California), larger, has longer tail and longer hindlegs.

Sign: Close-cropped feeding sites; a maze of runways connecting forms.

Habitat: Thick brushy areas, especially where brush has been cut.

Range: West Coast from nw Oregon to Baja California.

While the Brush Rabbit is primarily nocturnal, its young are often active by day. It does not dig burrows and rarely retreats into the burrow of another animal, even when pursued, but may climb into low brush to escape. Green clover is a favorite food, but it also eats grasses, plantain, and various berries, and in winter, woody vegetation, primarily salal and Douglas fir. It breeds February through August and has about 5 litters per year of 1–7 offspring (averaging 3). Before leaving the nest, the mother covers it with a blanket of grass. The young are mature in 4–5 months. Lynx, coyotes, hawks, and gopher snakes are among its predators.

248 Marsh Rabbit
(*Sylvilagus palustris*)

Description: *Dark brown above* with nape dark
cinnamon; belly white. Very *small tail,
gray mixed with brown below.* Short,
broad ears, 1⅛–2" (45–52 mm) long;
feet small, reddish-brown above.
L 14⅛–18" (352–450 mm); T 1¼–
1½" (33–39 mm); HF 3½–3⅝" (88–
91 mm); Wt av. 3½ lb. (1.6 kg).

Similar Species: Swamp Rabbit larger, with tail white
below like that of other cottontails.

Sign: Trails in marshy vegetation.
Tracks: In addition to the typical rabbit
tracks, alternating tracks are left when
it walks on hind legs, a practice
frequent for the Marsh Rabbit though
unusual for leporids.

Habitat: Bottomlands, swamps, lake borders,
coastal waterways.

Range: Florida northeast to se Virginia.

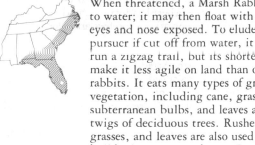

When threatened, a Marsh Rabbit takes
to water; it may then float with only
eyes and nose exposed. To elude a
pursuer if cut off from water, it will
run a zigzag trail, but its shorter legs
make it less agile on land than other
rabbits. It eats many types of green
vegetation, including cane, grasses,
subterranean bulbs, and leaves and
twigs of deciduous trees. Rushes,
grasses, and leaves are also used to
build a large, covered nest. Breeding
begins in February, and there are
several litters per year of 2–5 young.

238 Eastern Cottontail
(*Sylvilagus floridanus*)

Description: *Grayish-brown above,* interspersed with
some black; forehead often has white
spot. Distinct *rust-colored nape.* Short
tail cottony white below. Whitish feet.
Long ears, 1⅞–2¾" (49–68 mm).
L 14¾–18¼" (375–463 mm); T 1½–

2⅝" (39–65 mm); HF 3⅜–4⅛" (87–104 mm); Wt 2–4 lb. (900–1,800 g).

Similar Species: New England Cottontail usually lacks rust-colored nape and has black patch between ears; Desert Cottontail usually smaller with slightly longer ears; Marsh and Swamp rabbits have dark feet; Snowshoe Hare usually larger, dark brown in summer.

Sign: Small, woody sprigs cut off cleanly and at an angle (sprigs browsed by deer, which lack upper incisors, are raggedly torn). Young trees stripped of bark to height of 3–4' when snow is deep. *Scat:* Dark brown, spheroid, pea-size pellets sometimes found in piles. *Tracks:* In clusters of 4; foreprints almost round, about 1" wide, slightly longer hindprints oblong, about 3–4" long, depending on size and speed of rabbit. When sitting or standing: 2 foreprints side by side just ahead of 2 more widely spaced hindprints. When moving: one foreprint slightly ahead of the other; hindprints ahead of foreprints, as forefeet are fulcrums for hops. Hindprints relatively short when moving fast, as less of the leg touches down. Straddle 4–5"; stride variable with speed.

Habitat: Brushy areas, old fields, woods, cultivated areas; especially thickets and brush piles.

Range: Eastern U.S. except for New England, west through North Dakota, Kansas, Texas, n New Mexico, and into Arizona.

The most common rabbit in our range, the Eastern Cottontail breeds from February through September and usually produces 3–4 litters per year of 1–9 young (usually 4–5), which are nursed at dawn and dusk. Within hours after giving birth the female mates again. If no young were lost, a single pair, together with their offspring, could produce 350,000 rabbits in 5 years. However, this rabbit's death rate vies with its birth rate, and few rabbits live more than one year. Cottontails usually hop, but they can leap 10–15'; sometimes they stand on hindfeet to view their surroundings. When pursued, they usually circle their territory and often jump sideways to break their scent trail. They dislike getting wet but will swim if pressed. In winter, where brush is strong enough to hold a covering blanket of snow, they may make a network of runways beneath it. In cold weather, they often take shelter in the burrow of a woodchuck. During breeding season, males fight each other and perform dancelike courtship displays before the territorial females. On midwinter nights, groups of cottontails have been seen frolicking on crusted snow; as they are not mating aggregations, they may be purely playful gatherings to provide release after periods of forced inactivity.

245 New England Cottontail
(*Sylvilagus transitionalis*)

Description: *Brownish, heavily sprinkled with black. Black patch between ears.* Never a white spot on forehead. Short ears, 2¼–2¾" (56–71 mm) long, with outer edge bordered with a broad black stripe. L 14¼–19" (363–483 mm); T 1¼–1⅞" (31–49 mm); HF 3½–4" (90–102 mm); Wt 26¼–47⅛ oz. (750–1,347 g).

Similar Species: Eastern Cottontail lacks black patch between ears, often has white spot on forehead.

Habitat: Woods or brushlands.

Range: New England southwest through the Alleghenies.

The habits of this rabbit are very similar to those of the Eastern Cottontail, but it is much more secretive and rarely ventures from

cover. Its home range is about ½–¾ of an acre. There are several litters per year of 3–8 young. In recent years, its numbers have been declining and its range shrinking, probably because of loss of habitat and the widespread introduction of other rabbit species.

237 Nuttall's Cottontail
"Mountain Cottontail"
(*Sylvilagus nuttallii*)

Description: Grayish-brown above; white below. *Black-tipped ears,* 2⅛–2⅝" (54–65 mm) long, densely furred inside. L 13¾–15⅜" (350–390 mm); T 1¾–2" (44–50 mm); HF 3½–3⅞" (88–100 mm); Wt 23⅞–36⅜ oz. (678–1,032 g).

Similar Species: Desert Cottontail's ears sometimes longer, sparsely furred inside.

Habitat: Sagebrush; wooded areas particularly in southern parts of range; uplands.

Range: Eastern Washington and extreme s central British Columbia to e California east through s Saskatchewan, Montana, n New Mexico.

Nuttall's Cottontail rests in forms when dense vegetation is available but otherwise uses burrows and rocky crevices for shelter. It prefers grass but lives most of the year on sagebrush and will eat juniper berries. Breeding from February through July, it has 2–5 litters per year of 3–8 young born in a hair-lined cup nest and weaned at about 1 month.

242 Desert Cottontail
(*Sylvilagus audubonii*)

Description: Buff-brown above; white below. Nape bright rust. *Moderately long ears,* 2¼–2¾" (55–70 mm) long. L 13¾–16½"

(350–420 mm); T 1¾–2⅞" (46–74 mm); HF 3–3⅞" (75–100 mm); Wt 29½–42 oz. (835–1,191 g).

Similar Species: Nuttall's Cottontail's ears sometimes shorter; Brush Rabbit smaller, with shorter tail and shorter hindlegs; Pygmy Rabbit much smaller, with tail gray above and below; Eastern Cottontail often larger, with similar-size ears appearing shorter in proportion.

Sign: Fecal pellets deposited on logs and stumps, which the rabbits use as lookout posts after dark.

Habitat: Grassland to creosote brush and deserts.

Range: California to Texas, north to e Montana and sw North Dakota.

Unlike most cottontails, it seldom uses forms but will readily climb sloping trees. In areas of sparse vegetation it occasionally rests in the burrows of other animals such as prairie dogs or skunks. The home range of Desert Cottontails is up to 15 acres for males and 9 acres for females. Its running speed has been timed at 15 mph. Grasses, mesquite, other green plants, bark, twigs, and cactus are chief foods. Mating is year-round, with at least 2 litters per year of 1–6 young (averaging 3) born in a fur-lined depression.

247 Swamp Rabbit
"Cane-cutter Rabbit"
(*Sylvilagus aquaticus*)

Description: *Largest cottontail.* Short, coarse fur; *brownish-gray* mottled with black above; whitish below. Thin tail white below. Feet rust-colored. Ears, 2½–2⅝" (63–67 mm) long; L 20⅞–21¼" (530–540 mm); T 2⅝–2¾" (67–71 mm); Wt 3½–6 lb. (1.6–2.7 kg).

Similar Species: Marsh Rabbits much smaller, with tail dark below; other cottontails have whitish feet.

Sign: Fecal pellets on top of logs and stumps along waterways.

Habitat: Bottomlands, swamps, canebrakes.

Range: Eastern Texas and e Oklahoma east to s Illinois and n Georgia.

This excellent swimmer not only takes to water when pursued, as will other rabbits, but will swim simply to get about. To elude predators it may remain submerged except for its nose. It rests in a form under thick brush and will hide in hollow logs or the burrows of other animals. It feeds on green plants, both terrestrial and aquatic, with cane (*Arundinaria*) a favorite, and also forages among corn and other field crops. There are 2 litters per year of 1–4 young (usually 2–3) born in a shallow fur-lined form. Unlike other cottontails, which are born after a month's gestation naked and eyes closed, Swamp Rabbits are born furred after a longer gestation of almost 6 weeks, and their eyes open almost immediately.

244 European Rabbit
"Domestic Rabbit" "San Juan Rabbit"
(*Oryctolagus cuniculus*)

Description: Usually *brownish to grayish,* with tail dark above and white below, but coloration almost as variable as in the domestic cat. Ears, 2⅜–3⅞" (60–100 mm) long. L 18–24" (450–600 mm); T 2⅝–3½" (66–88 mm); HF 3⅝–4⅜" (92–112 mm); Wt 3⅛–5⅛ lb. (1.4–2.3 kg).

Similar Species: Cottontails generally smaller.

Sign: Warrens (extensive burrow systems with many entrances) in areas denuded of vegetation and littered with dark, round scat.

Habitat: Brushy areas, open fields.

Range: Introduced on Farallon Islands, California; San Juan Islands,

Washington; Middelm Island, Alaska; with mainland releases in Pennsylvania, Indiana, Illinois, New Jersey, Wisconsin, and Maryland; escaped individuals may be encountered in rural and suburban areas throughout North America.

On San Juan Island and in several other American areas, European Rabbits were introduced in an effort to establish a new game species, larger than the cottontail and with a reproductive capacity at least as great. These rabbits have generally thrived in the wild, but cannot rival the cottontail as game, for they are seldom active before late evening and retire before dawn. A high population can be destructive in agricultural areas, not only because of overbrowsing but because, unlike the cottontail, they dig extensive burrows, forming colonial networks called warrens. The lighthouse keeper who introduced them on his San Juan Island was almost literally overcome with success; there were soon so many rabbits and so many rabbit holes that the lighthouse nearly collapsed before thousands of the animals could be poisoned. Some escaped to a nearby island where their tunneling activities caused chunks of land along the edges to crumble into the sea. These incidents earned notoriety for the "San Juan Rabbit," as this species came to be called. They prefer short grass and leafy plants but when hungry will eat any available vegetation. This is the rabbit that "breeds like a rabbit," often having more than 6 litters per year of 4–12 young born in a grass nest in a special chamber in an underground den.

232, 235   Snowshoe Hare
"Varying Hare"
(*Lepus americanus*)

Description: *In summer, dark brown,* with tail dark
above and dusky to white below; *in
winter, white,* sometimes mottled with
brown (stays brown all year in w
Washington and Oregon). In the
Adirondack Mountains there are some
black (melanistic) hares that remain
black all year. *Moderately long ears, 2⅝–
3⅛″ (66–79 mm), black-tipped.* Large
hindfeet, 3⅞–5⅞″ (100–150 mm)
long, with soles well-furred, especially
in winter. L 15–20½″ (382–520 mm);
T 1–2¼″ (25–56 mm); Wt 2–3⅛ lb.
(896–1,400 g).

Similar Species: Arctic Hare larger, with tail always
white.

Sign: In snow, trails packed down as much
as 1′.
Tracks: Hindprints wider than other
hares in snow, due to snowshoe effect of
widely spread toes.

Habitat: Northern forests.

Range: Alaska and most of Canada south to n
California, n New Mexico, n
Minnesota, n Michigan, n New Jersey,
and south through the Alleghenies.

One of the smallest and shyest of the
hares, by day it rests in a form, hollow
log, or burrow of Woodchuck or
Mountain Beaver, though in overcast
weather it may venture out. If
disturbed, it may run in a circle
covering several acres, with bounds to
12′ and up to 30 mph, usually passing
close to its point of departure. It often
tries to hide in brush like a cottontail
instead of running into the open like
most hares. Although a good swimmer,
it avoids water. It enjoys dust bathing
and often uses the dusting wallows of
grouse. In summer, it feeds on grasses,
green vegetation, willow and berries
when available; in winter, on conifer
buds and bark of aspen, alder, and

willow. It also eats meat, and some become a nuisance to trappers by stealing bait. When alarmed, it may thump its hindfeet.

There are 2–3 litters per year of 1–6 young (averaging 3); they can run within hours but may nurse almost a month. The molt by which these hares (and other species displaying winter coloration) change coats is a photoperiodic phenomenon, governed by lengthening or shortening periods of daylight. When all goes well, it provides good protective coloration. As daylight diminishes in autumn, the hare begins to grow a white-tipped winter coat, at first patchy—excellent camouflage against patchy snow and by the time large expanses of ground are blanketed, the hare has turned white to match. When daylight lengthens in spring, the winter coat is gradually shed and replaced with brown. But when snow comes unusually late in fall or lasts unusually long in spring, the hare will have molted nonetheless; at such times it seems to know by instinct that it is conspicuous to predators and becomes less active than usual, seeking cover. While most leporid populations seem somewhat cyclic, that of the Snowshoe Hare appears especially so, becoming exceptionally plentiful every 9–10 years, then swiftly plummeting. The causes of these population fluctuations, while not fully understood, appear related to higher population densities and consequent crowding, which initiate a "stress syndrome" believed to retard the reproduction process and cause a dramatic decline in population. Predators include weasels, foxes, Mink, owls, hawks, wolverines, Bobcat, and, especially Lynx, which in Canada depend on these hares so heavily as a food supply that its population parallels the hare's, following it by 1 year.

234 Northern Hare
"Mountain Hare" "Blue Hare"
"European Varying Hare"
(*Lepus timidus*)

Description: *In summer, reddish-brown or brownish-gray
             above;* underparts, legs, tail, edge of
             ears, and *eye ring white;* eartips black. *In
             winter, white* except for black eartips.
             Ears, 3–3⅛" (75–78 mm) long.
             L 22¼–27¼" (565–690 mm);
             T 2⅛–4⅛" (53–104 mm); HF 5¾–
             7⅜" (147–189 mm); Wt 7–10 lb.
             (3.2–4.5 kg).
Similar Species: Snowshoe Hare's ears smaller.
Habitat: Open tundra, but uses brush when
             available.
Range: Western and n Alaska.

The Northern Hare is larger and has
shorter ears than hares in more
southerly areas; these are both energy-
saving adaptations, for they reduce the
ratio of the animal's surface area
(through which heat is lost) to its body
mass. It feeds primarily on green plants
in summer, woody vegetation, such as
bark, twigs, and shoots in winter. Its
cries include puffing and hissing sounds
and a "hoo-hoo" only given during the
mating season. The young are born in
June in a hollow in an open area or near
brush and are full grown by mid-
August.

233, 236 Arctic Hare
(*Lepus arcticus*)

Description: *Largest hare in North America. In summer,
             grayish-brown above;* underparts, tail,
             and back edge of ear white; eartips
             black. *In winter, white,* with hairs white
             to base, except black eartips. Remains
             white all year in Greenland and
             Ellesmere and northern Baffin Islands.
             Ears relatively short, 2¾–3¼" (70–
             84 mm) long. L 18⅞–26¾" (480–

678 mm); T 1¼–3⅛" (34–80 mm); HF 5¼–6⅞" (132–174 mm); Wt 6–15 lb. (2.7–6.8 kg).

Similar Species: Snowshoe Hare smaller, with tail brown in summer, white hairs dark at base in winter.

Sign: Cut willow shoots.
Tracks: Similar to other hares, but occasionally kangaroo-like prints made when hopping erect on hindfeet only.

Habitat: Tundra and rocky slopes.

Range: Northern Canada, from Mackenzie River to Newfoundland.

Relatively short ears (which help to conserve body heat), densely furred feet, and strong claws, used to dig through crusted snow for twigs and roots of dwarf willow (its chief food), sedges, and saxifrages, help equip this hare for the bitter cold of Arctic winters. Incisors, straighter than in other leporids, are used like tweezers to extract tiny plants from rocky crevices. More gregarious than other hares, it occurs in groups of 10–60, especially in windswept areas; on Canada's Arctic islands, it can be found in herds of several thousand. It takes shelter in depressions, especially on the leeward side of rocks, and faces into the wind so that cold air flows over its fur. In storms it may tunnel in the snow. During the breeding season, the first 2 weeks in April, males box with forefeet (jackrabbits mainly use hindfeet), slashing out with sharp claws. A single litter of 4–8 young is born in late June or July. Owing to food scarcity, they are cared for much longer than other hares, being nursed about 2 weeks.

231, 241 **White-tailed Jack Rabbit**
(*Lepus townsendii*)

Description: *Buffy-gray above;* white or pale gray below. *Tail white above and below,* or sometimes with dusky stripe on top but not extending onto rump. Long ears 3¾–4⅜" (96–113 mm); on outsides buff or gray on front, whitish with black stripe to tip on back. In winter, white or very pale gray in most of range (except most southern parts). L 22¼–25¾" (565–655 mm); T 2⅝–4⅜" (66–112 mm); HF 5¾–6¾" (145–172 mm). Wt 5¾–9½ lb. (2.6–4.3 kg).

Similar Species: Black-tailed Jack Rabbit with black on tail continuing up rump; Snowshoe Hare smaller, dark brown in summer.

Habitat: Barren, grazed, or cultivated land; grasslands.

Range: Eastern Washington and ne California east through Minnesota, Iowa, and Kansas.

Traveling in 12–20′ leaps, this jack rabbit can maintain a speed of 36 mph, with spurts up to 45 mph. Bucks fight furiously during the mating season in late April and early May, kicking out with their hindfeet for the most part and biting when they can. The 1–6 young (averaging 4) are born a month later in a form or on the ground; they soon forage for themselves and are independent in 3–4 weeks or even sooner. When cornered, this jack will swim, dog-paddling with all 4 feet. In summer, it eats grasses, clover, and other green vegetation; in winter, twigs, buds, and dried vegetation. It is a fine game species; the young White-tails make better table fare than the Black-tails.

240 Black-tailed Jack Rabbit
(*Lepus californicus*)

Description: Buffy-gray or sandy above, peppered with black; white below. *Tail has black stripe above, extending onto rump,* with white border. *Very long ears, 3⅞–5"*

(99–131 mm) brownish with black tips. Very large hindfoot, 4⅜–5¾″ (112–145 mm) long. L 18¼–24¾″ (465–630 mm); T 2–4⅜″ (50–112 mm); Wt 4–8 lb. (1.8–3.6 kg).

Similar Species: White-tailed Jack Rabbit lacks black on top of tail; Antelope Jack Rabbit with white sides and no black on ears.

Sign: Trails worn between feeding and resting sites; scarred or freshly nipped prickly-pear cactus or light tufts of fur on thorns; nesting forms: shallow scrapes often beneath sagebrush or rabbit bush.

Habitat: Barren areas and prairies, meadows, cultivated fields, also areas where vegetation exceeds height of 2′.

Range: Western U.S.: Texas and California north to s central Washington. Introduced in New Jersey and Kentucky.

This most abundant and widespread jack was originally called a "jackass rabbit," after its very large ears; like other jacks, it is not really a rabbit but a hare, as its young are born well furred and with eyes open. By day, it generally rests in dense vegetation or in a form, becoming active in late afternoon. Somewhat social, it often feeds in loose groups. In summer, it eats many kinds of plants, favoring alfalfa when available; in winter, it depends on woody and dried vegetation. When alarmed, it remains very still but may move its ears to catch sounds. It rarely walks but hops 5–10′ at a time, up to 20′ when panicked, and reaches speeds of 30–35 mph over short distances. When it runs at moderate speeds, every fourth or fifth leap is exceptionally high, allowing a better view of surroundings or pursuing predator; but at top speed there are no such special jumps. When escaping from a predator, it flashes the white underside of its tail, alerting other jacks of danger and perhaps confusing its enemy. After fleeing a short distance, it stops and looks back, evidently to see if it is still pursued, and may then give a danger signal by thumping its hindfeet. It can swim, dog-paddling with all 4 feet. Mating is year-round but more frequent in milder seasons; 1–4 litters per year of 1–8 young (usually only 2–4) are born in a relatively deep form lined with hair from the mother's chest. The mother places them in separate forms, thus decreasing a predator's chance of taking her entire litter. To avoid attracting attention, she keeps her distance by day but comes several times a night to nurse her young, which can fend for themselves in less than a month. Generally silent, these hares can squeal and give distinctive calls when fighting or distressed and when assembling their young. Coyotes, foxes, hawks, owls, and snakes are predators.

White-sided Jack Rabbit
(*Lepus callotis*)

Description: Grayish-brown above; *white on sides* and belly. *Long ears,* 4⅝" (117 mm), with little or *no black on tips.* Large hindfoot, 5¼" (133 mm). L 22" (560 mm); T 2¾" (71 mm).

Similar Species: Antelope Jack Rabbit has longer ears.
Sign: Depressions in tabosa grass.
Habitat: Stands of tabosa grass.
Range: Only in extreme s Hidalgo County, New Mexico.

This hare hides in tabosa grass by day and is active at night.

239 Antelope Jack Rabbit
(*Lepus alleni*)

Description: Grayish-brown above; *lower sides largely white.* Face, throat, and ears brownish.

Tail black above. *Very long ears,* 6–8″ (152–203 mm), *with no black on tips.* L 21⅝–26⅛″ (553–670 mm); T 1⅞–3″ (48–76 mm); HF 5–5⅞″ (127–150 mm); Wt of 3 animals ranged from 6½–9½ lb. (3–4.3 kg).

Similar Species: White-sided Jack Rabbit has shorter ears.

Habitat: Deserts.

Range: Southern central Arizona and sw New Mexico.

The Antelope Jack Rabbit, named for its ability to make enormous leaps, can "flash" its white sides as it runs, moving the white fur higher or lower at will. Flashing white at one spot, it comes to rest elsewhere with brown showing. This presumably confuses a predator, which heads for the last glimpse of white. The long ears play an important role in regulating body temperature: in hot weather, they stand erect, and their dilated blood vessels give off heat, thus cooling the jack; in cold weather, ears lay back close to the body, and blood vessels constrict to maintain body warmth. Despite this adaptation, in the hottest part of the day it avoids direct exposure to the sun and rests in the shade of plants. It feeds on various coarse grasses, prickly pear, mesquite, cat's-claw, and other desert vegetation.

---

243 Cape Hare or European Hare
"Brown Hare"
(*Lepus capensis*)

Description: Large. Thick, kinky fur. *In summer, brownish above* with black hairs interspersed, *white below;* in winter, grayish above. *Tail black on top,* light below. Moderately long ears, 3⅛–3⅞″ (79–100 mm). L 25¼–27⅝″ (640–700 mm); T 2¾–3⅞″ (70–100 mm); HF 5⅛–5⅞″ (130–150 mm); Wt 6½–20¼ lb. (3.0–9.1 kg).

Similar Species: Black-tailed Jack Rabbit has black on rump above tail; Snowshoe Hare smaller, with tail brown in summer.

Habitat: Open fields in rolling country; sometimes sparse woods.

Range: Great Lakes region east to New York and New England.

Introduced into Dutchess County, N.Y., in 1893, it is the largest hare in its range. By day, it rests in a form scratched out in an area with an unobstructed view and a gentle draft that carries sound so predators may be heard before they are glimpsed. As its first response to danger is to "freeze," it is often killed by farm machinery. When pursued, it seeks to elude a predator with confusing flight involving sharp turns, back-tracking, and recrossings of its path. Normally taking about 4′ per leap, when in a hurry it bounds to 12′ and can clear obstacles 5′ high. It has been timed at 30 mph over a quarter-mile stretch and can make bursts up to 45 mph. Like many lagomorphs, it is a good swimmer and will not hesitate to cross a river. It feeds on grass, clover, wheat, corn, apples, berries, and many green plants in summer, twigs and buds in winter. During the mating season, males battle fiercely. There are 3–4 litters per year of 2–4 young, with the first litter born during late winter in a grass-lined nest in a form. The mother scatters newborns in separate forms and visits each nightly to nurse. To assemble them she gives a low bugle-like call. Cape Hares scream when distressed and give a warning noise by grating their teeth. Foxes and bobcats are the major predators. This hare is the original "Easter Bunny." According to a Germanic legend, Eostre, goddess of spring, created the first hare from a bird, and to show its gratitude the hare has ever since laid eggs during the Easter festival in her honor.

Rodents
(Order Rodentia)

The nearly 3,000 species of rodents form the largest mammalian order. Over half of all mammal species are rodents; by sheer numbers of individuals they represent the majority of mammals on earth. North American species range in size from mice weighing a fraction of an ounce (less than 10 g) to the Beaver (*Castor canadensis*), which may weigh up to 110 lb. (49.5 kg), but most members of this order are generally relatively small. They are distinguished by having only two pairs of incisors—one upper and one lower—and no canines, which leaves a wide gap between incisors and molars. Because incisors are enameled on the front only, the working of upper teeth against lower ones wears away the softer inner surfaces more rapidly, producing a sharp, beveled edge ideal for gnawing. Incisors grow throughout the animal's life (if they didn't they would be worn away), and rodents must gnaw enough to keep them from growing too long. If wear fails to keep pace with growth, a tooth may grow completely out of the animal's mouth and prevent eating; or it may curve inwards, growing back into skull or jaw and eventually causing death. Rodents have bulbous eyes on the sides of the head, which enable them to see forward or behind, detecting danger over a wide arc. Most, but not all, have 4 toes on forefeet, 5 on hindfeet.

Most rodents are nocturnal. The majority are active throughout the year; but a number hibernate in winter, and a few in habitats of intense heat and sparse vegetation estivate in summer. In both hibernation and estivation, body temperature drops to within a degree or two of environmental temperature, and all other bodily functions are also greatly reduced, thus conserving energy. Most hibernators survive by metabolizing fat stored on their bodies, but some, such as the chipmunks, wake to eat stored food. Because the surface area of small animals is large in proportion to their bulk, rodents lose body heat rapidly through radiation. Most, however, are extremely active; but while activity temporarily warms an animal, it also expends energy. Rodents make up for their high energy losses by feeding voraciously. A reproductive capacity unmatched by other mammals helps compensate for the high rate of predation on them.

While certain rodents are among man's worst pests—carrying disease, eating or spoiling stored grain and other foods, and destroying vast amounts of property—others feed heavily on weed seeds and help to keep insects in check by eating great numbers, and a few are valuable fur-bearers.

MOUNTAIN BEAVER
(Family Aplodontidae)

The one living member of this family
—found only in the western U.S. and
British Columbia—is among the more
primitive living rodents. The family
name refers to its simple rootless
molars.

229 Mountain Beaver
"Aplodontia" "Sewellel"
(*Aplodontia rufa*)

Description: Woodchuck-like but smaller, with a
short, heavy body. Dark brown above;
lighter brown below. Blunt head; short
legs; small ears and eyes; *tiny tail.* 5
toes on all feet, with first toe on front
foot a flattened nail, other front toes
with very long strong claws. L 9⅜–
18½" (238–470 mm); T ¾–2¼"
(20–55 mm); Wt 1⅛–3⅛ lb. (0.5–
1.4 kg).

Similar Species: Woodchuck's tail longer, bushy;
Muskrat's tail much longer, naked,
scaly.

Sign: Burrows up to 19" in diameter,
surrounded by fan-shaped earth mounds
and pathways; in very wet areas, a
"tent" of sticks covered with leaves and
fern fronds erected over burrow
entrances; in late summer, "hay piles"
of ferns and other vegetation up to 2'
high on logs or ground; cylindrical
earth cores, to 6" in diameter, made
during winter tunneling and left on
surface after snow cover melts.
Tracks: Narrow, under 2" long;
hindprints larger than foreprints and
may overlap them. 5 toes on all feet,
but small first toe on forefeet may not
print.

Breeding: Mates late winter; 1 litter of 3–5 young
(usually 4 or 5) born in early spring,
weaned by autumn, disperse soon after;
females breed at 2 years.

Habitat: Moist forests, especially near streams.
Range: Extreme sw British Columbia, w Washington, w Oregon, n California, extreme w central Nevada.

The common name "Mountain Beaver" is misleading, as this rodent is neither a beaver nor does it prefer a mountainous habitat: the name may have derived from its beaver-like habit of diverting streams into its tunnels or from its occasional gnawing of bark and cutting of limbs. Active throughout the year, this mostly nocturnal animal occasionally browses during the day, especially in autumn. Its home range is small, averaging about one third of an acre, and it remains within a few yards of cover. Its labyrinthine burrow system is usually shallow, often near cover, and used by many other animals. It features a nest chamber 1–5' deep containing a nest of coarse vegetation lined with fine soft vegetation; dead-end tunnels where excrement and rejected bits of food are deposited; and separate chambers for storage of food and "Mountain Beaver baseballs," baseball-size balls of stone or clay encountered in digging, which the animal occasionally gnaws upon to sharpen its teeth and uses to close off nesting or feeding areas when vacated. It feeds solely on vegetation, particularly ferns such as swordfern and bracken, the bark of coniferous and hardwood trees, and grasses. It cuts vegetation when green, allows it to wilt, then transports it to its burrow where it is eaten or stored, remaining moist in the water-saturated air of the burrows. It is not a particularly good climber, although it does climb trees to cut off small limbs, leaving stubs which it uses as a ladder when it descends head first, carrying the wood; occasionally it lets the small limbs drop to the ground. It excretes both soft and hard fecal pellets and reingests the former. Vocalizations include a shrill whistle; if disturbed, it grates its incisors and may bite. The Bobcat, Long-tailed Weasel, and the Mink are its major predators. The Mountain Beaver sometimes causes severe damage to conifers by peeling off the bark and may raid nearby gardens or damage them with its burrowing activity.

SQUIRRELS
(Family Sciuridae)

Squirrels are a large and diverse group, varying in both appearance and habits. The family name means "shade-tail," alluding to the habit of many species of holding a bushy tail over their back, but some members—the Woodchuck, marmots, and prairie dogs—hardly conform to the image this suggests. Nevertheless, all have in common certain cranial characteristics. Most squirrels are strictly or mostly diurnal, many hibernate, and some estivate (hibernate during the summer). Some live in trees, some in burrows, usually in open areas. The family is well represented in our range, with 63 species, members of 9 genera. Among the "shade-tailed" tree squirrels are the relatively large gray squirrels (*Sciurus*), the much smaller red squirrels (*Tamiasciurus*), and the most arboreal and the only nocturnal members, the flying squirrels (*Glaucomys*), which have along the sides of their slender bodies furred folds of skin which spread to enable them to glide through the air. Chipmunks (*Tamias, Eutamias*) have large, internal cheek pouches, black and white facial stripes, and 5 dark stripes (separated by 4 light ones) on the back and sides of their small bodies; they generally live in forests. The genus names are descriptive: in Latin *tamias* means "storer" and the prefix *eu,* "most typical" or "true," and these hibernators do store a great deal of food, which they eat upon waking in winter and upon emergence in early spring. They live mostly on the ground, but their nests may be either in an underground burrow or a hollow limb. Most are highly vocal, having several calls—primarily chattering, twittering chirps, sometimes repeated very rapidly. The 19 western chipmunks (*Eutamias*) are all very similar, with the penis bone, or baculum, often serving as the basis for identification. Many inhabit overlapping ranges from lowland to mountaintop, with the palest chipmunks in the driest areas, and the darkest in the most humid; as with most species, protective coloration enhances likelihood of survival. The single Eastern Chipmunk (*Tamias striatus*) is larger than its western relatives and is distinguished from them by having molariform teeth all the same size; in western chipmunks the first upper molariform is reduced. Unlike chipmunks, most ground squirrels (*Spermophilus, Ammospermophilus*) have no stripes at all, but when they do, none are on the head. All are burrowers, nearly all hibernate, and many are colonial. Most feed mainly on seeds, which is why Audubon and his contemporaries called them "spermophiles," or "seed-lovers." (Later mammalogists regrouped them with their Old World relatives of the genus *Citellus,* a classification still seen in some books, but the use of *Spermophilus* is now generally accepted.) Members of these genera are distinguished by the way they hold their tails when running; spermophiles hold them horizontally and ammospermophiles (antelope squirrels) vertically, exposing their white undersides as the pronghorn antelope flashes its white rump. Prairie dogs (*Cynomys*) are also colonial burrowers, but their bodies are more stocky. Larger still are the solitary Woodchuck and the marmots (*Marmota*). Ground squirrels, prairie dogs, the Woodchuck, and marmots are all sometimes called "picket pins" because of the way they sit bolt upright to survey their domain.

8 Eastern Chipmunk
(*Tamias striatus*)

Description: Reddish-brown above; belly white.
1 *white stripe on sides (bordered by 2 black stripes); stripes end at rump.* Dark center stripe down back; light facial stripes above and below eyes. Tail brown on tip, edged with black. Prominent ears. Large internal cheek pouches. L 8½–11¾″ (215–299 mm); T 3⅛–4⅜″ (78–113 mm); HF 1¼–1½″ (32–38 mm); Wt 2¼–4⅞ oz. (66–139 g).

Similar Species: Least Chipmunk has 2 white stripes per side with stripes extending to rump.

Sign: Burrow entrances 2″ wide without piles of dirt, often on a woody slope or bank; occasional sprinklings of nutshells, opened on one side; bits of chaff on logs, stumps, and rocks.
Tracks: In mud, hindprint 1⅞″ long, foreprint considerably smaller; straddle 1¾–3½″; stride 7–15″, with hindprints closer together and printing ahead of foreprints.

Breeding: Mates in early spring; 3–5 young born in May; litter in late July–August, probably by first-year females not breeding in early spring.

Habitat: Open woodland; forest edges; brushy areas; bushes and stone walls in cemeteries and around houses.

Range: Southeastern Canada and ne U.S. west to North Dakota and e Oklahoma, and south to Mississippi, nw South Carolina, and Virginia.

Essentially a ground species, this pert chipmunk does not hesitate to climb large oak trees when acorns are ripe. Like the Gray and Fox squirrels, it often feeds on acorns and hickory nuts; the cutting sounds it makes as it eats can be heard for some distance. It is single-minded in its foodgathering, making trips from tree to storage burrow almost continuously. It was estimated that in 3 days one chipmunk stored a whole bushelful of chestnuts, hickory nuts, and corn kernels. It has two chattering calls, a trilling "chip-chip-chip" repeated very rapidly (about 130 trills per minute) and a lower-pitched, slower "chuck . . . chuck . . . chuck." Nuts, seeds, and other types of vegetation, as well as some invertebrates, slugs, snails, and small vertebrates, form its diet. The Long-tailed Weasel is the major predator, but hawks, foxes, the Bobcat, and house cats also take their share.

13 Alpine Chipmunk
(*Eutamias alpinus*)

Description: Small. Generally yellowish-gray, with *dark side stripes reddish or brownish,* not blackish. Dark stripe down middle of back may be black. *Tail bright orange below.* Ears ½–⅝" (12–14 mm) long. L 6½–7⅞" (166–203 mm); T 2½–3⅜" (63–85 mm); Wt 1–1¾ oz. (28–50 g).

Similar Species: Least Chipmunk has yellowish tail below, Yellow-pine and Lodgepole chipmunks larger.

Habitat: Talus slopes and subalpine forests, from timberline to 8,000′ elevation.

Range: Sierra Mountains of e central California.

In late summer it puts on a great deal of fat. Depending on latitude and altitude, it hibernates from about October to February. Its call is high pitched and weak.

4 Least Chipmunk
(*Eutamias minimus*)

Description: *Small.* Color varies: in drier regions, muted yellowish-gray above with tan dark stripes; in moister areas, brownish-gray with black side stripes. *Stripes continue to base of tail. Sides orange-brown;*

belly grayish-white. Long tail light brown above, yellowish below, with hairs black-tipped. Ears tawny in front. L 6⅝–8⅞" (167–225 mm); T 2¾–4½" (70–114 mm); HF 1–1⅜" (26–35 mm); Wt 1–2½ oz. (30–70 g).

Similar Species: Ears of Uinta, Yellow-pine, Lodgepole, and Colorado chipmunks dark in front, whitish behind; Gray-collared, Townsend's, and Eastern chipmunks larger; Cliff Chipmunk with side stripes indistinct or absent; Alpine Chipmunk's tail bright orange below.

Breeding: 1 litter of 5–7 young born in May in an underground nest; nest may also be in a tree.

Habitat: Sagebrush deserts; pastures; piney woods; rocky cliffs; often abundant in open coniferous forests.

Range: Most of s Canada from Ontario to s Yukon; w U.S. from w North Dakota to New Mexico, west to nw California and se Washington.

Lightest in color of all the western chipmunks, it often lives in the most desert-like habitats and generally enters hibernation much later than the Eastern Chipmunk. An excellent climber, it ascends trees to sun itself and may even nest in them. Acorns, seeds, fruits, berries, and grasses are its main foods, but it also eats fungi, invertebrates, and (rarely) small vertebrates. Its distinctive call, a series of high-pitched chipping notes, is similar to that of the Eastern Chipmunk.

---

6 Yellow-pine Chipmunk
(*Eutamias amoenus*)

Description: *Brightly colored,* from tawny to pinkish-cinnamon, with *distinct stripes:* light stripes white or grayish, dark stripes usually black. Sides and *underside of tail brownish-yellow.* Top of head brown. Ears blackish in front, whitish behind.

L 7⅛–9⅝″ (181–245 mm); T 2⅞–
4¼″ (73–108 mm); Wt 1–2½ oz.
(30–73 g).

Similar Species: Uinta Chipmunk larger, with head and
shoulders more grayish and with dark
brown side stripes; Panamint
Chipmunk has tawny ears; Alpine
Chipmunk smaller.

Sign: Remnants of nuts; burrow openings
with no loose soil at entrances.

Breeding: Mates in April; 5–7 naked and blind
young born May–early June in a nest of
leaves, grass, lichen, and feathers.

Habitat: Coniferous forests, particularly yellow
pine.

Range: Southern British Columbia south to n
California, east to w Montana and nw
Wyoming; in the yellow pine zone.

In the open forests where the sun casts
sharp shadows, the well-defined stripes
of the Yellow-pine Chipmunk afford
protective coloration. Before winter, it
puts on little fat, suggesting that it
may not hibernate, or at least does not
do so for long; some individuals are
active even on snow. It lives in
burrows, usually about 1½–3′ long
and 7–21″ underground in an open area
within the forest; there is generally one
entrance, though there may also be
short side openings. Seeds are its most
important food, eaten as available—
early, when green, and later, when
ripe. When pine cones open in the fall
it climbs the trees to get the seeds. It
also eats some insects, fungi, and, in
Washington, thistle, the thorns
apparently being no deterrent: first it
eats the seeds from the head, then cuts
the head, which falls to the ground
where it is consumed with impunity. In
the fall, it stuffs its cheek pouches with
food to be stored in its burrows; one
food cache contained an estimated
67,970 items, including 15 kinds of
seeds, corn, and part of a bumblebee.
Of its at least 10 different calls, one
sounds like a robin's chirp and another,

among the most common, is a sharp
accented "kwist."

2 Townsend's Chipmunk
(*Eutamias townsendii*)
Related species: Allen's, Siskiyou,
Yellow-checked

Description: Large. *Dark brown,* often with rather
wide, diffuse or indistinct blackish and
light *stripes on head and continuing down
body.* Lighter in summer than winter.
Backs of ears bicolor: dusky on front
half; gray on back half. Tail long and
bushy: blackish above with many
white-tipped hairs, bright reddish-
brown below bordered with black and
finely edged with white-tipped hairs.
Brownish stripe below ears. L 8⅛–12½"
(221–317 mm); T 3½–6" (90–
152 mm); HF 1¼–1 ⅝" (32–40 mm);
Wt 1¾–3⅞ oz. (51–109 g).

Similar Species: Long-eared Chipmunk has prominent
white patch behind ear; Sonoma
Chipmunk's backs of ears unicolor;
other chipmunks in range smaller, have
more distinct stripes.

Breeding: Mates in spring; 1 litter of 2–6 young
born May–June.

Habitat: Rank vegetation, usually among dense
hardwood or humid coniferous
forests.

Range: Extreme s British Columbia south
through most of w Oregon.

One of the largest western chipmunks
and the darkest in color (as is common
among species in moist climates), it has
a looser, less sleek coat than the others.
It is active all day, like other
chipmunks, but rather shy. It lives in a
burrow about 2" across and
comparatively short at 5' in length. A
very good climber, it often suns itself
in trees and may run up a tree to flee a
predator. It forages within a home
range of 1½ acres. In northern parts of

its range, this chipmunk may put on a layer of fat and remain in a nest burrow all winter, but in milder climates it puts on little or no fat and may be abroad most of the winter. In summer it eats many types of berries; in late fall switches to acorns, maple seeds, and seeds of various conifers; and in winter feeds on numerous subterranean fungi. Some insects are also eaten. One tagged specimen lived in the wild at least 7 years, longevity unusual for a small rodent. Major predators are the Long-tailed Weasel and Mink.

Closely related species, originally recognized as subspecies of Townsend's Chipmunk, include Allen's Chipmunk (*Eutamias senex*) in northeast California and west central Oregon; Siskiyou Chipmunk (*Eutamias siskiyou*), inland in northwest California and adjacent southern Oregon; and Yellow-cheeked Chipmunk (*Eutamias ochrogenys*) in northwest coastal California and southwest coastal Oregon.

Sonoma Chipmunk
(*Eutamias sonomae*)

Description: *Large. Dark brown,* with all *stripes on back indistinct,* about same width, light stripes yellowish. Tail reddish below, becoming paler toward base, edged with buff. On head, dark stripes reddish, black spots behind eyes and below ears. Backs of ears nearly uniform brownish color. L 8¾–10⅞" (220–277 mm); T 3¾–5" (93–126 mm); HF 1⅛–1½" (32–39 mm).

Similar Species: Townsend's Chipmunk has bicolor ears, dusky on front half, gray on back half; Yellow-pine Chipmunk has distinct black and white stripes.

Habitat: Brushy open ground in redwood or yellow pine forests, sea level to 6,000'.

Range: Northwestern California.

Its call, or "chirp," which drops then rises in pitch, is lower and slower than that of Townsend's and many other chipmunks. Many chipmunks, or at least those that occur together, as do Townsend's and Sonoma, may have distinctive calls, allowing them to distinguish members of their own species and help to keep related individuals in contact. It forages in small branches of bushes as well as on the ground.

14 Merriam's Chipmunk
(*Eutamias merriami*)
Related species: California

Description: Grayish-brown above; belly white. *Indistinct stripes* nearly equal in width: *dark stripes gray or brown,* usually not black; *light stripes grayish.* Dull black spots in front of and behind eyes; stripe below ear brownish. Long tail edged with buff or white. L 8¼–11″ (208–280 mm); T 3½–5½″ (89–140 mm); HF 1¼–1½″ (32–39 mm); Wt 2½–4 oz. (71–113 g).

Similar Species: Long-eared Chipmunk has dark stripe below ear and white patch behind it; Lodgepole and Yellow-pine chipmunks have distinct back stripes.

Habitat: Apparently most abundant at upper edge of chaparral, in rocky scrub areas; also brushland, forested foothills, or coniferous or piñon-juniper forests in lower mountains to about 7,000′.

Range: Much of s California.

Recent evidence indicates that there are two very similar forms of Merriam's Chipmunk occurring together over part of their range but remaining distinct. These chipmunks are distinguished by skull and penis bone characteristics; the form found in San Bernardino, Little San Bernardino, Eagle, San Jacinto, and the Santa Rosa Mountains is paler in summer and has more reddish dark stripes on back.

Closely related is the California Chipmunk (*Eutamias obscurus*), which is paler, with dark stripes more reddish, and occurs only in extreme south central California.

7 **Cliff Chipmunk**
(*Eutamias dorsalis*)

Description: *Grayish,* with *stripes on body indistinct* or absent, often more distinct on sides of head. Bushy *tail rust-red below.* L 7¾–10⅞" (195–277 mm); T 3¼–5½" (85–140 mm); HF 1¼–1½" (32–39 mm); Wt 2–3 oz. (57–85 g).

Similar Species: Merriam's and Townsend's chipmunks, which also have indistinct stripes on back, occur to the west of the range of this species. Other chipmunks in range —Least, Uinta, Gray-collared—all have distinct striping on back.

Habitat: Rocky areas and cliffs; piñon-juniper zones.

Range: Eastern Nevada, Utah, and extreme nw Colorado; Arizona and w New Mexico.

Like most chipmunks, it hibernates during winter, but it may emerge during warm spells. It feeds on nuts, seeds, fruits, and berries. Vociferous, it gives a sharp "bark" about 160 times per minute, each accompanied with a tail twitch. Like Merriam's Chipmunk and others of brushy areas where small twigs cast indistinct shadows, the Cliff Chipmunk's indistinct striping serves as protective coloration.

Red-tailed Chipmunk
(*Eutamias ruficaudus*)

Description: Large. Brightly colored: Deep tawny above and on sides; *rump gray,*

contrasting with front part of body.
Tail rufous above, dark reddish below.
Three median stripes on back black;
outer stripes brownish. Cheeks with 2
white and 3 brown stripes. L 8¾–10"
(223–248 mm); T 4–4¾" (101–122
mm); HF 1¼–1⅜" (32–36 mm);
Wt about 2⅛ oz. (60 g).

Similar Species: Least Chipmunk smaller, with rump
not contrasting with upper parts and
sides; Yellow-pine Chipmunk's
underside of tail yellowish.

Habitat: Spruce-fir, pine-larch-fir, or yellow pine
coniferous forests; boulder-covered
slopes and mountains below timberline,
particularly in dense forest areas.

Range: Southeastern British Columbia, ne
Washington, n Idaho, w Montana.

Little is known about the habits of this
species, which is more arboreal than
most chipmunks. It gives a short
warning bark when alarmed.

Gray-collared Chipmunk
(*Eutamias cinereicollis*)
Related species: Gray-footed

Description: Dark, grayish, with paler gray neck and
shoulders. Back stripe black; side
stripes pale gray and dark brown.
L 8¼–9¾" (208–250 mm); T 3½–
4½" (90–115 mm); HF 1⅜" (32–
36 mm); Wt 2–3 oz. (57–85 g).

Similar Species: Least Chipmunk smaller and lacks gray
"collar"; Cliff Chipmunk has indistinct
striping on back.

Habitat: Coniferous forest, especially around logs
near clearings.

Range: Eastern central Arizona, sw New
Mexico.

The common and Latin species names
of this small chipmunk refer to its pale
gray "collar." Its diverse diet includes
acorns, Douglas-fir seeds, currants,
gooseberries, green vegetation,

mushrooms, and insects. Apparently there is only one litter per year. The closely related Gray-footed Chipmunk (*Eutamias canipes*), in south central New Mexico, was formerly recognized as a subspecies of Gray-collared Chipmunk.

Long-eared Chipmunk
(*Eutamias quadrimaculatus*)

Description: Fairly *large. Brightly colored,* with indistinct body stripes. Tail reddish-brown below edged with white. *Long ears,* ¾–1" (18–26 mm) long, *with large white patch behind and dark, almost black, stripe below.* L 7⅛–10" (200–255 mm); T 3¼–4⅝" (85–118 mm); Wt 2½–3½ oz. (71–100 g).

Similar Species: Townsend's and Merriam's chipmunks have brown stripe below ear; other chipmunks in range smaller, with indistinct stripes.

Sign: Small pits dug for fungi.

Habitat: Pine and fir forests of Sierra Nevada Mountains at elevations from 3600–7300'.

Range: Eastern central California.

Its primary foods are fungi; cedar and gooseberry seeds; manzanita flowers and fruits; various nutlets; and arthropods, mainly caterpillars, but also termites. Sometimes underground fungi similar to truffles are eaten exclusively. It gleans leftover pine or cedar seeds from cone middens left by Douglas Squirrels and seeds that Douglas and Western gray squirrels have dropped from trees. Climbing cedar trees up to a height of 30', it cuts cones directly from the twigs, then gnaws out the seeds, letting seeds and cones drop to the ground. It then caches this food for consumption in winter and spring. The reduced numbers seen in November may indicate the beginning of hibernation. Its call note is sharper than that of the Lodgepole Chipmunk, which occurs with it.

3 Lodgepole Chipmunk
(*Eutamias speciosus*)

Description: Bright brown above, with distinct stripes; median dark back stripes black but outer ones brown or often missing; outer light stripe bright white and broader than inner light stripes; *top of head brown.* Black spots in front of and behind eyes; stripes on front of head often missing. Ears blackish in front, white behind. Tail with black band about 1″ (25 mm) wide on underside near tip. L 7¾–9½″ (197–241 mm); T 2⅝–4½″ (67–114 mm); HF 1¼–1⅜″ (35 mm); Wt 1¾–2⅛ oz. (51–62 g).

Similar Species: Uinta Chipmunk has top of the head gray and narrower black band beneath tail; Yellow-pine chipmunk has black side stripes; Least, Alpine, and Panamint chipmunks smaller; Merriam, Long-eared, and Townsend chipmunks larger.

Habitat: Lodgepole pine and red fir stands; often associated with manzanita.

Range: Eastern central California.

In the San Gabriel Mountains it often sits on the upper stems of snowbush to scan its environment. Manzanita flowers and berries, nutlets, subterranean fungi, and caterpillars are important foods. In the mountains, it occurs with Merriam's chipmunk, which it replaces at higher elevations. In captivity, between October and mid-April it hibernates for 5–6 days at a time.

Panamint Chipmunk
(*Eutamias panamintinus*)

Description: Brightly colored, *with reddish or tawny back; head and rump gray.* Outer dark stripes on back indistinct; inner ones reddish or grayish. Head gray on top, with upper eye stripe black, lower one brown. Ears tawny in front. L 7⅝–8¾" (192–220 mm); T 3¼–4" (80–102 mm); HF 1⅛–1¼" (28–33 mm); Wt 1½–2¼ oz. (42.5–65.2 g).

Similar Species: Yellow-pine Chipmunk more brightly colored, with top of head brown, and lower dark eye stripe black and distinct; Least Chipmunk grayer, generally smaller, with rump similar in color to back; Long-eared Chipmunk larger; Cliff Chipmunk averages much larger and has indistinct back stripes. Lodgepole and Uinta chipmunks' ears blackish in front, whitish behind.

Habitat: Piñon-juniper forest in rocky areas.

Range: Southwestern Nevada, s central California.

The habits of this species are believed to be similar to those of the Yellow-pine Chipmunk.

1, 5 Uinta Chipmunk
(*Eutamias umbrinus*)
Related species: Colorado, Palmer's

Description: Grayish above, including crown, with wide, dark brown side stripes; white below; tawny wash on sides. Tail black-tipped, white-bordered, tawny below. *Ears blackish in front, whitish behind.* L 7¾–9⅝" (196–243 mm); T 2⅞–4½" (73–115 mm); Wt 2–3 oz. (57–85 g).

Similar Species: Least Chipmunk smaller, underparts more grayish, and ears tawny in front; Townsend's, Long-eared, and Cliff chipmunks have indistinct side stripes; Panamint Chipmunk has tawny

shoulders, sides, and front of ears;
Yellow-pine Chipmunk has distinct
black side stripes; Lodge-pole
Chipmunk bright brown above, top of
head brown; Gray-collared more gray
on shoulders.

Breeding: Young born in early summer depending
on latitude and elevation.

Habitat: Coniferous forests, mixed woods, open
areas; in yellow pines, white pines,
junipers, scrub oaks.

Range: Wyoming, Nevada, w California,
Utah, n central Arizona, n central
Colorado.

This tree-dwelling species often occurs
together with the Golden-mantled
Ground Squirrel. It accumulates much
fat, which is used in hibernation during
the long winters of its range. Nuts,
seeds, fruits, and berries are chief foods.
Closely related species include the
similarly colored Colorado Chipmunk
(*Eutamias quadrivittatus*) in southeast
Utah, western Colorado, northern New
Mexico, and northeast Arizona; and
Palmer's Chipmunk (*Eutamias palmeri*),
found at elevations of 2,000–12,000'
on Charleston Peak in southern
Nevada.

---

227 Woodchuck
"Groundhog" "Marmot"
(*Marmota monax*)

Description: *Large. Grizzled brown* (or reddish to
blackish); *uniformly colored.* Prominent
bushy tail. Small ears. Short legs. *Feet
dark brown or black.* Incisors white.
L 16½–32¼" (418–820 mm); T 3⅞–
9⅞" (100–152 mm); Wt 4⅜–14 lb.
(2–6.4 kg).

Similar Species: Yellow-bellied Marmot usually yellower
or lighter, has whitish spots between
eyes, and occurs south and west of this
range.

Sign: Large burrow openings 8–12" across,

with mounds just outside main
entrance; often additional escape
entrances with no mound. When hay is
high, woodchucks tramp down trails
radiating from burrows.

Habitat: Pastures, meadows, old fields, woods.

Range: Eastern central Alaska, British
Columbia, most of s Canada, n Idaho, e
Kansas, ne North Dakota; in the East,
south to Virginia, n Alabama.

The sun-loving Woodchuck is active by
day, especially in early morning and
late afternoon. A good swimmer and
climber, it will go up a tree to escape
an enemy or obtain a vantage point but
never travels far from its den. Green
vegetation such as grasses, clover,
alfalfa, and plantain forms its diet; at
times it will feed heavily on corn and
can cause extensive damage in a garden.
Its burrow, up to 5' deep and 30' long,
has one or more tunnels terminating
in a chamber containing a large grass
nest and is used by other mammals
—including cottontail rabbits,
Opossums, Raccoons, skunks, and foxes
which enlarge it for use as a nursery
den. If alarmed, the Woodchuck often
gives a loud sharp whistle, then softer
ones as it runs for its burrow from
which it then peeks out. When
angered, it chatters its teeth, and it can
hiss, squeal, and growl. In late summer
or early fall, it puts on a heavy layer of
fat, which sustains it through
hibernation. It digs a winter burrow
with a hibernation chamber where it
curls up in a ball on a mat of grasses.
Body temperature falls from almost 97°
F. to less than 40°, breathing slows to
once every 6 minutes, and heartbeat
drops from over 100 beats per minute
to 4. It emerges in early spring
(according to legend, on February 2,
"Groundhog Day," but much later in
northern parts of its range). A male at
once seeks a mate; its brief stay in the
burrow of a receptive female is almost

the only time that two adults share a den. A litter of 4–5 blind and naked young is born in April or early May; the young open their eyes and crawl at about 1 month and disperse at 2 months. The hunter is the Woodchuck's major enemy, but the automobile and large predators, especially the Red Fox, also take their toll. Woodchuck meat is very good, although eaten by very few. While an overpopulation can damage cropfields, gardens, and pastures, Woodchucks are beneficial in moderate numbers, for their defecation inside the burrow, in a special excrement chamber separate from the nesting chamber, fertilizes the earth, and their digging loosens and aerates the soil, letting in moisture and organic matter while bringing up subsoil for transformation into topsoil (in New York State they turn over 1,600,000 tons of soil each year). The common name comes from a Cree Indian word, "wuchak," used to identify several different animals of similar size and color, including marmots; it denotes nothing about the Woodchuck's habits or habitat.

---

228 Yellow-bellied Marmot
"Yellow-footed Marmot" "Rockchuck" "Mountain Marmot"
(*Marmota flaviventris*)

Description: Heavy bodied. Yellowish-brown, with *yellowish belly*. Feet light to dark brown. *Whitish spots between eyes.* Buff patches below ear to shoulders. Tail bushy. L 18½–27⅝" (470–700 mm); T 5⅛–8¾" (130–220 mm); Wt 5–10 lb. (2.2–4.5 kg).

Similar Species: Woodchuck usually somewhat larger and darker with darker feet, has no white spots between eyes, and occurs north and east of the Yellow-bellied Marmot's range.

Sign: In open areas burrow entrances 8–9"

wide, with mounds or fans of packed earth.

Habitat: Rocky situations; talus slopes; valleys and foothills to 11,000′ elevations.

Range: British Columbia and s Alberta south through e California, west to Colorado and n New Mexico, north to Montana.

It lives in a den in a hillside, under a rockpile, in a crevice or rock shelter; if alarmed, the Yellow-bellied returns to its den and often chirps or whistles from its position of safety. It feeds entirely on many kinds of green vegetation. In the fall, it puts on a layer of fat which sustains it through hibernation from August (October in the mountains of New Mexico) through February or March. A litter of about 5 is born March–April. It is a host for the tick that carries Rocky Mountain spotted fever.

225, 226, 230 Hoary Marmot
"Rockchuck" "Mountain Marmot"
"Whistler"
(*Marmota caligata*)
Related species: Alaska, Olympic, Vancouver

Description: Large. Silver-gray above, with brownish rump, whitish belly. Distinctive *black and whitish markings on head and shoulders:* nose and large patch between eyes whitish; patches on forehead around eyes and ears black; and often band behind nose black. Tail large, reddish-brown, bushy. Ears small. Feet black or very dark brown; forefeet may have white spots. L 17¾–32¼″ (450–820 mm); T 6¾–9¾″ (170–250 mm); Wt 8–20 lb. (3.6–9 kg).

Sign: Large burrows 9–15″ wide with fans or mounds of dirt.

Habitat: Most often talus slopes in mountains.

Range: Alaska to Yukon south to Washington, n Idaho, w Montana.

This marmot feeds almost entirely on grasses and many other kinds of green plants and may chase others from feeding grounds it considers its own. It often engages in playful wrestling matches in which a pair stand erect on hindlegs, place forefeet together, then push. In late summer, it puts on a great deal of fat which sustains it through hibernation. In southern parts of its range it hibernates from October to February; in British Columbia, from September to April. Mating occurs soon after emergence, and 4–5 young are born about a month later. The silvery fur, good camouflage in its rocky habitat, gives rise to its common name and the dark feet to its Latin species name (*caligata* means "booted"). Its shrill alarm whistle, louder than that of the other marmots and similar to a man's, accounts for the nickname "Whistler." Many carnivores prey on it, and while its rocky habitat is good escape cover, bears often dig up chucks that are still hibernating in early spring. Indians and Eskimoes use its pelt, which has a soft dense underfur, to make parkas, and they eat its tasty flesh.

Closely related species, often regarded as subspecies, include the paler Alaska Marmot (*Marmota broweri*) in northern Alaska; the Olympic Marmot (*Marmota olympus*) which is brownish mixed with white and found only in the Olympic Mountains, Clallam Co., Washington; and the dark brown Vancouver Marmot (*Marmota vancouverensis*) found only on Vancouver Island, British Columbia.

11 Harris' Antelope Squirrel
(*Ammospermophilus harrisii*)

Description: Upperparts pinkish-buff in summer, gray in winter; underparts white. A single white stripe on sides. *Tail mixed black and white below.* Ears small. L 8¾–9¾" (220–250 mm); T 2⅞–3¾" (74–94 mm); HF 1½–1¾" (38–42 mm); Wt 4–5¼ oz. (113–150 g).

Similar Species: Other antelope squirrels have undersides of tail clear white.

Sign: Burrows with diverging pathways.

Habitat: Low deserts with little vegetation.

Range: Southern and w Arizona, extreme sw New Mexico.

Like the White-tailed Antelope Squirrel, the Harris' has pale coloration, helping it blend with its arid environment. It metabolizes its water from food.

10, 12 White-tailed Antelope Squirrel
(Ammospermophilus leucurus)
Related species: Nelson's, Texas

Description: Upperparts buff in summer, gray in winter; underparts white. 1 narrow white stripe on each side. *Underside of tail clear white* with black-tipped hairs forming narrow black border. Ears small. L 7⅝–9⅜" (194–239 mm); T 2⅛–3⅜" (54–87 mm); HF 1⅜–1¾" (35–43 mm); Wt 3–5½ oz. (85–156 g).

Similar Species: Harris' Antelope Squirrel's underside of tail a mixture of black and white; Mohave Ground Squirrel lacks stripes.

Sign: Burrows with pathways radiating from them and no mounds at entrances.

Breeding: 1 litter per year of 5–14 young born in early spring; sometimes a second litter.

Habitat: Deserts, foothills; hard gravelly surfaces.

Range: Southwestern Idaho, se Oregon, Nevada, Utah, w Colorado, s California, n Arizona, nw New Mexico.

Like the other antelope squirrels, it runs fast with its tail held over the back, exposing white underparts. It

usually lives in burrows but also in rock crevices and sometimes in abandoned burrows of other animals. Available material is used to build a nest, which may incorporate grasses, fur, and bark. Usually foraging on the ground but sometimes in yucca or cactus, it feeds on seeds and fruit. It hibernates in northern parts of its range but may not in southern parts.

Closely related species include the very similar but larger and more buff Nelson's Antelope Squirrel (*Ammospermophilus nelsoni*), found in southern California in the general areas of Kern, Kings, and W. Fresno Counties; and the Texas Antelope Squirrel (*Ammospermophilus interpres*), found in south central New Mexico and western Texas, and distinguished from adjacent populations of the White-tailed Antelope Squirrel by having two black bands instead of one on the tail hairs.

25 Townsend's Ground Squirrel
(*Spermophilus townsendii*)

Description: Plain gray above, tinged pinkish; belly whitish or buff. *Short tail reddish or tawny below, with white edge.* Face and hindlegs reddish. L 6⅝–10¾" (167–271 mm); T 1¼–2¾" (32–72 mm); HF 1⅛–1½" (29–38 mm); Wt 4½–11½ oz. (128–325 g).

Similar Species: Washington Ground Squirrel has indistinct flecking; Belding's, Richardson's, and Columbian larger; Uinta larger, with brown streak down middle of back, tail with mixed blackish above and below.

Sign: Burrow openings rimmed with dirt 4–6" high.

Breeding: 4–16 young born by mid-March; abroad by mid-April when half-grown.

Habitat: Open sagebrush.

Range: South central Washington, e Oregon, extreme ne and sw California, most of Nevada, w Utah, s Idaho.

These ground squirrels sometimes form large colonies, yet they are not very social. Each adult digs two burrows—a small one in the feeding area, evidently used as an escape hatch if predators approach, and a much bigger home burrow, 50' long or more and up to 6' deep. Diggings often extend from the sagebrush flats where the animals forage, onto nearby rock ridges. Summer estivation begins in June or July and continues unbroken through winter hibernation, which ends in early spring, depending on locality. In eastern Washington, spring comes early and squirrels emerge in late January or early February and breed soon after. Seeds of grasses and other green plants and green plant parts are favored foods. These squirrels often fall prey to badgers.

Washington Ground Squirrel
(*Spermophilus washingtoni*)

Description: Back gray, indistinctly flecked with whitish spots. *Tail short* with blackish tip. Hindlegs and patch on snout reddish. L 7¼–9⅝" (185–245 mm); T 1¼–2⅝" (32–65 mm); HF 1¼–1½" (30–38 mm); Wt 5⅜–10 oz. (152–284 g).

Similar Species: Townsend's and Belding's ground squirrels lack the flecking; Idaho Ground Squirrel is brownish above, with a banded tail, and occurs only in Weiser and Payette valleys in w Idaho; Columbian Ground Squirrel larger, with longer, bushier tail, and legs and front of face reddish.

Sign: Burrow openings in open ground with trails radiating from them.

Breeding: 5–11 young (averaging 8) in mid-

March; abroad by mid-April when half-grown.

Habitat: Open areas: grasslands, low sage areas, cultivated fields, hillsides.

Range: Eastern central Washington and n central Oregon.

In summer, it puts on a thick layer of fat which serves as its source of energy during both estivation, begun in June or July, and hibernation, which follows immediately and lasts through February. It mates soon after emergence. Weed and grass seeds, stems and leaves of such plants as mustards, mallows, plantain, and alfalfa form its diet. It often stands upright at its burrow entrances. Its call is faint and squeaky. Badgers are its chief predator.

Idaho Ground Squirrel
(*Spermophilus brunneus*)

Description: *Dappled grayish-brown above* with lower back mainly brown; belly grayish-yellow. Shoulders and forelegs golden-buff; outer hindlegs and underside of tail rust-brown. *Tail with 5–8 alternating light and dark bands.* Chin white; nose rust-brown. L 8¼–8¾" (211–220 mm); T 1¾–2" (46–50 mm); HF 1¼–1⅜" (33–35 mm).

Similar Species: Columbian Ground Squirrel much larger, lacks white on chin.

Sign: Entrances to burrows under rocks and logs.

Habitat: Dry open areas with low, sparse green vegetation.

Range: Known only from the Payette and Weiser valleys in w central Idaho.

This colonial ground squirrel feeds on green plants, including seeds and onion bulbs. Hibernation begins in July or August. Juveniles are abroad by late May and reach adult size by mid-July.

22 Richardson's Ground Squirrel
"Picket Pin" "Wyoming Ground
Squirrel" "Flickertail"
(*Spermophilus richardsonii*)

Description: *Gray* or yellowish-gray above, tinged
with brown or buff and indistinctly
mottled; whitish or pale buff below.
Tail bordered with white or buff; light
brownish or *buff below.* L 9¾–14"
(248–355 mm); T 2⅝–3⅞" (65–100
mm); HF 1½–1⅞" (40–49 mm);
Wt 13–16⅜ oz. (369–469 g).
Similar Species: Belding's Ground Squirrel's tail reddish
below; Townsend's Ground Squirrel
smaller with shorter tail; Franklin's
Ground Squirrel larger, with longer
tail, dark underparts; Uinta Ground
Squirrel's tail buff mixed with black
above and below; Columbia Ground
Squirrel larger, with reddish legs.
Breeding: 6–11 young (usually 7–8) born May;
forage with mother in June.
Habitat: Open prairies.
Range: Southern Alberta, Saskatchewan, and
Manitoba south to ne Idaho,
Wyoming, nw Colorado, ne South
Dakota, extreme w Minnesota.

This rather solitary squirrel sometimes
appears colonial in favorable habitats,
being especially abundant where
vegetation is short. Because it often
stands erect on its hindlegs to survey
surroundings, it has acquired the
nickname "Picket Pin." It is also called
"Flickertail," after the way it
accompanies its shrill whistle with a
flick of its tail. It eats many insects—
especially grasshoppers, crickets, and
caterpillars—and the seeds, leaves, and
stems of many kinds of plants. It stuffs
its cheek pouches with seeds, which it
stores in its burrow and probably
eats in spring after hibernation from
September through January–March.
(Estivation may begin in July.)
The pouches of one ground squirrel
contained 162 oat seeds, 140 wheat

seeds, and almost a thousand wild
buckwheat seeds. Major predators are
badgers, weasels, gopher snakes, and
hawks.

28 Uinta Ground Squirrel
(*Spermophilus armatus*)

Description: Brownish to buff above, with paler
sides; belly buff. *Tail buff mixed with
black above and below,* with pinkish-buff
edge. Head, front of face, and ears
cinnamon, with grayish dappling on
top of head. Sides of face and neck
gray. Forelegs and forefeet buff;
hindlegs cinnamon, hindfeet buff.
L 11–11⅞″ (280–303 mm); T 2½–
3¼″ (63–81 mm); HF 1¾″ (42–46
mm); Wt 10–15 oz. (284–425 g).

Similar Species: Richardson's Ground Squirrel's tail
buff, brownish, or clay below;
Townsend's Ground Squirrel's tail
reddish or tawny below and usually
shorter; Belding's Ground Squirrel has
brown streak down back.

Breeding: Average of 4–5 young born in May,
first year, 6–7 thereafter; they emerge
from burrow in 24 days.

Habitat: Dry sage, sage-grass; also on lawns.

Range: Southwestern Montana, w Wyoming, e
Idaho, n central Utah.

Adults begin estivation in July,
juveniles later; by September all
individuals have disappeared. From
estivation they directly enter the long
hibernation. In Utah, adult males
emerge first, in late March to mid-
April, and remain active only about 3½
months before reentering their sleep
cycles. Seeds, other types of vegetation,
invertebrates, and some vertebrates are
eaten. As with several other ground
squirrels, the Badger appears to be the
major predator.

27 Belding's Ground Squirrel
(*Spermophilus beldingi*)

Description: Gray washed with reddish or pinkish
above, with broad *brown streak down
middle of back,* top of head pinkish; pale
gray below washed with pinkish
especially toward front. *Tail* pinkish-
gray above, *reddish to hazel below,* edged
with pinkish-buff, tipped with black.
L 10–11¾" (253–300 mm); T 2¼–3"
(55–76 mm); Wt 8–12 oz. (227–
340 g).

Similar Species: Richardson's Ground Squirrel has tail
clay, light brownish, or buff below;
Townsend's Ground Squirrel smaller,
with buff or whitish underparts.

Breeding: 3–8 young born late June–early July,
depending on locale and spring
weather, conditions which determine
time of mating. Size of litter varies
with maternal age, with yearlings and
6- to 8-yr.-olds having 3–4 young, 2-
to 5-yr.-olds, 6–8. (Data for Tioga Pass
population.)

Habitat: Old fields, roadsides, and other grassy
areas, where vegetation is very short;
hay and alfalfa fields in Utah.

Range: Eastern Oregon, sw Idaho, ne
California, extreme nw Utah, n
Nevada.

This semicolonial hibernator feeds on
weed and grain seeds, leaves and stems
of green plants, and grasshoppers,
crickets, caterpillars, and other insects.
It often stands up on its hindlegs to
view its surroundings. Large colonies of
these ground squirrels may damage
pastures and grain fields. A ten-year
study of the Belding's Ground Squirrel
population at the summit of Tioga Pass
(9,941' elevation) in the High Sierras
of California indicates that there, at
least, males hibernate alone, females
often in groups, generally of close
relatives. Their 8-month hibernation is
one of the longest of any North
American mammal. Males emerge first,

tunneling through snow, females 1–2 weeks later after snow has melted from the tops of their burrows. Within 4–6 days females are sexually receptive but remain so only 3–6 hours. Males, ready for reproduction since their emergence, compete so fiercely for mates—even interrupting copulating rivals—that all are injured, some killed. Courtship and mating occur mostly above ground, which is unusual for ground-living squirrels. On the average, females mate 4 times with 3 different males, with most offspring sired by the first, or first and second partner. The female digs a nesting burrow, 10–15′ long, 1–2′ below ground, with at least 2 openings, and builds a grass-lined nest inside. Young are born 25 days later, nursed almost a month, and appear above ground in late July–early August. By then, some adult males have entered hibernation. Females follow in late September, and the young, which need more time to accumulate fat, at snowfall. Since food is not stored in the burrow, squirrels forage voraciously to nearly double body weight; three fourths of the stored fat provides energy during hibernation and the remainder is used after spring emergence. Coyotes, Badgers, bears, weasels, and hawks are predators; females that have lost their own young to them may migrate to other sites and kill but not eat offspring of unrelated females, then settle in that area, probably as a means of acquiring safer breeding places. Infanticide is also practiced by the relatively carnivorous yearling males, which kill and eat offspring of unrelated females. Males disperse after weaning, but females are sedentary, with several generations sharing an ancestral site, and among close relatives they are highly cooperative, seldom fighting over nest sites, sharing parts of territory, giving alarm calls, and even chasing intruders from each other's unguarded burrows.

Males have a shorter lifespan, 3–4
years, while females usually live 4–6
years. For all, the chief cause of death is
severe weather: 54–93% of juveniles
and 23–68% of adults perish during
hibernation and more may freeze or
starve during snowstorms after their
spring emergence.

29 Columbian Ground Squirrel
(*Spermophilus columbianus*)

Description: Grayish mixed with black above, with
indistinct buff spotting. Front of *face,
front legs, and belly reddish-brown.* Front
feet buff. *Bushy tail* mostly reddish, but
edged with white and with some black
hairs above, especially at base and tip. L
12⅞–16⅛″ (327–410 mm); T 3–4¾″
(77–120 mm); Wt 12–28 oz. (340–
812 g).

Similar Species: Richardson's, Townsend's, and
Washington ground squirrels tend to
be smaller, and none has reddish-brown
forelegs and feet; Idaho Ground
Squirrel much smaller, with white
chin.

Breeding: 1 litter per year of 2–7 young
(averaging 3–4).

Habitat: Variable: alpine meadows, arid
grasslands, brushy areas.

Range: Southeastern British Columbia and sw
Alberta south to ne Oregon, n Idaho,
nw Montana.

This colonial estivator and hibernator
sleeps 7–8 months of the year, starting
estivation as early as July in a chamber
it seals off from its main tunnels by a
plug 2′ long. While it puts on fat in
summer, it also stores some seeds or
bulbs in its hibernation chamber to eat
after spring awakening. As with many
hibernators, males emerge several days
before females. Many kinds of food are
eaten, including grasses, plant stems
and leaves, seeds, bulbs and tubers,

insects, birds and other small
vertebrates. Especially when in large
colonies, these squirrels sometimes
damage grain fields.

30 Arctic Ground Squirrel
"Parka Squirrel"
(Spermophilus parryii)

Description: Largest North American ground
squirrel. Head and shoulders tawny to
reddish; *back reddish to grayish-brown,
with numerous whitish flecks;* underparts
and legs yellowish or tawny. Grayer in
winter. Males slightly larger than
females. L 11¾–15¾" (300–395 mm);
T 3–5⅜" (77–135 mm); HF 2–2¾"
(50–68 mm). Males average 27⅞ oz.
(791 g), females 24⅝ oz. (698 g).

Breeding: Mates in May, soon after emerging from
hibernation; 5–10 young born blind
and hairless in late June, weaned at 20
days, dig own burrows by late summer.

Habitat: Subalpine brushy meadows, riverbanks,
lakeshores, sandbanks, but not in
permafrost areas.

Range: Alaska, Yukon, mainland Northwest
Territories, and n British Columbia;
the only ground squirrel in its range.

Despite the continuous light during
most of its active summer season, this
highly vocal colonial ground squirrel
follows a "daily" routine from about 4
a.m. to 9:30 p.m., wandering far from
its home range to forage. It spends
most of its time crawling through
vegetation to feed on stems and leaves,
seeds, fruits, and roots of grasses,
sedges, and other green plants, as well
as woody plants and mushrooms, but
may pause to sunbathe, sandbathe, or
swim. On rainy or cloudy days it keeps
to its burrow; the reduced intensity of
light at night may serve as a sleep
stimulus. The burrow, often used for
many years, is an extensive series of

tunnels, many just under the surface and most not more than 3' deep, with several entrances. Shorter temporary burrows are often dug to provide refuge from summer predators. In the fall, after putting on a layer of fat, Arctic Ground Squirrels enter hibernation, adults first, then juveniles, which need more time to accumulate fat. Hibernation lasts more than half the year, from September through April or May. Males emerge first, through the snow, and have been seen abroad at 22° F. Food stored in the burrow, such as seeds, willow leaves, and bog rush fruit, are eaten at this time. It is preyed upon by Ermine, wolves, Arctic Fox, and Grizzly Bear (which tears up the ground to find them in their burrows), and by Eskimos, who eat them and use the skins to line parkas.

15 Thirteen-lined Ground Squirrel
"Striped Gopher"
(*Spermophilus tridecemlineatus*)

Description: Brownish, with *13 alternating brown and whitish longitudinal lines* (sometimes partially broken into spots) on back and sides. *Rows of whitish spots within dark lines.* L 6¾–11¼" (170–297 mm); T 2⅜–5¼" (60–132 mm); HF 1⅛–1⅝" (27–41 mm). Wt 3⅞–9½ oz. (110–270 g).

Sign: Burrow openings with radiating runways; however, openings are often hidden under a clump and no mound marks them, for excess dirt is spread evenly over the ground.

Breeding: Mates in April; 1 litter of 8–10 young born in May.

Habitat: Originally shortgrass prairies; now along roadsides, in yards, cemeteries, golf courses, wherever grass is kept mowed.

Range: Much of central North America, from se Alberta and s Manitoba south to n

New Mexico, n and se Texas, and east
through Minnesota and Missouri to
Michigan and Ohio.

This handsome little spotted animal
was known as the leopard-spermophile
in Audubon's day. Strictly diurnal, it is
especially active on warm days. A
solitary or only somewhat colonial
hibernator, in late summer it puts on a
heavy layer of fat and stores some food
in its burrow. It enters its nest in
October (much earlier for some adults),
rolls into a stiff ball, and decreases its
respiration from 100–200 breaths per
minute to one breath about every 5
minutes. It emerges in March or early
April. The burrow may be 15–20′
long, with several side passages, but
seldom more than 1–2′ below ground
except for a special deeper section for
the hibernation nest. Shorter burrows
are dug as hiding places. The home
range is 2–3 acres. Its maximum
running speed is 8 mph, and it reverses
direction if chased. It often stands
upright to survey its domain; when it
senses danger it dives down its burrow,
then may poke out its nose and give a
birdlike trill. Caterpillars, grass and
weed seeds, and grasshoppers are
dietary staples, but bird flesh and even
mice and shrews may be eaten. Great
numbers are killed by automobiles. The
squirrels sometimes damage gardens by
digging burrows and eating vegetables,
but they also devour weed seeds and
harmful insects.

16 Mexican Ground Squirrel
(Spermophilus mexicanus)

Description: Brown, with *about 9 rows of squarish
white spots on back;* belly whitish or buff.
Long, moderately bushy tail. Small
rounded ears. Males larger than
females. L 11–15″ (280–380 mm); T

4¼–6½" (110–166 mm); HF 1½–2"
(38–51 mm); Wt 4¾–11⅝ oz. (137–
330 g).

Similar Species: Spotted Ground Squirrel has spots
evenly scattered, not in rows; Thirteen-
lined Ground Squirrel has stripes as
well as spots.

Breeding: 1 litter per year of about 5 young born
in May.

Habitat: Brushy or grassy areas, or mesquite or
cactus deserts, usually on sand or
gravel.

Range: Southeastern New Mexico, sw Texas.

This somewhat colonial ground squirrel
hibernates in winter in the cooler parts
of its range. Each has several burrows: a
home burrow, usually with two
entrances, in which the young are born
in the deepest part of a side tunnel, and
2 or more secondary refuges. It feeds
primarily on green vegetation in
spring, later on insects and often on
dead animals along the highway. One
Mexican Ground Squirrel was observed
killing a young cottontail rabbit almost
one fourth its own size. Timid and
usually silent, it has an alarm call
consisting of a short trilling whistle.
Around small farms, these ground
squirrels sometimes inflict crop damage
by digging up germinating seeds and
eating ripening grain.

---

18 Spotted Ground Squirrel
(*Spermophilus spilosoma*)

Description: Grayish or brownish above, with small,
squarish *indistinct light spots scattered on
back;* whitish below. Rather scantily
haired tail similar to back, with black
tip; buff below. Ears small. L 7¼–10"
(185–253 mm); T 2¼–3⅝" (55–92
mm); HF 1⅛–1½" (28–36 mm); Wt
3½–4⅜ oz. (100–125 g).

Similar Species: Mexican Ground Squirrel has spots in
definite rows; Thirteen-lined Ground

Squirrel has stripes as well as spots.

Sign: Burrows about 2″ wide, usually opening under bushes or overhanging rocks.

Breeding: 2 litters of 5–7 young abroad by late April.

Habitat: Dry sandy areas especially; also grassy areas, pine woods.

Range: Southwestern South Dakota south to w Texas, New Mexico, Arizona.

Active in the morning and late afternoon, in the heat of the day it often retires to its burrow. In southern parts of its range it is active all year but may hibernate in northern ones. Green vegetation and seeds are primary foods, but it also eats grasshoppers and beetles.

26 Franklin's Ground Squirrel
"Whistling Ground Squirrel"
"Gray Gopher"
(*Spermophilus franklinii*)

Description: Brownish-gray peppered with black above; almost as dark below. Tail blackish mixed with buff above and below, bordered with white. L 15–15⅝″ (381–397 mm); T 5⅜–6″ (136–153 mm); HF 2⅛–2¼″ (53–58 mm); Wt 17⅝–24⅝ oz. (500–700 g).

Similar Species: Richardson's Ground Squirrel smaller, with paler underparts, shorter tail.

Sign: Burrows concealed in tall grass, with some mounds.

Breeding: 1 litter of 5–8 young born in May; young are above ground at 1 month old and disperse several weeks later.

Habitat: Dense grassy areas; hedges; brush borders.

Range: Eastern central Alberta, s Saskatchewan, and s Manitoba south to n Kansas, n Illinois, nw Indiana.

The largest and darkest ground squirrel in its range, it sometimes gathers in

small colonies but usually is solitary. It is active on sunny days but usually retires when the sky is overcast. In summer it puts on a layer of fat, and it hibernates from about October to April, depending upon latitude. Although a good climber, it is believed to spend more than 90% of its life underground. Its birdlike whistling call is usually heard in mating season, with males doing most of the vocalizing. Males also fight frequently, biting each other on the rump; in spring, almost every male has a cut or bare spot near the base of its tail. It eats green vegetation, corn, clover, seeds, berries, caterpillars and other insects, but small birds and mammals may form a third of its diet.

190, 196 Rock Squirrel
(*Spermophilus variegatus*)

Description: Largest ground squirrel in its range. *Mottled above, grayish-brown in front, brownish behind;* buff-white or pinkish-buff below. Long *bushy tail variegated buff and brown* with white edges. L 16⅞–20¾" (430–525 mm); T 6¾–9⅞" (172–252 mm); Wt 21–28 oz. (600–800 g).

Breeding: 2 litters per year of 5–7 young born May–July.

Habitat: Open rocky areas; oak-juniper growth in canyons.

Range: Southern Nevada, Utah, Colorado, panhandle of Oklahoma, w Texas, Arizona, New Mexico.

Active in early morning and late afternoon. In the north it hibernates, but only for short periods, and is often abroad during winter warm spells; in the southern parts of its range it is active all year. The common name is apt, for it is often seen sitting on rocks; it runs among them and makes its den in a burrow beneath them. It climbs trees nearly as well as tree squirrels to feed on the fruit of juniper or mesquite. It has a sharp, clear, sometimes quavering whistle; its alarm call is short, followed by a lower-pitched trill. Acorns, nuts, and seeds of mesquite, cactus, agave, currant, and many other plants are eaten on the spot or stored in its den. It sometimes damages crops. Some people find young Rock Squirrels tasty eating.

---

17 California Ground Squirrel
(*Spermophilus beecheyi*)

Description: Brownish, with buff flecking; *whitish wash on sides of neck across shoulders to haunches* enclosing a *dark brown or black V pattern* on top of back shoulders, with V pointing forward. Rather bushy tail brownish-gray above and below, edged with white. L 14⅛–19¾" (357–500 mm); T 5¾–8⅞" (145–227 mm); HF 1⅞–2½" (49–64 mm); Wt 9⅞–26 oz. (280–738 g).

Similar Species: Other ground squirrels in its range smaller.

Sign: Burrows with entrance mound and radiating pathways.

Breeding: Mates in early spring; 1 litter of 5–8 young. Young first begin to burrow at about 8 weeks of age.

Habitat: Open areas, including rocky outcrops, fields, pastures, sparsely wooded hillsides.

Range: Southern central Washington, w Oregon, most of California, w central Nevada.

Active from dawn to dusk, California Ground Squirrels form loose colonies, but individuals tend to be antisocial. Several animals may occupy one burrow, 3–6" wide, 5–200' long, but each uses its own entrance. This hole, rather than the nearest, is the one the animal usually races for when alarmed. Burrows are usually under a log, tree, or rock when available, otherwise in the open, with a mound at the main entrance. Some are used for many years by successive occupants. While this ground squirrel may climb into brush or a tree to bask in early morning sunlight, it otherwise remains on the ground. It feeds primarily on plant material, including leaves, stems, flowers, bulbs, roots, seeds, fruits, and berries, but sometimes also on insects and small vertebrates. It hibernates from November to February but first-year animals often remain above ground. It often damages grain, fruit, and nut crops, and its fleas often carry bubonic plague.

Mohave Ground Squirrel
(*Spermophilus mohavensis*)

Description: *Pinkish-gray above; belly white.* No mottling or stripes. Short thin *tail cinnamon above, white below.* Cheeks brownish. L 8¾–9⅛" (219–230 mm); T 2¼–2⅞" (57–73 mm); HF 1¼–1½" (32–38 mm).

Similar Species: Round-tailed Ground Squirrel has longer tail, cinnamon or drab-colored. White-tailed Antelope Squirrel has 1 narrow white stripe on each side.

Habitat: Creosote bush scrub in sandy desert.

Range: Mohave Desert of s California.

Like the antelope squirrel, it carries its tail over its back when running; the white underside helps reflect the sun's rays. This mainly solitary squirrel estivates and hibernates from August to March when food is scarce. (The White-tailed Antelope Squirrel, which occurs with it, remains active during this period.) It is preyed upon by Badgers, foxes, Coyotes, hawks, and eagles.

19 Round-tailed Ground Squirrel
(*Spermophilus tereticaudus*)

Description: Various shades of *cinnamon* with drab grayish cast above; slightly lighter below. No stripes or mottling. *Round tail long, slender,* not bushy; cinnamon or drab below. L 8–10½″ (204–266 mm); T 2⅜–4¼″ (60–107 mm); HF 1¼–1½″ (32–40 mm); Wt 5–6½ oz. (142–184 g).

Similar Species: Mohave Ground Squirrel pinkish-gray above, with shorter tail white below.

Sign: Burrow entrance under creosote or mesquite bush.

Breeding: Mates in late March–April, gestation about 27 days; young above ground first week in May, weaned mid-May. Litter size varies with abundance of rainfall and vegetation: average of 3.3 young in one dry year, 9 young in one wet year.

Habitat: Flat sandy desert areas, creosote scrub.

Range: Southeast California, s Nevada, sw Arizona.

To avoid the most intense heat, it is most active mornings and evenings and in midday retires to its burrow or seeks out shade afforded by a plant. Seeds, other plant parts, and insects are chief foods. It hibernates from late September or early October to early January; in some areas it remains active all year. Predators are hawks, eagles, Coyotes, foxes, Badgers, and Bobcats.

9 Golden-mantled Ground Squirrel
"Copperhead"
(*Spermophilus lateralis*)
Related species: Cascade Golden-mantled

Description: Chipmunklike. Back gray, brownish, or buff; belly whitish. *Head and shoulders coppery red,* forming "golden mantle." *On sides 1 white stripe bordered by black stripes;* no facial stripes. L 9⅛–12⅛" (230–308 mm); T 2½–4⅝" (63–118 mm); HF 1⅜–1¾" (35–46 mm); Wt 6–9¾ oz. (170–276 g).

Similar Species: Chipmunks smaller, with facial stripes.

Breeding: 1 litter per year of 4–6 young born in early summer.

Habitat: Moist coniferous or mixed forest; in mountains to above timberline.

Range: Southeastern British Columbia and sw Alberta south through much of w U.S., east to se Wyoming, w Colorado, n and w New Mexico.

It cleans its brilliantly colored coat by rolling in dust, then combing itself with teeth and claws. Usually silent, it can chirp and squeal with fright and growls when fighting. In the fall it puts on a layer of fat, which helps maintain it through winter hibernation; it also carries food in its well-developed cheek pouches to be stored in its den and presumably eaten in spring when it awakes, or perhaps when it awakens periodically during hibernation to feed in the manner of chipmunks. It hibernates from about October to May, depending on latitude. Its varied diet includes green vegetation and insects, although seeds, nuts, and fruits are the mainstay. It nests in shallow burrows up to 100′ long, often opening under or near a log, tree roots, or boulder. This species often occurs with the Uinta Chipmunk.

The closely related Cascade Golden-mantled Ground Squirrel (*Spermophilus saturatus*) is larger, with a poorly defined mantle and the upper pair of dark lines very faint; it lives in central Washington and southern British Columbia in the Cascade Mountains.

23 Black-tailed Prairie Dog
(*Cynomys ludovicianus*)

Description: Large. *Pinkish-brown above;* whitish or buffy-white below. Slim, sparsely haired *tail* unique among prairie dogs for *black tip.* Short rounded ears; large black eyes. L 14–16¼″ (355–415 mm); T 2¾–4½″ (72–115 mm); Wt 31¾–48 oz. (900–1,360 g).

Sign: Conical entrance mound to burrow of hard-packed earth at least 1′ high, about 2′ wide, and often wider, resembling miniature volcano.
Tracks: Hindprint 1¼″ long, with 5 toes printing; foreprint slightly smaller, with 4 toes printing. White-tailed and other prairie dogs with similar tracks.

Habitat: Shortgrass prairies.

Range: Eastern Montana and sw North Dakota south to nw Texas, New Mexico, extreme se Arizona.

During the hot summers in most of its range the usually diurnal Black-tailed Prairie Dog often sleeps in its burrow to escape midday heat and is most active above ground mornings and evenings. In cool overcast weather it may be active all day, but it retreats to its burrow to wait out storms. While it does not hibernate, during periods of severe cold or snowstorm it undergoes a mild torpor and for a few days keeps to its burrow. Among the most gregarious of mammals, it lives in "towns" of several thousand individuals covering 100 acres or more. The town is divided into territorial neighborhoods, or "wards," which, in turn, are composed of several "coteries," or family groups of 1 male, 1–4 females, and their young up to two years of age. The Black-tail rarely wanders far from the safety of its burrow. The burrow has conical entrance and exit mounds, which prevent flooding and serve as vantage points at which prairie dogs often sit on their haunches to survey

their surroundings and scan for danger. The mounds are of different heights to facilitate the flow of air through the burrow. About 3–5' below the entrance, a short lateral tunnel serves as a listening post and turn-around point, and at the bottom of the entrance shaft, as much as 14' deep, a long horizontal tunnel features several nesting chambers lined with dry grass, and an excrement chamber. A prairie dog covers its scat with dirt, and as one excrement chamber is filled up, a new one is excavated. About 98% of its food consists of green plants, including various kinds of grasses such as gramagrass, bluegrass, brome grass, and, in Texas, burro grass and purple needle grass. It occasionally eats a few insects, especially grasshoppers, and may rarely eat meat. It eats all the vegetation around its burrow, both because it is convenient and in order to clear protective cover that could be used by predators. In the fall, prairie dogs put on a layer of fat which helps them through winter months when food is scarce.

Like many gregarious mammals, the Black-tail is highly vocal. Studies with a sound spectogram indicate that it has nine distinctive calls, which include chirps and chatters much like those of a tree squirrel, snarls when fighting, squeals when frightened, and a shrill bark that gives its common and genus names (*Cynomys* comes from Greek words meaning "dog mouse"). A staccato double-noted call consisting of a chirp followed by a wheezing sound accompanied by tail flicking is an alarm signal; it is chorused by other dogs before all dive for safety. The "jump-yip" display, in which the prairie dog leaps into the air with head thrown back and forelegs raised as it gives a wheezing, whistling "yip," seems to be an all-clear signal; this is also picked up by other prairie dogs and soon the whole community is jumping and yipping. Black-tails approach each other, touch noses, and turn their heads sideways to touch incisors; this "kissing" is not a part of courtship but a gesture of recognition and identification among ward members. Black-tails groom each other and cooperate in burrow-building. They breed from February to March and about a month later have their one annual litter, usually of 4–5 young born deaf, blind, and hairless. The young emerge from the burrow at about 6 weeks, leave parents to fend for themselves at about 10 weeks, and are full-grown at 6 months. Lifespan is 7–8 years.

In the past, dog towns covered vast expanses of the Great Plains. After great numbers of bison were killed off, the use of the prairie for agriculture and grazing caused a prairie dog population explosion. As the rodents competed with cattle for grass—250 can consume as much grass each day as a 1,000-lb. cow—they were the object of such fierce extermination campaigns that their number declined by over 90% (which, in turn, led to the decline in numbers of their chief predator, the Black-footed Ferret.) Now foxes and the Badger are chief predators, but Coyotes, Bobcats, eagles, hawks, and snakes take a share. However, a balanced population of the animals (controlled by predators, sport hunters, and modern methods of habitat modification) can actually improve rangeland, and today many ranchers take pains to maintain dog towns instead of exterminating them. Prairie dog meat, though seldom eaten, is quite palatable and provided food for Indians and early settlers.

20, 21, 24 White-tailed Prairie Dog
(*Cynomys leucurus*)
Related species: Gunnison's, Utah

Description: Stocky. Pinkish-buff mixed with black above; slightly lighter below. Short, *white-tipped tail.* Dark patches above and below eyes; yellowish nose. Small ears. L 13⅜–14⅝″ (340–370 mm); T 1⅝–2⅜″ (40–60 mm); HF 2⅜–2⅝″ (60–65 mm); Wt 1½–2½ lb. (675–1,125 g).

Similar Species: Black-tailed Prairie Dog with tip of tail black, no dark patches over and under eyes.

Sign: Burrow openings with mounds up to 3′ high, 8–10′ wide. Burrow mounds of White-tailed Prairie Dogs less conspicuous than those of Black-tailed Prairie Dogs, as well as looser and not tamped down as thoroughly. An occasional burrow may have no discernible mound at all, probably because the loose earth has washed away.
Tracks: Similar to those of the Black-tailed and other prairie dogs.

Habitat: Sagebrush plains at high elevations.

Range: Southeastern Utah, sw Colorado, ne Arizona, nw New Mexico.

Although the habits of the White-tail are similar to those of the Black-tailed Prairie Dog, the White-tail is less colonial, with only a few of its burrows interlinked with those of other individuals; it also engages in fewer social contacts such as "kissing," mutual grooming, and cooperative burrow-building. Unlike the Black-tail, it lives at higher, cooler elevations (mountain meadows and high pastures rather than level plains) and hibernates throughout the resulting longer winters, entering the burrows by late October and reemerging in March. It is believed to awaken occasionally, at which times it does not emerge but probably feeds underground on roots

and seeds. Preferred foods are grasses
and forbs, much the same as those eaten
by Black-tailed Prairie Dogs. In some
areas, White-tailed Prairie Dogs are
forced to rely heavily on saltbush. All
prairie dogs gain weight rapidly in
summer; a White-tail that weighs
1½ lb. when the grasses begin to
sprout may weigh twice as much before
hibernation.

Because of cold winters, White-tailed
Prairie Dogs breed slightly later—
chiefly in March at higher elevations—
than Black-tail. Gestation requires
only a month, but the young (an
average of 5 in an annual litter) do not
appear at burrow entrances until May or
June. The lifespan is about 4 or 5 years.
In some regions, burrowing owls and
rattlesnakes reside in vacated prairie-
dog burrows (as do Black-footed Ferrets
on the plains), and there is a
widespread belief that rattlers kill many
of the rodents. Without doubt, they
kill a few pups in spring, but mature
prairie dogs show surprisingly little fear
of them. If rattlesnakes killed as many
as some suppose, many "dog towns"
would soon become ghost towns.
Other predators include birds of
prey, Badgers, Bobcats, and Coyotes.
Floods and fires also kill a few. Circling
birds of prey elicit the most pronounced
alarm response: a few quick terrified
yaps and every prairie dog in sight
disappears down a hole. Vocalizations,
including alarm calls, resemble those of
Black-tailed Prairie Dogs.

Closely related species are Gunnison's
Prairie Dog (*Cynomys gunnisoni*), found
in western Wyoming, northwestern
Colorado, and northeastern Utah; and
the Utah Prairie Dog (*Cynomys
parvidens*), an endangered species, found
in south central Utah.

182, 188, 195 Gray Squirrel
(*Sciurus carolinensis*)

Description: Gray above, with buff underfur showing especially on head, shoulders, back, and feet; underparts paler gray. Black phase common in northern parts of range. Flattened *tail* bushy, gray *with silvery-tipped hairs*. Albino squirrel colonies in Olney, Illinois; Trenton, New Jersey; Greenwood, South Carolina. L 16⅞–19¾″ (430–500 mm); T 8¼–9⅜″ (210–240 mm); HF 2⅜–2¾″ (60–70 mm); Wt 14–25 oz. (400–710 g).

Similar Species: Fox Squirrel is larger and has yellow-tipped tail hairs.

Sign: Gnawed acorn husks or other nutshells, especially hickory, walnut, beechnut, or pecan, littering ground; in winter and spring, ragged little holes in snow or earth where squirrels have dug up nut caches; gnawings on tree trunks and limbs, similar to porcupine's but with smaller tooth marks and no droppings below; woodpecker holes as dens, especially in standing dead trees, leaf nests: big, round, ragged solid-looking but hollow balls in high tree crotches or limbs (obvious in winter in bare branches); summer "cooling beds" or "loafing platforms": flatter, smaller leaf nests without cavity; corn cobs with only germ end of kernels eaten. *Scat:* Small, dark, oval, but seldom noticed.

Tracks: Foreprints, round, 1″ long, hindprints, more triangular, 2¼″ long. On ground when bounding: paired hindprints slightly ahead of paired foreprints; sometimes foreprints between rear parts of hindprints, often directly behind them, leaving tracks like exclamation points (!!); bounding stride from a few inches to over 3′. On snow, foreprints 1½–1¾″, hindprints nearly 3″, with claws usually showing. On mud or soft ground: hindprints shorter and rounder because entire pad does not always print and long toes may print more distinctly. (Rabbit tracks are similar but longer and foreprints are not paired.)

Habitat: Hardwood or mixed forests with nut trees, especially oak-hickory forests.

Range: Eastern U.S. west to s Manitoba, e North Dakota, most of Iowa, e Kansas, e Oklahoma, e Texas.

Especially active in morning and evening, particularly in dry weather, the Gray Squirrel is abroad all year, even digging through snow to retrieve buried nuts. It does not remember where it buried nuts but can smell them under a foot of snow; when snow is deep, the squirrel tunnels under it to get closer to the scent. It feeds primarily on nuts, especially hickory nuts, beechnuts, acorns, and walnuts, but also eats heavily at times maple or tulip tree seeds, fruit, or opening buds, and can ravage a corn patch. It never caches nuts where it finds them but carries them to a new spot, burying each nut individually in holes dug with forefeet, then tamped with fore and hind feet and nose. In this fashion it propagates many trees. It dens in trees year-round, using either natural cavities, old woodpecker holes, or leaf nests in stout mature trees or standing dead ones, especially white oaks, beeches, elms, and red maples. Both males and females build winter nests and more loosely constructed summer nests, which are likely to be near dens but are not always in the same trees. Extremely ramshackle nests may have been damaged by the elements but are likely to be ones built by juveniles or temporary shelters near corn or other attractive crops. Young are born in a tree cavity den or leaf nest; females often move their litters back and forth between cavity dens and leaf nests, perhaps because of changes in the weather, perhaps to escape predation or parasite infestation. Mating is in midwinter; a litter of 2–3 young is born in spring, with a second litter often in late summer. Its characteristic bark—"que, que, que, que"—is usually accompanied by a flick of the tail. The tail serves as an umbrella in rain, a blanket in winter, and a rudder when swimming; it gives lift when the squirrel leaps from branch to branch and slows descent should the squirrel fall. Overpopulation may trigger major migrations; in the early nineteenth century, when vast tracts of the East were covered by dense hardwood forest, observers reported migrations in which squirrels never touched ground but moved great distances from tree to tree. One of the top game animals, this squirrel provides sport and meat for many.

---

191 **Western Gray Squirrel**
"California Gray Squirrel"
(*Sciurus griseus*)

Description: *Gray with numerous white-tipped hairs* above; *belly white.* Backs of ears reddish-brown. Long *bushy tail with bands of gray, white, and black, especially below.* L 17½–23¼" (445–593 mm); T 9⅜–12¼" (240–310 mm); HF 3–4" (76–101 mm). Wt 12–34 oz. (340–964 g).

Sign: Large leaf nests, obvious in winter, often high in trees. Sign is same as for Gray Squirrel.

Habitat: Woodlands.

Range: Pacific states, from Washington to California.

The only large gray tree squirrel in its range on the West Coast, it is active all year but during bad storms may remain in its nest. In summer it uses a nest of shredded bark and sticks, usually at least 20' above the ground; in winter it probably lives in a tree hollow. Pine

cones, acorns and other nuts, some
fungi, berries, and insects are chief
foods. One annual litter of 3–5 young
is born between March and June. Its
hoarse barking call is heard mostly in
late summer.

193, 194 Abert's Squirrel
"Tassel-eared Squirrel"
(*Sciurus aberti*)
Subspecies: Kaibab

Description: *Large.* Dark grizzled gray above with
darker sides, reddish back; *belly white.*
Tail above similar to back but with
whitish cast, bordered with white;
white below. *Tasseled ear* reddish on
back, about 1¾" (44 mm) long, with
tufts or "tassels" extending about ¾"
(18–20 mm) beyond eartips. L 18¼–
23" (463–584 mm); T 7¼–10" (185–
255 mm); Wt 1½–2 lb. (681–
908 g).

Similar Species: Arizona Gray Squirrel lacks ear tufts.

Sign: Nests, about 1' in diam., high in trees,
especially in pine or juniper. Sign is
much the same as for Kaibab Squirrel
and Gray Squirrel.

Habitat: Coniferous forests; yellow or ponderosa
pine, sometimes in piñon or juniper.

Range: Isolated mountainous areas in Arizona,
New Mexico, se Utah, Colorado; in
Grand Canyon in Arizona, only on
South Rim.

On a base of twigs placed in a crotch, it
builds a tree nest with two entrances
and lines the inside of the 5" chamber
with shredded bark. It repairs the nest
as necessary. Pine seeds and piñon nuts
are chief foods but it also eats
mistletoe, the inner bark (cambium) of
pine, and other vegetable items. Nuts
are buried in the ground but no food is
stored in the nest. Active throughout
the winter, in very cold weather it may
remain in its nest except for retrieving

buried seeds, especially at tree bases
where there is no snow. Mating chases
may be seen in February or March. A
litter usually of about four young is
born in March or April; young are on
their own by late June. These brightly
colored squirrels, often killed by
hawks and automobiles, are also hunted
for sport and food.

Formerly considered a separate species,
but now classified as a subspecies of
Abert's, is the Kaibab Squirrel (*Sciurus
aberti kaibabensis*). It has dark
underparts, an all white tail, and is
found only on the North Rim of the
Grand Canyon.

186 Fox Squirrel
(*Sciurus niger*)
Related species: Nayarit

Description: *Largest tree squirrel.* 3 color phases: in
northeastern part of range, gray above,
yellowish below; in western part,
bright rust; in South, black, often with
white blaze on face and white tail tip.
Large bushy tail with *yellow-tipped hairs.*
In South Carolina, typically black with
white ears and nose. L 17⅞–27½"
(454–698 mm); T 7⅞–13" (200–
330 mm); HF 2–3¼" (51–82 mm);
Wt 17⅝–37⅛ oz. (504–1,062 g).

Similar Species: Gray Squirrel is smaller and has silvery-
tipped tail hairs.

Sign: Large leaf nests in trees, fairly well
hidden in summer but obvious in
winter; remains of nuts, tulip tree
fruits. Other sign is similar to that of
Gray Squirrel except that food debris is
often much more evident, because fox
squirrels commonly carry nuts to a
favorite feeding perch such as a low
branch, log, or stump, where ground
may be heavily strewn with shells.
When squirrels raid cornfields it may
be possible to tell which species is the
robber. A Fox Squirrel usually cuts and

hauls an entire cob to a feeding perch, which is strewn with husks and bits of cob, while a Gray Squirrel bites the kernels from cob, then eats only germ of kernel, dropping the remainder.

Habitat: Woods, particularly oak-hickory; in the South, live oak and mixed forests, cypress and mangrove swamps, piney areas.

Range: Eastern U.S. except for New England, most of New Jersey, extreme w New York, n and e Pennsylvania; west to the Dakotas, ne Colorado, and e Texas.

The Fox Squirrel is most active in morning and late afternoon burying nuts which in winter it will locate by its keen sense of smell, even under snow. It eats mainly hickory nuts and acorns but also other nuts and seeds, including the fruit of tulip poplar, the winged seeds of maple trees, ripening corn along wooded areas, open buds, various berries in season, and some fungi. It spends much time in trees feeding or cutting (chewing on) nuts or sunbathing on a limb or in a crotch. In summer it makes a leaf nest in a tree crotch; in winter it lives in a nest in a tree hole, often with a family group of several other squirrels. Winter mating chases are begun by the males, who are ready to copulate before the females come into heat. There are usually 2–4 young born in late February or early March, sometimes in June and July, occasionally into August or early September. Two-year-old females may have two litters per year. Eyes remain closed for about a month, and the young keep to the nest for their first 7 or 8 weeks and first venture to the ground when nearly three months old. Fox squirrels are good sport for the hunter and good and plentiful food for the table throughout much of the South and Midwest. They are hunted by many methods: one can listen for falling nuts, their cutting sounds, the swishing of

tree branches, or their call, "que, que, que."
A closely related species is the Nayarit Squirrel (*Sciurus nayaritensis*) found only in the Chiricahua Mountains of extreme southeastern Arizona.

192 Arizona Gray Squirrel
(*Sciurus arizonensis*)

Description: A *plain gray, white-bellied* tree squirrel. Relatively long tail fringed with white. *No ear tufts.* L 20¼–22⅜" (506–568 mm); T 9⅜–12¼" (240–310 mm); Wt 1⅜–1⅝ lb. (605–706 g).
Similar Species: Abert's Squirrel has ear tufts.
Sign: Leaf nests in trees. Sign is same as for Gray Squirrel.
Habitat: Deciduous lowland forest including walnut, sycamore, and cottonwood trees.
Range: Three isolated areas of e Arizona and w central New Mexico, mostly in canyons and valleys.

Its habits are apparently similar to those of the Eastern Gray Squirrel. It feeds on pine cones, nuts, acorns, berries, and seeds.

187 Red Squirrel
"Pine Squirrel" "Chickaree"
(*Tamiasciurus hudsonicus*)

Description: Smallest tree squirrel in its range. *Rust-red* to grayish-red above, brightest on sides; white or grayish-white below. Tail similar to back color but outlined with broad black band edged with white. In summer, coat is duller and a *black line* separates reddish back from whitish belly. In winter, large ear tufts. L 10⅝–15¼" (270–385 mm); T 3⅝–6¼" (92–158 mm); HF 1⅜–2¼" (35–57 mm). Wt 5–8⅞ oz. (140–252 g).

Similar Species: Douglas' Squirrel has grayish to
orangish underparts.

Sign: Piles of cone remnants; small holes in
earth; tree nests, especially in conifer
stands, often built of grass and
shredded bark.
Tracks: In mud, hindprint about 1½"
long, with 5 toes printing; foreprints
half as long, with 4 toes printing. In
rapid bounds, front tracks appear
between hind; in slow bounds, front
tracks slightly behind hind. Straddle,
4". Unlike ground squirrels
(*Spermophilus*), which run with one
forefoot in front of the other, the Red
tends to keep forefeet parallel when
running.

Habitat: Often abundant in any kind of forest:
natural coniferous forest, pine
plantations, mixed forest, or hardwood;
often around buildings.

Range: Throughout much of Canada and
Alaska; in the U.S. through Rocky
Mountain States, in the Northeast
south to Iowa, n Illinois, n Indiana, n
Ohio, n Virginia, and south through
the Alleghenies.

In conifer forests it feeds heavily on
pine seeds and leaves piles of cone
remnants everywhere. In the fall, it
cuts green pine cones and buries them
in damp earth, sometimes up to a
bushel per cache. Other foods eaten or
stored are acorns, beechnuts, and other
nuts; seeds of hickory, tulip, sycamore,
maple, elm; berries; bird's eggs; young
birds; fungi, even amanita mushrooms,
deadly to man, which are often cached
in trees. It makes a nest, often of
shredded grape bark, in a hollow tree,
fallen tree, hole in the ground,
hummock, or tree crotch (like the leaf
nests of gray squirrels). After animated
nuptial chases, it mates in late winter.
A litter of 3–7 young is born in March
or April, and there is sometimes a
second litter in August or September.
Vocalizations include a slightly

descending, drawn-out, rather non-musical trill which can be heard for some distance, and a chatter of various notes and chucks. The smallest tree squirrel in its range, it is usually ignored by the hunter.

185 **Douglas' Squirrel**
"Pine Squirrel" "Chickaree"
(*Tamiasciurus douglasii*)

Description: *Upper parts reddish- or brownish-gray* grading into chestnut brown on middle of back; *underparts grayish to orangish.* Grayer in winter. Tail above like back, except last third blackish; tail below rusty in center, bordered by a broad black band with whitish edge. Blackish line on sides in summer, indistinct or absent in winter. Small ear tufts in winter. L 10⅝–14″ (270–355 mm); T 3⅞–6⅛″ (100–156 mm); HF 1¾–2¼″ (44–57 mm). Wt 5¼–10½ oz. (150–300 g).

Similar Species: Red Squirrel has white to grayish-white underparts and is usually brighter red above.

Sign: Summer nests resembling large balls in trees; middens (piles of cone remnants). Other signs similar to those of the Red Squirrel.

Habitat: Primarily coniferous forests.

Range: Southwestern British Columbia, w Washington, w Oregon, n California.

Very active throughout the year, it runs about through trees and on the ground, though during bad storms it will remain in its nest. It builds a summer nest mainly of mosses and lichens, twigs, and shredded bark, but sometimes caps deserted bird's nest; in winter it nests in tree holes. Noisier than most squirrels, it has a large repertoire of calls, including a trill. It eats new shoots of conifers, green vegetation, acorns, nuts, mushrooms, fruits, and berries. In late summer and fall, it cuts cones from tree limbs and feeds on the seeds at special feeding stations in trees, below which discarded scales pile into "middens." It stores green cones in moist places (which keep them tender) and caches mushrooms in forks of trees. Mating is in early spring, with litters usually of 4–6 young in May or June; sometimes there is a second litter. The young first venture to the ground in August, and families remain together for much of the first year. Martens, Bobcats, house cats, and owls are predators. Man harvests the cone caches for seeds to plant nursery trees.

181, 183 Southern Flying Squirrel
(*Glaucomys volans*)

Description: *Smallest tree squirrel.* Very silky coat *grayish-brown above, white below.* Flattened gray-brown tail. *Loose fold of skin between front and hind legs.* Large black eyes. L 8¼–10″ (211–253 mm); T 3¼–4¾″ (81–120 mm); Wt 1⅝–3½ oz. (45–100 g).

Similar Species: Northern Flying Squirrel is generally larger and a richer brown.

Sign: *Tracks:* Similar to those of the Red Squirrel, but slightly smaller. In snow, it is nearly impossible to distinguish tracks of the two species.

Habitat: Various forests such as beech-maple, oak-hickory, and in the South, live oak.

Range: Eastern U.S. (except for n New England and s tip of Florida) west to Minnesota, e Kansas, e Texas.

The Southern and Northern flying squirrels are the smallest tree squirrels, the only nocturnal ones, and the most carnivorous of the group. Woodpecker holes are favored nest sites, but the Southern Flying Squirrel may build a summer nest of leaves, twigs, and bark.

Active all year, it may remain in its nest in extremely cold weather; in winter, several may den together in one tree hole. It does not truly fly, but glides through the air, up to 80 yd. or more, from the top of one tree down to the trunk of another, with legs outstretched and the fold of skin spread between foreleg and hindleg acting as a combination parachute and sail (or glider wing). While gliding, it can turn or change its angle of descent. Just before landing, it drops its tail and lifts its forequarters, slackening the flight skin which then serves as an air brake. It lands very lightly on all four feet, and at once scurries around to the other side of the tree trunk, in case a predator has followed its flight. Agile and extremely sure-footed aloft, it is relatively clumsy on the ground. It feeds on nuts, acorns, seeds, berries, some insects, and sometimes vertebrate flesh. Mating is in early spring, with a litter of 2–6 young born after a 40-day gestation period; there is often a second litter in late summer. Its call is faint and birdlike. It makes an excellent and exceptionally clean pet.

184 Northern Flying Squirrel
(*Glaucomys sabrinus*)

Description: *Small.* Very soft fur, rich brown above, white below. A *loose fold of skin between fore and hind legs.* Large black eyes. L 10⅜–14½″ (263–368 mm); T 4½–7⅛″ (115–180 mm); Wt 1⅝–2½ oz. (45–70 g).

Similar Species: Southern Flying Squirrel is generally smaller and grayer.

Sign: Nuts stored on stumps or about tree bases.

Habitat: Coniferous forests, mixed forests; sometimes in hardwoods where old or dead trees have numerous woodpecker-type nesting holes, especially in stumps

6–20′ high with holes near top.

Range: Eastern Alaska, s Yukon, s Northwest Territories, southern tier of Canadian provinces, Labrador; south in w U.S. through California, Idaho, Montana, Utah, and n Wyoming; in e U.S. to Minnesota, Wisconsin, Michigan, New England, and New York, and through Appalachian Mountains.

This squirrel is quite common, but because it is nocturnal, it is seldom seen except by the woodcutter who chops down the hollow tree in which it lives. Tapping on tree stumps containing woodpecker holes will often bring out a squirrel. It makes a nest of shredded bark in tree hollows and may cap an abandoned bird's nest to provide a temporary shelter. It spreads its legs and stretches its flight skin in gliding from tree to tree, pulling upright at the last instant to land gently. (See account of Southern Flying Squirrel). It feeds primarily on various nuts and seeds, but also eats insects, and probably stores much food for winter use. It mates in late winter; after gestation of about 40 days, a litter of 2–5 young are born in spring, often in a hollow stump or limb, sometimes in a bark nest in a conifer crotch; sometimes there is a second litter in late summer. Its chirping, birdlike notes are similar to those of night-flying warblers.

POCKET GOPHERS
(Family Geomyidae)

Occurring only in North America, pocket gophers are among the continent's most highly evolved mammalian burrowers. Primarily as a result of pronounced specialization for their almost completely subterranean existence, all are very similar in both structure and habits. They have thickset bodies with short necks, short fur, small ears and eyes, a naked or sparsely haired tail, and large, external, fur-lined cheek pouches—the "pockets" that give the common name. These pouches, extending from cheeks to shoulders, are often crammed with food or bedding for nests. After proceeding to a storage or nesting chamber in its burrow, the animal empties the pouches by squeezing their contents forward with both forepaws and then turns them inside out and cleans them. A special muscle pulls them back into place. As in moles, the fur of a pocket gopher can lie either forward or backward, enabling the animal to move about in its burrow equally well in both directions. The lips close behind the large incisors, keeping dirt from the mouth during underground gnawing; consequently, the big yellow incisors are always on display. They grow throughout the animal's life—if they didn't, the constant gnawing would soon wear them away. They are coated with enamel only on the front, which ensures a sharp, beveled edge, as the back of each tooth wears down faster. The 3 genera, with 16 species in our range, are distinguished by their upper incisors: the western pocket gophers (*Thomomys*) have no conspicuous grooves down the middle of these teeth; the Yellow-faced Pocket Gopher (*Pappogeomys*) has one groove; and the eastern pocket gophers (*Geomys*) have two.

Pocket gophers make two kinds of burrows: those near the surface for food gathering and deeper ones for storage and shelter. Gophers use their incisors to cut through earth and roots and to pry rocks loose; the crescent-clawed forefeet dig and shovel; and the hindfeet push back the earth accumulated under the animal's body. Passages slant towards the surfaces; (verticle shafts are made by moles). Pocket gophers usually forage underground for roots and tubers or cut off stems below ground and pull the plant into the burrow from below. What is not eaten immediately is stored in side chambers for later use. Because they derive their water from vegetation, they do not need to drink. These solitary animals do not hibernate but retreat to deep burrows in winter. In spring, males emerge to seek a female, but after mating they separate. There are usually 1 or 2 litters per year of 2–11 young. Even before dispersing, juveniles start to dig their own tunnels; at 2 months they leave home, and at 3 months are sexually mature. Although pocket gophers damage crops, their tunneling aerates the soil, which helps conserve ground water and prevent erosion.

Southern Pocket Gopher
(*Thomomys umbrinus*)

Description: *Brown,* similar to color of local soil; *sides yellowish-brown.* In Arizona, often a *dark band above from snout to base of tail,* which includes eyes and ears. L 5¼–10¾" (132–272 mm); T 1¾–3⅞" (43–100 mm); HF ⅞–1½" (22–37 mm).

Similar Species: All other western pocket gophers are similar, but Botta's Pocket Gopher, which occurs with it in isolated colonies in Arizona and New Mexico, generally has no dark band above and its sides have a purplish cast.

Habitat: Oak belt in Huachuca Mountains of Arizona; higher elevations in Patagonia Mountains, Arizona, often in oaks; very shallow rocky soils in pine forest at high elevations in Animas Mountains of New Mexico.

Range: Mostly Central America, but occurs north to extreme sw New Mexico and in the Patagonia Mountains of se Arizona.

The habits of this gopher where it occurs in our range are presumably similar to those of Botta's Pocket Gopher.

34 Botta's Pocket Gopher
(*Thomomys bottae*)
Related species: Townsend's

Description: Usually *dark brown to grayish above,* with purplish cast on sides; slightly lighter below. Tail tan to gray, essentially hairless. Variable coloration includes white individuals in the Imperial Desert of southern California, almost black ones in some coastal areas. Individuals in Arizona have white spotting under chin. *Rounded ear,* ¼–⅜" (5–8 mm) long, with a *similar-sized dark patch behind it.* L 6⅝–10¾" (167–273 mm); T 1¾–3¾" (42–97 mm); HF ⅞–1¼" (22–34 mm); Wt 2½–8¾ oz. (71–250 g).

Similar Species: All other western pocket gophers are very similar and distinguishable mostly by range.

Habitat: Various: deserts to mountain meadows, in soils ranging from sand to clay, with loam preferred; in se Oregon, sandy soil in prairie, scrub, dunes.

Range: Extreme sw Oregon (Curry Co.) south through California, s and e Nevada, much of Utah, sw Colorado, most of Arizona and New Mexico, w Texas.

This pocket gopher spends most of its time in underground burrows, which may account for its ability to tolerate such a wide variety of habitats. Tunnels are extensive; one in Texas was 150' long and very close to the surface, although the nest was more than 2' down. Side branches serve as refuse and toilet areas as well as food caches. It is solitary, living one to the burrow, and often fights if it meets another. Most breed once a year, which helps balance the population, as the predation rate is low due to their protected environment. In Texas, however, breeding seems to occur throughout the year, with most young born in spring. A closely related species is the grayish Townsend's Pocket Gopher (*Thomomys townsendii*), the largest pocket gopher in its range, found in isolated areas in northeast California, northern Nevada, southeast Oregon, and southeast Montana.

35 Northern Pocket Gopher
(*Thomomys talpoides*)
Related species: Wyoming, Idaho

Description: *Color varies greatly: often rich brown* or yellowish-brown, but also grayish or closely approaching local soil color. White markings under chin. *Rounded ear, with dark patch behind about 3 times size of ear.* In some areas, *tips of upper incisors white.* L 6½–9¼" (165–233 mm); T 1⅝–3" (40–75 mm); HF ¾–1¼" (20–31 mm); Wt 2¾–4⅝ oz. (78–130 g).

Similar Species: While all western pocket gophers are similar, Botta's Pocket Gopher in Arizona has more white spotting under chin; Camas and Townsend's pocket gophers are larger; Western and Mountain pocket gophers have longer, pointed ears.

Sign: High fan-shaped mounds; in spring,

"gopher cores": long coils of earth used to plug burrows in snow and left on ground after snow melts.

Habitat: Usually good soil in meadows or along streams; most often in mountains but also in lowlands.

Range: Southern British Columbia to s Manitoba south to ne California, n Nevada; isolated portions of n Arizona and n New Mexico; most of Colorado, and northeast to w Nebraska, and most of North and South Dakota.

The Northern Pocket Gopher seldom appears above ground, but when it does, it rarely ventures more than 2½' from a burrow entrance. Except when seeking a mate, it is ferocious toward its own kind. Although usually strictly terrestrial, one was observed swimming across a Canadian river nearly 300' wide. It is preyed upon by Badgers, weasels, and gopher snakes.
Closely related are the Wyoming Pocket Gopher (*Thomomys clusius*), which is smaller, paler, and occurs only in Sweetwater and Carbon counties, Wyoming; and the very similar Idaho Pocket Gopher (*Thomomys idahoensis*), which occurs only in eastern Idaho.

Western Pocket Gopher
(*Thomomys mazama*)

Description: Reddish-brown or various shades of gray to black, depending on soil color. *Pointed ear, with dark patch behind 5 times size of ear.* L 7¼–9⅜" (183–239 mm); T 2⅛–3¼" (53–81 mm); HF 1–1⅜" (25–35 mm); Wt 1¾–3⅜ oz. (52–96 g).

Similar Species: The very similar Northern Pocket Gopher has a different range.

Habitat: Prairie to mountain meadow.

Range: Western Washington, nw Oregon, and south into n California.

Unlike most pocket gophers in its range, the Western spends a great deal of time above ground, mostly at night, but also on warm, dark days. Sometimes it simply pokes its nose up through the ground to cut vegetation, other times it bends down vegetation to collect the seeds. It prefers grasses, false dandelions, garlic, and lupine. Owls, some of the larger mammals, and gopher snakes are frequent predators.

Mountain Pocket Gopher
(*Thomomys monticola*)

Description: From *tawny to russet or brown above;* slightly buff to vividly golden below. *Snout darker than face.* Pointed ear, ¼–⅜″ (7–9 mm), with dark patch behind about 3 times size of ear. L 6⅝–10¾″ (167–273 mm); T 1¾–3⅛″ (42–97 mm); HF ⅞–1¼″ (22–30 mm); Wt 2½–3⅛ oz. (71–91 g).

Similar Species: Townsend's and Camas pocket gophers are larger; Western Pocket Gopher occurs farther north; Northern Pocket Gopher has shorter, rounded ears.

Habitat: Open areas in coniferous forests.

Range: Northeastern California, extreme w central Nevada.

In winter, it burrows under the snow for plants and builds a nest above ground in the snow. Its underground burrows, plugged to help maintain suitable temperature and moisture, are used by many other animals, both vertebrate and invertebrate.

31 Camas Pocket Gopher
(*Thomomys bulbivorus*)

Description: *Dark grayish-brown.* L 11¾″ (300 mm); HF 1¾″ (42 mm); T 3½″ (90 mm).

Habitat: Sandy areas south of Portland.
Range: Northwestern Oregon, confined to Willamette Valley in Portland area.

The habits of this pocket gopher, by far the largest in Oregon, are little known. Its common and Latin species names derive from its fondness for bulbs of the Camas Lily (*Camassia*).

32 Plains Pocket Gopher
(*Geomys bursarius*)

Description: Larger in North, smaller in South. Light brown to black (in Illinois), varying with color of soil; slightly lighter below. *Long, sparsely haired tail. White feet.* Upper incisors with 2 distinct grooves. L 7⅜–14⅛″ (187–357 mm); T 2–4¼″ (51–107 mm); HF ⅞–1¾″ (23–43 mm); Wt 4½–12½ oz. (127–354 g).

Similar Species: In Texas (the only area where its range is shared), Yellow-faced Pocket Gopher with only one groove on its upper incisors; Texas Pocket Gopher usually larger, Desert Pocket Gopher usually grayer where the 2 species overlap.

Sign: Mounds of dirt up to 1′ high, more than 2′ wide, often in a line, with fresh mounds indicating direction of excavation.

Habitat: Prairie areas with sandy loam or loam soils; pastures; lawns; sometimes plowed ground.

Range: Eastern North Dakota, Minnesota, and w Wisconsin south through central Illinois, nw Indiana, much of Missouri and Arkansas to w Louisiana; west and south through s South Dakota, se Wyoming, e Colorado, e New Mexico, ne two thirds of Texas.

In early spring, the male leaves his burrow to seek a female, and after having mated returns to his solitary ways. Its burrows are shallow in summer, usually within 1' of the surface, and deeper in winter, when dirt is pushed up into the snow, leaving earthen cores when the snow melts.

Desert Pocket Gopher
(*Geomys arenarius*)

Description: Pale *gray-brown* above; *belly and feet white. Upper incisors with 2 distinct grooves.* L 8¾–11" (221–280 mm); T 2¼–3¾" (58–95 mm); HF 1⅛–1⅜" (27–35 mm).

Similar Species: Botta's Pocket Gopher lacks grooves on incisors; Yellow-faced Pocket Gopher has 1 groove; Texas Pocket Gopher larger; Plains Pocket Gopher dark brown where the two species occur together in Texas.

Sign: Large conspicuous mounds.

Habitat: Sandy river bottoms, especially along irrigation ditches.

Range: South-central New Mexico, extreme w Texas.

Its habits are little known but presumably similar to those of other eastern pocket gophers. At times it may greatly damage crops.

Texas Pocket Gopher
(*Geomys personatus*)

Description: *Pale grayish above;* belly mixed white and grayish. Long tail, sparsely haired. Upper incisors with 2 grooves. L 8⅞–12¾" (225–326 mm); T 2¼–4¾" (59–121 mm); HF 1¼–1¾" (30–42 mm); Wt 10–14 oz. (284–397 g).

Similar Species: Botta's Pocket Gopher lacks grooves on incisors; Yellow-faced Pocket Gopher has only 1 groove; Desert and Plains pocket gophers are smaller.

Habitat: Sandy soils; not on silt loam.

Range: Southern Texas.

The tunnels of this accomplished burrower are from 4–5″ wide and can be over 100′ long. It feeds mostly from within the burrow on roots and other plant parts, especially grasses, by cutting off plants at the base and pulling them inside. Its activities sometimes cause erosion or interfere with cultivation.

---

36 Southeastern Pocket Gopher
(Geomys pinetis)
Related species: Colonial, Sherman's, Cumberland Island

Description: Various shades of *brown,* according to soil color. Relatively *short, nearly naked tail.* Upper incisors with 2 distinct grooves. L 9–13¼″ (229–335 mm); T 3–3¾″ (76–96 mm).
Habitat: Open fields; pasture; open woods.
Range: Southeastern Alabama, s Georgia, n Florida.

The sole pocket gopher over most of its range (except in Georgia), this species forms an extensive series of burrows, varying from just below ground surface to 2′ deep. In Florida, they are often called "Salamanders."
Three closely related species are found only in Georgia: the Colonial Pocket Gopher (*Geomys colonus*), along the coast in the extreme southeast; Sherman's Pocket Gopher (*Geomys fontanelus*), in a small area in Chatham Co., in the northeast; Cumberland Island Pocket Gopher (*Geomys cumberlandius*), from Cumberland Island.

---

33 Yellow-faced Pocket Gopher
(Pappogeomys castanops)

Description: Yellowish-brown. *Dark feet.* Hairless tail. *One groove on upper incisors.* L 8⅛–

12⅜″ (226–320 mm); F 2¾–4⅛″ (70–105 mm); HF 1¼–1¾″ (31–43 mm); Wt 7½–11⅝ oz. (213–330 g).

Similar Species: Western pocket gophers have no grooves on incisors and eastern pocket gophers have two grooves.

Sign: Dirt mounds often beneath bushes or cacti.

Habitat: Clay or sandy soils in open lands.

Range: Southeastern Colorado south through e New Mexico, w Texas.

Its burrows are 3–4″ wide and usually deeper than those of the western pocket gophers in the same area. It feeds on plant parts, including bark from tree roots, and is considered a pest in cultivated areas.

POCKET MICE AND
KANGAROO RATS
(Family Heteromyidae)

Pocket mice and kangaroo rats are
neither rats nor mice but are, in fact,
closely allied to ground squirrels and
pocket gophers. Found only west of the
Mississippi, they inhabit plains,
prairies, and deserts. Both pocket mice
(*Perognathus*) and kangaroo rats
(*Dipodomys*) are nocturnal, burrowing
animals with external, fur-lined cheek
pouches used for carrying food. They
subsist chiefly on seeds and some
greens, which they store in
underground chambers. From these
their bodies manufacture water; some
species never drink. They dig
underground tunnels with chambers for
sleeping, nesting, and food storage.
Among some species, the mounds are
large and conspicuous. The entrance
and escape holes tend to be small, and
some are plugged with soil or sand
during the day to help maintain proper
levels of temperature and moisture.
Populations are subject to periodic
fluctuations. While most do not
hibernate, some are inactive in cold or
extreme heat. The young are born in
burrow nests, usually in late spring
through early fall. A litter may
comprise from 1 to 8 offspring, and
there may be one to several litters per
year, fewer in the north. Enemies
include rattlesnakes, hawks, Coyotes,
foxes, Bobcats, Cougars, weasels,
Badgers, and skunks. Vocalizations are
thin, high-pitched squeaks.
Kangaroo rats are among our most
beautiful rodents. The many species are
remarkably alike in markings but may
be distinguished by their range, size,
and intensity of coloration. Upperparts
are pale yellow or tan to dark brown;
the belly is white; and the long tail,
which aids in balancing, is usually
dark, with a white stripe on each side

and crested or tufted with long hairs along its terminal fifth. Most kangaroo rats have a white band running across the thigh and joining the white side of the tail. Facial markings are usually black and white, though very pale in a few species. Hindfeet are large, and hindlegs very long and powerful; forelegs are short. Kangaroo rats scurry about when foraging, but when alarmed, they use their springlike hindlegs to make spectacular hops; some of the larger species can leap almost 9′, thus suggesting their common name. As they seldom forage more than 30′ from an escape hole, they can reach the comparative safety of a burrow in a few bounds. They also use their hindlegs when fighting and to make a drumming sound.

Kangaroo mice (*Microdipodops*), smaller editions of the Kangaroo rats, also have long hindlegs for jumping, but their tails are quite different, being broadest in the middle and without a terminal crest or tuft. The sole of the hindfoot is densely furred.

Pocket mice, smaller than kangaroo mice, look more mouselike and have only moderately long tails, haired but untufted or only slightly tufted, and shorter hindlegs; they are poor jumpers. Their pale yellowish to brown upperparts are separated from white lowerparts by a buff-colored side stripe. They prefer sandy soil. The Mexican Pocket Mouse (*Liomys*) differs from other members of this family in lacking grooves on its upper incisors.

Olive-backed Pocket Mouse
(*Perognathus fasciatus*)

Description: Soft-furred. *Grizzled olive-gray above;* white below. Buff or yellowish line on side; buff patch behind ear. Tail slightly less than half total length.

Large hindfeet, small forefeet. L 4½–5⅝" (115–143 mm); T 2¼–2⅝" (57–67 mm); Wt ⅜ oz. (8.9–9.9 g).

Similar Species: Great Basin Pocket Mouse much larger; Silky and Plains pocket mice generally smaller, and yellowish above.

Sign: Small burrow openings with piles of sand, usually under a plant.

Habitat: Dry, sandy grasslands with little vegetation.

Range: Southeastern Alberta, s Saskatchewan, and sw Manitoba south to extreme ne Utah, n Colorado, nw Nebraska.

While the Olive-backed feeds on some insects, its primary food is seeds, including those of foxtail grass, bugseed, knotweed, Russian thistle, blue-eyed grass, and tumbleweed. Summer nests and storage chambers are 12–15" below ground, while those for estivation or hibernation are as much as 6' deep.

---

108 Plains Pocket Mouse
(*Perognathus flavescens*)
Subspecies: Apache

Description: Soft furred. Yellowish-buff sprinkled with black hairs above; white below. *No yellow patches behind ears.* L 4⅜–5⅛" (113–130 mm); T 1⅞–2⅜" (47–62 mm); Wt ¼–⅜ oz. (8–11 g).

Similar Species: Silky and Merriam's pocket mice have yellow patches behind ears.

Sign: Tiny burrows leading in all directions from under plants in sandy areas.

Habitat: Sandy plains with sparse vegetation.

Range: Southeastern North Dakota, w and s Minnesota, and n Iowa southwest to e Colorado and Texas panhandle.

During the day it closes the main burrow entrance but usually leaves open other less conspicuous ones.
Formerly considered a separate species, but now classified as a subspecies of the

Plains Pocket Mouse, is the larger
Apache Pocket Mouse (*Perognathus
flavescens apache*), which is distinguished
from the former by its distinct buff side
stripe. It is found in southeastern Utah,
southwestern Colorado, northeast
Arizona, and western New Mexico,
ancestral lands of the Apache Indians.

97 Silky Pocket Mouse
(*Perognathus flavus*)

Description: *Soft-furred. Pale yellowish above,* often
with many black hairs; belly white.
Yellow patch behind ear, white spot
below ear. *Small-footed.* Juveniles gray.
L 3⅛–4¾″ (100–122 mm); T 1¾–
2⅜″ (44–60 mm); Wt ¼–⅜ oz.
(6–9 g).

Similar Species: Plains Pocket Mouse lacks yellow patch
behind ear; Arizona and Little pocket
mice are larger.

Sign: Tiny burrow openings as wide as a
finger, at the base of plants or in
vertical banks.

Habitat: Prairies; sandy, gravelly, or rocky areas
with sparse vegetation.

Range: Southeastern Wyoming and w
Nebraska south to w Texas, New
Mexico, Arizona, extreme se Utah.

Its small burrows are usually not more
than 4″ deep, often with 3–4 openings.
Blind passages near the surface enable
the Silky to break through to escape
snakes and other underground
predators. Abandoned burrows of other
pocket mice are also sometimes used.
Like many other pocket mice, it drinks
no water, metabolizing it from food.

95, 107 Little Pocket Mouse
(*Perognathus longimembris*)
Related species: Arizona

Description: Soft-furred. Grayish-yellow or buff
above interspersed with black hairs,
varying from lighter to darker with
color of soil; underparts buff, brownish,
or white. *Tail uniformly light brownish.
Two small white patches at base of ears.*
L 4¼–5⅞" (110–151 mm); T 2⅛–
3⅜" (53–86 mm); Wt ¼ oz. (7–9 g).

Similar Species: San Joaquin Pocket Mouse occurs only
in San Joaquin Valley, where this
species does not occur; White-eared,
Yellow-eared, Long-tailed, and Great
Basin pocket mice larger; Arizona
Pocket Mouse generally larger; Silky
Pocket Mouse generally smaller.

Habitat: Gravelly soils in desert areas.

Range: Southeastern Oregon, Nevada, w and s
Utah, s California, and isolated small
areas in n, s central and sw Arizona.

This seasonally active pocket mouse
may hibernate for long periods under
adverse conditions; in California it is
inactive from October to January. It
can survive in the wild 3–5 years, a
considerable time for such a small
animal. In Nevada, the Kit Fox is an
important predator.
Closely related is the Arizona Pocket
Mouse (*Perognathus amplus*), tawny
above with many interspersed black
hairs, whitish below. It occurs in
Arizona.

96 San Joaquin Pocket Mouse
(*Perognathus inornatus*)

Description: *Soft-furred. Orange-buff above;* whitish
below. *Tail nearly uniform light brown*
above and below and has a small tuft.
Ears may have light spots at base. L 5–
6⅜" (128–160 mm); T 2½–3⅛" (63–
78 mm).

Similar Species: The Little Pocket Mouse does not occur in the San Joaquin Valley; White-eared Pocket Mouse has white ears, occurs in pine zones.

Habitat: Weedy or grassy areas on fine soil.

Range: Western central California.

Under adverse conditions of great heat or cold it may become torpid and retire to its burrow. The Latin species name *inornatus* alludes to its uniform coloration, which lacks dramatic "ornamental" markings.

---

101 Great Basin Pocket Mouse
(Perognathus parvus)
Related species: White-eared, Yellow-eared

Description: Medium-sized. *Soft-furred.* Pinkish-buff or yellowish above, interspersed with blackish hairs, white or buff below; indistinct olive-greenish line on sides. *Long tail,* darker above, whitish below, *slightly crested toward tip.* L 5¾–7¾" (148–198 mm); T 3–4¼" (77–107 mm); Wt ⅝–1⅛ oz. (16.5–31 g).

Similar Species: Little Pocket Mouse smaller; Long-tailed Pocket Mouse has tufted tail more heavily crested along terminal third.

Sign: Burrow systems with several openings and packed piles of soil near entrance.

Habitat: Arid, sparsely vegetated plains and brushy areas.

Range: Southern central British Columbia south through e Washington, e Oregon, s Idaho, to ne and central California, Nevada, extreme nw Arizona, Utah, extreme se Wyoming.

It is active from April through September, eating many kinds of insects and collecting seeds to be stored in its burrow, including those of Russian thistle, pigweed, wild mustard, and bitterbrush. Water is metabolized from food. Summer nesting and storage burrows are shallow, but a deep tunnel is dug to a hibernation nest of dry vegetation in a chamber 3–6' deep, where it spends the winter. It mates in April, after emerging from hibernation, and may produce 2 litters per year of 2–8 young born May and August. Its many predators include snakes, owls, hawks, weasels, skunks, and foxes.

Closely related species include the White-eared Pocket Mouse (*Perognathus alticola*), which occurs in Kern and San Bernardino Counties, California, and has ears with white hairs outside and inside and white or whitish underparts; and the Yellow-eared Pocket Mouse (*Perognathus xanthonotus*), which is found in Kern Co., California, and has ears with white hairs outside and yellowish hairs inside.

100 Long-tailed Pocket Mouse
(*Perognathus formosus*)

Description: *Soft-furred.* Gray or brown above; belly white, tipped with yellowish. *Long tail,* grayish above, whitish below, distinctly *crested and tufted* on terminal third. *Large hindfoot (over 20 mm).* Ears not clothed with white hairs. L 6¾–8¼" (172–211 mm); T 3⅜–4¾" (86–118 mm); Wt ½–⅞ oz. (14–24 g).

Similar Species: Bailey's Pocket Mouse larger; Great Basin Pocket Mouse lacks crested and tufted tail and has olive line on side; White-eared and Yellow-eared pocket mice have ears clothed with white hairs and a pale tail; all other soft-furred pocket mice have smaller feet.

Sign: Small piles of sand at base of rocks.

Habitat: Usually rocky or gravelly ground, sometimes along riverbeds and sandy wastes in hard-packed sand; open mesquite.

Range: Nevada, w Utah, nw Arizona, s California.

In extreme heat or cold, the Long-tailed becomes torpid and stays in its burrow. Its life span is 4–5 years. In Nevada, the Kit Fox is an important predator.

---

105 Bailey's Pocket Mouse
(*Perognathus baileyi*)

Description: Rough-haired. Grayish with yellow hairs interspersed; rump with black hairs but usually not spines; underparts clear white. *Long tail tufted at tip.* Small white spot at base of ear. L 7⅛–9⅛″ (201–230 mm); T 4⅜–5⅜″ (110–136 mm); Wt ⅞–1⅜ oz. (24–38 g).

Similar Species: Desert Pocket Mouse yellowish rather than grayish and usually smaller; Long-tailed Pocket Mouse smaller; Rock Pocket Mouse is smaller and has distinct spines or bristles on rump.

Habitat: Rocky slopes in desert areas.

Range: Extreme s California, s Arizona, and Hidalgo Co., New Mexico.

It feeds on the seeds of various green plants and also carries some seed in its cheek pouches back to its burrow as reserves for winter. It does not hibernate.

Hispid Pocket Mouse
(*Perognathus hispidus*)

Description: *Large. Rough-haired.* Brownish mixed with yellowish above; buff below. *Short tail* (less than half total length) dark brown above, whitish below, sparsely haired, *not tufted.* Large foot, 1″ (25–28 mm) long, with naked sole. L 7¾–8¾″ (198–223 mm); T 3½–4⅜″ (90–113 mm); Wt 1–1⅝ oz. (30–47 g).

Similar Species: Mexican Pocket Mouse is gray and has a

tail that is at least half its total length.

Sign: Burrow openings the size of a quarter, usually plugged by day, surrounded by small mounds of dirt.

Habitat: Prairie areas with sparse or moderate but not dense vegetation.

Range: Extreme s central North Dakota south to w Louisiana, all of Texas, and west to se Arizona.

Active much of the year in the southern part of its range, it probably hibernates in the north. Burrows, which may be more than 15″ below ground, contain branches for food storage and a maternity nest. There are probably 1 or 2 litters per year of 2–9 young in the North, although in the South it may breed throughout much of the year. It eats seeds, including those of cactus, evening primrose, and winecup, but also grasshoppers and caterpillars.

104 Desert Pocket Mouse
(*Perognathus penicillatus*)

Description: Rough-haired. Yellowish-brown to yellowish-gray above, interspersed with black hairs; belly and underside of tail white. *Long tail* (over half total length) *crested* and *tufted. No spines on rump.* Sole of hindfoot naked. L 6⅜–8½″ (162–216 mm); T 3¼–5⅛″ (83–129 mm); Wt ½–¾ oz. (15–23 g).

Similar Species: Nelson's and Rock pocket mice have rump spines or bristles; Hispid Pocket Mouse generally larger, with a shorter uncrested tail.

Habitat: Sandy deserts, among cactus or mesquite, especially along stream beds or washes.

Range: Southern California, extreme s Nevada, s and w Arizona, s New Mexico, w Texas.

During the heat of the day, the Desert Pocket Mouse closes its burrow and

retires within; like other pocket mice, it is active at night. It feeds on weed and grass seeds, including mesquite, creosote bush, and broom weed, which it carries in cheek pouches to be stored in side passages of its burrow.

Rock Pocket Mouse
(*Perognathus intermedius*)

Description: *Rough-haired.* Yellowish-gray above (nearly black when on lava flows); whitish below. Long tail grayish above, white below, crested and tufted. *Weak rump spines.* Sole of hind foot naked. L 6–7⅛" (152–180 mm); T 3¼–4⅛" (83–103 mm); Wt ⅜–⅝ oz. (12–18 g).

Similar Species: Nelson's Pocket Mouse larger with stronger spines on rump; Bailey's, Desert, and Hispid pocket mice lack rump spines.

Sign: Tiny burrows under rocks with tiny trails leading from them.

Habitat: Rocky areas and lava flows in desert areas.

Range: Southern and n central Arizona, extreme s central Utah, sw New Mexico, w Texas.

Like other pocket mice, it feeds on various weed seeds and often closes its burrow by day. It is preyed upon by owls, snakes, and carnivorous mammals.

Nelson's Pocket Mouse
(*Perognathus nelsoni*)

Description: Medium-sized. *Rough-haired.* Grayish above with *numerous distinct blackish spines on rump;* white below. *Tail longer than head and body,* slightly darker above than below, *crested toward tip* and tufted. L 7¼–7⅝" (182–193 mm);

T 4⅛–4⅝" (104–117 mm); Wt ½–
⅝ oz. (14–17 g).

Similar Species: Hispid and Desert pocket mice lack
rump spines; Rock Pocket Mouse
smaller, with weak rump spines.

Habitat: Rocky areas.

Range: Extreme se New Mexico, w Texas.

This little-known species burrows in
rocky areas among chino grass, sotol,
and bear grass.

111 San Diego Pocket Mouse
(*Perognathus fallax*)

Description: *Rough-haired.* Dark brown above, with
black spines on rump, white spines on hips;
underparts white, separated from
upperparts by buff band. Tail dark
above with narrow light stripe below,
crested along terminal ½–¾" (12–
16 mm). Ear ⅜" (7–9 mm). L 6⅞–
7⅞" (176–200 mm); T 3½–4¾" (88–
118 mm).

Similar Species: Bailey's and Desert pocket mice lack
spines and bristles on rump; California
Pocket Mouse has larger ears and is
found on brushy slopes rather than low
desert; Spiny Pocket Mouse paler,
yellowish or grayish.

Habitat: Dry, open, sandy, weedy areas.

Range: Extreme sw California, in San Diego
area.

It carries seeds to its burrow and
deposits them in separate passages
reserved for their storage.

110 California Pocket Mouse
(*Perognathus californicus*)

Description: *Brownish-gray,* with *distinct white spines
or bristles on rump* and *brownish side line.*
Tail brownish above, whitish below,
with prominent tuft. Hindfoot large.

Large ears ½" (9–14 mm) long; L 7½–
9⅜" (190–235 mm); T 4⅛–5⅝"
(103–143 mm).

Similar Species: San Diego Pocket Mouse has smaller
ears and is usually found at lower desert
elevations; Spiny Pocket Mouse pale
yellowish, with side line faint or
absent; Desert and Bailey's pocket mice
lack spines or bristles.

Habitat: Chaparral slopes.

Range: Southwestern California.

Along the coast of Southern California
this is the most common pocket mouse.
It has one annual litter of 2–5 young
born between March and June;
sometimes there is a second litter.

106 Spiny Pocket Mouse
(*Perognathus spinatus*)

Description: *Rough-furred.* Grayish or yellowish-buff
above; whitish below. Distinct *white
and brown spines on rump and flanks; no
line on sides.* Tail with long crest ½–1"
(12–25 mm). Small ears ¼" (5–7 mm);
L 6½–8⅞" (164–225 mm); T 3½–5"
(89–128 mm); Wt ½–¾ oz. (12.8–
19.9 g).

Similar Species: Bailey's and Desert pocket mice lack
spines or bristles; California and San
Diego pocket mice have definite line on
sides.

Habitat: Usually hot desert; in Nevada, found in
seepage areas and near tamarisk or
mesquite trees.

Range: Southern California; extreme s Nevada
at Granite Springs.

Like other pocket mice, it stuffs its
cheek pouches with food, mainly seeds
and other plant parts, which it then
stores in special chambers of its burrow.

102 Dark Kangaroo Mouse
(*Microdipodops megacephalus*)

Description: *Blackish* or dark *grayish above* with hairs gray at base; white below. *Tail thickest in middle,* tapering at both ends, with *black tip,* no tuft. *Incisors not grooved.* Soles of hindfeet haired. L 5¾–7″ (148–177 mm); T 2⅞–3⅞″ (74–100 mm); Wt ⅜–⅝ oz. (10–17 g).

Similar Species: Pale Kangaroo Mouse has light pinkish-cinnamon upperparts; pocket mice and kangaroo mice have grooved incisors.

Sign: Burrows 2–4′ long and 1′ deep open among brush but are closed by day and hard to find.

Scat: resembles that of Ord's Kangaroo Rat but smaller, ⅛–¼″ long.
Tracks: Prints are almost round, slightly longer than wide, about ½″ long; forefeet usually print almost side by side, followed by hindfeet, also side by side. Trails may meander about colony area.

Habitat: Shadscale and sagebrush scrub.

Range: Southeastern Oregon, extreme ne California, much of Nevada, nw Utah.

This species apparently stores no food in its burrow. Reported to feed heavily on the black seeds of Desert Star (*Mentzelia*) when available, it eats many other kinds of seeds as well. Its enemies are owls, foxes, badgers, and weasels.

---

103 Pale Kangaroo Mouse
(*Microdipodops pallidus*)

Description: *Small. Light pinkish-cinnamon* above; hairs white to base on belly and underside of tail. Tail *thickest in middle* and lacking tuft, distinct markings, and black tip. *Incisors not grooved.* Soles of hindfeet haired. L 5⅞–6¾″ (150–169 mm); T 2⅞–3¾″ (74–94 mm); Wt ⅜–⅝ oz. (10–17 g).

Similar Species: Dark Kangaroo Mouse has blackish or

dark grayish upperparts and black-tipped tail. Pocket mice and kangaroo rats have grooved incisors.

Sign: Burrow entrances, usually at least 2, open in brushy areas but plugged with earth by day. Tracks and other signs are similar to those of Dark Kangaroo Mouse.

Habitat: Fine sand around scattered brush in deserts.

Range: Western Nevada and adjacent Mono and Inyo Counties, California.

Burrows are 4–6' long, 1' deep; no food is stored in them, at least in summer. Various seeds and other vegetation form its diet. The "kangaroo" tail stores fat, which serves as an energy source during estivation and hibernation, and also helps maintain balance during jumps.

86 Ord's Kangaroo Rat
(*Dipodomys ordii*)

Description: Buff above; white below. Long tail, usually not white-tipped. Usually conspicuous white spots at base of ears and above eyes. *5-toed. White tail stripes narrower than dark stripes.* Lower incisors rounded in front. L 8⅛–11⅛" (208–282 mm); T 3⅞–6⅜" (100–163 mm); Wt 1¾–3⅜ oz. (50–96 g).

Similar Species: Only other five-toed kangaroo rats occurring with this species are Panamint Kangaroo Rat, which is larger with a longer tail, and Chisel-toothed Kangaroo Rat, which has flat-edged lower incisors.

Sign: 3" burrow openings often in banks or sand dunes, with small mounds outside; small, shallow, scooped-out dusting spots, as well as burrows, reveal a colony area; a tap at a burrow entrance may get a response of "drumming," the occupant's foot thumping as an alarm signal.

Scat: Brown or dark green, hard, oblong, very small (⅛–½" long).

Tracks: When moving slowly, all four feet touch ground and heel of hindfoot leaves a complete print about 1½" long, somewhat triangular, much wider at front than rear; foreprints much smaller, round, and between hindprints; when resting on ground, tail leaves a long drag mark. When hopping, heel of hindfoot is off ground, so hindprints are shorter, little or no tail mark shows, and forefeet may or may not print. Width of straddle over 2". Trails radiate and crisscross.

Habitat: Sandy waste areas; sand dunes; sometimes hard packed soil.

Range: Southeastern Alberta, sw Saskatchewan, s Idaho, s central Washington, e Oregon south to extreme ne California, Arizona, New Mexico, w Texas, w Oklahoma.

This kangaroo rat is active all winter in Texas, but farther north it is seldom seen above ground in very cold weather. It spends its days in deep burrows in the sand, which it plugs to maintain stable temperature and humidity. Extra holes are dug throughout the home range as escape hatches. It eats the seeds of mesquite, tumbleweed, Russian thistle, sunflowers, and sandbur. Interesting behavior includes skirmishes between individuals, with each jumping into the air and striking out at the other with its feet; kicking sand into the face of an enemy, such as a rattlesnake; jumping 6–8' at a leap when speed is called for; drumming by pounding the hindfeet; and taking sandbaths, which keep the fur from becoming matted. Sometimes it takes seeds from newly planted fields. It makes a sound similar to a bird's soft chirping. Rattlesnakes, owls, Badgers, skunks, foxes, weasels, and Coyotes are its chief predators.

84 Chisel-toothed Kangaroo Rat
(*Dipodomys microps*)

Description: Buff to dusky above; whitish below. Long tail with white side stripe narrower than dark stripes. *Five-toed. Lower incisors flat in front.* Ear ¼–½" (9–12 mm). L 9⅝–11¾" (244–297 mm); T 5⅜–6⅞" (134–175 mm); Wt 1⅞–2⅝ oz. (55–75 g).

Similar Species: Among other five-toed kangaroo rats occurring with this species, Ord's and Panamint kangaroo rats have lower incisors rounded in front.

Sign: Burrow entrances often along banks or other raised areas.

Habitat: Sagebrush and shadscale scrub; piñon-juniper woodlands.

Range: Southeastern Oregon, sw Idaho near Murphy, e California, most of Nevada, w Utah, extreme nw Arizona.

A male drums on sand with its hindfeet, evidently to attract a female from her burrow and arouse her. Males fight over females, rolling in the sand, growling, and sometimes leaping high above the ground. In Nevada, Chisel-toothed and Merriam's kangaroo rats avoid each other. Lifespan is 4–5 years.

82 Agile Kangaroo Rat
(*Dipodomys agilis*)

Description: Dark brown. Dark stripe on underside of tail extending to tip. *Five toes on each hindfoot.* L 10⅜–12⅝" (265–319 mm); T 6⅛–8" (155–203 mm); HF 1⅝–1¾" (40–46 mm); Wt 1⅝–2¾ oz. (45–77 g).

Similar Species: Merriam's and Fresno kangaroo rats smaller, with 4 toes. Giant Kangaroo Rat larger; Panamint Kangaroo Rat's tail has dark stripe on underside tapering to point near tip; Stephen's Kangaroo Rat very similar, differing only by skull characteristics.

Habitat: Sand or gravel in brushy areas.
Range: Southwest California.

The Agile is very similar in habits and characteristics to Heermann's Kangaroo Rat; they may eventually be combined as the same species.

109 Heermann's Kangaroo Rat
(*Dipodomys heermanni*)
Related species: Big-eared, Narrow-faced, California

Description: Brownish above; *white below*. Tail uniformly dusky, with little or no crest. *5-toed*. Ears dusky or nearly black. Juveniles gray. L 9¾–13⅜″ (250–340 mm); T 6⅜–8½″ (160–217 mm); Wt 1¾–3⅜ oz. (50–94 g).
Similar Species: Giant Kangaroo Rat usually larger.
Sign: *Tracks:* When resting on hindlegs, base of tail forms drag marks between complete hindprints, 1½–2″ long; when moving slowly, smaller round foreprints made between or just in front of hindprints; when making long jumps, only fronts of hindfeet touch ground, leaving small round prints 1″ across.

Habitat: Open sloping terrain; grassland and woodland in foothills; live oak and pines in low valleys.
Range: Central and s California.

Burrow systems may be 6–10′ long, with 2–3 passages, usually with a nest in one, and with 2–3 blind "escape" passages, ending an inch below the surface. It eats seeds of many plants, as well as the green parts of *Lotus, Dudleya, Lupine,* and *Bromus.* This fast-moving species has been clocked running 12 mph.
Closely related species, both with 5 toes on the hindfoot, include the Big-eared Kangaroo Rat (*Dipodomys elephantinus*),

which is larger and brownish, with big ears and a heavily crested tail, and occurs only in the San Benito County area of California; the Narrow-faced Kangaroo Rat (*Dipodomys venustus*), which has large ears and a white band across its flanks, and occurs in the Monterey and Santa Cruz areas of southwestern California; and the California Kangaroo Rat (*Dipodomys californicus*), which has 4 toes, a distinctly white-tipped tail, and occurs only in southern central Oregon and northern California.

---

87 Giant Kangaroo Rat
(*Dipodomys ingens*)

Description: *Largest kangaroo rat.* Dusky above; white below. Dusky-tipped tail, with dark brown stripe above and below, white side stripe. *Five-toed.* Ear about ½" (13 mm). L 12¼–13¾" (311–348 mm); T 6¼–7¾" (157–198 mm); Wt 4⅝–6¼ oz. (131–180 g).

Habitat: Open desert grasslands in valleys; often a dominant species in areas lacking brush.

Range: Southern California, in w San Joaquin Valley.

The Giant Kangaroo Rat often is nearly the only small mammal in its habitat. Its burrow system has 1–4 entrances and special chambers in which large quantities of food are stored. Near the entrances it makes tiny holes, which it fills with partially ripened seeds to dry, then covers with loose soil; 875 holes were dug by one individual. It has been heard to drum from within its burrow and has been induced to do so by a person drumming on top of the burrow. The Kit Fox is a common predator.

90 Panamint Kangaroo Rat
(*Dipodomys panamintinus*)
Related species: Stephens'

Description: Brownish-gray above, cinnamon on sides; white below. Dark stripe on bottom of tail tapering to point near tip. Light cheek patches and *white spot behind ear. Five-toed. Lower incisors rounded in front.* L 11¼–13⅛" (285–334 mm); T 6⅛–8" (156–202 mm); Wt 2 oz. (56.9 g).

Similar Species: Chisel-toothed Kangaroo Rat has lower incisors flat in front.

Habitat: Creosote bush scrub and piñon-juniper woodlands.

Range: Extreme w Nevada south through scattered areas in s California, and in s Nevada near Searchlight.

Like other kangaroo rats, it has a prominent oil-secreting gland on its back between the shoulders and regularly bathes in dust, which prevents its fur from becoming matted with excess oil. It has been heard to drum. It probably stores seeds and other plant parts, eating softer foods as found.
The closely related Stephens' Kangaroo Rat (*Dipodomys stephensi*) is slightly smaller and found only in the San Jacinto Valley area of California.

83 Banner-tailed Kangaroo Rat
(*Dipodomys spectabilis*)

Description: Dark buff above; white below. *Long tail* with narrow, white side stripes extending only ⅔ its length and with *a prominent white tip preceded by black band. Four-toed.* L 12¼–14⅜" (310–365 mm). T 7⅛–8¼" (180–208 mm); Wt 3½–4⅝ oz. (98–132 g).

Similar Species: Ord's and Merriam's kangaroo rats smaller, with no white tip on tail; Texas Kangaroo Rat smaller.

Sign: Large mounds of earth and vegetation up to 4' high and 15' wide (sometimes only 6" high and 5' wide) with several entrances opening to burrow systems and trails leading from them. Other signs resembling those of Ord's Kangaroo Rat.

Habitat: Scrub or brush-covered slopes, often with creosote bush or acacias on hard or gravelly soil.

Range: Southeastern Arizona, most of New Mexico, w Texas.

This kangaroo rat with the spectacularly white-tipped tail usually lives alone in its impressively mounded burrow system, which may have as many as a dozen openings to provide convenient retreat from predators. It eats green plants, and it stores seeds in side passages of its burrow for times of food scarcity. Needle grass, gramagrass, mesquite, and many other kinds of grasses and seeds have been found in Texas burrows.

Texas Kangaroo Rat
(*Dipodomys elator*)

Description: Buff above; white below. Long thick *white-tipped tail. Four-toed.* L averages 12½" (317 mm); T 7¾" (196 mm).

Similar Species: Ord's Kangaroo Rat, only other kangaroo rat sharing its range, has five toes and no white tip on tail.

Sign: Burrow openings among mesquite.

Habitat: Scrub areas, especially in mesquite.

Range: Southwestern Oklahoma, Clay and Wilbarger Counties in n central Texas.

Burrows are dug among mesquite and prickly pear plants to a depth of 3'. It stuffs its cheek pouches with plant parts, then stores them in the burrow system.

89 Desert Kangaroo Rat
(*Dipodomys deserti*)

Description: Yellowish-buff above; white below.
Tail crested, with *tip white,* sometimes
preceded by a short, dark cinnamon
stripe on top only. *No dark facial
markings. Four-toed.* L 12–14¾" (305–
377 mm); T 7⅛–8½" (180–215 mm);
Wt 2¾–4⅞ oz. (80–138 g).

Sign: Well-worn trails often leading away
from burrows.

Habitat: Areas of soft sand, such as dunes;
creosote bush or shadscale scrub.

Range: Southern Nevada, s California, sw
Arizona.

When excited, it kicks sand and drums
the ground with its large hindfeet. Like
all kangaroo rats, it is abroad at night
when humidity is highest but keeps to
its burrow when the moon is bright and
it could easily be spotted by predators.

85, 88 Merriam's Kangaroo Rat
(*Dipodomys merriami*)
Related species: Fresno

Description: *Smallest kangaroo rat.* Light yellowish-
buff above; white below. Long tail with
white side stripe wider than dark
stripes and *dusky tufted tip.* Facial
markings paler than in most species;
dark line on either side of nose but not
connected across it. *Four-toed.* L 8¾–
10¼" (220–260 mm); T 4¾–6¼"
(123–157 mm); Wt 1⅜–1⅝ oz.
(38–47 g).

Similar Species: Among four-toed species, Desert and
Banner-tailed kangaroo rats are much
larger.

Sign: Burrow openings near shrub bases.
Other signs similar to that of Ord's
Kangaroo Rat.

Habitat: Sagebrush, shadscale, creosote bush
desert scrubs, on a great variety of soil
types.

Range: Western Nevada, s California, sw
Utah, nw and s Arizona, s New
Mexico, w Texas.

There is one adult per burrow system;
females also display territorial behavior.
They feed mostly on seeds, especially of
mesquite, creosote bush, purslane,
grama grass, and ocotillo. When
Merriam's Kangaroo Rat occurs with
another kangaroo rat, Merriam's is
often found in areas of hard soil and the
other on sand.
Closely related is the Fresno Kangaroo
Rat (*Dipodomys nitratoides*), which occurs
only in the San Joaquin Valley,
California.

115 Mexican Spiny Pocket Mouse
(*Liomys irroratus*)

Description: *Dark gray grizzled with orange* above;
whitish below. Rough coat on back and
rump, with *spiny hairs* flattened,
grooved, and sharp-pointed. Tail
brownish above, whitish below, about
half total length. *Incisors not grooved.*
L 8–11⅝" (202–295 mm); T 4¼–
6½" (105–163 mm); Wt 1¼–1¾ oz.
(34–50 g).

Similar Species: True pocket mice (*Perognathus*) have
grooved incisors.

Sign: Burrows, sometimes with small
mounds closing the entrances.

Habitat: Dense brush on ridges of banks of Old
Rio Grande River; often in prickly pear
thickets.

Range: Extreme s Texas, in Cameron and
Willacy Counties near Brownsville.

It feeds on seeds of shrubs, such as
mesquite and hackberry, as well as
weed seeds. Unlike most species in its
family, it may take an occasional drink
of water.

BEAVER
(Family Castoridae)

This exclusively North American family comprises one species, which is described below.

224 Beaver
(Castor canadensis)

Description: Very large rodent. Dark brown. Large black *scaly tail*, horizontally flattened, paddle-shaped. Large hindfeet, black, webbed, with inner two nails cleft. Small eyes and ears. Large chestnut-colored incisors. L 35½–46" (900–1170 mm); T 11¾–17⅜" (300–440 mm); Wt usually 45–60 lbs (20.3–27 kg), but sometimes up to 109 lbs. (49.5 kg).

Similar Species: Muskrat and Nutria are much smaller and have slender tails.

Sign: Alarm signal: Tail "slaps" on water loud enough to be heard at a considerable distance; dams of woven sticks, reeds, branches, saplings, caulked with mud; domelike lodges of same materials in water, 6′ high or higher, up to 40′ wide; scent mounds: heaps of mud, sticks, and sedges or grass, up to 1′ high, 3′ wide, where Beaver deposits scent from anal glands, apparently to mark family territory; logs and twigs peeled where bark is eaten; felled trees; gnawed tree trunks: gnawings at heights no Beaver standing on the ground could reach are made when beavers stand on surface of deep winter snow—successive gnawings, made when snow at different levels, may produce totem-pole effect.
Scat: Seldom deposited on land but distinctive: oval pellets, 1″ long or longer, almost as thick, of coarse sawdust-like material that decomposes quickly; may contain undigested pieces of bark.

Tracks: Distinctive when not obliterated by wide drag mark of tail. Usually only 3 or 4 of the 5 toes print, leaving wide, splay-toed track 3″ long. Webbed hindfeet leave fan-shaped track often more than 5″ wide at widest part, at least twice as long as forefeet; webbing usually shows in soft mud.

Habitat: Rivers, streams, marshes, lakes, ponds.

Range: Most of Canada and U.S., except for most of Florida, much of Nevada, and s California.

Active throughout the year, the Beaver is primarily nocturnal and most likely to be observed in the evening. Beavers living along a river generally make burrows with an underwater entrance in the riverbank; those in streams, lakes, and ponds usually build dams that generally incorporate a lodge, which has one or more underwater entrances and living quarters in a hollow near the top; wood chips on the floor absorb excess moisture and a vent admits fresh air. The chief construction materials in the northern parts of its range—poplar, aspen, willow, birch, and maple—are also the preferred foods. To fell a tree, the Beaver gnaws around it, biting out chips in a deep groove. Small trees 2–6″ in diameter are usually selected, though occasionally larger ones as much as 33″ thick are felled; a willow 5″ thick can be cut down in 3 minutes. It trims off branches, cuts them into convenient sizes (about 1–2″ thick, 6′ long), and carries them in its teeth to the dam site. There it either eats the bark, turning branches in its forefeet as humans eat an ear of corn, or stores them for winter use by poking the ends into the muddy bottom of pond or stream. Dam designs vary widely; to lessen water pressure in swift streams, dams may be bowed upstream; in times of flood, temporary spillways may be constructed. Dam repair is constant.

Well adapted to its highly aquatic life, the Beaver swims with webbed hindfeet up to 6 mph, with tail serving as rudder and forefeet held close to the chest, free to help hold objects against the chest or to push aside debris. When submerged, valves close off ears and nostrils; skin flaps seal the mouth, leaving front incisors exposed for carrying branches, and clear membranes slide over eyes, protecting them from floating debris. It can remain submerged up to 15 minutes before surfacing for air. The Beaver combs its fur with the split nails on its hindfeet and waterproofs it by applying castoreum, an oily secretion from scent glands near the anus; a thick layer of fat beneath the skin provides insulation from chilly water in winter. On land the Beaver is far less at ease and frequently interrupts activity to sniff the air and look for signs of danger.

Believed to pair for life, it mates late January–late February, and 4 months later a litter of 1–8 kits (usually 4 or 5) are born well-furred, with eyes open, and weighing about 1 lb. They may take to the water inside their lodge within a half hour and are skillful swimmers within a week, though if tired may rest or be ferried upon their mother's back. On land, the mother often carries kits on her broad tail and sometimes walks erect and holds them in her forepaws. The young remain with their parents two years, helping with housekeeping chores until they are sent away just before the birth of a new litter.

Great expanses of the U.S. and Canada were first explored by trappers and traders in search of Beaver pelts, the single most valuable commodity in much of North America during the early nineteenth century. The fur was in constant demand for robes and coats, clothing trim, and top hats (sometimes

called "beavers") fashionable in
continental capitals and the relatively
urban areas of the eastern U.S. Some of
America's greatest financial empires and
real-estate holdings were founded on
Beaver profits. Unregulated trapping
continued for so long—well into the
twentieth century in some areas—that
the beaver disappeared from much of its
original range. Now reestablished over
most of the continent and protected
from overexploitation, it has become an
agricultural pest in some regions. It
kills many trees, most of little value as
timber; its dams may block the
upstream run of spawning salmon and
flood stands of commercial timber,
highways, and croplands, or change a
farmer's pond or stream into a slough
that will eventually become a meadow.
However, the dams also help reduce
erosion, and the ponds formed by the
dams may create a favorable habitat for
many forms of life: insects lay eggs in
them, fish feed on the insect larvae, and
many kinds of birds and mammals—
including otters, Minks, Moose, and
deer—come to feed and drink. The
Beaver's fine, soft fur is highly prized;
its flesh is quite tasty, and the tail,
though fatty, is considered a delicacy
by some residents of the far north.
Aside from trappers, the otter is the
beaver's most important enemy, though
the Coyote, the Red Fox, and the
Bobcat also prey upon it.

NEW WORLD RATS AND MICE
(Family Cricetidae)

This is the largest family of mammals
in North America, comprising 19
genera of 70 species with members
found in every available habitat. These
highly adaptable, mouselike creatures
range in size from the ¼-oz. (8 g)
Northern Pygmy Mouse (*Baiomys
taylori*) to the 4-lb. (1.8 kg) Muskrat
(*Ondatra zibethicus*). They vary greatly
in habits and form, though most use
burrows and none hibernate, and all
share certain cranial characteristics,
features not readily apparent to the field
observer. However, by examining
dental structure, they can be identified
as belonging to one of two groups: the
cricetines and the microtines. The
cricetines comprise all North American
species except the voles and lemmings.
They generally have long tails, large
eyes and ears, and teeth with well-
developed cusps. As a group they
are omnivorous and nocturnal.
Most breed throughout the year,
especially in warmer climates and
produce several litters of 2–7 young per
year. The tiny harvest mice
(*Reithrodontomys*) are distinguished by
the deep grooves in their incisors. They
live mainly in open grassy areas,
feeding on grass seeds and building
apple-sized nests of shredded grass
above ground in vegetation. Deer or
white-footed mice (*Peromyscus*) have 2
rows of cusps on their teeth and
internal cheek pouches. Most of these
mice are good climbers. They have
adapted to every possible North
American habitat, where they are often
the most abundant mammals present.
Many of the 16 species are so similar
that they can be distinguished only by
careful examination of their internal
bone structure. There are two species of
grasshopper mice (*Onychomys*), both
with short tails with white tips. The

most predaceous of rodents, they eat mostly insects but also kill small mammals up to their own size. Three genera are rat-sized: rice rats (*Oryzomys*), cotton rats (*Sigmodon*), and woodrats (*Neotoma*). Rice rats and cotton rats are similar in appearance, with the cotton rats having shorter, heavier tails and coarse grizzled fur. Rice rats live in marshy habitats; cotton rats favor grasslands. Woodrats, with large ears and soft brownish or grayish pelts, resemble overgrown deer mice. Often called pack or trade rats after their habit of collecting and hoarding all sorts of objects—especially shiny ones, a woodrat will often put down the twig it is holding and "trade" it for a shiny coin, which it carries off instead. It stores its trinkets in large houses resembling small Beaver lodges.

The second group, the microtines, comprises the voles and lemmings. These rodents have stout bodies with short legs and tails, and inconspicuous ears and eyes. Their teeth have flattened crowns with ridges in "loop and triangle" patterns suitable for constantly grinding the fibrous grasses and leaves that make up the bulk of their diet. The molariform teeth and incisors grow throughout the animal's life. Microtines are active day and night, and throughout the year. The meadow voles (*Microtus*), primarily inhabit open grassy areas, although two genera, red-backed voles (*Clethrionomys*) and heather voles (*Phenacomys*) generally frequent woodlands. Most breed throughout the year, and many, including the prolific meadow voles, produce several litters per year, usually of 4–9 young. Lemmings (*Lemmus, Dicrostonyx*) are stouter than voles and have shorter tails; most are restricted to the far northern regions of North America. The mass migrations of the Scandinavian Lemming (*Lemmus lemmus*) are one of the most amazing phenomena of the natural world. When food is plentiful, lemming populations increase enormously; however, when food supplies diminish, vast hordes leave their native regions to seek food in new areas. Swarms of lemmings pass through forests, towns, and cities, crossing rivers and streams. They travel in one direction only and allow no obstacle to stop them. Many reach the sea, which to them is merely another barrier to be conquered in their frenzied drive for food. They dive in, swim until they become exhausted, and eventually drown. These cyclical migrations occur every 3 to 4 years. The closely related Brown Lemming (*Lemmus sibiricus*) of northern North America undergoes similar population cycles, but instead of joining a mass migration, individuals disperse separately after the population reaches its peak.

Voles and lemmings consume all varieties of vegetable matter; they, in turn, are the major food source for many of the larger northern carnivores. Also included in this group are the muskrats (*Ondatra*), which, although classed as voles, differ from them in form and habits. Muskrats are large aquatic rodents with long, vertically flattened tails used as rudders when they swim. They live either in houses in open swamps or in burrows in banks along rivers, streams, or lakes. Their dens are built above the high water line, with a separate tunnel leading into the water. They breed from spring to autumn in the north; year-round in the south. Vegetable matter is their chief food, although they will occasionally eat mussels, fish, and crayfish.

Muskrats are the most valuable fur-bearers for North American trappers; their pelts are among the most durable.

121 Marsh Rice Rat
(*Oryzomys palustris*)
Related species: Coue's

Description: Grayish-brown above; pale buff below. *Long sparsely furred tail,* showing scales brown above, paler below. *Feet whitish.* Ears and eyes medium-sized. L 7⅜–12″ (187–305 mm); T 3¼–6⅛″ (84–156 mm); Wt 1–2¾ oz. (30–78 g).

Similar Species: Cotton rats have longer, more grizzled fur, shorter tail; Norway Rat larger, with proportionately shorter, thicker tail; Black Rat's tail longer and uniformly dark; woodrats larger, pure white below, with longer ears.

Sign: Extensive runways among marsh vegetation; feeding platforms made of plants bent over the water, often surrounded by remnants of crabs; nest of shredded grass, 12–18″ wide, often in vegetation above water.

Tracks: In soft mud or dust, hindprint ⅜″ long, with 5 toes printing; foreprint slightly smaller, with 4 toes printing. Walking stride, 2″, with hindprint directly behind foreprint, or slightly overlapping. Those of other rice rats (*Oryzomys*) similar.

Habitat: Mostly marshes; also drier areas among grasses or sedges.

Range: Mainly se U.S.: e Texas (with isolated populations in extreme s Texas) north to se Kansas, se Missouri, s Illinois, s Kentucky, e North Carolina, and north along the East Coast to se Pennsylvania and s New Jersey.

The Marsh Rice Rat swims underwater with ease, foraging on the tender parts of aquatic plants. Also included in its diet are crabs, fruits, insects, snails, and the subterranean fungus *Endogone*. Closely related is the Coue's Rice Rat (*Oryzomys couesi*), which is larger, darker, and occurs only in Cameron and Hildalgo counties, Texas.

Key Rice Rat
(*Oryzomys argentatus*)

Description: Silvery-gray. *Long sparsely haired tail,*
showing scales; gray above, paler
below. L 9⅞–10¼" (251–259 mm);
T 4¾–5¼" (121–132 mm); Wt to 3
oz. (84 g).
Similar Species: Marsh Rice Rat browner.
Habitat: Freshwater marshes.
Range: Cudjoe Key, Florida.

The Key Rice Rat was described in
1978 as a distinct species; it is
distinguished from the Marsh Rice Rat
by its silvery-gray coloration and
differences in skull characteristics. It is
presently considered an endangered
species because of its restricted range
and habitat reduction.

Plains Harvest Mouse
(*Reithrodontomys montanus*)

Description: *Brownish above* with *slightly darker,
indistinct middorsal stripe;* white below.
Tail usually less than one-half total length.
Grooved incisors. L 4¼–5⅜" (107
–143 mm), T 1⅞–2½" (48–63 mm);
HF ⅝" (14–17 mm); Wt ¼–⅜ oz.
(6–10 g).
Similar Species: Western Harvest Mouse usually has
longer tail; Fulvous Harvest Mouse
always has longer tail; House Mouse has
ungrooved incisors.
Habitat: Prairies, especially those with bluestem
grass.
Range: Northern Texas, New Mexico, and se
Arizona north to w Wyoming, sw
North Dakota.

The Plains Harvest Mouse is
herbivorous, living mainly on seeds.
Most harvest mice nest on or above the
ground, but this species frequently
builds its nest in burrows. The nest is
occupied year-round.

113 Eastern Harvest Mouse
(*Reithrodontomys humulis*)

Description: *Brownish above*, with dark middorsal
stripe; *dusky below*. Tail about half total
length and not sharply bicolored.
Grooved upper incisors. L 4¼–5⅛"
(107–150 mm); T 1¾–2¾" (45–
68 mm); HF ⅝" (15–17 mm); Wt ⅜–
½ oz. (10–15 g).

Similar Species: Fulvous Harvest Mouse has longer tail;
House Mouse has ungrooved incisors.

Habitat: Old fields; brushy areas; briar patches;
broom sedges; low areas.

Range: Southeastern U.S.: e Texas, nw
Arkansas, Mississippi, Tennessee,
Kentucky, s Ohio, West Virginia,
Virginia, Pennsylvania, Delaware.

These mice feed on seeds and young
sprouts. They store surplus seeds in
their nests and, occasionally, in an extra
cache nearby.

---

118 Western Harvest Mouse
(*Reithrodontomys megalotis*)

Description: *Brownish above, buff along sides; white
below*. Grooved incisors. L 4½–6¾"
(114–170 mm); T 2–3⅞" (50–
96 mm); HF ¾" (14–20 mm); Wt ⅜–
¾ oz. (9.1–21.9 g).

Similar Species: Fulvous Harvest Mouse has longer tail;
Salt-marsh Harvest Mouse pinkish-
cinnamon or tawny below; Plains
Harvest Mouse has somewhat shorter
tail and indistinct middorsal stripe;
House Mouse has ungrooved incisors.

Habitat: Early-stage dry weedy or grassy areas.

Range: Much of w U.S. and extreme sw
Canada east to sw Wisconsin, nw
Indiana, ne Arkansas and w Texas.

The Western frequently makes use of
the ground runways of other rodents
and is a nimble climber. Although
primarily a seed-eater, in spring it also

eats new growth and in summer
consumes many insects, especially
grasshoppers. It stores surplus food,
such as seeds, in underground caches.

122 Salt-marsh Harvest Mouse
(Reithrodontomys raviventris)

Description: *Dark brown above; pinkish-cinnamon or
tawny below.* Tail similarly bicolored.
Upper incisors grooved. L 4¾–6⅜"
(120–162 mm); T 2½–3½" (64–
88 mm); HF ⅝–¾" (15–19 mm).

Similar Species: Western Harvest Mouse has pure white
belly.

Habitat: Salt marshes.

Range: San Francisco Bay area of California.

This mouse is especially active on
moonlit nights. It builds a nest of grass
lined with softer grass or down in a
clump of vegetation above the ground,
or sometimes in an old bird's nest. It
feeds mainly on seeds, including those
of many grasses, and can drink sea
water. Owls, snakes, and many
mammals prey upon it.

116 Fulvous Harvest Mouse
(Reithrodontomys fulvescens)

Description: Reddish-brown interspersed with black
above, shading to yellowish on sides;
white below. *Tail more than half total
length. Feet reddish above.* Grooved
incisors. L 5¼–7⅞" (134–200 mm);
T 2¾–4⅝" (72–116 mm); HF ⅝–⅞"
(15–22 mm); Wt ½–1 oz. (14–
30 g).

Similar Species: Other harvest mice usually have shorter
tails; Western Harvest Mouse less
reddish-yellow on sides.

Habitat: Grassy or weedy areas; arid inland
valleys.

Range: Southeastern Arizona, sw and e Texas, e

Oklahoma, se Kansas, sw Missouri, w
Arkansas, Louisiana, w Mississippi.

In arid areas, these mice live in
burrows; elsewhere they inhabit nests
constructed up to 4′ above ground.
Nests have only one opening. This
species eats mostly seeds and the soft
parts of green plants.

133 Cactus Mouse
(*Peromyscus eremicus*)

Description: *Pale gray above;* white below. Tail
sparsely haired, indistinctly bicolored,
longer than head and body. Ears nearly
hairless. L 6¾–8⅝″ (169–218 mm);
T 3⅝–5″ (92–128 mm); HF ¾–⅞″
(18–22 mm); Wt ⅝–1⅜ oz. (18–
40 g).

Similar Species: Canyon Mouse's tail tufted at tip;
Brush Mouse has long hairs toward tip
of tail; White-ankled Mouse's tail more
clearly bicolored; Piñon Mouse has
larger ears.

Habitat: Deserts, especially rocky outcroppings
with cactus or yucca stands.

Range: Southern California, extreme s Nevada,
extreme sw Utah, Arizona, s New
Mexico, sw Texas.

Well adapted to desert living, the
Cactus Mouse tolerates higher
temperatures and needs less water than
most other North American deer mice.
It may nest in clumps of cactus, among
rocks, or in the abandoned burrows of
other small animals. Often climbing to
forage, this mouse is known to eat the
seeds of mesquite and hackberry,
insects, and some green vegetation.

Merriam's Mouse
(*Peromyscus merriami*)

Description: *Pale grayish;* tail bicolored and more
than half total length. L 7¾–8⅝"
(197–218 mm); T 4–4¾" (102–
118 mm); HF ¾–⅞" (20–24 mm).

Habitat: Low desert; mesquite flats.

Range: In U.S., known from Pima, Pinal, and
Santa Cruz counties in extreme s central
Arizona.

In the field, this species is almost
impossible to distinguish from the
similar Cactus Mouse. It can be
distinguished from most other deer
mice, however, by its grayer fur.

120 California Mouse
(*Peromyscus californicus*)

Description: *Largest North American deer mouse.*
Yellowish-brown or gray mixed with
black above; whitish below, often with
buff spot on breast. Tail usually not
sharply bicolored. Ears large. Feet
white. L 8⅞–11⅛" (220–285 mm);
T 4⅝–6⅛" (117–156 mm); HF 1–
1⅛" (25–29 mm); Wt 1⅛–2 oz.
(33.2–54.4 g).

Similar Species: All other deer mice smaller.

Habitat: Brushy hillsides and ravines; chaparral.

Range: Southwestern California.

The California Mouse often lives in the
house of a Woodrat. Territorial, it
actively defends its nest from members
of its own sex, although a male and
female will share a nest for extended
periods. The large nest is made of
grass, weeds, and sticks—often as
much as half a bushel—and maintained
by an individual for a long time. It eats
the fruits, seeds, and flowers of shrubs,
as well as fungi, laurel seeds, berries,
and arthropods. Weasels and barn owls
are among its chief predators.

124, 128   Deer Mouse
(*Peromyscus maniculatus*)
Related species: Sitka

Description: Grayish to reddish-brown above; white below; tail distinctly bicolored and short-haired. Woodland forms usually larger, with tail longer and feet larger than prairie form. L 4¾–8¾" (119–222 mm); T 1¾–4¾" (46–123 mm); HF ⅝–1" (16–25 mm); Wt ⅜–1⅛ oz. (10–33 g).

Similar Species: White-footed Mouse's tail shorter than woodland form, and tail and hindfeet longer than prairie form.

Sign: *Tracks:* Similar to those of the White-footed Mouse.

Habitat: Prairies; brushy areas; woodlands.

Range: In the West, Mexico to s Yukon and Northwest Territories; in the East, Hudson Bay to Pennsylvania, the southern Appalachians, central Arkansas and central Texas.

Highly variable, this species comprises numerous subspecies, which differ both in structure and habitat. There are, however, two primary forms: the prairie and the woodland. The smaller prairie form (*P. m. bairdii*) occurs through much of the Midwest, whereas the many woodland forms occur to the north, presumably forming a series of interconnecting populations with the prairie form. These mice feed on various foods, including seeds and nuts, small fruits and berries, insects, centipedes, and the subterranean fungus *Endogone*. Seeds and small nuts are routinely stored in hollow logs or other protected areas. The most important foods of the prairie form include the seeds of foxtail grass and wheat, caterpillars, and corn. This form is common in cultivated situations and remains even during harvesting and plowing periods. It digs small burrows in the ground or sometimes nests in a raised area, if available; it may also have additional small refuge burrows. The woodland forms generally nest in hollow logs. Closely related is the larger Sitka Mouse (*Peromyscus sitkensis*), which occurs only on several islands off the coast of British Columbia.

112 Oldfield Mouse
(*Peromyscus polionotus*)

Description: *Whitish to fawn above;* white below. *Tail short, bicolored.* L 4¾–6" (122–153 mm); T 1⅝–2⅜" (40–60 mm); HF ⅝" (15–19 mm); Wt ¼–½ oz. (8–15 g).
Similar Species: White-footed, Cotton, and Florida mice larger, darker, with longer tails.
Habitat: Waste fields; beaches.
Range: Southeastern U.S. from e Alabama, Georgia, and sw South Carolina south through n and e coastal Florida.

This burrowing species plugs up the entrance to its tunnels with sand while inside. At the far end of the burrow, above the nest, a branch of the tunnel extends upward, ending just below the ground surface. A predator digging into the burrow will often cause the mouse to "explode" through this escape hatch, thereby eluding the startled predator. Seeds and insects form the bulk of the Oldfield's diet, although blackberries and wild pea (*Galactia*) are also eaten.

127 White-footed Mouse
"Wood Mouse"
(*Peromyscus leucopus*)

Description: Grayish to dull orange-brown above; white below. Tail similarly bicolored, nearly one-half total length. Large ears, ½" (13–14 mm) long. *Juveniles gray above; white below.* L 6⅛–8⅛" (156–205 mm); T 2½–3¾" (63–97 mm);

HF ⅞″ (19–24 mm); Wt ⅜–1½ oz.
(10–43 g).

Similar Species: Deer Mouse (woodland form) generally
larger, with longer hindfeet and tail;
Deer Mouse (field form) smaller, with
shorter tail, smaller hindfeet. Oldfield
Mouse smaller, lighter colored; Cotton
Mouse slightly larger, with larger
hindfoot.

Sign: Black cherry pits stored in, around, and
under logs and tree trunks.
Tracks: In dust, hindprint ⅝″ long,
with 5 toes printing; foreprint ¼″ long
and wide, with 4 toes printing;
straddle, 1⅜″, with foreprints printing
behind and between hindprints. In
mud, fore and hind prints each
approximately ⁵⁄₁₆″ wide;
straddle 1½″.

Habitat: Wooded and brushy areas.

Range: Eastern U.S.: mid-Maine south to w
North Carolina, n South Carolina, n
Georgia, n Alabama; west to e
Montana, n Colorado, central Arizona.

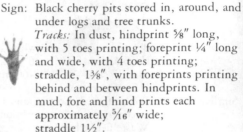

White-footed Mice are active year-
round, though they may remain in
their nests during extremely cold
weather; a few may hibernate. They
construct nests in any concealed
location, with birds' nests, abandoned
burrows of other small mammals, and
buildings used as nesting sites on
occasion. When a nest becomes soiled,
it is abandoned and a new one is
constructed in a different location.
Omnivorous, they feed on nuts, seeds,
fruits, beetles, caterpillars, and other
insects. Two favorite foods are the
centers of black cherry pits and jewel
weed seeds, the latter coloring the
stomach contents blue. Caches of nuts
and seeds are stored near the nest in
autumn. An alarmed individual will
drum its forefeet rapidly.

126 Cotton Mouse
(*Peromyscus gossypinus*)

Description: Reddish-brown above; white below. *Tail short-haired, usually bicolored, slightly less than half total length.* L 6–8⅛" (152–205 mm); T 2½–3¾" (63–97 mm); HF ¾–1" (20–26 mm); Wt ¾–1⅝ oz. (20–46 g).

Similar Species: White-footed Mouse slightly smaller, with smaller hindfoot; Florida Mouse has 5 (not 6) pads on sole of foot; Oldfield Mouse smaller and lighter-colored.

Habitat: Woodlands; swamps; brushlands; rocky areas; beaches.

Range: Southeastern U.S.: from e Texas and se Oklahoma east to se Virginia, e North Carolina, e South Carolina, Georgia, Florida.

Skillful climbers, Cotton Mice run up trees like Gray Squirrels and are fairly strong swimmers, both useful adaptations for the southern swamps where they are most abundant. These nocturnal rodents nest on sandy ridges along the bayous, often in or under logs or palmetto scrub, and have been known to invade buildings. Omnivorous, they eat many invertebrates, as well as seeds, fruits, and nuts.

Canyon Mouse
(*Peromyscus crinitus*)

Description: Grayish or yellowish-brown above; whitish below. *Tail more than half total length, well-furred, with tufted tip. Ears small.* L 6¼–7⅝" (161–192 mm); T 3¼–4¾" (80–118 mm).

Similar Species: Cactus Mouse has tail sparsely furred; Piñon, Rock, and Brush Mice have longer ears; prairie form of Deer Mouse usually has shorter tail where the ranges of the 2 species overlap.

Habitat: Rocky canyons, from below sea level to over 10,000' (3,050 m).

Range: Southeastern Oregon and sw Idaho south through Nevada and Utah to s California, n and w Arizona, w Colorado, nw New Mexico.

Little is known of the habitats of this secretive species, which lives among the barren rocks and crevices lining canyon walls.

125 Brush Mouse
(*Peromyscus boylii*)

Description: Brownish or grayish above to buff or tawny on sides; white below. *Tail distinctly bicolored,* hairy, *equal to or longer than head and body.* Ankles dusky. Large ears, about ¾" (16–20 mm). L 7⅛–9⅜" (180–238 mm); T 3⅝–4¾" (91–123 mm); HF ¾–1" (20–26 mm); Wt ¾–1¼ oz. (22–36 g).

Similar Species: Deer and White-footed mice in range of this species have tails shorter than head and body; Piñon, Palo Duro, and Rock mice have longer ears; Cactus and Canyon mice have smaller ears.

Habitat: Arid to semiarid brushlands, especially rocky areas.

Range: California, s and extreme w Nevada, Utah, sw Colorado, Arizona, New Mexico, w Texas, Oklahoma, nw Arkansas, sw Missouri.

A skilled climber, this mouse often runs up trees to avoid predators. Its nest, constructed of dried vegetation, is often found under brushpiles or in rocky crevices. Foods include conifer seeds, acorns, berries, and insects. Cactus fruit are eaten extensively when in season.

Texas Mouse
(Peromyscus attwateri)

Description: Brown above with sides pinkish-cinnamon; white below. *Tail half or more of total length, bicolored, hairy with prominent tuft at tip. Ankles dark or dusky.* Ears large. L 6¼–8⅝" (160–218 mm); T 2¾–4⅜" (68–111 mm); HF ¾–1" (20–26 mm); Wt ⅝–1⅜ oz. (19–41 g).

Similar Species: White-footed Mouse's tail less than half total length; White-ankled Mouse has white ankles; Cotton Mouse, difficult to differentiate, only in e Oklahoma.

Habitat: Rocky or grassy areas with red cedar or scrub woodlands; high cliffs among oak stands.

Range: North central Texas, e Oklahoma, se Kansas, extreme sw Missouri, nw Arkansas.

The Texas Mouse was recently recognized as a species separate from the Brush Mouse. A good climber, it uses its long, tufted tail for balance and support while scaling cliff faces. It builds a nest of grass and dry leaves in a crevice or rock pile and travels over a home range of about half an acre. This mouse feeds heavily on acorns, camel crickets, pine and grass seeds, and beetle larvae. Broad-winged hawks and coachwhip snakes are among its many predators.

White-ankled Mouse
(Peromyscus pectoralis)

Description: Gray to brown above; creamy white below. *Tail more than half total length,* thinly haired and indistinctly bicolored. Ears small. *Ankles white.* L 7⅛–9⅛" (180–232 mm); T 3¾–4¾" (94–123 mm); HF ⅞" (20–23 mm); Wt ⅞–1⅜ oz. (24–39 g).

Similar Species: Brush Mouse has larger ears and dusky

ankles; Canyon Mouse's tail has tufted tip; Deer Mouse has shorter tail.

Habitat: Rocky areas, especially in oak and juniper woodlands.

Range: Extreme se New Mexico, sw and central Texas, extreme s Oklahoma.

Little is known about the habits of this species. It constructs its nest in rock piles and other protected areas, including debris around human settlements. Juniper berries, acorns, hackberries, cactus fruit, and various invertebrates are its known foods.

130 Piñon Mouse
(*Peromyscus truei*)

Description: *Large.* Grayish-brown above; whitish below. *Tail bicolored, tufted, less than half of total length. Ears very large.* L 6¾–9⅛" (171–231 mm); T 3–4¾" (76–123 mm); HF ¾–1⅛" (20–27 mm); Wt ⅝–1¹⁄₁₆ oz. (19–31 g).

Similar Species: Rock Mouse more brownish, with longer tail; Palo Duro Mouse with longer tail; Brush, Canyon, and Cactus mice have smaller ears; California Mouse larger.

Sign: Small piles of piñon nut and juniper seed remnants on rocks and logs and around the bases of trees.

Habitat: Piñon-juniper areas, preferably rocky and with shrubby understory.

Range: Southwestern Oregon and California east to Colorado, New Mexico, extreme w Oklahoma.

Piñon Mice live in hollow juniper trunks, or under rocks, in a nest made of grasses, leaves, and shredded juniper bark. They frequently have small secondary nests made of juniper bark scattered about their home range. Agile climbers, these mice often forage in trees for the piñon nuts and juniper seeds that are their staple diet. They also eat other seeds, leafy plants, berries, and insects. Seeds and nuts are often stored in the primary nest. Coyotes and Gray Foxes are among their many predators.

Rock Mouse
(*Peromyscus difficilis*)

Description: *Large.* Brownish above; white below. *Tail more than half total length. Large ears.* L 7⅛–10¼" (180–260 mm); T 3⅝–5¾" (91–145 mm); HF ⅞–1⅛" (22–28 mm); Wt ⅞–1¹⁄₁₆ oz. (24–32 g).

Similar Species: Piñon Mouse usually grayer, with shorter tail; Palo Duro Mouse usually grayer; Brush, Canyon, and Pocket mice have longer tails and smaller ears.

Habitat: Rocks, canyons, and lava cliffs, generally with piñon nut trees and junipers.

Range: Southeastern Utah, w Colorado, e Arizona, New Mexico, w Texas.

As its name suggests, the Rock Mouse is very skillful at climbing about on rocky cliff faces. Much of its diet is piñon and juniper nuts and fruits, but in summer it feeds heavily on insects. Its former scientific name was *Peromyscus nasutus.*

Palo Duro Mouse
(*Peromyscus comanche*)

Description: *Large.* Grayish-brown above; whitish below. *Tail distinctly bicolored,* as long as, or longer than, head and body. *Large ears and feet.* L 7¼–8⅝" (183–218 mm); T 3¾–4½" (93–114 mm); HF ⅞–1" (22–25 mm).

Similar Species: Rock Mouse more brownish; Piñon Mouse with shorter tail; Brush,

Canyon, and Cactus mice have shorter ears.

Habitat: Rocky, cedar-covered cliffs and hillsides; cliffs and canyons.

Range: Briscoe, Garza, and Randall counties in West Texas.

At various times in the past this species has been considered to be a subspecies of both the Rock Mouse and the Piñon Mouse. Although it is structurally similar to the Piñon Mouse, it is at present classified as a separate species on the basis of differences in its body proteins. Its habits are similar to those of the Piñon Mouse.

---

132 Florida Mouse
"Gopher Mouse"
(*Peromyscus floridanus*)

Description: *Large.* Brownish above; white below. Large ears. Nearly naked *large hindfeet with five pads.* L 7¼–8¾" (186–221 mm); T 3⅛–3¾" (80–95 mm); HF ⅞–1⅛" (24–29 mm).

Similar Species: Other deer mice have 6 pads on hindfeet.

Habitat: High sandy ridges with abundant blackjack and turkey oak; scrub palmetto.

Range: Northern peninsular Florida.

The Florida or "Gopher" Mouse is almost exclusively a burrow dweller, most often using the burrows of the Gopher Tortoise (*Gopherus polyphemus*) or pocket gophers (*Geomys*). These large burrows provide good protection from climatic changes and predators. The typical burrow nest is simpler than the surface nests of deer mice that live above ground. It consists of a platform composed of leaves, Spanish moss, and possibly some feathers. Omnivorous, the Florida Mouse feeds on seeds, nuts, insects, and other invertebrates.

129 Golden Mouse
(Ochrotomys nuttalli)

Description: *Golden-cinnamon above;* white below, often tinged with yellowish-brown. *Tail long. Southern populations generally smaller-sized.* L 5⅞–7½" (150–190 mm); T 2¾–3¾" (68–93 mm); HF ¾" (17–20 mm); Wt 2⅜–3¼ oz. (68–93 g).

Habitat: Greenbrier thickets; boulder-strewn hemlock slopes; brushy hedgerows; swamps.

Range: Extreme e Texas and Oklahoma; s Missouri and s Illinois to East Coast; s Virginia south to midpeninsular Florida.

This highly arboreal, gregarious mouse often climbs trees to 30' or more. It runs about the high branches with ease, using its long prehensile tail for balance and support. The globe-shaped nests are constructed of leaves, pine needles, grass, or Spanish moss and lined with finely shredded bark, grass, or fur. They vary in diameter from 3–12" and may be found in tangled vegetation or high in trees. Larger nests often provide quarters for several individuals, while smaller ones serve mainly as feeding shelters. Its diet consists of invertebrates, acorns, and many other types of seeds, including sumac, poison ivy, greenbrier, and wild cherry.

114 Northern Pygmy Mouse
(Baiomys taylori)

Description: *Smallest tree mouse in North America.* Body and tail *grayish-brown above; slightly lighter below. Tail nearly one half total length.* L 3⅜–4⅞" (87–123 mm); T 1¼–2⅛" (34–53 mm); Wt ¼–⅜ oz. (7–10 g).

Similar Species: Harvest mice *(Reithrodontomys)* have grooved upper incisors; deer mice

(*Peromyscus*) white below; House Mouse
has nearly naked, unicolored tail.

Habitat: Grassy or weedy areas.

Range: Eastern and s Texas, extreme se
Arizona, extreme sw New Mexico.

Pygmy Mice utilize small home ranges,
usually less than 100′ in diameter. For
reasons not yet known, populations
occur in isolated pockets, frequently
separated by areas seemingly suitable
for habitation. They construct nests
either underground or in low tangled
vegetation; a typical nest consists of a
ball of grass, usually with two
entrances. These mice also maintain
networks of tiny runways beneath the
matted grass. They feed mostly on
vegetation, with prickly pear cactus
stems and fruit heavily eaten when
available. The fruit frequently stains
their mouths and urine red. Grass
blades and seeds, mesquite beans, and
granjeus berries are common foods;
snails may also be eaten.

99 Northern Grasshopper Mouse
(*Onychomys leucogaster*)

Description: *Heavy-bodied. Two color phases above:
grayish, or cinnamon-buff;* white below.
Short, thick, *bicolored tail with white tip,*
usually less than ⅓ total length.
Juvenile pelage dark gray. L 5⅛–7½″
(130–190 mm); T 1⅛–2⅜″ (29–
61 mm); HF ¾–1″ (17–25 mm);
Wt 1–1⅛ oz. (27–52 g).

Similar Species: Southern Grasshopper Mouse smaller,
with longer tail; Deer Mice (*Peromyscus*)
have longer tails lacking white tip.

Sign: *Tracks:* In mud or dust, fore and hind
prints overlap partially or completely,
each about ⅝″ long, ½″ wide, with
hindprint sometimes slightly longer;
straddle 1¼″.

Habitat: Low valleys; deserts; prairies.

Range: Much of w North America from se

Washington, s Alberta and sw
Manitoba south to ne California, e
Arizona, w Texas.

These mice are most active on moonless
nights or under heavy cloud cover. As
their name suggests, they feed heavily
on grasshoppers, but they also eat other
insects, scorpions, mice, and a small
amount of plant material. Grasshopper
Mice either dig burrows or take over
those abandoned by other animals.
They maintain a complex system of
burrows throughout their rather large
territories, including a nest burrow,
retreat burrows, cache burrows,
defecation burrows, and signpost
burrows. The nest burrow is the center
of activity and is sealed during the day
to retain moisture. Retreat burrows are
8–10″ long and extend into the ground
at a 45° angle to ensure speedy escapes
from predators. Seeds are stored in the
cache burrows for use when insect
foods are not available. Signpost
burrows are short, usually only 1–2″
long, and located at the edge of the
territory. They are used to designate
territorial boundaries and marked by
glandular secretions. Grasshopper Mice
have several calls, one of which is high-
pitched, prolonged, and made in a
wolflike fashion with raised nose and
open mouth. Another common call is a
sharp barklike alarm chirp, rapidly
repeated.

---

98 **Southern Grasshopper Mouse**
   "Scorpion Mouse"
   (*Onychomys torridus*)
   Related species: Mearn's

Description: Stocky. *Grayish or pinkish-cinnamon
above;* white below. *Tail white-tipped,*
thick, short, between one third and one
half total length. Juveniles gray.
L 4¾–6½″ (119–163 mm); T 1¼–

2⅝" (32–68 mm); HF ¾" (18–23 mm); Wt ¾–1 oz. (22–30 g).

Similar Species: Northern Grasshopper Mouse larger with shorter tail; deer mice (*Peromyscus*) have longer, thinner tails lacking white tips.

Habitat: Low deserts with creosote bush, mesquite, and yucca.

Range: Southern California, s Nevada, extreme sw Utah, w and s Arizona, s New Mexico, w Texas.

The Scorpion Mouse digs its own burrows or appropriates those of other small mammals. Its home range, up to 8 acres for males, is unusually large for a small rodent. The highly territorial males employ a high-pitched, wolflike call to ward off other males. Like the large carnivores, Grasshopper Mice have developed efficient strategies for dispatching prey: small mammals are killed by a bite through the back of the neck; before killing scorpions, the deadly tail is immobilized.
Closely related is Mearn's Grasshopper Mouse (*Onychomys arenicola*), which is slightly smaller and drab brown above; it occurs only in southwestern New Mexico, where its populations overlap with those of the Southern Grasshopper Mouse.

---

136 **Hispid Cotton Rat**
(*Sigmodon hispidus*)
Related species: Arizona

Description: *Dark brown or blackish coarse grizzled fur above; grayish below. Tail less than one-half total length,* scaly, scantily haired, slightly lighter below. L 8¼–14⅜" (207–365 mm); T 3–6½" (75–166 mm); Wt 2¾–4¼ oz. (80–120 g).

Similar Species: Rice rats (*Oryzomys*) have longer tails; Yellow-nosed Cotton Rat has yellowish-colored nose; Tawny-bellied Cotton Rat buff below.

Sign: *Tracks:* In mud, fore and hind prints overlap; combined prints about ½" wide and long; straddle to 1½"; walking stride 1¼". Those of other cotton rats (*Sigmodon*) similar.

Habitat: Grassy and weedy fields.

Range: Southeast Virginia south through Florida, west to se Colorado, se New Mexico, se Arizona.

Hispid Cotton Rats are one of the most prolific mammals. They begin breeding at 6 weeks and produce several litters per year; however, their enormous reproductive potential is kept in check by their many predators, including birds, reptiles, and other mammals. Omnivorous, Cotton Rats consume vegetation, insects, and small animals. They can cause great destruction to crops, such as sugar cane and sweet potatoes; at times they reduce quail populations by eating the eggs and chicks.

Closely related is the Arizona Cotton Rat (*Sigmodon arizonae*), occurring only in central Arizona. Originally considered a subspecies of the Hispid, it was established as a separate species when cellular examination revealed it to have a reduced number of chromosomes. In appearance, the two species are nearly identical.

Tawny-bellied Cotton Rat
(*Sigmodon fulviventer*)

Description: Speckled black and buff above; *tawny below*. Tail uniformly brownish-black. Measurements of one specimen: L 10⅝" (270 mm); T 4¼" (108 mm); HF 1¼" (33 mm).

Similar Species: Other cotton rats gray below; woodrats white below, with larger ears.

Habitat: Mesquite grasslands and cattail areas.

Range: Southeast Arizona, sw New Mexico.

This species lives in nests of woven grasses, which are placed in runways among dense vegetation. Since it prefers grasslands, its populations now exist in scattered areas where domestic stock is not grazed.

---

141 Yellow-nosed Cotton Rat
(*Sigmodon ochrognathus*)

Description: Grizzled brownish above; grayish below. *Nose orange or buff. Tail bicolored:* very dark above; grayish-buff below. L 9¼–10¼″ (233–260 mm); T 3⅞– 4½″ (100–117 mm); HF 1⅛″ (28–29 mm); Wt 1¾–4 oz. (50–112 g).

Similar Species: Other cotton rats lack orange or buff nose.

Sign: Runways among vegetation, radiating from burrow entrances.

Habitat: High grasslands; rocky slopes with patches of grass.

Range: Southwest Texas through n Mexico to extreme sw New Mexico, extreme se Arizona.

These cotton rats feed on green vegetation. Their nests, which are composed of grasses and agave fibers, can be found under piles of dead leaves, or in the abandoned burrows of Southern Pocket Gophers.

---

131 Eastern Woodrat
(*Neotoma floridana*)

Description: Grayish-brown above; white or grayish below. Bicolored tail less than half total length. L 12¼–17⅜″ (310–444 mm); T 5⅛–8″ (129–203 mm); HF 1½– 1¾″ (37–40 mm); Wt 7–16 oz. (200– 455 g).

Similar Species: Bushy-tailed Woodrat has a flattened squirrel-like tail; Southern Plains Woodrat steel gray above; White-throated and Stephens woodrats have white throat.

Sign: Stick houses in crevices or caves in the North; in brush, trees, palmetto, or holes in ground in the South; piles of fecal pellets, bones, sticks, cedar or other wood cuttings on ledges.

Habitat: Rocky cliffs, caves, tumbled boulders in the North; Osage-orange and other hedges and wooded low areas in the South.

Range: Much of se U.S. from mid-peninsular Florida north to Pennsylvania and s New York (excluding coastal area from New Jersey to North Carolina and west to n Georgia); west to sw South Dakota, w central Nebraska, e Colorado, most of Kansas, e Oklahoma, e Texas.

The Eastern Woodrat usually constructs its stick house in a protected location. When built in a cave, the house may be open at the top. It feeds mostly on green vegetation, but also eats various fruit, nuts, fungi, ferns, and seeds. Young woodrats cling tenaciously to their mother's teats; if alarmed, she often drags the whole litter with her as she flees. These woodrats have a host of predators, including snakes, owls, weasels, and Bobcats, but only the snakes and sinuous weasels can get to a woodrat while it is inside its house.

135 Southern Plains Woodrat
(*Neotoma micropus*)

Description: *Steel gray above; pale gray below.* Tail heavy, dark grayish above; white below. *Throat, chest, and feet white.* Males larger than females. L 11¾–15″ (300–380 mm); T 4¾–7⅜″ (120–185 mm); HF 1¼–1⅝″ (34–41 mm); Wt 7⅛–10⅞ oz. (204–310 g).

Similar Species: Other woodrats browner.

Sign: Large houses (may be 4–5′ high), or

sticks, cactus parts, thorns, and other debris, usually placed by a cactus; trails radiating from its house may also be visible.

Habitat: Semiarid brushlands; cactus, mesquite, and thornbush thickets.

Range: Western Texas, w Oklahoma, sw Kansas, se Colorado, most of New Mexico.

If vegetation is sparse, this woodrat will dig a burrow in the earth below its house instead of constructing the usual surface runways. It feeds heavily on prickly pear leaves and the fruit of many cacti, along with seeds, nuts, and the leaves of sotol and agave. All the water it needs is obtained from succulent plants.

139 White-throated Woodrat
(*Neotoma albigula*)

Description: Brownish-gray above; white or grayish below. Tail bicolored brownish-gray above; whitish below. Feet white. *Hair gray at base except white to base on throat.* L 11⅛–15¾" (283–400 mm); T 3–7¼" (76–185 mm); HF 1¼–1½" (30–39 mm); Wt 4¾–10¼ oz. (136–294 g).

Similar Species: Desert, Eastern, and Mexican woodrats have throat hairs gray at base; Southern Plains Woodrat steel gray; Dusky-footed Woodrat has dusky hind ankles, tail blackish above; Stephens Woodrat has longer hairs at tip of tail.

Sign: Large houses of sticks, cactus parts, and other debris under cactus or other plants; well-worn trails leading from houses.
Tracks: In mud, hindprint ¾" long, with 5 toes printing; foreprint ½" long, with 4 toes printing. Hindprints ahead of foreprints; distance between individual walking prints, approximately 1¾–3".

Habitat: Brushlands of southwestern dry plains and deserts.

Range: Extreme se California east to w Texas, but extending north into se Utah and s Colorado.

The White-throated Woodrat generally chooses the base of a prickly pear or cholla cactus as the site for its house; however, if vegetation is scarce, it will build in rocky crevices and sometimes add an underground chamber. It is skilled at climbing spiny cacti and uses the needles to help cover the entrance to its houses. Several houses may be present in a small clump of cactus, but no more than one adult resides in each. Cactus figures strongly in the diet, along with some mesquite and various leafy plants. Very little grass or animal material is consumed. A small amount of food is stored in its house. Highly adapted to desert living, the White-throated obtains its water from the food it eats. It is preyed upon by gopher snakes, rattlesnakes, Coyotes, owls, Bobcats, Ringtails, and weasels.

134 Desert Woodrat
(*Neotoma lepida*)
Related species: Stephens', Arizona

Description: *Buff-gray above;* grayish below, often washed with buff. Tail similarly bicolored. Hindfeet white. *All hairs gray at base.* L 8¾–15⅛″ (225–383 mm); T 3¾–7⅜″ (95–188 mm); HF 1⅛–1½″ (28–41 mm).

Similar Species: White-throated Woodrat's throat hair white at base; Mexican Woodrat's tail white below; Dusky-footed Woodrat is larger, with hindfeet that are dusky above.

Habitat: Deserts; piñon-juniper areas.

Range: Southeastern Oregon, sw Idaho, Nevada, Utah, s and extreme ne California.

The Desert Woodrat often appropriates
an old burrow of a ground squirrel or
kangaroo rat, fortifying the entrance
with a house constructed of sticks and
cactus spines. The house is used both
for protection and for food storage,
with the nest placed underground in a
deep cool chamber. It is adept at
moving about on and among spiny cacti
without injuring itself. Its diet is
composed of spiny cacti, along with
yucca pods, bark, berries, piñon nuts,
seeds, and any available green
vegetation. It produces an alarm rattle
by vibrating its tail against dry
vegetation.

Closely related is the slightly smaller
Stephens' Woodrat (*Neotoma stephensi*),
with throat hair white to base and long
hairs at tip of tail. It is often found in
piñon-juniper areas of northeastern
Arizona, northwestern New Mexico,
and extreme southeastern Utah. It
shelters among rocks. Also considered a
separate species is the similar Arizona
Woodrat (*Neotoma devia*), which occurs
only in western Arizona.

119 Mexican Woodrat
(*Neotoma mexicana*)

Description: *Grayish to brownish above;* white or
yellowish below. May be blackish above
when inhabiting lava flows. *Tail
distinctly bicolored. Throat hair gray at
base.* L 11⅜–16⅝" (290–417 mm);
T 4⅛–8⅛" (105–206 mm); HF 1¼–
1½" (31–41 mm); Wt 4⅞–6½ oz.
(140–185 g).

Similar Species: White-throated and Southern Plains
woodrats have throat hair white at base;
Desert Woodrat difficult to distinguish,
although grayish below and tail less
strongly bicolored.

Habitat: Rocky situations in mountains;
ponderosa pine forests and piñon-
juniper areas.

Range: Southeastern Utah, s Colorado, w
Arizona, most of New Mexico, w
Texas.

The Mexican Woodrat prefers to nest in
rocky crevices, fortifying these with a
blockade of sticks, vegetation, and
other debris. In less rocky areas, nests
may be in hollow trees, brushpiles, or
buildings. Its diet includes green
plants, berries, nuts, acorns, and fungi.
Cactus is also eaten, though it is not
present in many of the higher areas
inhabited by this species.

138 Dusky-footed Woodrat
(*Neotoma fuscipes*)

Description: Buff-brown above, grayer on face;
grayish to whitish below; belly often
washed with tan. *Feet and ankles dusky;*
toes and claws white. *Tail brown above,
slightly lighter below,* nearly half total
length. L 13¼–18¾" (335–475 mm);
T 6¼–12¾" (158–322 mm); Wt 8⅛–
9⅜ oz. (233–267 g).

Similar Species: Desert and White-throated woodrats
have white feet; Bushy-tailed Woodrat
has flattened bushy tail.

Habitat: Conifer and hardwood forests;
chaparral.

Range: Western two thirds of California,
w Oregon except n coast.

These woodrats build their houses or
"lodges" on the ground in open areas
and in trees up to a height of 50' when
they dwell in woodlands. These houses
can be up to 8' high and 8' in
diameter. Nests are constructed
within their houses and have several
compartments, often providing homes
for various frogs, small mammals, and
invertebrates as well. A semi-colonial
species, several rats may occur together
in the same area. The Dusky-footed
apparently establishes pair bonds for the

mating season, but after mating occurs the males live separately in small tree nests. Like the other woodrats, its diet is mostly green vegetation, but also includes fruit, nuts, and seeds. Their main predators are owls, Coyotes, weasels, skunks, and Bobcats.

189 Bushy-tailed Woodrat
"Mountain Pack Rat"
(*Neotoma cinerea*)

Description: Varies from pale grayish to blackish above, but often brownish peppered with black hairs; whitish below. *Tail squirrel-like,* bushy, and flattened. L 11½–18½" (292–472 mm); T 4¾–9¼" (120–236 mm); Wt 5½–15½ oz. (156–444 g).

Similar Species: All other woodrats have rounded short-haired tails.

Sign: Stick houses concealed in crevices or abandoned buildings.
Scat: Piles of fecal pellets on ledges; black tarlike concretions of older fecal material and white calcareous encrustations from urine often evident on cliff faces.

Habitat: Rocky situations; coniferous forests.

Range: Northwestern U.S. from n California and nw New Mexico north to sw North Dakota and Washington, then north through extreme sw Saskatchewan, sw Alberta, British Colombia, extreme sw Mackenzie, se Yukon.

This is the original "pack rat," the species in which the trading habit is most pronounced. It has a strong preference for shiny objects and will drop whatever else it may have in favor of carrying off a coin or a spoon. In coniferous forests this woodrat may build its house as high as 50′ up a tree. In some areas the houses are used only for caching large quantities of dried vegetation, and the nest itself is

concealed in a rocky crevice behind a
barricade of sticks. Green vegetation is
the preferred food, but twigs, nuts,
seeds, mushrooms, and some animal
matter are also eaten. These woodrats
engage in a hindfoot-stomping behavior
when alarmed. They will also stomp
their hindfeet when undisturbed,
producing a slow tapping sound. The
bushy tail is used for balance when
climbing and jumping. They are
heavily preyed upon by spotted owls
and Bobcats.

61, 62 Southern Red-backed Vole
(*Clethrionomys gapperi*)
Related species: Western, Northern

Description: *Rust-reddish above;* sides buff or grayish;
gray to buff-white below. Tail short,
slender, slightly bicolored. Gray phase
sometimes occurs in the Northeast.
L 4¾–6¼" (120–158 mm); T 1¼–2"
(30–50 mm); HF ¾" (16–21 mm);
Wt ⅝–1½ oz. (16–42 g).

Similar Species: Meadow voles (*Microtus*) lack rust-red
coloration; Woodland Vole
distinguished from gray phase by
softer, molelike fur; Red Tree Vole
arboreal.

Sign: Runways and burrows on forest floor
under rocks and logs and in moss;
pieces of cut green vegetation in
runways.

Habitat: Cool, damp forests; bogs, swamps.

Range: Southern tier of Canadian provinces
south into Oregon; entire Rocky
Mountain system to Arizona and New
Mexico; Allegheny Mountain system to
North Carolina, North and South
Dakota, Minnesota, Wisconsin, upper
half of southern peninsular Michigan,
and New England south to Maryland.

These voles use natural runways along
rocks and logs and the burrows of other
animals when available; they do not

make elaborate burrow systems like those of the meadow voles (*Microtus*). They are often seen running across a bed of moss or up an old tree stump. They feed on green herbaceous plants such as false lily of the valley, bunchberry, goldthread, and various berries when ripe. Bulbs, stems, tubers, and nuts are stored for later use.

Closely related is the Western (or California) Red-backed Vole (*Clethrionomys occidentalis*), which occurs mostly in coniferous forests from w Washington south to nw California, west of the Cascade Mts. Unlike the Southern Red-backed, it is primarily a burrower. Also closely related is the Northern Red-backed Vole (*Clethrionomys rutilus*), which is bright reddish above and found in the tundra of northern Canada and Alaska.

Heather Vole
"Mountain Phenacomys"
(*Phenacomys intermedius*)

Description: *Grizzled brown above; silvery below.* Proportionately *short tail* distinctly bicolored. *Feet white.* Yellow-faced individuals in some populations. L 5⅛–6" (130–153 mm); T 1–1¾" (26–41 mm); HF ¾" (16–18 mm); Wt ½–1⅜ oz. (15–41 g).

Similar Species: Long-tailed, White-footed, Tree, Yellow-cheeked, and Rock voles all have longer tails; Montane Vole difficult to distinguish, though tail usually longer and feet white.

Habitat: Open grassy heather; blueberry patches in scattered clearings on mountaintops.

Range: Southern tier of Canadian provinces plus s Yukon and Northwest Territory; in U.S., south to n California, Idaho, Utah, Wyoming, Colorado, n New Mexico, w Montana; also in far ne Minnesota.

In winter, this species nests on the ground surface in runways covered with snow; the rest of the year it nests in burrows. Nests are built of fine dry snowgrass and lichens. The diet consists of plants such as bearberry, reargrass, lousewort, and huckleberry, supplemented with twigs, bark, and seeds.

White-footed Vole
(*Phenacomys albipes*)

Description: Rich brown above; gray often washed with brown below. *Tail slender, sparsely haired, distinctly bicolored.* Tops of feet usually pure white. L 5¾–7¼″ (149–182 mm); T 2¼–3″ (57–75 mm); HF ¾″ (18–21 mm); Wt ⅝–1 oz. (17–29 g).

Similar Species: Creeping Vole has shorter tail; Montane Vole difficult to distinguish, but inhabits high mountain meadows; Townsend's and Long-tailed voles usually larger; red-backed and tree voles reddish.

Habitat: Along small streams in alder associations.

Range: Coastal Oregon, extreme nw California.

Probably the rarest of North American voles, little is known of the habits of this secretive species. Its tiny eyes and claw structure indicate that it is a burrowing form. The White-footed feeds on green vegetation and roots; major predators include weasels, Mink, skunks, and house cats.

64, 66   Red Tree Vole
"Tree Phenacomys"
(*Phenacomys longicaudus*)
Related species: Dusky

Description: *Bright reddish above;* whitish below. *Long
tail blackish, well-haired.* L 6¼–8⅛"
(158–206 mm); T 2⅜–3¾" (60–
94 mm); HF ¾–⅞" (18–24 mm);
Wt ⅞–1⅝ oz. (25–47 g).

Similar Species: Red-backed voles (*Clethrionomys*) have
shorter tails, are more terrestrial;
meadow voles (*Microtus*) grayish to
brownish.

Sign: Bulky nests in Douglas fir trees.

Habitat: Primarily Douglas fir forests; also
redwood or Sitka spruce–salal areas if
ample Douglas fir not available.

Range: Coastal Oregon, nw California.

This highly specialized tree-dweller
rarely descends to the ground. Its nests
are built 6–150' above ground, usually
in Douglas fir. Nests are composed of
twigs from the host tree, though the
voles may base them on old nests of
squirrels, woodrats, or birds, with the
inner nest composed of resin ducts from
leaves discarded by the vole when
feeding. Additional twigs and food
refuse are used to enlarge the nest
continually, with urine and fecal pellets
helping to mold it together and secure
it to the tree. Generations of voles may
use the same nest, and a large one may
have several chambers with connecting
passageways. One passage leads to the
bottom of the nest; an escape exit is
next to the trunk; others lead upward
toward foraging areas. When leaping, a
tree vole may spread its legs for balance
and land uninjured on the ground. This
ability seems to be learned, as young
voles seldom land on their feet. This
vole depends upon the Douglas fir for
nest site and food, although it also eats
the needles of grand or lowland white
fir, Sitka spruce, and western hemlock.
Food may be consumed where found

but usually is eaten at the nest.
Douglas fir needles have resin ducts
along each edge which the vole bites off
and discards, eating the remainder,
although young needles may be eaten
entirely. Sexes remain in separate nests
except for breeding. Spotted owls are
the main predator, along with Saw-
whet and Long-eared owls. Populations
are widely separated and are
disappearing due to logging and forest
removal.

Closely related is the sooty brown
Dusky Tree Vole (*Phenacomys silvicola*),
which occurs in northwestern coastal
Oregon.

76 Meadow Vole
"Field Mouse"
(*Microtus pennsylvanicus*)
Subspecies: Beach

Description:
Color variable: from yellowish- or
reddish-brown peppered with black, to
blackish-brown above; usually gray
with *silver-tipped hair below*. Tail long,
dark above, lighter below. Feet dark.
Third upper malariform tooth with 4
triangles. L 5½–7¾" (140–195 mm);
T 1¼–2½" (33–64 mm); HF ¾–⅞"
(18–24 mm); Wt ¾–2½ oz. (20–
70 g).

Similar Species:
Montane Vole difficult to distinguish,
but usually found in mountains; Prairie
Vole buff below, with shorter tail;
Tundra Vole more yellow; Singing Vole
has shorter tail, occurs above
timberline; Yellow-cheeked and Rock
voles have yellow noses.

Sign:
Grass cuttings, 1–1½" long, in piles in
runways 1" wide found in dense
vegetation.
Scat: Small elongate fecal pellets, dark-
colored.
Tracks: In light snow, hindprint ⅝"
long, with 5 toes printing; foreprint ½"
long, with 4 toes printing; hindprints

ahead of foreprints, with distance between individual walking prints ½–⅛"; straddle, approximately 1½". Print patterns vary greatly, from an overlapping two-two pattern to the four-print pattern shown. Jumping distances between tracks range from 1¾–4¼".

Habitat: Lush grassy fields; also marshes, swamps, woodland glades, mountaintops.

Range: Canada and Alaska (except for northern portions) south and east to n Washington, Idaho, Utah, New Mexico, Wyoming, Nebraska, n Missouri, n Illinois, Kentucky, ne Georgia, South Carolina.

This vole lives in a system of surface runways and underground burrows, often nesting in the burrows during the summer; it may also nest in a depression on the surface under matted vegetation. In winter, the Meadow Vole usually places its spherical grass nest on the surface as long as there is snow cover for protection and insulation. Its diet consists almost entirely of green vegetation and tubers, including many grasses, clover, and plantain. Grass cuttings are produced as the vole reaches up and cuts off the stalk, pulls it down and cuts it again, until the seed heads are reached. The voles apparently consume any flowers and leaves and all but the tough outer layer of the stalk. They eat almost their own weight daily. When alarmed, Meadow Voles stamp their hindfeet like rabbits.
Often considered as a separate species is the Beach Vole (*Microtus pennsylvanicus breweri*), larger, more grizzled and pale brown; it is the only vole found on Muskeget Island, Massachusetts.

75 Montane Vole
"Mountain Vole" "Montana Vole"
(*Microtus montanus*)

Description: Grizzled brown to blackish above, often with buff tint; white to gray below. *Moderately long tail bicolored. Feet dusky* or silvery-gray. Second upper molariform tooth with 4 closed triangles and no loop. L 5½–7½" (140–192 mm); T 1¼–2¾" (31–69 mm); HF ¾–1" (18–25 mm); Wt 1¼–3 oz. (37–85 g).

Similar Species: Creeping Vole usually smaller, not grizzled; Meadow Vole difficult to distinguish, usually darker brown with darker feet, not found in mountains; Mexican Vole buff to cinnamon below; Prairie Vole buff below with shorter tail; California Vole in lowlands, but difficult to distinguish, except for pale feet; White-footed Vole usually with white feet, occurs in alder thickets along streams.

Habitat: High mountain meadows; valleys associated with dry grassy areas.

Range: South central British Columbia, e Washington, most of Oregon, ne California east to se Montana, e Wyoming and w Colorado, extending south into New Mexico and extreme e central Arizona.

The little-known Montane Vole lives in runway and burrow systems under grassy cover. This grass, including sedges and rushes, is the mainstay of its diet during most of the year. In summer it prefers to eat leafy plants, though it does not forsake the cover of the grassy areas; it also eats some fungi. Populations undergo dramatic fluctuations from year to year, depending on the availability of adequate amounts of food.

70 California Vole
(*Microtus californicus*)

Description: Grizzled brownish with scattered black
hairs above; gray below with hairs often
white-tipped. Long tail bicolored. *Feet
pale.* L 6¼–8⅜" (157–214 mm);
T 1½–2¾" (39–68 mm); HF ¾–1"
(20–25.5 mm); Wt 1½–3½ oz. (42–
100 g).

Similar Species: Montane Vole has dusky feet; Creeping
Vole not grizzled; Townsend's Vole has
dusky feet and blackish tail; Long-
tailed Vole has longer tail; Heather
Vole smaller; White-footed Vole
usually smaller.

Habitat: Grassy meadows from sea level to
mountains.

Range: California and sw Oregon.

This vole feeds on grasses and other
green vegetation when available; in
winter it eats mostly roots and other
underground parts of plants. Hawks,
owls, weasels, and snakes are its main
predators.

Townsend's Vole
(*Microtus townsendii*)

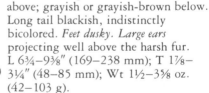

Description: Dark brown sprinkled with black
above; grayish or grayish-brown below.
Long tail blackish, indistinctly
bicolored. *Feet dusky. Large ears*
projecting well above the harsh fur.
L 6¾–9⅜" (169–238 mm); T 1⅞–
3¼" (48–85 mm); Wt 1½–3⅝ oz.
(42–103 g).

Similar Species: California and Long-tailed voles have
more distinctly bicolored tails and
lighter feet; Montane and Creeping
voles smaller, with proportionately
shorter tails.

Sign: Piles of grass cuttings in runways.

Habitat: Moist grassy areas.

Range: Northwestern California north to se
British Columbia and Vancouver Is.

A good swimmer, Townsend's Vole often constructs the entrances to its burrow system underwater, with the nest inside a hummock above water level. In winter, nests are placed on dry ground away from water, which might freeze and prevent access. Its varied diet includes velvet grass, horsetail, alfalfa, rushes, sedges, and buttercups. In winter it occasionally causes damage in nurseries, killing saplings by eating off their bark. Owls and hawks are its main predators.

74 Tundra Vole
(*Microtus oeconomus*)

Description: Grayish to brownish above with *yellowish or fulvous cast; white below. Tail bicolored:* dusky to black above, whitish to buff below; relatively short. L 6–8⅞" (153–225 mm); T 1⅜–2⅛" (36–54 mm); HF ¾–1" (19–25 mm); Wt ⅛–2¾ oz. (25–80 g).

Similar Species: Meadow Vole lacks yellowish cast; Singing Vole has shorter tail; Long-tailed Vole has longer tail; Yellow-cheeked Vole has yellowish nose.

Habitat: Tundra areas around streams, lakes, marshes; sometimes thick grass in drier areas.

Range: Alaska, w Yukon, n Mackenzie.

This burrowing species builds a nest of sedges and grasses within its burrows. Moving about on the surface, it sometimes uses frost cracks as extensions of the runway system. Droppings are deposited in specific areas off the main runways. In summer it feeds primarily on green grasses and sedges, while storing rhizomes (especially knotweed and licorice root) and grass seeds for later use. At one time Eskimos trained dogs to find the Tundra Vole's caches of licorice.

71 Long-tailed Vole
(*Microtus longicaudus*)
Related species: Coronation Island

Description: Large. Grayish-brown above; light grayish below. Feet dusky-white. Long tail bicolored. L 6¼–10⅜″ (155–265 mm); T 2–4½″ (50–115 mm); HF ¾–1⅛″ (20–29 mm); Wt ¾–3 oz. (22–87 g).

Similar Species: Townsend's Vole has blackish, indistinctly bicolored tail; other voles generally have shorter tails.

Habitat: Dry grassy areas far from water; mountain slopes; alder and willow sedge areas.

Range: From se Alaska through Yukon and sw Mackenzie to California, Nevada, ne Arizona, New Mexico; also in w South Dakota.

In winter these voles spread out across the mountain slopes in search of food; in summer they usually retreat into grassy areas. They feed on roots and bark when green vegetation is scarce.
Closely related is the Coronation Island Vole (*Microtus coronarius*), with body and tail brown above, dark gray below. It is found only on Coronation Island, off the coast of British Columbia.

Mexican Vole
(*Microtus mexicanus*)

Description: *Grizzled cinnamon-brown above; buff to cinnamon below.* Short tail. L 4¾–6″ (121–152 mm); T ⅞–1⅜″ (24–35 mm); HF ¾″ (17–21 mm); Wt ⅞–1¾ oz. (26–48 g).

Similar Species: Montane Vole white to gray below; Long-tailed Vole has longer tail.

Habitat: Clearings in yellow pine forests; arid grasslands; wet boggy situations.

Range: Southwestern half of New Mexico, e Arizona (including Hualpai Mts.),

w central Arizona, extreme se Utah,
extreme sw Colorado, extreme w Texas.

The Mexican Vole is active mostly by
day. Its grass nests are located in
clumps of vegetation, under logs, in
cuplike depressions in the ground, or in
underground chambers. This vole is
preyed upon by Gray Foxes, Bobcats,
Badgers, skunks, and Coyotes.

68 Rock Vole
"Yellownose Vole"
(*Microtus chrotorrhinus*)

Description: Brownish above; gray below. *Relatively
long tail* slightly lighter below. *Nose
orangish.* L. 5⅜–7¼″ (137–185 mm);
T 1¾–2⅛″ (42–53 mm); HF ¾–⅞″
(19–23 mm); Wt 1–1⅜ oz. (30–40 g).
Similar Species: Yellow-cheeked Vole larger; Meadow,
Red-backed, and Woodland voles lack
yellowish nose.
Habitat: Moist, rocky, woodland slopes;
mountains in southern part of range.
Range: Southeastern Ontario to Labrador,
south to extreme ne Minnesota, w
Maine, and e New York south through
the Smoky Mountains of North
Carolina.

Although primarily diurnal, the
secretive Rock Vole is rarely seen. It
occurs in scattered pockets of moist
woodland, feeding mainly on green
plants, including bunchberry, thread
moss, grasses, and blueberry; it also
eats some caterpillars and subterranean
fungi.

69 Yellow-cheeked Vole
(*Microtus xanthognathus*)

Description: *Large.* Dull brown above; gray below.
Long tail. Nose orangish. Upper incisors

of adults grooved. L 7¼–8⅞″ (186–226 mm): T 1¾–2⅛″ (45–53 mm); HF ⅞″ (9–23 mm); Wt 4–6 oz. (113–170 g).

Similar Species: Rock Vole smaller.

Sign: Burrows with 3–9′ wide dirt piles at entrances; wide radiating runways extending 50–75 yds.

Habitat: Forests (especially spruce) bordering bogs or marshes.

Range: Eastern central Alaska, central Yukon, and s Mackenzie south to n Alberta, Saskatchewan, Manitoba.

The Yellow-cheeked is colonial and undergoes major population fluctuations; a very large colony will often disappear within one year. These voles are very vocal, chirping when alarmed, and are most active around dusk. Grasses, horsetails, and lichens are important in their diet; blueberries are also eaten.

72 Creeping Vole
"Oregon Vole"
(*Microtus oregoni*)

Description: *Short-haired. Brown above; silvery below.* Short tail indistinctly bicolored. Ears protrude from fur. L 4¾–6⅛″ (120–156 mm); T 1¼–2″ (30–52 mm); HF ½–⅞″ (14–21 mm); Wt ½–1⅛ oz. (14–31 g).

Similar Species: California, Montane, Long-tailed, and Townsend's voles have longer tails and longer fur.

Sign: Small subsurface burrows appearing as raised ridges; similar to those of a small mole.

Habitat: Coniferous forests; brushy and grassy areas usually on drier upland slopes.

Range: Northwest California, w Oregon, w Washington, sw British Columbia.

This vole spends most of its time in shallow burrows. Its grass nests are

usually constructed underground, although occasionally they may be placed in hollow logs or under pieces of bark or other debris. Its diet is mainly green vegetation; it also eats blueberries and other berries and subterranean fungi. Owls and weasels are its chief predators.

Singing Vole
"Alaska Vole"
(*Microtus gregalis*)
Related species: Insular

Description: *Pale grayish or buff above;* gray below. *Very short tail, heavily furred.* Ear spot usually buff or tawny; feet gray or buff. L 4–6¼" (101–161 mm); T ¾–1⅛" (19–41 mm); HF ¾" (18–21 mm); Wt ¾–2⅛ oz. (22–60 g).

Similar Species: Tundra, Yellow-cheeked, Long-tailed, and Meadow voles larger, with longer tails.

Sign: Burrows, about 1" in diameter, with fresh dirt at entrances; surface runways; stacks of cut vegetation around willows and birches.

Habitat: Above timberline; subarctic tundra; willow clumps along water, often drier ground near water.

Range: Alaska, Yukon, w Mackenzie.

This vole's common name refers to its high-pitched trill, which is usually sounded while the animal stands in its burrow entrance. A colonial animal, it also gives warning chirps when danger approaches. The burrows, up to 3' long, lead to a large nest and storage chamber. This chamber may be 1' long and is often within 2" of the surface. The voles carry out the excess soil in their mouths and deposit it next to the burrow entrance. This species climbs well for a vole and forages in low bushes. It feeds mainly on lupines, arctic locoweed, horsetails, sedges, and the leaves and twigs of willows. Tubers are cached underground, whereas green vegetation is cut and stacked on the surface where willow or birch boughs hang low; these piles sometimes contain a half bushel of material. Eskimos frequently collect the tubers from its storage chambers. It was formerly known as *Microtus miurus*.

Closely related is the Insular Vole (*Microtus abbreviatus*), known only from Hall and St. Matthew islands in the Bering Sea off Alaska.

77 Prairie Vole
(*Microtus ochrogaster*)

Description: *Grizzled yellowish-brown above;* buff below. Relatively *short tail bicolored.* 2 triangles between front and back loops on third uppercheek tooth. Incisors ungrooved. L 5⅛–6¾" (130–172 mm); T ⅞–1⅝" (24–41 mm); HF ¾–⅞" (17–22 mm): Wt 1¼–1¾ oz. (37–48 g).

Similar Species: Meadow Vole has silvery-gray belly, longer tail, and usually 4 triangles on third uppercheek tooth; bog lemmings have shallowly grooved upper incisors.

Habitat: Dry grass prairie or mixed grassy-weed situations.

Range: Southeastern Alberta, s Saskatchewan, and s Manitoba south to e Colorado, n Oklahoma, nw Tennessee, nw Kentucky. Isolated populations in se Texas and sw Louisiana.

Like many microtines, Prairie Voles are subject to cyclical population fluctuations, with populations peaking, then declining, every 3–4 years. Their diet mainly consists of green vegetation and tubers, which they often cache in underground chambers or tree stumps. These voles often damage orchards and other crops.

67 Woodland Vole
"Pine Vole"
(*Microtus pinetorum*)

Description:	Reddish-brown above with *short soft fur;* grayish, washed with buff below. *Tail short,* reddish-brown, about the length of hindfoot. Incisors not grooved. L 4⅛–5¾" (105–145 mm); T ¾–1" (17–25 mm); HF ¾" (16–20 mm); Wt ⅞–1⅜ oz. (25–39 g).
Similar Species:	Prairie Vole has long grizzled fur; Meadow and Red-backed voles have longer tails; bog lemmings have shallowly grooved upper incisors.
Habitat:	Deciduous woodlands with thick leaf mold or thick herbaceous ground cover; sometimes parklike grassy areas.
Range:	Eastern U.S. west to central Iowa and central Texas, north to central New England and central Wisconsin; in southern states except for most coastal areas.

The Woodland Vole spends most of its time in tunnel systems one to several inches below the surface. It usually constructs these burrows itself, digging with forefeet and incisors and pushing back the dirt with the hindfeet. It is somewhat colonial, although colonies sometimes disband and disappear for no apparent reason. Roots and tubers are its dietary mainstays, but it will also eat leaves, stems, and other portions of plants. Large amounts of food are stored in underground caches. This vole may be a problem in orchards, where it can damage roots; however, since its burrows are so close to the surface, it can often be controlled by cultivation. The alternate common name Pine Vole and the Latin species name *pinetorum* are misleading, as this species is rarely found in or around pine woods.

73 Water Vole
(Arvicola richardsoni)

Description: *Large.* Long fur, grayish- to reddish-
brown above; grayish with white or
silvery wash below. *Long bicolored tail.*
L 7¾–10¼" (198–261 mm); T 2¾–
3⅝" (69–92 mm); HF 1–1¼" (25–
30 mm).

Similar Species: Other voles smaller, most with shorter
tails.

Sign: Large burrows, up to 5" in diameter,
linked to edge of water by wide, damp
runways.

Habitat: Along upland streams and lakes.

Range: Southeastern and sw British Columbia
and sw Alberta south through central
and e Washington to central and e
Oregon, n Idaho, n central Utah, w
Wyoming, w Montana.

This large, semiaquatic vole is an
excellent swimmer and often enters
water to avoid predators. It lives in
colonies along waterways, constructing
its burrows among sedges or below
alders or willows. In winter, it moves
farther from water and builds grass
nests in its runways under the snow
cover. It feeds on various leafy plants,
including valerian, lousewort, lupine,
sneezeweed, and the buds and twigs of
willows.

Sagebrush Vole
(Lagurus curtatus)

Description: *Pale gray above;* whitish to silvery or
buff below and on feet. Bicolored, well-
furred *tail usually less than 1" (2.5 cm)
long.* Ears and nose buff. L 4¼–5⅝"
(108–142 mm); T ⅝–1⅛" (16–
28 mm); HF ⅝" (14–18 mm); Wt ⅝–
1⅜ oz. (17–38 g).

Similar Species: Other voles larger, darker-colored, with
longer tails and rarely found in
Sagebrush Vole's habitat.

Sign: Burrow entrances, often under sagebrush clumps, containing greenish scat; grass cuttings; paths between burrows.

Habitat: Sagebrush and grass-sage communities.

Range: Eastern Washington, s Alberta, and sw Manitoba south through e Oregon to Nevada, Utah, ne Colorado.

These voles are usually found in colonies, which vary greatly in size and density from year to year. There are several entrances to their relatively short burrows, which are often under 2' long and usually less than 12" deep with a nest chamber 7–10" in diameter. The nest is constructed of shredded sagebrush bark lined with grass. It feeds on grass heads and other green plants in summer, bark and twigs of sage and various roots in winter. It does not store food.

221 Round-tailed Muskrat
"Water Rat" "Florida Water Rat"
(*Neofiber alleni*)

Description: *Large aquatic rodent.* Dense fur, dark brown above and below, with silky sheen when dry. *Tail long and round.* Ears and eyes small. Hindfeet slightly webbed. L 11¼–15" (285–381 mm); T 3¾–6⅝" (95–168 mm); HF 1½–2" (38–50 mm); Wt 5½–12¼ oz. (155–350 g).

Similar Species: Muskrat larger with vertically flattened tail.

Sign: Houses 1–2' in diameter, similar to Muskrat's but smaller and built without mud, located in shallow water or on wet ground near water; cattail or other plant cuttings in marshes; feeding platforms consisting of floating masses of cut vegetation.
Tracks: Smaller than Muskrat's and longer in proportion to width, with more sole printing; in mud, hindprint

approximately 1½" long; foreprint to 1"
long, printing slightly ahead of
overlapping hindprint; distance
between sets of prints 2½".

Habitat: Marshes.

Range: Southeastern Georgia, peninsular
Florida.

Although primarily nocturnal, this
squeaky-voiced rodent is sometimes
active by day and tends to be
gregarious. Its house of tightly woven
grasses or sedges usually rests on a base
of decayed vegetation with two
entrances just below the surface of the
water. Houses are sometimes
constructed in fields of broom sedge a
short distance from water; these are
connected to a series of runways
beneath the sedge. Occasionally larger
and more complex houses are
constructed with several chambers,
instead of the usual one, and with
several entrances. Abandoned houses are
used by Cotton and Rice rats. During
the breeding season, more material is
added to the walls and floor of the
house, and fine grass is added to the
nesting chamber. The young may be
produced in any month, and each year
there are probably 4–5 litters of 1–4
young (usually 2). Known foods include
maiden cane and other aquatic plants
such as sea purslane, pickerelweed, and
arrowhead. Feeding platforms are
frequently constructed from the debris
left over from eating, with plunge holes
leading directly into the water; these
holes are sometimes covered by
vegetation. Crayfish remains are often
common on the feeding platforms, but
they are left there by Rice Rats, not the
Round-tailed. Nests and feeding
platforms are popular sunning sites for
many snakes, such as the cottonmouth,
which prey upon this species. Other
predators include the Marsh Hawk and
the Barn Owl.

222 Muskrat
(*Ondatra zibethicus*)

Description: Large, volelike rodent. Dense glossy fur, dark brown above, lighter on sides; finer, softer, and paler below to nearly white on throat. Small dark patch occasionally on chin. *Long tail* scaly, nearly naked, *vertically flattened and tapering to a point.* Eyes and ears small. Hindfeet partially webbed and larger than forefeet. L 16⅛–24⅜" (409–620 mm); T 7⅛–12⅛" (180–307 mm); HF 2½–3½" (64–88 mm); Wt 1¼–4 lb. (541–1816 g).

Similar Species: Round-tailed Muskrat smaller, with round tail, restricted to se Georgia and peninsular Florida; Nutria larger, with round tail.

Sign: Houses, similar to beaver lodges, constructed of aquatic plants, especially cattails, up to 8' in diameter and 5' high, on top of piles of roots, mud, or similar support in marshy areas, streams, or lakes, or along water banks; feeding platforms of cut vegetation in water, or on ice, slightly smaller than houses and marked by discarded or uneaten grass and reed cuttings. Other signs include floating blades of grass, sedges, and similar vegetation near banks or feeding platforms; piles of clamshells sometimes found at feeding sites in freshwater areas; scent posts along banks composed of small mats of leaves and grass blades mixed with mud and musk secretions.
Scat: Oval, generally ½" long, frequently in clusters on rocks, along banks, on logs in or next to water, and on feeding platforms.
Tracks: Hindprint in mud 2–3" long, with all 5 toes printing; foreprint half as long, narrower, generally with only 4 toes printing (fifth toe is vestigial). Hindprint can be ahead or behind foreprint, sometimes overlapping. Distance between sets of walking prints approximately 3". Tail often leaves drag

mark between prints, or may
alternately be lifted and dropped, or
held up completely, leaving no mark.

Habitat: Fresh, brackish, or saltwater marshes,
ponds, lakes, rivers, canals.

Range: Most of U.S. and Canada, except for
southern parts of U.S., especially s
Georgia, Florida, Texas, California, and
arctic regions of Canada.

Active primarily at night, and at dusk
and dawn, Muskrats nonetheless may
be seen at any time of day in all
seasons, especially spring. Excellent
swimmers, these aquatic rodents spend
much of their time in water. Propelled
along by their slightly webbed
hindfeet and using their rudderlike tail
for guidance, they can swim backward
or forward with ease; they dislike
strong currents and avoid rocky areas.
Their mouths close behind protruding
incisors, thus allowing them to chew
underwater. They can remain
submerged for long periods, traveling
great distances underwater. One
individual was filmed underwater for 17
minutes, coming to the surface for air
for 3 seconds, then submerging for
another 10 minutes. Their large houses
commonly contain one nesting chamber
with one or more underwater entrances.
Houses constructed along banks may
have several chambers, each with one or
more tunnels leading underwater. The
houses and feeding platforms are added
to as long as they are used; they usually
house only one individual, though
several may live together harmoniously
except in the late winter to early
September breeding season. Scent posts
covered with musky secretions from the
perineal glands help identify the sexes.
Females produce 1–5 litters per year of
1–11 young (usually 4–7) and often
breed while still nursing. Gestation is
generally 3–4 weeks. The naked young
become furred about 2 weeks after birth
and can then swim and dive. In a

month they are weaned and soon driven away by the mother. Muskrats primarily eat aquatic vegetation, such as cattails, sedges, rushes, water lilies, and pond weeds, though some terrestrial plants may also be eaten. In some areas freshwater clams are eaten, along with crayfish, frogs, and fish. Food is commonly towed out to the feeding platforms, which can be distinguished from the houses by plant cuttings and other scattered debris from eating. Houses and feeding platforms are kept immaculately clean, with droppings deposited on logs and rocks outside. Droughts and flooding are common hazards faced by these rodents, causing periodic population fluctuations. Overcrowding, especially when it occurs during fall or winter, causes fighting among individuals, forcing many to travel several miles overland to seek a new place to live. Raccoon, Mink, and man are the Muskrat's major enemies, though it is also preyed upon by many other animals. Both the Raccoon and the Mink open up Muskrat houses to devour the young. Because of its durability and waterproof qualities, Muskrat fur is considered extremely valuable, and it is of great importance to the fur trade; nearly ten million Muskrats are trapped annually. Their flesh, sold as "marsh rabbit," provides good eating, though its popularity has declined. Muskrats often cause damage to dams or dikes with their tunneling activities; they may also feed upon crops.

63 Brown Lemming
"Common Lemming" "Black-footed Lemming"
(*Lemmus sibiricus*)

Description: *Robust chestnut-brown above* with grayish head; buff-gray below. *Tail stubby.* Feet silvery. Ears hidden in thick coarse fur. L 4¾–6⅝" (122–168 mm); T ⅝–1" (16–26 mm); HF ¾–⅞" (18–23 mm); Wt 1¾–4 oz. (48–113 g).

Similar Species: Collared Lemming has black stripe down back, all white in winter; bog lemmings have grooved incisors; voles have longer tails.

Sign: Nests of woven balls of grass 6–8" wide. *Tracks:* Located among rocks or on grassy hummocks. Prints ½" long, look like miniature bear tracks. Pattern irregular, like voles', but vole tracks are characteristically half-asterisk shape.

Habitat: Wet tundra; alpine meadows.

Range: Alaska and n tier of Canadian provinces south into n British Columbia.

The Brown Lemming is closely related to the Scandinavian Lemming (*Lemmus lemmus*), which is famous for its mass migrations. Brown Lemming populations reach a peak every 3–4 years, usually in summer, with breeding continuing throughout the winter. The following summer, overcrowding is severe, food supplies depleted, and the lemmings become nervous and hyperactive. They then undergo a frenzied dispersal, but do not migrate *en masse* like the Scandinavian form.
Individuals encountering water barriers attempt to swim across, though many become exhausted and drown if the distance is too great. Predation, disease, and starvation, however, take the major toll. Weakened and distracted by dispersal, lemmings are easily caught by predators, which include foxes, Grizzly Bears, weasels, and Snowy Owls. Within a few weeks

the swarms have dwindled to a few
individuals and the cycle begins again.
Brown Lemmings use runways and
tunnels, the latter leading to 2–3
chambers about 6″ in diameter. One
chamber contains a nest of grass lined
with fur; the others are empty and
probably used for resting and toilet
areas. Their surface nests, made of
woven balls of grass, are frequently
abandoned and new ones built.
Lemming home ranges are very small,
from 3½–6 square yards. They feed on
grasses, along with sedges and leafy
plants in summer, bark and twigs of
willow and birch in winter.

65 Southern Bog Lemming
(*Synaptomys cooperi*)

Description: *Brown above;* silvery below. *Very short
tail* brownish above, lighter below. Ears
and eyes inconspicuous. *Upper incisors
shallowly grooved.* L 4⅝–6⅛″ (118–
154 mm); T ½–⅞″ (13–24 mm); HF
⅝–⅞″ (16–24 mm); Wt ¾–1¾ oz.
(21–50 g).

Similar Species: Northern Bog Lemming has rust-
colored hair at base of ears; other
volelike animals have ungrooved upper
incisors.

Sign: Grass cuttings about 3″ long.
Scat: Bright green fecal pellets.

Habitat: Grassy meadows; sometimes burrows in
northeastern forests; bogs.

Range: Southeastern Manitoba east to
Newfoundland, south to Kansas, ne
Arkansas, w North Carolina, ne
Virginia.

This lemming lives in a system of
subsurface runways and burrows about
6″ below the ground; it also commonly
uses the runways of other small
mammals. Its globular grass nest, up to
7″ in diameter with 2–4 entrances, may
be in an underground chamber or

above-ground among vegetation. Grass and clover form the bulk of its diet, although fungi and algae are sometimes eaten. A host of mammals, birds of prey, and snakes feed upon them. The populations of this lemming fluctuate greatly; in some years they are highly abundant, at other times they seem nonexistent in the same locality. Although called a bog lemming, this species seldom occurs in bogs.

Northern Bog Lemming
(*Synaptomys borealis*)

Description: *Brown above;* grayish below. *Short bicolored tail.* Rust-colored hairs at base of ears; ears hidden in fur. Eyes small. *Upper incisors grooved.* Males often have patch of white hair on flank. L 4¾–5½″ (118–140 mm); T ¾–1⅛″ (19–27 mm); HF ⅝–⅞″ (16–22 mm); Wt ¾–1¼ oz. (23–34 g).

Similar Species: Southern Bog Lemming lacks rust-colored hairs at base of ears. Other volelike animals have ungrooved incisors.

Sign: 1½″ grass cuttings; spherical grass nests, 8″ in diameter; piles of green fecal pellets in runways.

Habitat: Bogs; spruce woods; alpine meadows; tundra.

Range: Southern Alaska and British Columbia including extreme n Washington, n Idaho, and nw Montana, east through s Yukon, s Mackenzie, much of southern tier of Canadian provinces.

This colonial lemming is active day and night year-round. Like the meadow voles (*Microtus*), it uses surface runways and burrow systems. Summer nests are placed within burrows; winter nests, on ground surface. Diet includes sedges, grasses, and leafy plants.

78 Collared Lemming
"Varying Lemming" "Pied Lemming"
"Banded Lemming"
(*Dicrostonyx torquatus*)
Related species: Labrador

Description: Buff-gray above with black stripe down
back; buff-gray to white below. *Pale or
tawny ruff across throat ("collar"). Tail
short.* Small ears hidden in fur. All
white in winter, with elongated
hardened footpads below middle two
foreclaws for digging in snow. L 5¼–
6⅜" (132–162 mm); T ⅜–¾" (10–
20 mm); HF ⅝–⅞" (15–22 mm);
Wt 2–4 oz. (56–112 g).

Similar Species: Brown Lemming lacks black stripe
down back; bog lemmings have
grooved upper incisors; most voles have
longer tails.

Sign: Surface nests of balls of grass 6–8"
wide, usually among rocks or in
snowdrifts.

Habitat: Arctic tundra.

Range: Northern and w Alaska; n tier of
Canadian provinces east to Hudson
Bay.

This is the only North American rodent
that turns white in winter. It is often
found together with the Brown
Lemming in runways beneath the snow.
The Collared's tunnel systems include
rest and toilet areas, as well as deep
nesting chambers down to the
permafrost line. Breeding occurs from
March to September, with several
litters of 1–7 young born per year; both
parents care for young. In summer, its
diet includes grasses, sedges, bearberry,
and cottongrass; in winter, twigs and
buds of willow are eaten. Sometimes
whole trees are denuded. It is a major
food source for Arctic carnivores, with
foxes, wolves, wolverines, owls, and
gulls among its many predators.
Closely related is the Labrador Collared
Lemming (*Dicrostonyx hudsonius*), found
in Labrador and northern Quebec.

OLD WORLD RATS AND MICE
(Family Muridae)

The Old World rats and mice are the world's most fertile and adaptable mammals; no other mammal family includes more species. The three species accidentally introduced into the New World from the Old World—the Black Rat, the Norway Rat, and the House Mouse—have long tails, large ears, and are distinguished from native rats and mice by their molariform teeth, which have 3 rows of cusps rather than 2. Like most rodents, they are active all year and primarily nocturnal. They are among the major scourges of mankind, damaging millions of dollars of goods each year and carrying diseases such as plague, typhus, and food poisoning; it has been estimated that disease-causing organisms borne by rats have probably cost more lives in the past 10 centuries than all the wars and revolutions ever fought. Today, however, these animals also have a beneficial aspect, for the white rat bred from the Norway Rat and the white mouse bred from the House Mouse play important roles in biological and medical laboratory research.

117 Black Rat
"Ship Rat"
(*Rattus rattus*)

Description: Brownish or grayish above; underparts grayish to whitish, but not white. *Scaly, sparsely haired tail* uniformly dark and longer than half total length. Prominent ears. L 12¾–17⅞" (325–455 mm); T 6¼–10" (160–255 mm); Wt 4–12¼ oz. (115–350 g).

Similar Species: Norway Rat has tail proportionally shorter (less than half total length); rice rats have tail darker above than below; woodrats have white underparts.

Sign: Similar to those of the Norway Rat.
Habitat: Mainly around seaports and buildings; sometimes in natural habitats.
Range: Most abundant in the South and along Atlantic coast north to e Maine and along Pacific coast to extreme sw British Columbia. In the East: inland to e Arkansas, w Kentucky, n Alabama, n Georgia, and most of North Carolina and Virginia; in the West: inland as far north as w Nevada.

The Black Rat occurs in a great many varieties and races, or subspecies, of which few are actually black, despite the common name. Believed to have come from southeast Asia, it spread through Europe centuries ago, long before the arrival of the Norway Rat; appeared in Central and South America in the mid-sixteenth century, evidently carried there aboard Spanish ships; arrived in North America with the early colonists at Jamestown in 1609; and gradually spread across the continent. Formerly much more common, it has often been displaced by the slightly larger and far more aggressive Norway Rat. As Black Rats are far more common than Norway Rats on ships, they continue to be reintroduced at seaports. Excellent climbers, in the South they live in the upper stories of buildings. Nests are also made in tangled vines and in trees.
Omnivorous, but partial to grain, the Black Rat does enormous damage in docks and warehouses, contaminating with droppings what it does not eat. It breeds throughout the year, producing several litters of 2–8 young. Like other rats, it carries a number of diseases, including bubonic plague transmitted by its fleas. Snakes, owls, dogs, and cats are its chief predators.

137, 140   Norway Rat
"Common Rat" "Brown Rat" "Water
Rat" "Sewer Rat"
(*Rattus norvegicus*)

Description: Brownish-gray above; *grayish below.*
Scaly tail slightly less than half total
length, darker above than below. Small
eyes. Prominent ears. L 12⅜–18⅛"
(316–460 mm); T 4¾–8½" (122–
215 mm); Wt 6⅞–17 oz. (195–
485 g).

Similar Species: Black Rat has tail proportionally longer
(more than half its total length);
woodrats have white underparts.

Sign: Dirty smudges around holes in walls
and other passageways; damaged goods;
tunnels under boards or in riverbanks;
pathways from tunnels to food supplies.
Scat: Dark brown, about ¾" long.
Tracks: Hindprint to 2" long, with 5
long, pointed toes printing; foreprint
less than half as long, narrower, with 4
toes printing. Sets of tracks in alternate
pairs, hindprints slightly ahead of fore;
approximately 3".

Habitat: Farms, cities, many types of human
dwellings; in summer: often cultivated
fields.

Range: Entire U.S., s Canada to central British
Columbia and along Pacific Coast to
Alaska.

While early scientific descriptions of
this species came from Norway and it
was once believed to have arrived in
England in the eighteenth century
aboard Norwegian ships, the Norway
Rat is neither a native of Norway nor
more common there than elsewhere.
Probably originating in Central Asia,
from the sixteenth to the eighteenth
century it spread across Europe both
overland and aboard trading vessels and
arrived in North America about 1776
in boxes of grain brought by the
Hessian troops hired by Britain to fight
the American colonists. This loosely
colonial rat is a good climber and

swimmer. Omnivorous, it feeds on meat, insects, wild plants, seeds, and stored grain, contaminating with its droppings what it does not eat. It will kill chickens and eat their eggs. It makes a network of interconnecting tunnels 2–3″ across and up to 1½′ deep and 6′ long, with one or more chambers for nesting or feeding, one or more main entrances, and several escape exits. It digs by cutting roots with its incisors, freeing dirt, pushing it under its body with forefeet and out behind with hindfeet, then turning around and pushing it out with head and forefeet. Sometimes mating within hours of giving birth, a female may bear up to 12 litters per year of 2–22 young (but usually has about 5 litters of 7–11, as food shortages and unfavorable climate usually limit realization of its reproductive potential). Young are born naked and blind, open their eyes at 2 weeks, are weaned at 3–4 weeks; females may breed at 3 months or even earlier if food is abundant. Lifespan is about 3 years, but few live that long; at 2 years, females stop breeding and males' reproductive powers diminish. If local populations become severely overcrowded, mass migrations occur. In 1727, hordes of them were observed crossing the Volga River in Russia; though millions drowned, many survived. The German nursery legend about the Pied Piper of Hamelin who rid the town of rats by musically charming them into the Weser River, where they drowned, evidently grew from observation of rat migrations coupled with efforts toward their extermination. Vocalizations include squeaks, whistles, and chirps. Snakes, owls, hawks, skunks, weasels, Minks, and dogs are predators. Rats are a major carrier of diseases such as typhus, spotted fever, tularemia, and bubonic plague, and their destructive powers are enormous: as well as eating grain and ruining property, rats have started fires by gnawing matches and caused floods by tunneling through dams. The white rats used in laboratories are specially bred albino strains of the Norway Rat.

123 House Mouse
(*Mus musculus*)

Description: *Grayish-brown above; nearly as dark below.* Long tail dusky above and below, nearly naked. *Ungrooved incisors.* L 5⅛–7¾" (130–198 mm); T 2½–4" (63–102 mm); Wt ⅝–¾ oz. (18–23 g).

Similar Species: White-footed mice (*Peromyscus*) have white underparts; harvest mice have grooved incisors.

Sign: In buildings: damaged materials and shredded nesting material ; in fields: small dark droppings, small holes in the ground.

Habitat: Buildings; areas with good ground cover, including cultivated fields. Uncommon in undisturbed or natural habitats.

Range: Throughout U.S. and sw Canada north to central British Columbia, and along the Pacific coast north to Alaska.

The House Mouse originated in Asia and spread through Europe many centuries ago. In the early sixteenth century, it arrived in Florida and Latin America on ships of the Spanish explorers and conquistadors and about a century later came to the northern shores of this continent along with English and French explorers, traders, and colonists. It makes its own nest but lives in groups, sharing escape holes and areas for eating, urinating, and defecating. It takes turns grooming its fellows, especially on the head and back where it is difficult for the animal to groom itself. If population grows too dense, many females, particularly adolescents, become infertile. A highly migratory existence and rapid rate of reproduction enable it to thrive by taking advantage of situations not readily available to other species, including cultivated fields which offer a rich if temporary habitat. As a crop develops, the mice move in and have several litters of 3–16 young in quick succession (gestation is only 18–21 days), building large populations quickly; when the field is harvested or plowed, they move out. Many perish, many find other fields, still others invade buildings. Sometimes these migrations assume plague proportions: in 1926–27 an estimated 82,000 mice per acre wreaked havoc in the Central Valley of California. In such densities, mice, though generally timid, have been known to bite people and even to run over them. In cultivated fields, some of their actions are beneficial, as they feed heavily on weed seeds, with foxtail grass a favorite, along with caterpillars and other insects; but they are entirely destructive in houses, barns, and storage buildings. They consume, or their droppings contaminate, quantities of grain and other valuable foodstuffs. Their scientific name derives from the Sanskrit *musha,* meaning "thief." They chew or shred anything chewable or shreddable, including furniture and wires, sometimes starting fires; gnaw holes in walls, floors, and baseboards; and, like other rodents, can spread disease. They can scurry up rough vertical walls and even pipes. In the wild, birds and mammals are predators. Centuries ago, cooked mouse meat was a folk remedy for colds, coughs, fits, and fevers, but it is not recommended. The white mice used in research laboratories are albinos bred from this species.

JUMPING MICE
(Family Zapodidae)

Jumping mice are beautiful yellowish
or reddish mice with very long tails,
large hindfeet, and deeply grooved
orange incisors. They are good runners
and agile jumpers, with the long tail
helping them to maintain balance in
the air. The three species of meadow
jumping mice (*Zapus*) probably seldom
jump more than 3–4', but the
Woodland Jumping Mouse
(*Napaeozapus*) can make spectacular
leaps of at least 6–8'. The seeds of
grasses and other green plants, berries,
insects, and fungus scratched from
surface litter are chief foods. They are
primarily nocturnal and are long and
deep hibernators, sleeping 6–8 months
of the year. During this period they
draw upon reserves of stored body fat
for energy, as they do not store food.

---

93 Meadow Jumping Mouse
(*Zapus hudsonius*)

Description: *Yellowish sides;* brownish back; white
belly. *Long tail* with *tip usually not
white.* 1 small molariform tooth
precedes 3 large molariform teeth.
L 7¼–10" (187–255 mm); T 4¼–6⅛"
(108–155 mm); HF 1⅛–1⅜" (28–
35 mm); Wt ½–1 oz. (13–28 g).

Similar Species: Woodland Jumping Mouse has tip of
tail white and lacks the reduced first
molariform tooth.

Habitat: Mainly moist fields; but also brush,
brushy field, marsh, stands of touch-
me-not (*Impatiens*), woods with thick
vegetation (especially ones in which
Woodland Jumping Mouse does not
occur).

Range: Southern Alaska and most of southern
tier of Canadian provinces; ne U.S.
west to e Wyoming, and south to ne
Oklahoma, ne Georgia.

When startled from a hiding place, it may take a few long jumps of 3–4' then shorter ones, but generally soon stops and remains motionless, which is its best means of eluding predators. In spring, animal foods are particularly important, with caterpillars, beetles, and other insects constituting about half of its diet. It feeds on the seeds of grasses and many other green plants as they ripen, either by cutting off grasses at the base, then pulling the stem down to reach the head, or by climbing a stalk, cutting off the head, and carrying it to the ground in its mouth. In summer and fall, the subterranean fungus *Endogone* forms one eighth its diet. It stores no food, but in the two weeks before entering hibernation puts on about 6 grams of fat. By the end of October nearly all Meadow Jumping Mice have retired to hibernation nests of shredded grass in a protected place, under a board, in a hollow log, beneath a clump of grass, often in a bank, mound, or other raised area. Many later-born, smaller mice—those unable to accumulate adequate fat reserves—apparently perish during hibernation. In late April or early May, males emerge first; 1–2 weeks later females emerge and the first mating takes place. Gestation is 19 days. There are often two litters of 2–9 young (usually 5–6) per year, with most produced in June and August.

91, 94 Western Jumping Mouse
(*Zapus princeps*)
Related species: Pacific

Description: Yellow sides; dark band down middle of back; belly white, sometimes tinged yellow. *Long tail* darker above, whitish below. *Enlarged hindfeet.* L 8½–10¼" (215–260 mm); T 5–6¼" (126–160 mm); HF 1⅛–1¼" (28–34 mm);

Wt ½–1⅜ oz. (15–38 g).

Similar Species: Meadow Jumping Mouse smaller, occurring in the East and farther north.

Habitat: Variable: primarily moist fields, thickets, or woodlands, especially where grasses, sedges, or other green plant cover is dense; grassy edges of streams, ponds, or lakes.

Range: Western North America from s Yukon, all of British Columbia, s half of Alberta and Saskatchewan, extreme sw Manitoba, south through ne South Dakota, ne and w Montana, to central New Mexico and e central Arizona, Utah, n Nevada, w California, w Oregon.

Although it often runs on all four feet, the Western Jumping Mouse may make a series of jumps 3–5′ long when startled from its hiding place, then "disappear" by remaining motionless in a new one. It can swim and climb. Although primarily nocturnal like other jumping mice, by day it has been observed 1′ or more off the ground while foraging in salal thickets. The seeds of grasses, dock, and many other green plants, strawberries, blueberries, blackberries, and subterranean fungi are chief foods. It lives in burrows it digs itself or in those of other animals. While it makes no runways, it will use those of other animals. When alarmed, it may drum on the ground with its tail. Mating occurs soon after emergence from hibernation. The young are usually born in June or July, sometimes much later, in a spherical nest of interwoven broad-leaved grasses or, if in a bog, of sphagnum moss, constructed in a depression in the ground; they weigh less than 1 gram at birth. Between August and October the mouse fattens up, then retires to a winter burrow to hibernate curled into a ball wrapped around with its long tail. Those young born too late in the year to acquire sufficient fat reserves probably perish during hibernation. Owls and Bobcats are chief predators. A closely related species is the Pacific Jumping Mouse (*Zapus trinotatus*) found in southwestern British Columbia south through northwestern California.

92 Woodland Jumping Mouse
(*Napaeozapus insignis*)

Description: Brightly colored: *orange sides* with scattered dark hairs; brownish back; white underparts. *Long tail with white tip.* Forefeet small. Three large molariform teeth. L 8–10″ (204–256 mm); T 4½–6¼″ (115–160 mm); Wt ⅝–⅞ oz. (17–26 g).

Similar Species: The 3 species of meadow jumping mice generally lack white tail tip, are more yellowish, and have a small molariform tooth preceding the three large molars.

Habitat: Coniferous and hardwood forests in cool moist environments, especially with dense green vegetation.

Range: Southeastern Canada from Manitoba to e Labrador, south to e West Virginia and northwest to ne Minnesota; also in the Alleghenies to ne Georgia.

This good swimmer and superlative jumper usually walks but when in a hurry takes great leaps of 6–8′. When frightened, it drums its tail on the ground. It lives in a burrow either of its own construction or takes over one of another small mammal. Its consumption of the subterranean fungus *Endogone,* which forms about a third of its diet, providing water as well as food, also benefits the fungus; excretion of the fungal spores aids in their dispersal, and the mouse's digestive juices are probably essential for their germination. Seeds, caterpillars, beetle larvae, and berries are other major foods. It begins to put on a layer of fat about 2 weeks before hibernation, which starts in September or October. Emergence is in April or May, with males preceding females by a few days, and breeding soon follows. Gestation is 23–29 days. Most females have one litter per year of 2–7 young (usually 4–5), but there is often a second smaller litter, especially in the South; young are born hairless and blind, are weaned at 34 days. Predators include skunks, weasels, the Mink, the Bobcat, owls, rattlesnakes, and the domestic cat.

NEW WORLD PORCUPINES
(Family Erethizontidae)

The single North American species is described below.

219, 220 **Porcupine**
(Erethizon dorsatum)

Description: Large chunky body with high-arching back, short legs. Long guard hairs in front half of body; black or brown in the East, yellowish in the West. *Quills on rump and tail.* Feet have unique soles with small, pebbly-textured fleshy knobs and long curved claws; 4 toes on forefeet, 5 toes on hindfeet. L 25½– 36½" (648–930 mm); T 5¾– 11¾" (148–300 mm); Wt 7¾–39⅝ lbs. (3.5–18 kg).

Sign: Large irregular patches of bark stripped from tree trunks and limbs with neatly gnawed edges, plentiful tooth marks.
Scat: Similar to that of deer but more variable; in winter: rough-surfaced irregular pellets, sometimes connected when food is relatively soft; in summer: pellets softer, more elongate, often curved, sometimes segmented. Accumulations found at entrances to crevice shelter or cave among rocks and, in winter, at base of single tree where porcupine has fed for a long time.
Tracks: Distinctive; toe in, almost like a badger's; pebbled knobs on soles leave stippled impression, long claws mark far ahead of oval main prints; foreprint, including claw marks, about 2½" long, hindprint well over 3" long, usually but not always printing ahead of foreprint. Stride is short and waddling, with prints 5–6" apart; straddle up to 9" wide. In snow, feet may drag or shuffle, connecting prints. Trail occasionally blurred, as if swept by a small broom when belly brushes ground and stiff

heavy tail swishes from side to side in waddling walk.

Habitat: Woods.

Range: Most of Canada and western U.S.; in the East, south to New England, New York, and most of Pennsylvania, n half of Michigan, Wisconsin.

The solitary Porcupine is active year-round, though in bitter cold it may den up in a hole in a rocky bluff, sometimes with other Porcupines in the area. Primarily nocturnal, it may also rest by day in a hollow tree or log, underground burrow, or treetop, for it is an excellent if slow and deliberate climber. On the ground, it has an unhurried, waddling walk, relying on its quills for protection against predators which can move more swiftly, though it prefers to retreat or ascend a tree rather than confront an enemy. On its body there are about 30,000 quills, which are modified hairs solid at tip and base, hollow for most of the shaft, and loosely attached to a sheet of voluntary muscles beneath the skin. The Porcupine's generic name means "one who rises in anger," and while a porcupine cannot throw its quills at an enemy, when forced to fight it erects them, lowers its head, and lashes out with its tail. If the tail strikes the enemy, the loosely rooted quills detach easily and are driven forcefully into the victim, whose body heat causes the microscopic barblets on the end of the quill to expand and become ever more firmly embedded. Wounds may fester or, depending on where it enters, a quill may blind the victim or prevent it from eating. Cutting the end off the hollow quill releases air pressure and allows it to be more easily withdrawn. A few carnivores, notably the Fisher, are adept at flipping a porcupine over to attack its wiry-haired but unquilled underside, but even a Fisher occasionally receives a fatal injury. A strict vegetarian, in spring the Porcupine feeds on leaves, twigs, and such green plants as skunk cabbage, lupines, and clover; in winter, it chews through the rough outer bark of various trees, including pines, fir, cedar, and hemlock to get at the inner bark (cambium) on which it then mainly subsists. Fond of salt, the Porcupine has a great appetite for wooden tool handles that have absorbed human perspiration through use. It mates mainly in October and November when it is most vocal, giving a variety of squeaks, groans, and grunts. The jocular answer to the question "How do Porcupines mate?" is "Carefully." In fact, mating occurs in the same fashion as in other mammals, but not until the female is sufficiently aroused that she relaxes her quills before raising her tail over her back and presenting herself. After a gestation of nearly 7 months— an unusually long period for a small mammal—the single young is born in May or June. Quills are well formed but not injurious to the mother, as the baby is born head first in a placental sac and the short quills are soft; quills harden within half an hour. Lifespan is 7–8 years. In addition to the Fisher, Porcupine predators include the Mountain Lion, the Bobcat, and the Coyote. The Porcupine may kill trees by stripping away the bark, and its gnawing may damage buildings, furniture, and tools. In some states, the Porcupine is protected because it provides an easily obtained source of food to a person lost in the woods: a sharp blow on the nose with a stick kills it. Its quills, both natural and dyed, have been used in brilliantly executed decorative appliqué by Indians, who also ate the animal's flesh.

NUTRIA
(Family Capromyidae)

Members of this family are native to
South America and the Caribbean; the
single species has been introduced into
North America.

223 Nutria
"Coypu"
(*Myocastor coypus*)

Description: *Large aquatic rodent. Brown above;*
somewhat lighter below. Long, scaly,
sparsely haired *round tail*. Muzzle and
chin whitish. Ears and eyes small.
Incisors dark orange, protruding
beyond lips. Hindfeet longer than
forefeet, with inner 4 toes webbed.
Males larger than females. L 26⅜–
55⅛" (67–140 cm); T 11¾–17¼"
(30–44 cm); HF 4⅜–5½" (112–
140 mm); Wt 5–25 lb. (2.3–11.4 kg).

Similar Species: Muskrat smaller, with vertically
flattened tail, which is higher than
wide; Beaver larger, with large,
horizontally flattened tail.

Sign: Feeding platforms of aquatic vegetation
and debris, 5–6' across; well-
established trails of flattened vegetation
along marshy shores; at dusk, a chorus
of piglike grunts may be heard.
Scat: Elongated droppings found on
feeding platforms or shoreline.
Tracks: Similar to those of Muskrat but
larger, with hindfeet showing webbing
between inner 4 toes; easily confused
with Beaver's when the Beaver's fifth
toe webbing does not print.

Habitat: Marshes; ponds; streams.

Range: Widely introduced, especially in the
Southeast, but also in Maryland, s New
Jersey, scattered locations in the Great
Plains, n Oregon, Washington.

The generic name for this nocturnal
aquatic rodent comes from Greek words

for "mouse" (*myo*) and "beaver" (*castor*). Although it often feeds on land, when disturbed the Nutria returns to the water, often with a loud splash. It can remain submerged for several minutes and often floats just under the surface with only eyes and nose exposed. Its nest of plant materials is made either in a burrow dug in a riverbank with entrance above water, above ground or in shallow water, or in the burrows of other animals or the lodges of Beavers or Muskrats. Feeding on almost any terrestrial or aquatic green plants, it also eats some grain, sometimes dipping its food into water before eating. Nutria may occupy feeding platforms to rest and to avoid terrestrial predators. Like the lagomorphs, it reingests fecal pellets in order to digest food more completely while at rest. Breeding occurs year-round in the South, and courtship features much chasing, fighting, and biting. After gestation of about 130 days, a litter of 1–11 young (usually 4–6) are born fully haired and with eyes open; litters are largest when food is most abundant. Within 24 hours, the well-developed young swim with their mothers and nibble green plants. Introduced in Louisiana in the 1930's as a fur-bearer, many Nutria escaped from captivity during the hurricane floodings in the 1940's, multiplied enormously in the wild, and are now more important than the Muskrat in the extensive trapping industry in Louisiana. The long coarse guard hairs are used in making felt for hats; the soft belly fur, resembling Beaver, is used for coats and coat linings. When populations are high, Nutria may undermine stream banks, deplete wild vegetation, and raid rice and other crops.

Carnivores
(Order Carnivora)

Most of the major predators, as well as the domestic dog and cat, are in this order. North American terrestrial species range from the world's smallest land carnivore, the Least Weasel (*Mustela nivalis*), scarcely more than 1 oz. of sinuous energy, to the largest, the Alaskan Brown Bear (*Ursus arctos middendorffi*), a massive 1,700 lb. Terrestrial carnivores vary greatly in size and appearance and include many of the animals most familiar to man. The name of the order is somewhat misleading, however, for while many canivores live mainly on freshly killed prey, others are omnivorous, eating a great deal of vegetation. All North American carnivores have 3 pairs of relatively small incisors above and below, and large strong canines. Most have one annual litter with offspring born blind and requiring a relatively extended period of parental care. Carnivores generally live on land, but some spend part or nearly all of their time in water. Except for the European Badger (*Meles meles*), none truly hibernate, though several remain in their nests for long periods during exceptionally cold weather. The dwindling of habitat, and with it, the decrease of prey, has diminished the populations of many carnivores. A few of the large species, such as Cougars, have also suffered undue persecution by man, and others, such as the Coyote, have been hunted because of predation on livestock, sometimes real, sometimes exaggerated. In former times, species with valuable pelts were often decimated by unregulated trapping. Some carnivores, including the Ocelot and the Gray Wolf, are now considered endangered or threatened, and are fully protected; many others receive some protection as game or fur-bearers.

Also included in this order are seals, sea lions, and the Walrus—aquatic carnivores sometimes classified as belonging to a separate order, Pinnipedia.

WOLVES, FOXES, AND THE COYOTE
(Family Canidae)

All North American canids have a doglike appearance characterized by a lithe body; long, narrow muzzle; erect, triangular ears; long, slender legs; and bushy tail. Most are social animals: wolves travel in packs with a clearly established hierarchy of dominance; Coyotes hunt in smaller groups or pairs; and only foxes are solitary. Most canids chase down their prey, but foxes also rely on stalking and pouncing. Although sight and hearing are keen, canids rely heavily on their acute sense of smell, both for scenting the prey itself and "reading" scent posts marked with the urine or secretions of other animals. Most species have only 1 annual litter of 2–7 young. As a result of years of persecution, wolves have decreased greatly. The Coyote, however, has thrived alongside man, increasing both in numbers and range. When a "wolf" is reported where none has been seen for at least a century, it is usually a Coyote, a dog, or a coydog (a dog-coyote hybrid). The canid family has given rise to the domestic dog (*Canis familiaris*), which some believe to be derived from the wolf (or wolf and jackal) while others suggest it is descended from an extinct wild dog quite different from any living canid.

263, 264 **Coyote**
(*Canis latrans*)

Description: *Grizzled gray* or reddish-gray with buff underparts; long, rusty or yellowish legs with dark vertical line on lower foreleg; *bushy tail with black tip.* Nose pad to 1″ (25 mm) wide. Ears prominent. Height at shoulder 23–26″ (58–66 cm). L 41⅜–52″ (105–

132 cm); T 11¾–15½" (30–
39 cm); HF 7¾–8¾" (18–22 cm);
Wt 20–40 lb. or more (9.1–18.1 kg).

Similar Species: Gray and Red wolves are larger, with
larger nose pads. "Coydogs," hybrids of
Coyotes and domestic dogs, especially
shepherd mixtures, are larger, usually
lack dark vertical line on lower foreleg,
and have relatively shorter and thicker
snouts.

Sign: *Dens:* Favored sites are riverbanks, well-
drained slopes, sides of canyons or
gulches. Den mouths usually 1–2'
wide, often marked by mound or fan of
earth and radiating tracks.
Scat: Typically canine, but often full of
hair and usually deposited on
"runway," a long, meandering,
habitually used hunting trail.
Tracks: Similar to dog's, but in a nearly
straight line; 4 toes, all with claws;
foreprint about 2½" long, slightly
narrower; hindprint slightly smaller;
stride 13" when walking, 24" when
trotting, 30" or more when running,
often with much wider gaps signifying
leaps. Tracks and scat most often seen
where runways intersect or on a hillock
or open spot, vantage points where
Coyotes linger to watch for prey.

Breeding: Mates February–April; may pair for
several years or life, especially when
populations are low; 1–19 young born
April–May; in a crevice or underground
burrow.

Habitat: In the West, open plains; in the East,
brushy areas.

Range: East Alaska, n and w Canada, all of
w U.S. east to at least New England,
n New York, New Jersey, Ohio,
Tennessee, and Louisiana. Additional
isolated records of Coyotes all over the
East.

The best runner among the canids, the
Coyote can leap 14' and cruises
normally at 25–30 mph and up to 40
mph for short distances; tagged Coyotes
have been known to travel great

distances, up to 400 miles. The Coyote runs with its tail down, unlike wolves, which run with tail horizontal. A strong swimmer, it does not hesitate to enter water after prey. Vocalizations are varied, but the most distinctive are given at dusk, dawn, or during the night and consist of a series of barks and yelps followed by a prolonged howl and ending with short, sharp yaps. Seldom heard in the East but common in the West, this call keeps the band alert to the locations of its members and reunites them when separated. One call usually prompts others to join in, resulting in the familiar chorus heard at night throughout the West. Barking alone, with no howling, seems to be a threat display employed in defense of a den or a kill. Its scientific name means "barking dog"; its common name comes from *coyotl,* the term used by Mexico's Nahuatl Indians.

In feeding, the Coyote is an opportunist, eating rabbits, mice, ground squirrels, pocket gophers and other small mammals, birds, frogs, toads, snakes, insects, many kinds of fruit, and carrion. To bring down larger prey, such as a deer or Pronghorn, the Coyote may combine efforts with 1 or 2 others, running in relays to tire prey or waiting in ambush while others chase prey toward it. Sometimes a Badger serves as involuntary supplier of smaller prey: while it digs for rodents at one end of their burrow, a Coyote waits to pounce on any that may emerge from an escape hole at the other end. It stalks like a pointer, "freezing" before it pounces. The typical den is a wide-mouthed tunnel, 5–30′ long, terminating in an enlarged nesting chamber. The female may dig her own den, enlarge a fox or Badger burrow, or use a cave, log, or culvert; if the den area is disturbed, the female will move pups to a new home. Predators once included Grizzly and

Black bears, Mountain Lions, and wolves, but with their declining populations these are no longer a threat. Man is the major enemy, especially since Coyote pelts have become increasingly valuable; but the Coyote population continues to increase, despite trapping and poisoning.

256 Red Wolf
(*Canis rufus*)

Description: *Reddish fur,* with interspersed blackish hairs; also black, brown, yellowish, or gray. *Nose pad more than 1″ (25 mm) wide.* Height at shoulder 15–16″ (38–41 cm). L 55¼–65″ (140–165 cm); T 13½–16½″ (34–42 cm); HF 8¼–10″ (21–25 cm); Wt 40–90 lb. (18.2–40.9 kg).

Similar Species: Coyote is smaller, with a smaller nose pad and smaller hindfoot; Gray Wolf is larger and grayer.

Sign: *Scat:* Similar to that of Coyote.
Tracks: Fore and hind prints 4½″ long; 4 toes with claws; outer toes smaller than middle ones.

Breeding: 4–7 young born April–May in protected den area.

Habitat: Prairies, brush, forested areas, coastal plains, swamps, bayous.

Range: Southwestern Louisiana and se Texas.

Little is known of this species, but its habits are presumably similar to those of the Gray Wolf. Occasionally it pursues deer, but like the Coyote, it feeds primarily on hares and rabbits, small rodents, and birds. Den sites include stream banks, enlarged burrows of other mammals, hollow trees, and sandy knolls in coastal areas. This southwestern wolf was formerly persecuted as a threat to livestock, but ranchers are now cooperating with wildlife researchers in gathering

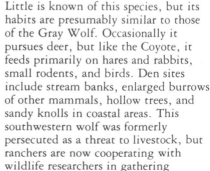

information about its habits and trying to preserve the species. Since it interbreeds readily with the Coyote, it may be doomed to extinction by hybridization rather than by man.

250, 261, 262, **Gray Wolf**
266   "Timber Wolf"
(Canis lupus)

Description: Usually *grizzled gray* but shows great variation in color, ranging from white to black. *Long, bushy tail with black tip. Nose pad 1" (25 mm) wide.* Males larger than females. Height at shoulder 26–38" (66–97 cm). L 39½–80⅝" (100–205 cm); T 14–19¾" (35–50 cm); HF 8¾–12¼" (22–31 cm); Wt 57–130 lb. (26–59 kg).

Similar Species: Coyote much smaller, with smaller nose pad.

Sign: Heavily used trails where prey is plentiful.
Scent posts: Scrapes, rocks, or stumps, all marked with urine.
Den: Entrance 20" x 26", with burrow 6–30' deep, often marked by fan or mound of earth and sometimes by bones or scraps of prey brought for pups.
"Rendezvous," or rest area: Usually a grassy expanse—dry marsh, old burn, or meadow with good mousing and a wide view—where pack gathers when den is vacated; it is marked by scat, tracks, beaten trails, and sometimes diggings where food has been cached and later uncovered.
Scat: Resembles a large dog's but often contains hair of prey.
Tracks: Similar to domestic dog's but larger. Foreprint 4¼–5" long; hindprint slightly smaller. Walking stride 30"; sometimes hindfeet come down in forefeet prints.

Breeding: Mates February–March; 5–14 young, averaging 7, born April–June in den in

an enlarged chamber without nesting
material; at 1 month pups emerge to
play near den entrance guarded by an
adult. Rest of pack leaves den site in
late afternoon or at dusk to hunt,
usually returning next morning with
food. Pups jump and bite at snouts and
throats of returning hunters,
stimulating them to regurgitate
undigested meat, which pups and their
guardian devour. Some juveniles leave
adults at 1 year, some at 2 years, when
mature.

Habitat: Open tundra, forests.

Range: Once most of North America, but now
only Alaska, Canada, n Washington, n
Idaho, n Montana, Isle Royale National
Park in Lake Superior, and ne
Minnesota.

A social animal, the Gray Wolf mates
for life and lives in packs of 2–15,
usually 4–7, formed primarily of family
members and relatives. The strongest
male is normally the leader; all
members of the pack help to care for
the young. The Gray Wolf possesses
various whines, yelps, growls, and
barks—the usual one short, harsh, and
uttered in a brief series; not all wolves
are capable of barking. Howls, used to
keep the pack together, may be at a
constant pitch, rise and fall, or rise and
break off abruptly; they sound dismal
to some, but beautiful and haunting to
others. The howl of one wolf seldom
lasts more than 5 seconds, but others in
the pack may take it up, producing a
chorus continuing until the animals tire
or disperse. Many wolves answer a bark
—even a poor human imitation of one
—by howling. A communal howl is
heard sometimes in early morning but
most often in the evening, when it may
stimulate the urge to hunt. It usually
begins with a few sharp barks by one or
more pack members, which are often
followed by a low, rather querulous
howl that, in turn, stimulates steadier,

louder communal howling that dies away after a few minutes, often ending with a few more barks before the pack goes off together to hunt. A wolf separated from its pack may give the "lonesome howl"—a shortened call that rises in pitch and ten dies away plaintively. If answered, the wolf switches to a "location," or "assembly," howl; this is deep, even, and often punctuated by barks. Wolves seldom call when actually chasing prey; rather, they stop to vocalize in order to maintain contact and sometimes call to signal arrival at an ambush point toward which other pack members will then attempt to deive prey. Wolves run with a bounding gait with tail held horizontally. Except perhaps for Caribou, they probably travel more often and for greater distances than any other terrestrial animal. A large pack's territory covers 100–260 sq. mi., which is traveled at regular intervals over such runways as animal trails, logging roads, and frozen lakes. Territories may overlap slightly, but groups usually avoid one another. If food is adequate, a pack may use the same range for many generations. Usually hunting at night, the wolf feeds primarily on large mammals—Moose, Caribou, deer—but will also catch smaller ones, and sometimes eats berries, birds, fish, and insects. The pack works together on a hunt, either chasing down its victim, usually by slashing tendons in the hindlegs, or driving it to circle back to waiting pack members. Wolves gain an advantage over large prey in deep, crusted snow: the crust may support wolves but a moose or deer may break through and be unable to run fast enough to escape. Myth notwithstanding, wolves do not attempt long chases. They can gallop and bound over short distances at speeds more than 30 mph, but if they cannot capture running prey within about 1,000 yards, they usually abandon the attempt. A healthy deer outruns wolves unless hindered by deep, semicrusted snow.

Wolves try to surprise prey, cut off its retreat, or ambush it. Whatever seems to be running away arouses in the wolf the instinct to dash after it, but wolves are soon apt to give up such a chase unless the creature pursued stops and starts again. Wolves, like many other carnivores, test prey: a Moose that stands and fights often persuades a pack to seek easier prey, but one that intermittently defends itself and runs— perhaps because it is injured, sick, defective, or very young or old— signals the possibility of its defeat, and the pack often continues to pursue it. What appears to be pursuit by wolves may be instead wolves' inquisitive trailing to identify prey or competition for prey; in deep snow wolves will follow men or dog teams in order to take advantage of the tamped trail. Even in winter the wolf rarely dens up; during a blizzard, it curls its tail over paws and nose and soon becomes covered with snow, which provides insulation from the cold. While man has long feared wolves, there have been few attacks on man, the wolf's only important predator. Lifespan is 10–18 years.

251, 252, 265 **Arctic Fox**
(*Alopex lagopus*)

Description: In summer, *bluish-brown or grayish with white underparts;* in winter, white or creamy white. A rare blue phase is dark blue-gray in summer, pale blue-gray in winter. Tail bushy. Black nose pad, eyes, and claws. Snout blunt. Ears rounded and short, usually 2¼" (56 mm) long. Males larger than females. Height at shoulder 10–12"

(25–30 cm). L 29½–35⅞″ (75–91 cm); T 10⅜–13⅜″ (27–35 cm); HF 5⅛–6¼″ (13–16 cm); Wt 5½–8¾ lb. (2.5–4 kg).

Similar Species: Other foxes have larger, more pointed ears. Red Fox has white tail tip; Gray Fox has black "mane" on top of tail.

Sign: *Den:* Burrows in sandy soils with several entrances about 1′ wide. *Scat:* Small, narrow, roughly cylindrical, tapered at one end, similar to Red and Gray foxes'; when Arctic Fox feeds on crustaceans, may be pinkish bleaching to white. *Tracks:* Similar to Red Fox's but without barlike impression that often shows in its heel-pad track. Fore and hind prints 2–3½″ (5–9 cm) long; 4 closely spaced toes, all with claws; sometimes slightly blurred because of densely haired foot pads, especially in winter.

Breeding: 4–25 young, averaging 6.4, born April–June; cared for by both parents until family disperses in mid-August; male brings food for young and mate and guards family.

Habitat: Tundra at edge of northern forests; in winter, far out on ice floes. Rare blue phase usually in areas without permanent snow cover, where its color would be disadvantageous.

Range: Northern and w Alaska and n Canada south to n Northwest Territories, ne Alberta, n Manitoba and n Quebec; a few records indicate presence farther south.

The Arctic Fox's adaptations to its subzero habitat include a compact body with short legs and short ears (heat loss occurs mostly through extremities), dense fur, and thickly haired foot pads, which insulate against the cold and provide traction on ice. Although individuals are relatively solitary, several will congregate around a large carcass or dump. It dens in a bank or hillside and in winter may tunnel into a

summer

winter

snowbank. The female builds a summer nest in a new den with several entrances. Populations peak about every 4 years, paralleling and following by roughly 1 year that of lemmings, a chief food. In summer, when prey is abundant, the Arctic Fox gluts itself but still keeps hunting. It stores surplus food by clawing through the soil and deep-freezing it on the permafrost below or caching it in a crevice or under a rock. In winter, it follows Polar Bears, eating leftovers from their kills and, if food is scarce, even their droppings. It also eats voles, ground squirrels, young hares, birds, bird's eggs, fish, berries, occasionally the young of seals and sea lions, and, in winter, carrion. When prey is scarce and hunting territories are consequently expanded, young and old foxes unable to defend their territories may be forced to emigrate. They travel south up to several hundred miles; few return north, as many are trapped for their pelts. Winter pelage develops in October: the coat thickens, and the new hairs are much lighter. The long-haired pelts are valuable, especially the rare blue phase, and much sought. Arctic Foxes are raised commercially on islands off Alaska. Their flesh is often eaten by Eskimoes.

249, 253, 254, 255   **Red Fox**
(*Vulpes vulpes*)

Description: Small, doglike. *Rusty-reddish above; white underparts, chin, and throat. Long, bushy tail with white tip.* Prominent pointed ears. Back of ear, lower legs, feet black. Elliptical pupils. Color variations include a black phase (almost completely black), a silver phase (black with silver-tipped hairs), a cross phase (reddish-brown with a dark cross across shoulders), and intermediate phases, all with white-tipped tail. Height at shoulder 15–16″ (38–41 cm). L 35⅜–40⅜″ (90–103 cm); T 13¾–17″ (35–43 cm); HF 5¾–7″ (146–178 mm); Wt 7⅞–15 lb. (3.6–6.8 kg).

Similar Species: Other foxes lack the conspicuously white-tipped tail.

Sign: *Den:* Maternity den usually in sparse ground cover; commonly enlarged den of marmot or Badger on slight rise, providing view of all approaches, but also in stream bank, slope, or rock pile; less often in hollow tree or log. Typical earthen mound has main entrance up to 1′ wide, slightly higher, with littered fan or mound of packed earth and 1–3 less conspicuous smaller escape holes. Den well marked with excavated earth, cache mounds where food is buried, holes where food has been dug up, and scraps of bones and feathers. Dens established shortly after mating (usually late January or February), abandoned by late August when families disperse.
Scat: Similar to and often indistinguishable from that of Gray Fox, but often paler.
Tracks: Similar to those of Gray Fox, but usually slightly larger, with smaller toeprints. Foreprint about 2¼″ long, hindprint slightly smaller, narrower, more pointed. Often blurred, especially in winter, with lobes and toes less distinctly outlined than those of Gray Fox, as Red Fox's feet are more heavily haired. In heavy snow, tail may brush out tracks.

Breeding: Mates January–early March. After 51–53 days gestation, 1–10 kits, average 4–8, born March–May in maternity den. When about 1 month old, they play aboveground and feed on what is brought them by their parents. At first, meat is predigested by mother and regurgitated, but soon live prey is brought, enabling kits to practice killing. Kits disperse at 4 months, males up to 150 miles away or more, females usually less widely. Adults also disperse, remaining solitary until the next breeding season.

Habitat: Varied; mixed cultivated and wooded areas, brushlands.

Range: Most of Canada and U.S. except for much of West Coast: Southwest (s California, n Nevada, Arizona); s Alberta and sw Saskatchewan to sw Oklahoma; nw Texas and Southeast (coastal North Carolina to peninsular Florida).

Even when fairly common, the Red Fox may be difficult to observe, as it is shy, nervous, and primarily nocturnal (though it may be abroad near dawn or dusk or on dark days). Omnivorous, it eats whatever is available, feeding heavily on vegetation in summer, including corn, berries, apples, cherries, grapes, acorns, and grasses; in winter on birds and mammals, including mice, rabbits, squirrels, and Woodchucks. Invertebrates such as grasshoppers, crickets, caterpillars, beetles, and crayfish compose about one fourth of its diet. Food not consumed at once is cached under snow, leaves, or soft dirt.

In winter, adult foxes rarely den up. In the open, they curl up into a ball, wrapping bushy tail about nose and foot pads, and at times may be completely blanketed with snow. Regarded as the embodiment of cunning, the Red Fox is believed by many field observers merely to be extremely cautious and, like other canids, capable of learning from experience.

In the mid-eighteenth century, Red Foxes were imported from England and released in New York, New Jersey, Maryland, Delaware, and Virginia by landowners who enjoyed riding to the hounds. (At the time, the Gray Fox— not a good substitute for the Red, as it cannot run as fast or as long—had not yet expanded its range north into these areas). The Red Foxes that now populate almost all of the states are combined strains derived from the interbreeding of imported foxes with native races, which, encouraged by settlement, gradually expanded their range south from Canada. For years, unregulated trapping and bounty payments took a heavy toll on foxes. Now that foxes are to some extent bred commercially and poultry farms made nearly predator proof, trapping is regulated in many regions, and most bounty payments have been abolished. The Red Fox in America (perhaps 3–4 million) may be expanding its range, although competition with the Coyote, which is also expanding its range, may have a restraining effect.

258, 259, 260   **Swift Fox**
(*Vulpes velox*)
Related species: Kit

Description: *Buff-yellowish* above, whitish below. *Tail with black tip* and often a black spot at upper base. *Feet light colored;* ears large, triangular; dark spots below eye. Height at shoulder 12″ (30 cm). L 23⅜–31½″ (60–80 cm); T 8⅞–11¾″ (23–30 cm); Wt 3–6 lb. (1.4–2.7 kg).

Similar Species: Red Fox has a white tail tip and black feet; Gray Fox is larger, darker, and has a black "mane" on top of tail.

Sign: *Den:* In ground with 3–4 entrances 8″ wide; usually with mound of earth; sometimes scattered with small bones or scraps of prey. *Scat:* Small, irregular, cylindrical. *Tracks:* Similar to Gray Fox's but smaller, usually less than 1½″ long; all prints show 4 toes and claws.

Breeding: Mates January–February, usually for life; 3–5 young born March–April in chamber 3′ below ground with no nesting material.

Habitat: Shortgrass prairies, other arid areas.
Range: South Alberta, Saskatchewan, and Manitoba south through e Montana and Wyoming, ne Colorado, the Dakotas, Nebraska, w Kansas and Oklahoma, e New Mexico, n Texas.

This mostly nocturnal, solitary fox excavates its own den or enlarges a Badger or marmot den in open country. Its calls include a shrill yap, several whines, purrs, and growls. For short distances, it can run as fast as 25 mph (hence its common name). It eats rabbits, ground squirrels, rats and mice, birds, insects, grasses, and berries; in winter it caches food under snow. It attempts to evade predator dogs and Coyotes by entering burrows or suddenly changing direction of flight.

Closely related and considered a subspecies by some taxonomists is the Kit Fox (*Vulpes macrotis*), found mainly in the Southwest but also north to southeastern Oregon and southwestern Idaho. It is similar in coloration but smaller and faster. The names Kit Fox and Swift Fox are used interchangeably for both species.

257 **Gray Fox**
(*Urocyon cinereoargenteus*)
Related species: Insular

Description: *Grizzled gray above, reddish below* and on back of head; throat white. *Tail with black "mane" on top* and black tip; feet rusty colored. Prominent ears. Height at shoulder 14–15″ (36–38 cm). L 31½–44¼″ (80–113 cm); T 8¾–17⅜″ (22–44 cm); HF 3⅞–5⅛″ (10–15 cm); Wt 7¼–13 lb. (3.3–5.9 kg).

Similar Species: Red Fox has a white tail tip; Kit and Swift foxes are smaller and have yellowish-buff fur with black tail tip.

Sign: *Tree and scent posts:* Marked with urine,

noticeable on snow by spattered urine stains and melting.

Caches: heaped or loosened dirt, moss, or turf, frequently paler than surrounding ground; dug-up cache holes are shallow and wide, since foxes seldom bury very small prey except near a den in whelping season.

Den: Entrance size varies considerably, as most dens are in natural cavities, with entrance occasionally marked by snagged hair or a few telltale bone scraps; several auxiliary or escape dens nearby. Dens are in rare instances conspicuously marked with mounds like those of the Red Fox.

Scat: Small, narrow, roughly cylindrical, usually sharply tapered at 1 end. Because Gray Fox eats more berries than Red Fox, its stool is darker, particularly where wild cherries abound.

Tracks: When in straight line, similar to those of a very large domestic cat, except that nonretractile claws may show. Similar to Red Fox's, but often smaller with larger toes and more sharply defined because of less hair around pads. Foreprint about 1½" long; hindprint as long, slightly narrower; 4 toes with claws. On fairly hard ground, hind heel pad leaves only a round dot if side portions fail to print. A fox digs in when running, leaving claw marks even in hard ground, where pads do not print.

Breeding: Mates February–March; 2–7 young, average 3–4, born in March or April; weaned at 3 months, hunting for themselves at 4 months, when they weigh about 7 lb. Male helps tend young; however, he does not den with them.

Habitat: Varied, but associated much more with wooded and brushy habitats than are Red Foxes.

Range: Eastern U.S. west to e North and South Dakota, Nebraska, Kansas, Oklahoma, most of Texas, New Mexico, Arizona

and California, north through Colorado, s Utah, s Nevada, and w Oregon.

Although primarily nocturnal, the Gray Fox is sometimes seen foraging by day in brush, thick foliage, or timber. The only American canid with true climbing ability, it occasionally forages in trees and frequently takes refuge in them, especially in leaning or thickly branched ones. Favored den sites include woodlands and among boulders on the slopes of rocky ridges. It digs if necessary but prefers to den in clefts, small caves, rock piles, slash piles, hollow logs, and hollow trees, especially oaks; sometimes it enlarges a Woodchuck burrow. Unlike the Red Fox, the Gray uses dens all winter for shelter and safety. It growls, barks, or yaps, but less frequently than the Red Fox. Omnivorous, it feeds heavily on cottontail rabbits, mice, voles, other small mammals, birds, insects, much plant material, including corn, apples, persimmons, nuts, cherries, grapes, pokeweed fruit, grass, and blackberries. The most important predators are domestic and wild dogs, Bobcats where abundant, and man.
A closely related species, the Insular Gray Fox (*Urocyon littoralis*) occurs as 6 subspecies on 6 islands off southern California; it is similar in appearance to the Gray Fox but smaller.

BEARS
(Family Ursidae)

The three species of North American bears—the Black, the Grizzly, and the Polar—are the largest of all terrestrial carnivores. They range from 600 to 1,700 lb. and have powerful, densely furred bodies; small, rounded ears; and small eyes set close together. They have 5 claws on each foot and, like man, walk on the entire sole with the heel touching the ground. While their vision is poor, their sense of smell is keen. Although classed as carnivores, bears tend to be omnivorous, eating leaves, twigs, berries, fruit, and insects as well as small mammals. Commonly believed to hibernate, bears enter a protected area and sleep away the harshest part of winter, but their sleep is not deep and their temperature falls only a few degrees below normal. The young are born while the female is denned up. Although the eggs are fertilized when the female mates in late spring or early summer, 6 or 7 months may pass before the embryos become implanted in the uterine wall, after which they develop rapidly. When born, bears are the size of rats, generally weighing only ½–1 lb., which makes the magnitude of their eventual growth greater than that of all other mammals except marsupials. North American bears produce 1 litter every other year. All bears are dangerous in the following situations: when accompanied by cubs, surprised by the sudden appearance of humans, approached while guarding kill or feeding, fishing, hungry, injured, breeding, or when familiarity has diminished their fear of man, as in some Canadian and U.S. parks. Once distributed over much of North America, bears have been eliminated from most areas of human habitation.

292, 293 Black Bear
(*Ursus americanus*)

Description: In the East, *nearly black;* in the West, *black to cinnamon* with white blaze on chest. A "blue" phase occurs near Yukatat Bay, Alaska; and individuals are nearly white on Gribble Island, British Columbia, and neighboring mainland. *Snout tan* or grizzled; in profile *straight* or slightly convex. Males much larger than females. Height at shoulder 3–3½′ (90–105 cm). L 4½–6¼′ (137–188 cm); T 3–7″ (77–177 mm); HF 9⅛–14⅜″ (23–37 cm); Wt 203–595 lb. (92–267 kg).

Similar Species: Grizzly Bear is usually larger and has a facial profile that is generally somewhat concave, an outer pair of upper incisors much larger than 2 inner pairs, a muscular hump above the shoulder region, and longer foreclaws.

Sign: Feeding signs are common: logs or stones turned over for insects; decayed stumps or logs torn apart for grubs; ground pawed up for roots; anthills or rodent burrows excavated; berry patches torn up; fruit-tree branches broken; rejected bits of carrion or large prey, such as pieces of skin, often with head or feet attached.

"Bear Trees": Scarred with tooth marks, often as high as a bear can reach when standing on its hindlegs; also higher, longer claw slashes, usually diagonal but sometimes vertical or horizontal. In spring, furrowed or shaggy-barked trees used repeatedly and by several bears as shedding posts—to rub away loose hair and relieve itching—show rub marks and snagged hair.

Scat: Usually dark brown, roughly cylindrical, sometimes coiled, similar to a dog's; often showing animal hair, insect parts, fruit seeds, grasses, root fibers, or nutshell fragments; but where bears have fed heavily on berries, their scat may be a liquid black mass.

Trails: Those used by generations of

bears are well worn, undulating, and marked with depressions.

Tracks: Broad footprints 4″ long, 5″ wide turning in slightly at the front and showing 5 toes on fore and hind feet. Hindprints 7–9″ long, 5″ wide. Individually, prints (especially hindprints) look as if made by a flat-footed man in moccasins, except that large toe is outermost, smallest toe innermost and occasionally fails to register. In soft earth or mud, claw indentations usually visible just in front of toe marks. Bears have a shuffling walk; hind and front tracks are paired, with hindtrack several inches before front track on same side. Stride about 1′ long. Sometimes when walking slowly, hindfeet either partially or completely overlap foreprints; when running, hindfeet brought down well ahead, with gaps of 3′ or more between complete sets of tracks.

Breeding: Mates June–early July; 1 litter of 1–5 (usually twins or triplets) born January–early February, generally every other year. Sows mate during their third year, with most producing 1 cub the first winter, 2 on subsequent breedings. While the mother sleeps in the den, the almost naked newborns nestle into her fur. The mother often lies on her back or side to nurse, but sometimes sits on her haunches, with cubs perched on her lap, almost like human infants. Young weigh ½ lb. at birth.

Habitat: In the East, primarily forests and swamps; in the West, forests and wooded mountains seldom higher than 7,000′ (2,100 m).

Range: Most of Canada, Alaska, south on West Coast through n California, in Rocky Mountain states to Mexico, n Minnesota, Wisconsin, and Michigan; in New England, New York, and Pennsylvania south through Appalachians; in Southeast, most of Florida, and s Louisiana.

This uniquely American bear, although primarily nocturnal, may be seen at any time, day or night, ranging in a home area of 8–10 sq. miles, sometimes as many as 15. It is solitary except briefly during mating season and when congregating to feed at dumps. Its walk is clumsy, but in its bounding trot it attains surprising speed, with bursts up to 30 mph. A powerful swimmer, it also climbs trees, either for protection or food. Though classed as a carnivore, most of its diet consists of vegetation, including twigs, buds, leaves, nuts, roots, various fruit, corn, berries, and newly sprouted plants. In spring, the bear peels off tree bark to get at the inner, or cambium, layer; it tears apart rotting logs for grubs, beetles, crickets, and ants. Small to medium-size mammals or other vertebrates are also eaten. A good fisherman, the Black Bear often wades in streams or lakes, snagging fish with its jaws or pinning them with a paw. It rips open bee trees to feast on honey, honeycomb, bees, and larvae. In the fall, the bear puts on a good supply of fat, then holes up for the winter in a sheltered place, such as a cave, crevice, hollow tree or log, roots of a fallen tree, and, in the Hudson Bay area, sometimes a snowbank. Excrement is never found in the den: the bear stops eating a few days before retiring, but then consumes roughage, such as leaves, pine needles, and bits of its own hair. These pass through the digestive system and form an anal plug, up to 1′ long, which is voided when the bear emerges in the spring. Bears are often a problem around open dumps, becoming dangerous as they lose their fear of man, and occasionally people have been killed by them. Hunting Black Bear is a popular sport; the flesh is good, and the hides are used for rugs. The helmets of Britain's Buckingham Palace guards are made of its fur.

294, 295 Grizzly Bear, including Brown Bears
(*Ursus arctos*)

Description: *Yellowish-brown to black,* often with white-tipped hairs, giving grizzled appearance. *Hump over shoulders.* Facial profile usually somewhat concave. Outer pair of incisors larger than inner 2. Claws of front feet nearly 4″ (10 cm) long. Height at shoulders about 4¼′ (130 cm). L 6–7′ (180–213 cm); T 3″ (76 mm); HF 10¼″ (26 cm); Wt 323–1,496 lb. (147–680 kg).

Similar Species: Black Bear is smaller, lacks shoulder hump, and has all 3 pairs of upper incisors equal in size. Alaskan Brown Bear (*U.a. middendorffi*), once regarded as a separate species, is a typically brown northwestern coastal Grizzly, usually 800–1,200 lb. at 8–9 years of age, but reaching 1,700 lb., making it the world's largest terrestrial carnivore.

Sign: Shallowly dug depression and a high, loose mound of branches, earth, or natural debris heaped over it conceal a cache of carrion or a kill. Beware of this sign, for a bear will not be far away. Other signs include overturned rocks, torn-up berry patches, raggedly rooted round, torn logs, girdled, bark-stripped, clawed, and bitten "bear trees" (marks higher than those made by Black Bears, with largest tooth marks higher than a man's head and claw slashes perhaps twice as high). Hair tufts on trees, which may be polished from rubbing over several seasons. Large, gaping pits indicate that Grizzlies have dug for rodents. A wide, deep snowslide is occasionally gouged by a Grizzly sliding down a short incline on its haunches. *Bed:* Usually in thickets, oval depression about 1′ deep, 3′ wide, 4′ long, matted with leaves or needles and sometimes small boughs. *Scat:* Usually cylindrical, often more

than 2″ wide; and, like Black Bear's, possibly showing animal hair, vegetation fibers or husks. Droppings may be rounded, or massed in areas where vegetation is the primary food.

Trail: Trampled in tall grass, may undulate, and is marked by deep depressions.

Tracks: Shaped and placed like those of Black Bear but larger and with different claw marks; the long, relatively straight foreclaws print farther ahead of toe pads, and hindclaws register only occasionally. Hindprint of a large Grizzly may be 10–12″ long and 7–8″ wide in the front; foreprint often as wide, about half as long. In soft mud, tracks may be even larger. Even on hard ground, Alaskan Brown Bears often leave bigger prints, with hindtracks more than 16″ long, 10½″ wide, and sunk 2″ deep in hard sand. Stride averages 2′, may be 8–9′ during a bounding run.

Breeding: Mates late June–early July; 1 litter of 1–4, average 2, born January–March every other year. Young are exceptionally small, the size of rats, and weigh only 1 lb.

Habitat: Semi-open country usually in mountainous areas.

Range: Alaska, Yukon, and Mackenzie District of Northwest Territories south through most of British Columbia and w Alberta to s central Nevada.

Primarily nocturnal, the great, shaggy Grizzly has a low, clumsy walk, swinging its head back and forth, but when necessary it can lope as fast as a horse. Grizzly cubs can climb, though not as nimbly as Black Bear cubs, but lose the ability during their first year. In winter, Grizzlies put on a layer of fat, as much as 400 lb., and become lethargic. They den up in a protected spot, such as a cave, crevice, hollow tree, or a hollow dug out under a rock, returning year after year to a good den.

Not being true hibernators, they can be awakened easily. Omnivorous, they feed on many kinds of plants, including roots or sprouts, fungi, berries, fish, insects, large and small mammals, and carrion. When salmon migrate upstream to spawn, these normally solitary bears congregate along rivers, and vicious fights may erupt among them. More often, they establish dominance through size and threats, spacing themselves out, with the largest, most aggressive individuals taking the choicest stations. The Grizzly is adept at catching fish with a swift snap of its huge jaws. Occasionally it will pin a fish underwater with its forepaws, then thrust its head underwater to clasp the catch in its teeth. It digs insects from rotting logs and small mammals from their burrows, sometimes tearing up much ground in the process. It caches the remains of larger mammals, such as Elk, Moose, Mountain Goats, sheep, or livestock, returning to the cache until all meat is consumed. While the Grizzly normally avoids man, it is the most unpredictable and dangerous of all bears. Although in captivity a Grizzly has lived 47 years, the life span in the wild is 15–34 years.

296 Polar Bear
(*Ursus maritimus*)

Description: *White fur;* black nose pad, lips, and eyes. Relatively long legs and long neck. Ears very small. Males considerably larger than females. Height at shoulder about 4' (120 cm). L 7–11' (213–335 cm); T 3⅛–5⅛" (8–13 cm); HF 13" (33 cm); Wt 924–1,100 lb. (420–500 kg).

Sign: A seal carcass, partly eaten but with no blubber remaining. Wheeling, calling gulls sometimes mark the location of

such a carcass, as may the presence of Arctic Foxes or their tracks in association with bear tracks.

Scat: Large, dark, cylindrical, like that of big Grizzly.

Tracks: Similar to those of the largest Grizzlies but smaller, rounder, blurred by hair. Hindprint 12–13" long, usually at least 9" wide. Claws, though sharp enough to grip ice or slippery snow when the bear runs, are short and seldom leave marks in front of prints. Any bear track on an ice floe is a Polar Bear's.

Breeding: Mates April–May; litters of 1–4 (average 2) born November –January every other year (or sometimes every third year) while females are in their winter dens, excavations in snowbanks, ice ridges, or hillsides. Cubs weigh about 2 lb. at birth; they remain with mother about 1½ years, denning with her the winter after their birth.

Habitat: Broken ice packs at northern edge of the continent, near North Pole; seldom far inland.

Range: Extreme n Canada and Alaska and on Arctic islands.

Unlike most North American bears, which are primarily nocturnal, the Polar Bear is active at all times of the year, searching for prey on both long summer days and long winter nights. Adaptations to its Arctic existence include color, which blends with the snowy environment and so provides useful camouflage for avoiding enemies and capturing prey; large size, which helps maintain temperature by reducing surface-heat loss; and furred feet, which insulate against cold and provide traction on icy surfaces. Because the hairs of its waterproof fur are hollow, they are especially insulating and increase the bear's buoyancy when swimming. An excellent swimmer, it paddles at about 6½ mph with front feet only, hindfeet trailing—a trait

unique among 4-footed land animals—
and can remain submerged about 2
minutes. While swimming or treading
water, it stretches its long neck for a
better view, as it does on land. Owing
to the scarcity of plants in its icy
habitat, it is the most carnivorous
North American bear, with canine
teeth larger and molariform teeth
sharper than in other bears. Acute
scenting ability enables the Polar Bear
to locate prey even when hidden by
drifts or pressure ridges. It stalks seal
young and sometimes adults and young
Walrus often by swimming underwater
to their ice floes. While Hair Seals are
its staple, it also feeds on fish, birds
and their eggs, small mammals, dead
animals (including whales), shellfish,
crabs, starfish, and mushrooms, grasses,
berries, and algae, when available. It
hollows out a winter den in a protected
snowbank, where it remains in a
lethargic condition from November to
March. Males den for much shorter
periods, from late November to late
January, or may be abroad occasionally
at any time of the year. One of the
world's largest denning areas for Polar
Bears, on the lowlands of Hudson Bay
and James Bay, was discovered in 1969
and is the only known region where
they den in earth rather than in snow.
They excavate caves in lake and stream
banks and peat hummocks by digging
down to the permafrost. This area is far
south for the species, and it is believed
that they use the permafrost dens again
in summer to cool off. No large
denning areas have yet been found in
Alaska; some Polar Bears in that region
may winter in Siberia, drifting across to
Alaska on ice floes in spring. Polar
Bears are a source of food and hides for
Eskimoes. There are several recorded
cases of attacks on men by Polar Bears.

RACCOON, RINGTAIL, AND COATI
(Family Procyonidae)

The procyonid family comprises a diverse group of animals, ranging from the lesser pandas (*Ailurus*) of Asia to the olingos (*Bassaricyon*) of Central and South America. Most species, however, occur in the southern parts of the New World; only 3 species are found in our range. North American procyonids are characterized by their long tails with dark and light banding. Their cheek teeth are blunt rather than sharp, indicating that these carnivores have adapted to eat a wide variety of foods, including vegetable matter. They all have 5 clawed toes on each foot and, with the exception of the Ringtail (*Bassariscus astutus*), walk flat on the soles of their feet, as do bears and men. The Ringtail, which walks on its toes, is the only species with retractible claws. Most are good climbers and will den in hollow trees, when available; if not, they may use ground burrows or caves. With the exception of the Coati (*Nasua nasua*), all are nocturnal. Most tend to be social, often remaining together as family groups and, in the case of the Coati, in larger bands.

---

201 **Ringtail**
"Miner's Cat" "Civet Cat"
"Cacomistle"
(*Bassariscus astutus*)

Description: *Yellowish-gray* above; whitish-buff below. Body catlike; face somewhat foxlike. Very long, bushy tail with 14–16 bands, alternately black and white, ending with black at tip; black bands do not meet on underside. Relatively large ears and eyes. *No black mask;* white or pale eye ring. Five toes on each foot; claws partially retractile.

L 24¼–31⅞″ (616–811 mm); T 12¼–17¼″ (310–438 mm); HF 2¼–3⅛″ (55–78 mm); Wt 1⅞–2⅜ lb. (870–1,100 g).

Similar Species: Coati is larger, with a thin, indistinctly banded tail. Raccoon is much larger, with a black mask and shorter tail.

Sign: Tree holes, usually small, with a gnawed rim.

Den: In cliffs, between or under rocks, and in hollow trees, stumps, and logs.

Scat: Usually elongated and cylindrical, but with great variations in size and shape; in dry habitat, tends to crumble.

Tracks: Unlike its relatives, the Ringtail leaves no long heel prints. Prints 1–2¾″ long, 2″ wide, catlike, with no noticeable differences between fore and hind prints. Five toes on each foot, with no claws showing. Because habitat is usually dry and often rocky, tracks are not easily found.

Breeding: In Texas, mates early April; litter of 2–4 young born late May–early June, sometimes in a nest. After 3–4 weeks, male joins mate in bringing food to den for offspring. Young at birth are white haired, fuzzy, and stubby tailed but soon acquire adult coloration and longer tails. They hunt independently at about 4 months and disperse in late fall.

Habitat: Various; most common in rocky situations, such as jumbles of boulders, canyons, talus slopes, rock piles; less common in wooded areas with hollow trees; sometimes about buildings.

Range: Southwestern Oregon, California, s Nevada, s two thirds of Utah, w Colorado, and s Kansas south through Arizona, New Mexico, Oklahoma, and Texas.

In a narrow den often padded with moss, grass, or leaves, the Ringtail sleeps by day, either on its side, its back (summer), or with its tail wrapped about its curled body (winter). Upon awakening, it grooms itself, scratching with a hindleg and licking its fur and forepaws, which it then uses to clean ears, cheeks, and nose. By night the Ringtail ambushes its prey, then pounces, forcing the prey down with its forepaws and delivering a fatal bite to the neck. It generally begins by devouring the head of its victim. Better mousers than cats, Ringtails were placed in frontier mines to control rodents, earning the name "Miner's Cat." Its varied diet includes grasshoppers and crickets; small mammals, such as rats, mice, squirrels, and rabbits, including carrion; small birds; fruit, such as persimmons, hackberries, juniper, and mistletoe; spiders, scorpions, centipedes; snakes, lizards, toads, and frogs. It can leap like a squirrel, and its extraordinarily sharp claws permit it to climb walls or trees. Young Ringtails squeak; adults bark, scream, and snarl. When threatened or fighting, the Ringtail screams and secretes a foul-smelling fluid from the anal glands, earning the name "Civet Cat," an allusion to the African carnivore *Civetticus civetta,* which produces a musky substance, civet, used in perfumes. The name "Cacomistle" derives from *tlacomiztli,* which in the language of Mexico's Nahuatl Indians means "half mountain lion." Neither its fur nor meat is valuable, but man is one of its chief predators along with the Bobcat and the Great Horned Owl.

202 Raccoon
(*Procyon lotor*)

Description: Reddish-brown above, with much black; grayish below. Distinguished by a *bushy tail with 4–6 alternating black and brown or brownish-gray rings* and a *black mask* outlined in white. Ears relatively small. L 23¾–37⅜" (603–950 mm); T 7½–16" (192–406 mm);

HF 3¼–5⅜″ (83–138 mm); Wt 12–
48 lb. (5.4–21.6 kg).

Similar Species: The Coati has a long, thin, indistinctly
banded tail and lacks the black mask;
the Ringtail lacks mask, is much
smaller.

Sign: Along shores, streams, or ponds,
crayfish leavings; in cornfields, broken
stalks, shredded husks, scattered
kernels, and gnawed cob ends.
Den: Usually in a hollow tree, which
may have scat accumulated about its
base and trunk scratched or bark torn.
Scat: Droppings inconsistent in shape,
but generally cylindrical, uniform in
diameter, about 2″ long, granular,
varying from black to reddish and
sometimes bleached white. They
resemble the Opossum's and skunk's,
but are often deposited on large tree
limbs, stones crossing a stream, or logs.
Tracks: Hindprint 3¼–4¼″ long,
much longer than wide; resembles a
miniature human footprint with
abnormally long toes. Foreprint much
shorter, 3″, almost as wide as long;
claws show on all 5 toes. Tracks are
large for animal's size because Raccoon
is flat-footed, like bears and men.
Stride 6–20″, averaging 14″. When
walking, left hindfoot is almost beside
right forefoot. When running, makes
many short, lumbering bounds,
bringing hindfeet down ahead of
forefeet in a pattern like oversize
squirrel tracks.

Breeding: Though Raccoons are sedentary, males
travel miles in search of mates. Female
accepts only 1 male per season, usually
in February in the North, December in
the South. He remains in her den a
week or more, then seeks another mate.
Lethargic during pregnancy, the female
prefers to make a leaf nest in large
hollow trees but may also use such
protected places as culverts, caves, rock
clefts, Woodchuck dens, or under
wind-thrown trees. Litter of 1–7
young, average 4–5, born April–May,

weighing about 2 oz. at birth, open eyes at about 3 weeks, clamber about den mouth at 7–8 weeks, are weaned by late summer. At first, mother carries them about by nape of neck, as a cat carries kittens, but soon leads them on cautious foraging expeditions, boosting them up trees if threatened but attacking ferociously if cornered. Some young disperse in autumn; others may remain but are driven away by the female before she bears her next litter, as den space is limited. Some yearling females may be pregnant themselves and must quickly find dens of their own.

Habitat: Various, but most common along wooded streams.

Range: Southern edge of s provinces of Canada; most of U.S. except for portions of the Rocky Mountain states, central Nevada, and Utah.

Native only to the Americas, the Raccoon is nocturnal and solitary except when breeding or caring for its young. Although territories overlap, when 2 meet, they growl, lower their heads, bare their teeth, and flatten their ears; the fur on the backs of their necks and shoulders stands on end, generally with the result that both back off. During particularly cold spells, the Raccoon may sleep for several days at a time but does not hibernate. Its vocalizations are varied, including purrs, whimpers, snarls, growls, hisses, screams, and whinnies. Omnivorous, it eats grapes, nuts, grubs, crickets, grasshoppers, voles, deer mice, squirrels, other small mammals, birds' eggs, and nestlings. It spends most nights foraging along streams but may raid Muskrat houses to eat the young; prey on rice rats nesting in walls (afterward perhaps taking the lodge as its den); prowl woodland streams and swim, but not dive, for crayfish, frogs, worms, fish, dragonfly larvae, clams, turtles, and turtle eggs;

climb trees to cut or knock down acorns; and in residential areas, tip over or climb into garbage cans. The Raccoon's nimble fingers, almost as deft as a monkey's, can easily turn doorknobs and open refrigerators. If water is conveniently close, it sometimes appears to wash its food, getting its scientific name, *lotor,* which means "a washer." The objective, however, is not to clean the food, but rather to knead and tear at it, feeling for matter that should be rejected; wetting the paws enhances the sense of touch. In fact, its common name comes from *Aroughcoune,* used in colonial times by the Algonquin Indians of Virginia to mean "he scratches with his hands." "Coon hunting" is a popular sport in late autumn, when Raccoons are very active, fattening themselves for winter. At night, dogs trail the Raccoon until it is treed; then hunters make their way to the tree and shoot the animal out. If the Raccoon is young or small, the hunters may spare it; for many, the sport lies in listening to their hounds and observing the skill of their performance. Sometimes, instead of treeing, a Raccoon leads hounds to a stream or lake. A dog that swims well can easily overtake a Raccoon in the water, but the Raccoon, a furious fighter, can then whip a single dog.

Raccoon meat is good (tasting somewhat like lamb), but nearly all fat should be removed. Pelts are valuable, and during the 1920's a coonskin coat was a collegiate craze.

205 Coati
(*Nasua nasua*)

Description: Grayish-brown. *Long, thin, somewhat indistinctly banded tail* (6–7 bands). Long, pointed snout; white toward tip and around eye, sometimes with black or dark brown patches on upper part. Ears small; dark feet. Male twice as large as female. L 33⅜–52¾" (85–134 cm); T 16½–26¾" (42–68 cm); HF 3¾–4¾" (95–122 mm); Wt 16½–27 lb. (7.5–12.2 kg).

Similar Species: Raccoon is stouter, with a black mask and shorter, bushy, distinctly banded tail; Ringtail is smaller, with a bushy tail and much larger ears.

Sign: *Scat:* Usually cylindrical, similar to Raccoon's, and equally variable.

Tracks: 3" long, 2" wide, hind and fore prints; all with 5 toes; claws show on foreprints only. Because not quite as fully plantigrade as the Raccoon, less of hind heel pad registers, and prints are shorter.

Breeding: Mates January–March; 4–6 young, with coats darker than adults, born in maternity den in rocky niche or similar shelter in spring, after gestation of about 77 days.

Habitat: Mountain forests, usually near water; also rocky, wooded canyons.

Range: Southeastern quarter of Arizona, sw New Mexico, Big Bend and Brownsville areas of s Texas. Abundant in Huachuca, Patagonia, and Tumacacori mountains of se Arizona.

More active by day and more gregarious than other members of the raccoon family, Coatis are fairly conspicuous, as they travel about in troupes of 4–25, usually females and their young. They hold their long tails high and nearly erect, except for the curled tip, and their young engage in constant noisy play, chasing each other up and down trees. As is usual among social animals, the Coati is much more vocal than the Raccoon and snorts, grunts, screams, whines, and chatters. It spends its days foraging for food, which includes invertebrates and lizards found in soil surface litter. Extremely fond of fruit, including that of the manzanita, juniper, and prickly pear, a troupe may ignore customary foods and visit a fruit-bearing tree daily until it is stripped. Grooming sessions frequently interrupt feeding; a Coati combs its fur with its teeth or the claws of either feet or hands. During the hottest part of the day, it may nap in a shady spot. It swims well and climbs excellently, using its long, semiprehensile tail to help balance on branches and, by wrapping the tail around vines or small branches, slow its descent. When startled, it generally climbs a tree; but when treed by man, it descends rapidly and may injure dogs. It spends the night in trees, ascending toward dusk. As it inhabits warm latitudes, it remains active in winter and needs no den for warmth. The Coati is abundant in the Huachuca Mountains of Arizona where it is believed to have damaged orchards and killed chickens and dogs. Although a record of this species dates from 1892 at Fort Huachuca, its abundance in the area may be a relatively recent phenomenon.

WEASELS, SKUNKS, BADGERS, OTTERS, AND ALLIES
(Family Mustelidae)

Members of this family, which vary greatly in appearance and habits, include the arboreal Marten, the aquatic otters, and the burrowing Badger. Most mustelids are relatively small animals, with long, low-slung bodies, short legs, short, rounded ears, and a thick silky coat that makes them valuable fur-bearers. All are solitary, primarily nocturnal, and active throughout the year. Most have paired anal scent glands; in skunks these are highly developed for defense and can spray their powerful secretion accurately as far as 15'. In many other species, the secretions, while often pungent, are used more as social and sexual signals. In their reproductive cycles, many mustelids exhibit delayed implantation, which means that the fertilized egg floats free in the uterus for an extended period (180–200 days in the Spotted Skunk) instead of immediately implanting in the uterine wall. Development of the embryo is suspended until implantation finally occurs, after which it proceeds rapidly. This delay is advantageous, allowing animals to mate in summer or autumn and bear young in spring, when food is plentiful and conditions for growth and survival are optimal. While valued for their fur, most mustelids have a poor public image. Skunks are disliked because of their highly effective means of self-defense. Weasels and their kin are mainly thought of as killers of poultry and nesting game birds, although modern poultry-raising methods have minimized such predation. In fact, these carnivores more often serve to control rodents.

211 Marten
"Pine Marten" "American Sable"
(*Martes americana*)

Description: *Weasel-like. Brownish,* varying from
dark brown to blond, with paler head
and underparts, darker legs, *orange or
buff throat patch.* Long, *bushy tail;*
pointed snout; small ears. Males larger
than females. L 19¼–26⅞" (490–682
mm); T 5¼–9½" (135–240 mm); HF
2¾–3⅞" (70–98 mm); Wt 1–3½ lb.
(448–1,568 g).

Similar Species: Fisher is much larger and lacks orange
throat patch. Mink is darker, with
shorter tail and white on chin; lacks
orange throat patch.

Sign: *Scat:* Resembles Mink's but often
contains bits of fruit or nuts; scat
stations, where droppings are left
repeatedly.

Tracks: like Mink's but slightly larger,
1½–1⅞" wide; straddle 2½–3", to 6"
in snow; walking stride 9" for males, 6"
for females, more than doubles when
running.

Breeding: Mates midsummer; delayed
implantation; 2–4 young born blind,
naked, around April in leaf nest.

Habitat: Forests, particularly coniferous.

Range: Most of Canada; in the West, south to
n California through Rocky Mountains;
in the East, to n New England and n
New York.

Martens are active in early morning,
late afternoon, and on overcast days,
traversing a home range of 5–15 sq.
mi. They spend much of their time in
trees. Both sexes establish scent posts
by rubbing their scent glands on
branches. Usually Martens avoid each
other; if 2 meet, they bare their teeth
and snarl. They pounce on prey; the
Red Squirrel is favored, but flying
squirrels, rabbits, mice, and birds are
also taken. The varied diet also includes
carrion, eggs, berries, conifer seeds,
and honey. Surplus meat is sometimes

buried, though Martens are generally poor diggers. Inquisitive, they can be coaxed from their dens in fallen logs or tree holes by squeaking like a mouse. Their valuable pelts have led to their extirpation in many areas, and in others lumbering has destroyed their habitats and reduced populations. Martens are now protected and making comebacks in many localities.

213 Fisher
(*Martes pennanti*)

Description: Long, thin body; *dark brown above and below with grayish cast on head. Bushy tail;* broad head with pointed snout; small ears. Males larger than females. L 31⅛–40¾″ (790–1,033 mm); T 11¾–16⅝″ (300–422 mm); HF 3½–5⅝″ (89–143 mm); Wt 3–18 lb. (1.4–8.2 kg).

Similar Species: Marten smaller with orange throat patch; Mink much smaller with white chin patch.

Sign: Porcupine kills.
Scat: 4–6″ long, dark, roughly cylindrical, often segmented; may show fur, bone, berries, nuts. Scat with Porcupine quills is almost a sure sign of Fisher.
Tracks: Similar to Mink's and Marten's but larger; wider than long, with claws showing; 2″ wide on dirt, more than 2½″ on snow. May end abruptly where tree is climbed.

Breeding: Mates March–April, right after giving birth in a rock crevice or hollow tree; delayed implantation, with gestation of nearly a year; 1–5 young born blind the following spring; weaned at 3–4 months.

Habitat: Mature forests.

Range: Southern tier of Canadian provinces south to n California and in the Rocky Mountains to Utah; in the East, to n New England and New York.

Although primarily nocturnal like most mustelids, the Fisher is sometimes abroad by day. A good climber and swimmer, it travels a home range of 50–150 sq. mi., even larger in winter when food is scarce, using well-established trails or running on fallen logs, and moving between trees, from branch to branch. Snowshoe Hares and Porcupines are its main prey. Although Fishers are adept at flipping Porcupines over, ripping them open, and then feeding along the unprotected abdomen, occasionally one is injured or even killed by the quills. Squirrels, mice, chipmunks, carrion, fruit and other plants are also eaten. Although the origin of its common name is unknown, the Mink's habit of fishing may have been mistakenly ascribed to the Fisher. It dens in hollow trees or rocky crevices, shifting sites occasionally, and may use underbrush or a hole dug in snow as a temporary den. If disturbed, it hunches its back like a cat and may hiss, growl, snarl, or spit. A valuable fur-bearer, with female skins especially prized, in many areas it has been extirpated; loss of habitat has also depleted populations, for it requires extensive wilderness.

208, 210 **Ermine**
"Short-tailed Weasel"
(*Mustela erminea*)

Description: Elongated body, *dark brown above, white below*. Tail brown with black tip; *feet white*. In winter, throughout northern range, white with black tail tip, nose, and eyes. Males almost twice as large as females. L 7½–13½" (190–344 mm); T 1¾–3½" (42–90 mm); HF 1⅛–1¾" (28–43 mm); Wt 1⅝–6⅜ oz. (45–182 g).

Similar Species: Least Weasel is smaller, with shorter tail that lacks black tip; Long-tailed

Weasel is usually larger, with longer
tail and brownish feet in summer;
Black-footed Ferret yellowish-brown,
with dark mask around eyes.

Sign: *Scat:* Similar to Long-tailed Weasel's
but slightly smaller.
Tracks: Similar to Long-tailed Weasel's
but usually slightly smaller.

Breeding: Mates in July; 4–9 young born blind,
with fine hair, in spring in some
protected area, such as under a log, a
rockpile, or tree stump; eyes open at 35
days; young play among themselves,
cared for by both parents.

Habitat: Varied: open woodlands, brushy areas,
grasslands, wetlands, farmlands.

Range: Most of Canada south to n California, w
Colorado, and n New Mexico in West;
to n Iowa, Michigan, Pennsylvania, and
Maryland in East.

Though the Ermine hunts mainly on
the ground, often running on fallen
logs, it can climb trees and occasionally
even pursues prey into water. After a
rapid dash, it pounces on its victim
with all 4 feet, biting through the neck
near the base of the skull. Mice are its
main food, but it also eats shrews, baby
rabbits, and birds. Its den—which may
be found beneath a log, stump, roots,
brushpile, or stone wall—usually has
several entrances and contains a nest of
vegetation mixed with hair.
Vocalizations include grunts, hisses,
chatters, and a shrill call note. In the
southernmost parts of its range it does
not turn white in winter. The winter-
white fur of both the Ermine and Long-
tailed Weasel is known as ermine and
highly valued; the black-tipped tails are
the traditional trim on the robes of
royalty.

207 Least Weasel
(*Mustela nivalis*)

Description: *Tiny. Brown above, white below. Tail very short, brown; feet white.* All white in winter except in southern part of range. L 6¾–8⅛″ (172–206 mm); T ⅞–1½″ (24–38 mm); HF ¾–⅞″ (19–23 mm); Wt 1¼–1¾ oz. (37–50 g).

Similar Species: Ermine and Long-tailed Weasel are both larger with black tail tips; Black-footed Ferret yellowish-brown, with dark mask around eyes.

Sign: *Scat:* Similar to that of larger weasels but smaller.
Tracks: Similar to those of larger weasels but much smaller; straddle 1¼–1¾″; leaps occasionally 2′.

Breeding: Mates year round; up to 3 litters per year; 3–6 young born in any month, usually in the abandoned burrow of another animal; weaned at 4–7 weeks.

Habitat: Grassy and brushy fields, marsh areas.

Range: Most of Canada south in Midwest to e Montana, Nebraska, Iowa, n Illinois, n Indiana, Ohio, Pennsylvania, West Virginia, through the s Appalachian Mountains.

The Least Weasel is the smallest carnivore in North America and one of the most ferocious. Previously known as *Mustela rixosa,* it is now considered to be the same species as the European Least Weasel. Although primarily nocturnal, it is abroad by day over its home range of less than 2 acres. It feeds almost entirely on meadow mice, chasing them over their runways, pouncing upon them, and killing them with a swift bite at the base of the skull; it also takes an occasional shrew or mole. Despite the legend, weasels do not suck blood; this notion probably arose from the fact that a weasel's snout is often bloodied when it bites its prey. It dens in the abandoned burrow of another small mammal, such as a mouse, gopher, or ground squirrel, using the rodent's grass nest but lining it with mouse hair. When disturbed, it gives a shrill squeaking call, and it may hiss when threatened. Foxes, cats, and owls are its chief predators.

209 Long-tailed Weasel
(*Mustela frenata*)

Description: *Brown above, white below.* Tail brown with black tip; *feet brownish.* In Southwest, white on face. During winter in northern latitudes, entirely white except for black nose, eyes, and tail tip. Males almost twice as large as females. L 11–21¾″ (28–55 cm); T 3⅛–6⅜″ (8–16 cm); HF 1⅛–2″ (29–51 mm); Wt 3–9⅜ oz. (85–267 g).

Similar Species: Ermine is smaller, with shorter tail and white feet in summer; Black-footed Ferret yellowish-brown, with black mask around eyes.

Sign: Cache of several dead mice under log or in burrow. Drag marks in deep snow; holes where weasel plunged under snow.
Scat: Dark brown or black, long, slender, often tapering at one end, often segmented; frequently showing hair or bits of bone; deposited on rocks, logs, or stumps.
Tracks: hindprints ¾″ wide, 1″ long or more, usually with only 4 of the 5 toes printing; foreprints slightly wider, but approximately half as long. Hindfeet usually placed in or near foreprints, but prints are sometimes side by side, more often with 1 slightly ahead; straddle 3″. Stride varies as weasels run and bound, often alternating long and short leaps: when carrying prey or stalking, 12″; when running, 20″.

Breeding: Mates in midsummer; 4–9 young born blind, nearly naked, in early May in abandoned dens of other small mammals; disperse at 7–8 weeks, when males are already larger than mother.

Females mate in first year, males not until second season.

Habitat: Varied: forested, brushy, and open areas, including farmlands, preferably near water.

Range: Southern British Columbia, Alberta, Manitoba, and Saskatchewan south through most of U.S. except se California and much of Arizona. Range extends to Bolivia.

Weasels are wholly carnivorous, preying mainly on mice but also taking rabbits, chipmunks, shrews, rats, and birds, including poultry. They attack prey several times their size, climb 15–20′ up a tree after a squirrel, and occasionally go on killing sprees. Their killing instinct is triggered by the smell of blood; even an injured sibling will be killed and eaten. Furtive hunters, weasels move so sinuously that they seem to flow over rocks and logs; and in their relentless pursuit of prey, their supple bodies slip through the smallest burrows or crannies. Vocalizations are varied: weasels squeak and hiss when annoyed, make a purring sound when content, and sometimes utter a rapid chatter; during mating season, females give a reedy, twittering call. When alarmed, enraged, or excited by the mating urge, their anal glands release a powerful malodorous musk. Sometimes a weasel drags its rump, presumably to leave scent that informs other weasels of its sex and perhaps even its identity. Weasels den in the abandoned burrows of other mammals, often chipmunks but also ground squirrels, moles, or pocket gophers. But they make their own grass nests, usually lined with mouse hair. In the northern part of their range, weasels turn white in winter; but to the south, within a 600-mile-wide transcontinental belt, some molt to white while others remain brown. The color change is evidently genetically determined: if a northern weasel is captured and taken south, it still turns white in winter, and a southern weasel transported north remains brown. The time of the molt is governed by the length of the period of daylight; weasels are piebald before the color change is completed. Hawks, owls, cats, foxes, and snakes prey upon these weasels, which are also taken by trappers, though their pelts are not of great value.

212 Black-footed Ferret
(*Mustela nigripes*)

Description: Minklike in shape. *Yellowish-brown or buff above*, with brownish wash on back; slightly paler below. *Tip of tail and feet dark or black*. Dark or black *mask around eyes*, with *face white* above and below mask. Males larger than females. L 19¾–22⅝″ (500–573 mm); T 4½–5½″ (114–139 mm); HF 2–2⅞″ (51–73 mm); Wt 18¾–22⅛ oz. (535–633 g).

Similar Species: Weasels brown above, white below; Mink uniformly brown. Both lack dark mask.

Sign: Fresh, untamped earth at entrance of prairie dog burrow often indicates occupancy by a Black-footed Ferret. (Prairie dogs tamp down mounds of excavated earth.)
Scat: Approximately 3″ long, usually segmented when it contains much hair.
Tracks: Similar to Mink's, but longer and narrower with more of heel printing. Hindprint approximately 2″ long, 1½″ wide; foreprint nearly as long, but about half as wide. Both prints show 5 toes with claw marks visible.

Breeding: Little known; females nesting in prairie dog burrows observed with 3–5 young born late spring–early summer.

Habitat: Arid prairies; prairie dog towns.

Range: Great Plains: s Alberta and s
Saskatchewan south to w Oklahoma,
nw Texas, New Mexico, nw Arizona.

The Black-footed Ferret is the rarest of
North American mammals. The
Department of the Interior Fish and
Wildlife Service lists the Black-footed
Ferret as one of the Ten Most Wanted
endangered species in North America.
Its range originally extended as far
north as Alaska, but the slaughter of
prairie dogs—its primary food source
—has reduced its range considerably
and driven it to near extinction.
A Ferret prefers living in a prairie dog
town surrounded by its favorite source
of food. Sometimes it sits erect, looking
about for a burrow to raid. A prairie
dog that catches sight of it will dart
quickly underground. The Ferret,
keeping its body close to the ground,
stalks to the prairie dog's burrow and
peers into the plunge hole. If the prey
is near the surface, the Ferret lunges for
it. Otherwise, it slithers down the
tunnel. It quickly dispatches its prey,
burying any remains. Having occupied
its victim's home, the Ferret will
sometimes poke its head from the
burrow to scan its territory. If it
decides to set up residence in the
burrow, it redecorates extensively,
enlargening the entrance and building
additional living chambers. When
prairie dogs are scarce, the Ferret will
eat other rodents, including mice,
gophers, and ground squirrels. It may
also eat birds, their eggs, and small
reptiles. Attempts are being made to
restore Ferret populations in the West,
notably in South Dakota, where Wind
Cave National Park offers the best
opportunity for seeing this species in
the wild.

214 Mink
(*Mustela vison*)

Description: Sleek-bodied with lustrous fur, *uniformly chocolate brown to black* with *white spotting on chin and throat.* Tail long, somewhat bushy. Males larger than females. L 19¼–28¼" (491–720 mm); T 6¼–7⅜" (158–194 mm); HF 2¼–3" (57–75 mm); Wt 1½–3½ lb. (700–1,600 g).

Similar Species: Marten has longer tail, orange throat patch; weasels have light underparts; Black-footed Ferret yellowish-brown, with dark mask around eyes.

Sign: Hole in snow where it plunged after prey; trough in snow, similar to otter slide but smaller.
Den: In streambanks with 4" openings.
Scat: Dark brown or black, 5–6" long, roughly cylindrical, sometimes segmented; often with bits of fur or bone especially of muskrat; deposited on beaver lodges, rocks, logs, and around den.
Tracks: Fairly round, 1¼–1¾" wide, more than 2" in snow. In clear print, heel pad and all 5 slightly webbed toes show separately; semiretractile claws may show. Hindfeet 2¼" long in mud, 3½" in snow, and placed nearly in prints of forefeet; trail of twin prints 12–26" apart depending on animal's size and speed.

Breeding: Mates in midwinter, males mating with several females but eventually living with 1; 3–6 young born blind, naked, in fur-lined nest in spring; weaned at 5–6 weeks; remain with mother until family disperses in fall.

Habitat: Along rivers, creeks, lakes, ponds, and marshes.

Range: Most of U.S. and Canada except Arizona, s California, s Utah, s New Mexico, and w Texas.

Minks of both sexes are hostile to intruders, and males fight viciously in

or out of breeding season. They maintain hunting territories by marking with a fetid discharge from the anal glands, which is at least as malodorous as a skunk's, although it does not carry as far. They swim very well, often hunting in ponds and streams, and can climb trees but do so rarely. Like weasels, Minks kill by biting their victims in the neck. Muskrats are preferred prey, but many rabbits, mice, chipmunks, fish, snakes, frogs, young snapping turtles, and marsh-dwelling birds are taken; Minks occasionally raid poultry houses. They eat on the spot or carry prey by the neck to their dens, where any surplus is cached. They den in protected places near water, often in a Muskrat burrow, an abandoned Beaver den, or hollow log, or they may dig their own den in a streambank; all dens are temporary as Minks move frequently. Foxes, Bobcats, and Great Horned Owls are known predators. If angered or alarmed, Minks may hiss, snarl, or screech and discharge their anal glands (as they do when trapped); if contented, they produce a purring sound. Pelts are highly valued. Most of those used commercially come from Minks raised on ranches, and their range of natural color reflects man's selective breeding.

206 Wolverine
"Glutton" "Skunk Bear"
(*Gulo gulo*)

Description: *Bulky,* somewhat bearlike. *Dark brown,* with *broad yellowish bands* from shoulders back over hips and meeting at base of tail; light patches in front of ears. Males larger than females. L 31½–44¼" (800–1,125 mm); T 6¾–10¼" (17–26 cm); HF 6½–8" (165–

205 mm); Wt 18–42 lb. (8.2–19.1 kg).

Sign: *Scat:* Often more than 5″ long, more or less cylindrical, usually tapering at 1 or both ends, semisegmented; often showing hair or bone.
Tracks: If perfect, all 5 toes and semiretractile claws print; small toe often does not print. Foreprint 4½–7″ long, varying with size of animal or condition of snow, and about as wide; heel pad often showing 2 lobes, a wide lobe in front of smaller round lobe, which does not always register; hindprint similar to foreprint; stride extremely variable; straddle 7–8″. Wolf's track is similar but has only 4 toes, different lobing.

Breeding: Mates April–September; implantation delayed till January; 2–5 young born early spring in some protected area, such as a thicket, or a rock crevice; remain with mother 2 years. Extended mating season increases the probability that these solitary and sparsely distributed animals will find a mate.

Habitat: Forests, tundras.

Range: Northern Canada south in West to nw Washington. Spotty distribution in se U.S.

Perhaps the most powerful mammal for its size, the ferocious Wolverine is capable of driving even a bear or Cougar from its kill. It prefers carrion but eats anything it can kill or find, including Moose or Elk slowed down in heavy snow, Beavers, deer, Porcupines, birds, squirrels, eggs, roots, and berries. It trails Caribou herds, eating the remains of wolf kills; follows trap lines, eating bait, trapped animals, and cached food; and raids cabins, marking everything it cannot eat with musk and sometimes urine and droppings. The Wolverine was once popularly called the "Glutton"; even its species name, *gulo,* means "glutton," but its truly voracious appetite may be an adaptation for survival where food is often scarce. Careless about concealing its own food caches, it marks them with a foul-smelling musk that repels other carnivores. Its den, which may contain leaves or grass, is under an uprooted tree or in a crevice, thicket, or other protected place. Alternating periods of activity and rest every 3–4 hours, a male traverses a vast home range of more than 1,000 sq. mi., which is shared with 2 or 3 females. A Wolverine can cover great distances at a slow lope, swims capably, and climbs quickly, often pouncing on prey from a tree. Its eyesight is poor, but its senses of smell and hearing are excellent. Wolverine fur is used to line or trim parka hoods, as the oils in it make it frost resistant.

204 Badger
(Taxidea taxus)

Description: *Flattish body,* wider than high, with short, bowed legs. *Shaggy coat grizzled gray to brown. White stripe* from shoulder to pointed, slightly upturned snout. *Short, bushy, yellowish tail;* cheeks white with black patch; ears small; dark feet with *large foreclaws.* Males larger than females. L 20½–34¼" (521–870 mm); T 3⅞–6¼" (98–157 mm); HF 3½–5⅛" (89–130 mm); Wt 7⅞–25⅛ lb. (3.6–11.4 kg).

Sign: *Den:* "Badger hole" or burrow with 8–12" elliptical entrance to accommodate Badger's flattish shape, surrounded by large mound of earth scattered with bone, fur, rattlesnake rattles, and droppings. Vicinity of burrow marked by other elliptical holes dug when foraging. Burrows of prairie dogs with openings enlarged to capture occupants.
Scat: Cylindrical, usually segmented; showing bits of bone and fur; definitive

only in association with other badger sign.

Tracks: Turn in sharply. Foreprint 2″ wide (as long as wide even though little heel pad shows), longer when claw tips show; hindprint narrower than foreprint, 2″ long. Gait variable, with hindfoot printing before or behind forefoot. Stride 6–12″; straddle 5–7″, wider in snow.

Breeding: Mates in late summer; delayed implantation; 2–5 young born well furred, blind, March–April; weaned June; disperse late summer.

Habitat: Open plains, farmland, sometimes edge of woods.

Range: Western U.S. east to e Texas, Oklahoma, n Missouri, n Illinois, n Indiana, n Ohio, north to se British Columbia, Alberta, Manitoba, and s Saskatchewan.

This powerful burrower has become nocturnal in areas where it encounters man, but otherwise it is often active by day, usually waddling about but occasionally moving at a clumsy trot. It feeds mainly on small mammals—especially ground squirrels, pocket gophers, rats, and mice—which it usually captures by digging out their burrows. Occasionally a Badger will dig itself into a deserted burrow and await the occupant's return. A Coyote sometimes watches attentively as the Badger digs for prey and may steal the rodent that pops from an escape exit, but it cannot be said that Coyote and Badger hunt together. The Badger captures some prey above ground and also eats birds, invertebrates, and carrion; it buries surplus meat for future use. Fond of rattlesnake, the Badger is evidently unharmed by the venom unless the snake strikes its nose. It buries its droppings and cleans itself frequently, swallowing loose hair licked from its coat.

Although primarily terrestrial, it swims

and even dives and on hot days sprawls in shallow water to cool off. Few animals will attack the Badger, because it is a formidable adversary: thick fur, loose, tough hide, and heavy neck muscles protect it as it bites, claws, and exudes (not sprays) a skunklike musk—while snarling, squealing, growling, and hissing. Despite such ferocity, it seldom picks a fight, preferring to retreat if necessary. A poor runner, it will back into a nearby burrow and face its tormentor with sharp teeth and strong claws; once inside it plugs the entrance hole. With no burrow convenient, it may dig one, showering dirt in the face of its attacker and excavating so quickly that it can outpace a man with a shovel. During the coldest part of winter, Badgers may become torpid, remaining in nest chambers deep within their burrows, but they do not hibernate.

The Badger probably gets its common name from the white mark borne like a badge on its forehead. In Europe it was once considered sport to bait Badgers, and the verb "to badger" (meaning to tease, annoy, or persecute) derives from that cruel practice. Badger hair is used to make the best quality paintbrushes, and the coarse bristles were formerly used in shaving brushes. Stockmen dislike Badgers because their many excavations pose hazards for hoofed animals, but in agricultural areas they are a valuable control on rodent populations.

---

197 Eastern Spotted Skunk
(*Spilogale putorius*)
Related species: Western Spotted

Description: Small. Black with horizontal white stripes on neck and shoulders, *irregular vertical stripes and elongated spots on sides.* Tail with white tip; white spots on top

of head, between eyes. L 13½–22¼"
(343–563 mm); T 2¾–8⅝" (68–219
mm); HF 1¼–2¼" (33–56 mm); Wt
27½–35 oz. (784–999 g).

Similar Species: Other skunks are larger, with
horizontal stripes or bands only.

Sign: *Scat:* Dark, small (¼" diameter),
irregularly cylindrical.
Tracks: Like Striped Skunk's but
smaller. Hindprint 1¼" long; heel pad
shows more definite lobing. Unlike
other skunks, stride very irregular.

Breeding: Mates in late winter; 4–5 young born
in spring, blind, furred, and achieve
adult coloration in early summer.

Habitat: Mixed woodlands and open areas,
scrub, farmlands.

Range: In the Midwest and Southeast,
Minnesota and South Dakota south to
Texas and Louisiana; in the East, s
Illinois and s central Pennsylvania south
to Mississippi, w South Carolina and
Florida.

Faster and more agile than the larger
skunks, the Spotted Skunk is also a
good climber, ascending trees to flee
predators and occasionally to forage.
More social than other skunks, several
may share a den in winter. The Spotted
Skunk's spraying behavior is unique: if
a predator refuses to retreat when it
raises its tail, the skunk turns its back,
stands on its forefeet, raises its tail
again, spreads its hindfeet, and sprays,
often for a distance of 12'. Although
most carnivores will kill and eat it if
they can do so without being sprayed,
they usually back off when the skunk
starts its threat display. The Great
Horned Owl, its chief predator, can
strike from above without warning to
carry off a young skunk before its
mother can spray. Dens are in the
burrows of other animals, hollow logs,
brushpiles, or other protected places.
Highly carnivorous, the Spotted Skunk
feeds mainly on small mammals but
also eats grubs and other insects, as

well as corn, grapes, and mulberries.
Its fur is the finest and silkiest of the
skunks, and pelts are valuable.
The closely related and similarly
colored Western Spotted Skunk
(*Spilogale gracilis*), found in the western
half of the U.S., is considered a
subspecies by some taxonomists.

198 Striped Skunk
(*Mephitis mephitis*)

Description: *Black with 2 broad white stripes on back
meeting in cap on head and shoulders;* thin
white stripe down center of face. Bushy
black tail, often with white tip or
fringe. Coloration varies from mostly
black to mostly white. Males larger
than females. L 20½–31½" (522–800
mm); T 7¼–15½" (184–393 mm); HF
2¼–3½" (57–90 mm); Wt 6–14 lb.
(2.7–6.3 kg).

Similar Species: Hog-nosed Skunk has white back and
tail, snout naked on top, and no white
facial stripe; Hooded Skunk has longer
tail and is usually mostly black with
narrow white stripes (in white-backed
phase, black hairs are interspersed).

Sign: Strong odor if skunk has recently
sprayed. Den entrance sometimes
marked with nesting material, snagged
hairs. Small pits in ground or patches
of clawed-up earth from foraging may
be skunk signs if confirmed by tracks or
hair.

Scat: Variable (like most omnivores),
generally dark, cylindrical, sometimes
segmented, varying in size.
Tracks: Show 5 toes when clear,
sometimes claws. Hindprints 1¼–2"
long, less wide, broadest at front, more
flat-footed; foreprints 1–1¾" long,
slightly wider; stride 4–6" (because
skunk shuffles and waddles, tracks are
closer than in other mustelids, and fore
and hind prints usually do not overlap);
when running, stride longer and

hindfeet print ahead of forefeet. Trail
undulates slightly because of waddling
walk.

Breeding: Mates in late winter; in mid-May, 4–7
young born blind, with very fine hair
clearly marked with black-and-white
pattern; weaned at 6–7 weeks when
scent has developed but is not yet very
potent.

Habitat: Deserts, woodlands, grassy plains,
suburbs.

Range: Most of U.S., s tier of Canadian
provinces.

Whereas most mammals have evolved
coloration that blends with their
environment, the Striped Skunk is
boldly colored, advertising to potential
enemies that it is not to be bothered.
Its anal glands hold about a tablespoon
of a fetid, oily, yellowish musk, enough
for 5 or 6 jets of spray—though 1 is
usually enough. When threatened, it
raises its tail straight up and sprays
scent 10–15'; the mist may reach 3
times as far, and the smell may carry a
mile. Fluid in the eyes causes intense
pain and fleeting loss of vision.
Ammonia or tomato juice can be used
to remove the odor; carbolic soap and
water are best for washing skin. Sudden
movement, noise, or too close an
approach can trigger the spray, and the
Striped Skunk can spray even when
held aloft by the tail. A mother skunk
is fiercely protective of her young, and
at the approach of an intruder will
snarl, stamp, raise her hindlegs, click
her teeth, and finally, arching her tail
over her back and turning her rump
toward the enemy, brace hindfeet to
spray. The procession of a mother
followed by her young in single file,
comical by day, is mysterious by night:
with the black bodies invisible, all one
sees is a series of ghostly, undulating
streaks of white. Pelts of this species are
not highly valued, but the musk, once
its odor is removed, is used as a

perfume base because of its clinging quality. These skunks usually den in a burrow abandoned by another animal, though they also dig their own and may use any protected place, such as a hollow log, crevice, or beneath a building. Omnivorous, they feed on a wide variety of vegetable matter: insects and grubs, small mammals, eggs of ground-nesting birds, and amphibians. Although they feed on many insect pests, they also root up lawns in the process; mothballs sprinkled on the ground discourage them from visiting homes or campsites, since they and many other small animals are repelled by the smell of camphor. Skunks gorge themselves in the fall to fatten up in preparation for the lean winter months. They do not hibernate but during extremely cold weather may become temporarily dormant. The Striped Skunk is currently the chief carrier of rabies in the U.S. Its only serious predator is the Great Horned Owl.

200 Hooded Skunk
(*Mephitis macroura*)

Description: Usually *black except for 1 or 2 widely separated narrow white stripes along upper side;* one phase has back and tail white with black hairs interspersed. Hair on back of neck often forms ruff. L 22–31⅛″ (558–790 mm); T 10⅞–17⅛″ (275–435 mm); HF 2¼–2⅞″ (58–73 mm).

Similar Species: Striped Skunk usually has 2 broad white stripes close together and shorter tail; Hog-nosed Skunk has back and tail white without black hairs and top of snout naked.

Breeding: 3–5 young born May–early June.

Habitat: Rocky ledges, tangles of vegetation along streams.

Range: Southeastern Arizona, sw New Mexico, and extreme w Texas.

Its habits are not well known but are probably similar to those of the Striped Skunk. The common name refers to the hoodlike ruff of long white hair that often forms at the back of the neck.

199 Hog-nosed Skunk
"Rooter Skunk"
(*Conepatus mesoleucus*)
Related species: Eastern Hog-nosed

Description: *Top of head, back, and tail white;* lower portions black. *Long snout, naked on top,* with broad nose pad. Foreclaws enlarged. Males larger than females. L 20¼–35¾" (51.3–90 cm); T 6⅛–16⅛" (17.4–41 cm); HF 2⅝–3½" (6.5–9 cm).

Similar Species: Striped Skunks and most Hooded Skunks have black tails; when Hooded Skunk has white tail and back, these show scattered black hairs.

Sign: Extensive patches of ground torn up and pitted by rooting.
Scat: Similar to Striped Skunk's.
Track: Similar to Striped Skunk's but forefeet toeprints are longer, often longer than heel pad.

Breeding: Mates in March; 2–4 young born April–May in den in rocky crevice; weaned August.

Habitat: Foothills, brushy areas.

Range: South Arizona, se Colorado, much of New Mexico, and s Texas.

Although primarily nocturnal like other skunks, in winter the Hog-nosed Skunk may forage by day. Its broad nose pad is an adaptation for rooting up the insects that are its chief food; vegetation, arachnids, reptiles, mollusks, and small mammals are also eaten. It dens in rocky crevices. The Eastern Hog-nosed Skunk (*Conepatus leuconotus*) found in extreme southern Texas is closely related and, because it probably intergrades with the

Hog-nosed, is sometimes considered a subspecies.

215 River Otter
(*Lutra canadensis*)

Description: Elongated body. *Dark brown (looks black when wet)* with paler belly; *throat often silver-gray;* prominent whitish whiskers. *Long tail thick at base and gradually tapering to a point; feet webbed.* Males larger than females. L 35–51⅜" (889–1,313 mm); T 11¾–20" (300–507 mm); HF 3⅞–5¾" (100–146 mm); Wt 11–30 lb. (5–13.6 kg).

Similar Species: Sea Otter is yellowish or grayish on head and neck.

Sign: Holes in snow where otter plunged in flight from predator, rough trough where otter plowed through loose snow.
Rolling places: Areas of flattened vegetation up to 6' wide, with twisted tufts of grass marked with musk and sometimes droppings. Slides on riverbanks 8" wide, much wider with heavy use. Slides in snow 1' wide or wider; often on flat ground, as much as 25' long, sometimes pitted with blurred prints where otter has given itself a push for momentum.
Scat: Irregular, sometimes short, rounded segments, sometimes flattened masses; showing fishbones, scales, or crayfish parts; when fresh, often greenish and slimy; most often found on banks of stream or pond, logs or rocks in water.
Trail: Meandering, about 8" wide, between neighboring bodies of water or other favored spots, such as rolling areas or slides. Trail may show sidling walk.
Tracks: 3¼" wide or more; often show only heel pad and claws; toes fan out widely, but webbing rarely prints, except in mud. Running stride 1–2'.

Breeding: Mates in early spring, just after birth of litter; delayed implantation; 1–4 young born blind, fully furred in nest of sticks in bank burrow; weaned at 4 months, disperse at 8. Male, evicted while young are small, returns to help care for them when half grown.

Habitat: Primarily along rivers, ponds, and lakes in wooded areas, but will roam far from water.

Range: Alaska and most of Canada south to n California and n Utah; in the East, from Newfoundland south to Florida; extirpated from most areas of Midwest.

The River Otter is active by day if not disturbed by human activity. Well adapted to its aquatic life, it has a streamlined body, rudder-like tail, and ears and nostrils valved to keep out water. It swims rapidly both underwater and on the surface, moving like a flexible torpedo, either forward or backward, with astonishing grace and power. To observe its surroundings, it raises its head high and treads water. It can remain submerged for several minutes. Also at ease on land, the River Otter runs fairly well, although not as nimbly as the Mink. Its permanent den is often dug into banks, with underwater and exposed entrances, and contains a nest of sticks, grass, reeds, and leaves. It also uses resting places under roots or overhangs, in hollow logs, burrows of other animals, or Beaver lodges, which if heavily used may also contain a nest. Feeding mainly on fish, often caught in a quick broadside snap, it also eats small mammals, such as mice and terrestrial invertebrates. A pair of River Otters may work together to drive a school of fish into an inlet where they can be caught easily. Large catches are carried to land to be eaten; smaller ones consumed as the otter floats on its back.
Vocalizations include a whistle,

probably given to communicate over distances, and a shrill, chattering call, emitted during mating season; otters chuckle softly to siblings or mates apparently as a sign of affection and also chirp, grunt, snort, and growl. Among the most playful of animals, a lone River Otter often amuses itself by rolling about, sliding, diving, or "body surfing" along on a rapid current. In family groups they take turns sliding, and they frolic together in the water. A River Otter makes the most of a snowslide by first running to get speed, then leaping onto the snow or ice with its forelegs folded close to its body for streamlined tobogganing. While sociable most of the year, during breeding season competing males may battle. Some anglers suspect River Otters of depleting game fish stocks, but while otters will eat bass or trout, they prefer the slower-moving "trash fish," which are caught more easily. Because their fur is durable, thick, and beautiful, excessive trapping in the past has greatly diminished the number. More recently, water and even air pollution, including mercury fallout, have taken a toll. Some River Otters, however, may be developing a tolerance to certain toxic substances, and their populations are slowly increasing.

---

216 **Sea Otter**
(*Enhydra lutris*)

Description: *Dark brown with head and back of neck yellowish or grayish.* Old males may have white heads. Fairly short tail, thick at base, gradually tapering. Feet webbed; *hindfeet flipper-like.* Males somewhat larger than females. L 30–71¼" (76–181 cm); T 10¼–14¼" (26–36 cm); HF 5⅞–8¾" (150–222 mm); Wt 25–80 lb. (11.4–36.3 kg).

Similar Species: River Otter is smaller, with silver-gray

throat and longer tail; it lives mainly in fresh water.

Sign: A loud rapid tapping: the sound of shellfish being cracked open by stones. *Scat:* When fresh, massed or cylindrical, thick, 4–5" long; showing bits of shellfish or shell; crumbles easily; occasionally found on beaches. *Tracks:* Rarely seen; hindprint fan shaped, 6" long, almost equally wide at front; foreprint smaller, roundish; rarely seen.

Breeding: 1, rarely 2, young born at sea in spring, with fur, teeth, eyes open; weaned at 1 year; may remain with mother even after she has new pup. Mother floats on back to let offspring nurse, nap, or play on her chest.

Habitat: Coastal waters within mile of shore; especially rocky shallows with kelp beds and abundant shellfish.

Range: Pacific coast from California to Alaska.

Highly aquatic, the Sea Otter eats, sleeps, mates, and even gives birth at sea. Flipper-like hindlegs make it clumsy on land, and it takes to the beach only to wait out storms. By day it feeds while floating on its back, sculling with its tail; but if in a hurry, it swims on its belly, using feet and tail like a River Otter. It can remain submerged 4–5 minutes. Apart from primates, the Sea Otter is a greater user of tools than any other mammal. When it dives for food, it also brings up a small rock. It then floats on its back, places the rock on its chest, and cracks the shell against it. Abalone, sea urchins, crabs, mussels, and fish are its chief foods. At night it wraps strands of kelp about its body to secure its position in the kelp beds where it sleeps. It watches for danger by standing in the water and shading its eyes with both forefeet; if it spots such predators as sharks and Killer Whales, it hides in kelp beds. If a female is alarmed, she may tuck her pup under a foreleg and dive for safety. A playful animal, the Sea Otter may interrupt a meal to dive and frolic underwater; it consorts amiably with seals and sea lions, sometimes touching noses.

Unlike these oceangoing mammals, the Sea Otter has no insulating blubber; the air trapped in its fine fur keeps it warm as well as increasing buoyancy; if the fur is damaged in an oil spill or by other pollution, the otter can die from exposure or cold. Once abundant, the Sea Otter was so heavily hunted for its highly prized pelts that by 1911, when international treaty forbade its massacre, it had nearly become extinct. Not seen in California for almost a century, in the spring of 1938 a herd appeared in the sea south of Carmel; today the population there is perhaps 1,000, and even larger herds are found off the coast of southern Alaska and the Aleutian Islands.

CATS
(Family Felidae)

Cats are well equipped for the hunt.
Although coloration varies, all have
long, sleek bodies, powerful legs, short
heads with relatively small rounded ears
and eyes that face forward, providing
the binocular vision and depth
perception so crucial to locating prey.
Their night vision is superb; the pupils,
contracted into vertical slits by day,
expand almost to fill the eye, while a
layer of cells behind the retina absorbs
even the dimmest light. Cats move
about confidently in the dark, using
their sensitive whiskers to gauge spaces
through which they can pass. Their
molariform teeth have well-developed
shearing edges, and the canines are
large fangs. Rough tongues, with
which they groom their fur, can also
rasp meat from bones of prey. The 5
toes on the forefoot and 4 on the
hindfoot have retractile claws, usually
withdrawn to keep from being blunted
but extended to slash prey. Soft foot
pads surrounded by fur permit stealthy
stalking. Cats can swim, though most
do not like getting wet, and they climb
well. Most cats are nocturnal and
solitary, except during the mating
season. They mark out territory with
feces as well as urine and tree scratches.
Most North American species mate in
winter or spring; copulation generally
stimulates ovulation. Gestation is 50–
110 days, with most having 1 annual
litter of 1–6. The kittens, born blind
and helpless, receive extended parental
training in the ways of the wild. Cats
are native to most parts of the world
except Australia and New Zealand; 7
species of *Felis* are found in our range,
though only the Mountain Lion, the
Lynx, and the Bobcat are frequently
found north of Mexico.

274 Jaguar
(*Felis onca*)

Description: Yellowish to tawny, *spotted with black rosettes or rings* in horizontal rows along the back and sides; inside most rings tan with 1 or 2 black spots. Legs, head, and tail have smaller, solid spots, usually giving way to incomplete bands near end of tail. L 62–95¼" (157–242 cm); T 17–26¼" (43–67 cm); HF 8⅞–11⅞" (225–302 mm); Wt 119–300 lb. (54–136 kg).

Similar Species: Mountain Lion unspotted; Ocelot smaller; Margay much smaller, lacks rosettes.

Sign: *Scat:* Similar to Mountain Lion's. *Tracks:* Very difficult to distinguish from those of average-size Mountain Lion. Foreprint 4–4½" long, about equally wide; hindprint slightly smaller.

Breeding: Mates December–January in northern part of range; 2–4 young born April–May in dens in cave, rock shelter, dense thorn thicket, under tree roots, or similar shelter. They are born fur covered, heavily spotted, and with eyes closed. At first, male keeps distance but soon brings food for nursing mate and later for young.

Habitat: Brush, forested areas, jungles, swamps, and arid mountainous scrub.

Range: Southeastern and central California, s Arizona, New Mexico, and into s Texas. Very rare in U.S.; increasingly seen from Mexico to Brazil and n Patagonia.

The biggest and most powerful North American cat, it is the only one that roars. The Jaguar moves over a large home range, 3–15 miles in diameter where prey is abundant, larger where prey is scarce. Though a great traveler, it has been sighted only once in the U.S. since the 1940's. It hunts mostly on the ground but climbs well and sometimes ambushes prey by leaping from tree limb or ledge. It is, however, less arboreal than the Mountain Lion, and its tail, less needed for balancing, is proportionately shorter. Unlike most cats, it is extremely fond of water, delighting to play in shallow pools on hot days and unhesitatingly entering ponds and streams after fish and other aquatic life. Jaguars are solitary except when breeding and rearing young. While some mated pairs remain together, it is more common for them to separate after a year, when the young disperse. Their diet includes deer, peccaries, rabbits, large ground birds, sea turtle eggs dug up along the coast, and livestock where available. The name "Jaguar" derives from an American Indian word meaning "the killer that takes its prey in a single bound." In pre-Columbian civilizations in Mexico, Guatemala, and Peru, the Jaguar was worshiped as a god.

270, 271   Mountain Lion
"Cougar" "Puma" "Catamount"
(*Felis concolor*)

Description: *Yellowish to tawny* above; white overlaid with buff below. *Unspotted. Long tail with black tip.* Backs of ears and 2 whisker patches on upper lip, dark. Head fairly small; ears small and rounded; feet large. *Young buff with black spots.* L 59⅛–108" (150–274 cm); T 21–36" (53–92 cm); HF 8¾–12" (22–31 cm); Wt 75–275 lb. (34–125 kg).

Similar Species: Jaguar is spotted; Jaguarundi is much smaller.

Sign: Scratches or gashes on trees used as scratching posts are longer and higher than those left by Bobcat or Lynx. Remains of a kill, often loosely covered with branches, leaves, and litter, making a conspicuous cache, to which the cat may return.

Scat: Usually copious; varies from masses to irregular cylinders and pellets; frequently with traces of hair or bone scraps showing. Sometimes covered with earth but often left exposed or partly exposed as a scent post; if so, scratchings on the ground probably indicate general direction of movement, as Mountain Lions habitually face their line of travel as they scratch. Scent posts may also be a more conspicuous "scrape," where a male lion has loosely piled leaves or debris and urinated on pile to mark his territory.

Tracks: Prints quite round, usually with all 4 lower toes showing but no claw marks, as claws are retracted. Foreprint 3¼–4″ long; hindprint slightly smaller. Lobed heel pad has single scalloped edge at front, double scalloped edge at rear. Tracks usually in a fairly straight line, staggered in pairs, with hindfoot track close to or overlapping forefoot track but seldom registering precisely within it. Straddle 8–10″; length of stride 12–28″. Longer gaps indicate bounding, when all feet come down close together. In snow, prints slightly larger, sometimes blurred by thicker winter fur, and elongated by foot drag marks; in deep snow, tail may drag and leave trace between prints.

Breeding: No fixed mating season; 1–6 young usually born midsummer in a maternity den lined with moss or vegetation in rock shelters, crevices, piles of rocks, thickets, caves, or other protected place. Kittens raised only by the female and remain with her for 1 year, sometimes 2.

Habitat: Originally varied, now generally mountainous areas. Adaptable to hilly northern forests; mountainous, semiarid terrain; subtropical and tropical forests and swamps.

Range: Western North America from British Columbia and s Alberta south through

w Wyoming to California and w Texas. Also s Texas, Louisiana, s Alabama, Tennessee, and peninsular Florida.

The most widely distributed cat in the Americas, the Mountain Lion is a solitary, strongly territorial hunting species that requires isolated or undisturbed game-rich wilderness; it has therefore declined or become extinct in much of the habitat where it once thrived. There have been a few sightings of animals or tracks in Canada's Maritime Provinces, upper New England, and New York State. Unlike most cats, it may be active by day in undisturbed areas. A good climber and excellent jumper (it can leap more than 20′), it swims only when necessary. It feeds primarily on large mammals, preferring deer, but also eats Coyotes, Porcupines, Beaver, mice, marmots, hares, Raccoons, birds, and even grasshoppers. Sometimes it waits for passing game but more often travels widely after prey; a male may cover up to 25 miles in 1 night. It can outrun a deer, but only for short distances. After locating large prey by scent or sound, it usually slinks forward slowly and silently, with belly low to the ground and legs tensed to leap. It tries to stalk within 30′ before pouncing from its hiding place or running at prey; it then leaps onto its victim's back, biting into the neck and gashing with sharp claws. Where deer abound, an adult Mountain Lion may kill an average of 1 per week, helping to keep the herd from overpopulating. Usually silent, it has many kinds of calls, including screams, hisses, and growls. It also utters a shrill, piercing whistle, evidently an alarm, sometimes used when it has been treed or cornered or when females signal their cubs. The bloodcurdling mating call has been likened to a woman's scream. Mountain Lions pair only during breeding season;

for about 2 weeks they hunt together and sleep side by side. Occasionally they have been known to injure or even kill people, usually children, but they tend to avoid man unless cornered or extremely hungry. There have been rare, unexplained killing orgies, when a Mountain Lion has slaughtered several deer or a flock of domestic sheep in 1 night. For many years they were bountied and persecuted as a threat to livestock, but now they are fully protected where rare and classified as game animals where abundant.

---

273 Ocelot
(*Felis pardalis*)

Description: Grayish to tawny or gold, heavily marked with *black-bordered brown spots, tending to form lines.* Spots include rosettes, rings, speckles, slashes, and bars. Long tail. L 36¼–53⅞" (92–137 cm); T 10⅜–15¾" (27–40 cm); HF 5¼–7⅛" (13–18 cm); Wt 20–40 lb. (9.1–18.2 kg).

Similar Species: Jaguar is much larger and marked almost entirely with rosettes. Margay smaller, with similar coloration and markings.

Sign: Scratchings and other sign similar to Bobcat's.
Scat: Similar to Bobcat's.
Tracks: Similar to Bobcat's but slightly larger and wider: 2–2½" long, about equally wide. Front and rear edges of print of heel pad less scalloped than Bobcat's and sometimes even convex.

Habitat: Forested or brushy areas, dense chaparral.

Range: Southern Oklahoma, sw Arkansas, w Louisiana, Texas and extreme se Arizona (much more common in Mexico south into Paraguay). The Santa Ana National Wildlife Refuge, along Rio Grande River in s Texas, offers best opportunity for viewing in the wild.

Ocelots sometimes travel and hunt in
pairs, probably as mates, maintaining
contact and signaling each other with
meows like those of domestic cats.
Principal foods include mice, rats,
rabbits, birds, snakes, lizards, fish,
frogs, and young or small domestic
animals. They climb well and silently
and sometimes even catch birds perched
in trees. Good swimmers, they
occasionally hunt along streams.
Populations declined drastically owing
to habitat loss, efforts at eradication in
order to protect small livestock and
poultry, and, more importantly, the
trade in exotic furs and pets. Mother
Ocelots were often killed in the process
of capturing kittens, which, while
affectionate and easily tamed, become
unpredictable and sometimes dangerous
when mature. Ocelots are now fully
protected in the U.S., and the
importation of skins and the selling of
live Ocelots as pets are banned.

Margay
(*Felis wiedii*)

Description: *Ocelot-like, but smaller.* Ground color
grayish or yellowish to tawny; belly
white with brown spots. *Long-tailed.*
Spotting on sides brown and irregular-
shaped, often with dark buff centers.
4 dark brownish stripes on back, 1 on neck.
L 51¼–71⅛" (130–180 cm); T 13–
20" (33–51 cm); HF 3½–5¼" (89–
132 mm); Wt 5–7 lb. (2.3–3.2 kg).

Similar Species: Ocelot larger, with similar color and
markings; Jaguar larger, with rosettes.

Sign: Believed to be similar to Ocelot's.

Habitat: Forested areas.

Range: Rarely in U.S.; only known sighting
occurred at Eagle Pass in Maverick
County, Texas in the 1850s.

Skilled at climbing, the Margay is the
only North American cat known to go

down a tree headfirst. This arboreal
acrobat can hang from a bough by one
unusually long-clawed hindfoot. Little
else is known of this nocturnal species'
habits, although they are believed to be
similar to those of the Ocelot.

---

272 Jaguarundi
(Felis yagouaroundi)

Description: Small, unspotted. *Three color phases:
black, gray (entirely grayish), and reddish
(white or pale below).* Long body and tail;
legs short. L 35–54″ (89–137 cm); T
13⅛–24″ (33–61 cm); HF 4¾–6″
(12–15 cm); Wt 15–18 lb. (6.7–
8.1 kg).

Similar Species: Mountain Lion is much larger; other
long-tailed cats are spotted.

Sign: *Tracks:* Foreprint 1½–1¾″ long;
hindprint almost as large; both slightly
longer than wide. Typical cat tracks,
with 4 toe prints and no claws
showing.

Breeding: Mates at any time of year; 2 annual
litters, generally of 2–3 young, usually
born in spring and late summer in dens
made in thickets, brush, or under fallen
trees. Kittens born with distinct light
spots, which soon disappear, and may
display all color phases within the same
litter.

Habitat: Brushy thickets or cactus, catsclaw,
mesquite, and other spiny plants.

Range: Rare in U.S.; only in extreme s Texas
and extreme se Arizona. More common
from Mexico south to n Argentina.

The habits of this elongated and elegant
cat are little known. It is occasionally
active during the day, especially in the
morning. Solitary, it pairs only for
breeding. Though it will climb, it
spends most time on the ground,
preying on birds, including poultry and
small- to medium-size mammals, such
as rats, mice, and rabbits. Stalking and

ambushing less than most cats, it is an
excellent runner, sprinting after and
overtaking even the fastest prey. It
swims well, crossing rivers when
necessary, and probably preys on fish
and other aquatic species. Its diet also
includes fruit.

---

268 **Lynx**
(*Felis lynx*)

Description: Buff or tawny with mixed blackish
hairs; underparts cinnamon-brownish.
*Short tail tipped with black. Long black
ear tufts. Large, pale cheek ruffs,* whitish
with black barring, forming a double-
pointed beard at throat. Feet very large
and well furred. Males larger than
females. L 29⅛–41⅞" (74–107 cm); T
2–5⅜" (5–14 cm); HF 7⅛–12¾" (18–
33 cm); Wt 11¼–40 lb. (5.1–
18.1 kg).

Similar Species: Bobcat has shorter legs, smaller ear
tufts, less bushy tail tipped with black
above but not below.

Sign: Scratching posts and kill caches
resemble Bobcat's. It creates scent posts
by urinating on trees and stumps.
Scat: Similar to Bobcat's.
Tracks: Foreprint 3–4¼" long, almost
as wide; hindprint slightly smaller;
both with 4 toes, no claws showing.
Because of well-furred paws, prints are
much larger and rounder than Bobcat's
and especially large when toe pads
spread and blur in powdery snow.
Straddle usually less than 7", almost as
narrow as Bobcat's. Normally short
stride 14–16", but may have long gaps,
as Lynx occasionally leaps as if
practicing pounce.

Breeding: Mates mid-March–early April; usually
1 litter of 2 young born May–July.
Kittens remain with mother through
first winter.

Habitat: Deep forest.

Range: Much of Canada and Alaska south into

much of Washington, n Oregon, n Idaho, and extreme nw Montana. Also Rocky Mountain areas of Wyoming and n Colorado. In the East, n New England and extreme n New York; in the Midwest, n Michigan and n Wisconsin.

By day the Lynx rests under a ledge, the roots of a fallen tree, or a low branch. It frequently, and expertly, climbs trees and sometimes rests in them, waiting to leap down on passing prey. The long ear tufts serve as sensitive antennae, enhancing hearing. Large, thickly furred feet permit silent stalking and speed through soft snow, in which some prey may flounder, though not the well-named Snowshoe Hare, the Lynx's chief prey. Big feet also help make the Lynx a powerful swimmer. Its populations are characteristically cyclic, peaking about every 9–10 years, paralleling that of the Snowshoe Hare. It also eats birds, Meadow Voles, the remains of dead Moose and Caribou, and occasionally small, winter-weakened deer, Caribou, or sheep. It caches meat, especially a large kill, by scantily covering it with snow or ground litter. Usually silent, during mating season it may shriek or utter a scream that ends in a prolonged wail. Although the Lynx occasionally preys on domestic animals in remote areas, it is usually no threat to man or livestock. Its main predators are the wolf, Mountain Lion, and man, who values its long, silky fur.

267, 269 **Bobcat**
(*Felis rufus*)

Description: Tawny (grayer in winter), with *indistinct black spotting. Short, stubby tail* with 2 or 3 black bars and *black tip above;* pale or white below. *Upper legs*

have dark or black horizontal bars. Face
has thin, often broken black lines
radiating onto *broad cheek ruff. Ears
slightly tufted.* Males larger than
females. L 28–49⅜″ (71–125 cm); T
3¾–6¾″ (10–17 cm); HF 5¼–8¾″
(13–22 cm); Wt 14⅛–68¼ lb. (6.4–
31 kg).

Similar Species: Lynx has tail tip black above and
below, larger feet, longer legs, more
pronounced ear tufts, and longer fur
with less distinct spots.

Sign: Scent posts, established by urinating,
visible only on snow and identifiable
only by tracks; tree trunks used as
scratching posts, with low claw marks;
a cache covered somewhat haphazardly
and scantily with ground litter.
Scat: Similar to a domestic dog's, often
buried, but sometimes merely with dirt
scraped about and scratch marks left on
ground.
Tracks: Fore and hind prints about same
size, 2″ long, slightly longer than wide,
with 4 toes, no claw marks. If clearly
outlined, heel pad distinguishes from
canine print: dog's or Coyote's is lobed
only at rear; Bobcat's is lobed at rear
and concave at front, giving print
scalloped front and rear edges. Trail
very narrow, sometimes as if made by a
2-legged animal, because hindfeet are
set on, close to, or overlapping
foreprints; 9–13″ between prints. This
manner of walking may be an
adaptation to stalking: hunting as it
travels, cat can see where to place its
forefeet noiselessly, then brings down
hindfeet on same spots.

Breeding: Mates in spring. Litter of 1–7 young,
usually 2–3, born late April–early May
in maternity den of leaves or other dry
vegetation in hollow log, rock shelter,
under fallen tree, or other protected
place. Some southern populations
produce a second litter.

Habitat: Primarily scrubby country, broken
forests, but adapts to swamps,

farmlands, arid lands if rocky or brushy.

Range: Spottily distributed from coast to coast, s Canada into Mexico. Probably most plentiful in Far West, from Idaho, Utah, and Nevada to Pacific and from Washington to Baja. Scarce or absent in most of central and lower Midwest.

Found only in North America, where it is the most common wildcat, the Bobcat gets its common name from its stubby, or "bobbed," tail. It "lies up" by day in a rock cleft, thicket, or other hiding place. The Bobcat spends less time in trees than the Lynx but is also an expert climber. Sometimes it rests on a boulder or a low tree branch, waiting to pounce on small game that passes; its mottled fur provides excellent camouflage. If hard pressed, it will swim. It uses the same hunting pathways repeatedly to prey mostly on the Snowshoe Hare and cottontail rabbit but also eats mice, squirrels, Porcupines, and cave bats. Unless prey is very scarce, it will not eat carrion. Small prey is consumed immediately; larger kills are cached and revisited. The Bobcat occasionally preys upon livestock, especially poultry. Its variety of calls sound much like those of the domestic cat, although its scream is piercing and when threatened, it utters a short, sudden, and resonant "cough-bark." It yowls loudest and most often during breeding season. Males are sexually active all year, but most females are in heat in February or March. Bobcat hunting with hounds is popular in some areas. Its fur is used for trim. Populations are stable in many northern states, reviving in other states where intensive trapping formerly decimated them, and being reestablished in some states, such as New Jersey, where stock has been transplanted from New England.

Seals, Sea Lions, and the Walrus

The aquatic carnivores, formerly placed in their own order—Pinnipedia, meaning "fin feet"—are believed to have evolved from the same ancestral groups as the bears and the mustelids. Although unlike terrestrial carnivores in appearance, their dentition is similar; they feed solely on flesh, mainly fish and aquatic invertebrates. These carnivores are distinguished by adaptations for their aquatic life: torpedo-like bodies; legs modified as flippers; and nostrils and ears, when present, that close when submerged. There are 5 bones in the fore and hind feet; these are elongated, flat, and connected by webbing, which gives a finlike appearance. Tails are reduced or vestigial.

Aquatic carnivores are generally larger than terrestrial carnivores, ranging from 200 lb. to several tons, and in most species males are larger than females. Large size and a streamlined body are believed to be adaptations to the cold environments where these aquatic carnivores evolved, as both reduce the relative amount of surface area through which body heat is lost. Fine fur covers the skin (except in the adult Walrus) and is molted at regular intervals. Appearing much darker wet than when dry, the fur provides insulation against the cold, as does a layer of blubber directly beneath the skin. This oily fat also increases buoyancy and acts as a reservoir of energy when the animals fast during molting and breeding. When water is very cold, blood vessels in the skin contract; this also reduces the amount of heat lost through the skin. Skillful and graceful swimmers and divers, aquatic carnivores are clumsy on land and ice, to which they return to give birth and to molt. When animals make deep dives, down to almost 2,000' (600 m), remaining submerged for extended periods, up to 45 minutes, their heartbeats slow to 7–13% of the normal rate and blood vessels constrict, sending the available oxygen mainly to the brain and heart. Delayed implantation occurs in most species, extending the gestation period so that the birth of the young and mating can occur when the herds assemble at the same time and place each year. There is usually a single pup, rarely 2, which grows rapidly on its mother's unusually rich milk, about 50% fat (cow's milk is about 3.5% fat). Pinnipeds usually have adult pelage near the end of the first summer, are sexually mature at 2–5 years, and may live up to 40 years. An animal's age is determined by counting the number of dentine rings around the root of an extracted tooth, as 1 ring is added each year.

EARED SEALS
(Family Otariidae)

Occurring nearly worldwide except in the Arctic Ocean and Antarctica, the eared seals, which include sea lions and fur seals, have small but noticeable external ears; long, slender bodies; longer necks than the earless seals; and longer, more supple forelimbs. Among the aquatic carnivores, they are the least specialized for an aquatic life-style and the most agile on land. Hind flippers can rotate forward under the body, and long fore flippers turn out at the wrist at right angles; all 4 limbs can be used to move on land in either a somewhat doglike walk or a "gallop" in which fore flippers and hind flippers work together. In the water, they use fore flippers for propulsion, holding hind flippers together to serve as rudder. Flippers are thick and hairless, with nails well developed on the middle 3 digits of the hind flippers. All have a coarse coat of guard hairs, and the fur seals also have a dense underfur. Coloration varies, but there are no stripes or distinct markings.

Although they remain at sea most of the year, eared seals are highly gregarious and form large herds on marine beaches during the breeding season, June–July. The much larger bulls maintain harems of 3–40 cows, depending on the species and particular bull. Mating occurs shortly after the cows give birth. The single calf is born hairy, not woolly like the young phocids. They usually begin swimming at 2 weeks, and those in our range are weaned in 3–4 months. This family is believed to have evolved from the same ancestral group as the bears.

300 Northern Fur Seal
"Alaska Fur Seal"
(*Callorhinus ursinus*)

Description: Bulls with greatly enlarged necks, *blackish above with massive grayish shoulders,* reddish below; females gray above, reddish below. *Very large flippers.* Tiny tail. Small head with short, pointed nose, large eyes, long whiskers. L males 6'3"–7'3" (190–220 cm), females 3'8"–4'8" (110–140 cm); Wt males 330–594 lb. (150–270 kg), females 84–119 lb. (38–54 kg).

Similar Species: Sea lions and Elephant Seal larger; Harbor Seal spotted.

Habitat: At sea most of the year; in summer breeds on rocky island beaches.

Range: Point Barrow, Alaska, on the Arctic Ocean south in winter to San Diego, California; in summer breeds on the Pribilof islands in the Bering Sea; Commander and Robben islands (USSR); and San Miguel Island, off California.

One of the most oceangoing of the aquatic carnivores and the greatest traveler, sometimes migrating up to 6,200 miles (10,000 km), this fur seal returns to land only during the breeding season. At sea it is not gregarious and is rarely seen in groups of more than 3. When resting in the water, it takes a "jug handle" position, lying on its back with hind flippers bent up over the belly and held there by a fore flipper. By day it rests and preens and may swim slowly with a flipper waving in the air. Feeding at night, when fish swim closer to the surface to eat, it often dives 60–450', remaining submerged several minutes. Small fish and squid are swallowed whole, but the seal surfaces with prey more than 10" long, then bites and shakes it into manageable pieces. About 30 species of marine mammals and oceanic birds are used as food.

This fur seal's major rookery on the Pribilofs is enormous, with more than a million seals within a 31-mile radius. Older bulls arrive first, in late May—June, and battle savagely to establish territories in the best places, near the water and with best access to cows; females arrive mid-June—mid-July, and the biggest bulls may form harems of up to 100 cows (some of these cows may be stolen by bulls farther from shore). Within a few days, cows give birth; they mate 4–7 days later, usually with the bull in whose territory they have given birth. A single pup is born glossy black and weighing 10–12 lb. After remaining with it 1 week, the cow goes on feeding forays several times weekly, often more than 100 miles out to sea, returning regularly to nurse the pup with her rich milk. In August female yearlings come ashore and breed with the bachelor bulls too young and small to maintain their own territories; these bulls will join the territory scramble when 9–10 years old. Bulls, battle scarred and thin from their 2-month fast during breeding season, barely have strength to return to the water in August; they winter south of the Aleutians or in the Gulf of Alaska, with some migrating to Asian waters. Females and juveniles traveling separately leave the beaches by November, with some wintering as far south as southern California.

The Pribilof breeding grounds were discovered in 1786, and by 1834 overhunting had greatly reduced fur seal populations. As early as 1835, the seals were afforded some protection and the taking of females forbidden. Now the harvest of fur seals is carefully managed and limited to excess males in bachelor herds. The pelts are prized for their fine, soft fur; blubber is rendered for oil; and flesh and bones are used for meal. Since 1973 there has been no hunting on 1 of the 2 major Pribilof islands, which has been designated a study area in order to compare a natural population with the managed one.

303 Guadalupe Fur Seal
(*Arctocephalus townsendi*)

Description: Brownish-gray above, *with silvery cast on yellowish-gray head and neck;* brownish-black below, with chest lighter in adult males. *Snout pointed,* rust-orange on sides; flippers large. L males to 6′3″ (190 cm), females 4′6″ (140 cm); Wt males to 350 lb. (159 kg), females to 100 lb. (45 kg).

Similar Species: Sea lions and Elephant Seal much larger and lack pointed snout; Harbor Seal spotted.

Habitat: Rocky coastal islands.

Range: California's Channel Islands to Credros Island off Baja California; only known to breed on Guadalupe Island.

Nearly exterminated by sealers in the 1800's, by 1892 only 7 individuals were known to exist. Although a fisherman sold 2 males to the San Diego Zoo in 1928, and 1 seal was seen on San Nicolas Island in 1949, very few were found until 1954, when 14 were sighted on Guadalupe Island. Today they are protected, and the population numbers about 1,000. This seal prefers rocky caves as breeding sites, and while the male will defend his territory, unlike other eared seals he occasionally oversees his harem from the water. Pups are born in late June—July and can swim shortly after birth, although they do so only in emergencies.

298, 299 Northern Sea Lion
"Steller Sea Lion"
(*Eumetopias jubatus*)

Description: *Largest eared seal* (males larger than any bear). *Bulls buff above, reddish-brown below;* with dark brown flippers and massive necks and forequarters. *Cows uniformly brown,* one third the size of males, and more cylindrical in shape. *Snout and face otter-like;* low forehead. L males 8′10″–10′6″ (270–320 cm), females 6′3″–7′3″ (190–220 cm); Wt males to 2,200 lb. (999 kg), females 600–800 lb. (272–365 kg).

Similar Species: Elephant Seal larger, has relatively small flippers, and male has large proboscis; fur seals and California Sea Lion smaller, and latter browner and usually barking.

Habitat: Rocky shores and the coastal waters along them.

Range: Pacific coast from s Alaska and Aleutian and Pribilof islands south to s California.

These sea lions usually stay in the water during poor weather but otherwise spend much time "hauled out" on rocky shores, they will dive into the sea if a boat approaches. Occasionally they swim up rivers. They eat fish, including blackfish, rockfish, greenling, and—more rarely—commercially valuable ones, such as salmon, squid, clams, and crabs, generally feeding at night in water less than 600′ deep and within 10–15 miles from shore. During breeding season (May–August), fasting bulls often fight fiercely to defend their territories and harems of 10–30 cows. Nonbreeding females and bachelor bulls herd separately from breeding colonies. One pup is born in late May–June, weighing 40–45 lb.; it can swim its first day but lacks enough body fat to insulate against chill water. Mating follows within 2 weeks of birth.

Females mate in their third year; although males are sexually mature at 6–7 years, they are not large enough to compete for cows until they are 9 or 10 years old. The young and sometimes adults frolic in the water, and pups may play "king of the mountain" on rocks along the beach. Adults have a deep, bellowing roar; pups, a lamblike bleat. Males leave rookeries in August, females and pups in early fall, and most animals from southern populations migrate north. Killer Whales and some sharks are predators. It is sometimes called the Steller Sea Lion, after the German naturalist Wilhelm Steller, who first described the species in 1741, calling it a "lion of the sea" because of its leonine eyes with golden pupils and lion-like, bellowing roar.

301, 302 California Sea Lion
(*Zalophus californianus*)

Description: *Slender. Buff to brown; appears black when wet.* Head becomes paler with age. *Males* much larger than females, *with high foreheads.* L males 6'6"–8'2" (200–250 cm), females 5'–6'6" (150–200 cm); Wt males 440–660 lb. (200–300 kg), females 100–220 lb. (45–100 kg).

Similar Species: Northern Sea Lion larger, paler, and with low forehead; Guadalupe Fur Seal smaller.

Sign: Continual barking by territorial males.

Habitat: Sandy or rocky beaches, occasionally caves, protected by high cliffs; preferably on islands.

Range: Pacific coast from Vancouver south to Baja California and into Gulf of California; breeds on islands from California's Channel Islands south through gulf.

The trained seal of zoo and circus, in the wild this sea lion often indulges in similar antics, throwing objects and catching them on its nose and cavorting in the water. The fastest of the aquatic carnivores, it can swim up to 25 mph when pressed, often "porpoising" along at the surface. It can descend to 450' and stay submerged for 20 minutes. It uses sonar for underwater navigation and finding prey. Spending much of the day sleeping on islands, it hunts primarily at night. It feeds on squid, octopus, abalone, and many types of fish, which it eats by snapping off the head and swallowing the remainder "head" first. While highly gregarious, outside of the breeding season the sexes remain segregated, males traveling north as far as British Columbia and females and young remaining in the waters off rookeries. The bulls are probably the most vocal of all mammals, continually giving a honking bark while defending their territories. Cows make a quavering wail to summon their pups and bark and growl in aggressive interactions with other cows. A pup, which recognizes its mother's voice, responds with a call resembling a lamb's bleat. During the breeding season (June–July), fasting bulls maintain territories but do not attempt to keep specific harems. In June a single pup is born, blue eyed and weighing about 36 lb.; cows mate shortly thereafter. A pup may nurse nearly a year, though it also eats fish; while learning to swim, it often rests on its mother's back. Females breed at 4 years; males must wait several more years before they are big enough to compete for territories. Killer Whales and sharks are predators. Once sold primarily for the oil rendered from their blubber and also for dog food, today the much-reduced numbers of California Sea Lions are fully protected by law.

WALRUS
(Family Odobenidae)

Fossils indicate that the Walrus evolved from an ancestral eared seal perhaps 7 million years ago. Like eared seals, its hind flippers can rotate forward for terrestrial locomotion, and bulls are polygamous; but unlike them, the Walrus has no external ears and has nails on all 5 toes. It is most obviously distinguished by its tusks, which grow throughout the animal's life; the enamel on top when the tusks erupt soon wears off, leaving pure ivory. In this family there is only 1 species.

297 Walrus
(Odobenus rosmarus)

Description: *Yellowish to reddish brown hide,* essentially hairless except on muzzle about 400 bristles up to 1' long. No external tail. Short, round head. Upper canines are *2 large tusks,* up to 40" long in Pacific bulls, 14" in Atlantic bulls; cows' tusks somewhat shorter, narrower, more curved in middle. L Atlantic males 8'2"–11'10" (250–360 cm); females 7'6"–9'6" (230–290 cm); average Wt males 1,650 lb. (750 kg), females 1,254 lb. (570 kg). Pacific race larger; Wt males 2,783 lb. (1,265 kg), females 1,870 lb. (850 kg).

Sign: Bellows heard up to a mile away.

Habitat: Along continental shelf of northern seas, especially along edge of pack ice; preferred water depth less than 60' (18 m).

Range: Atlantic race in Arctic seas around Greenland south to Hudson Bay; Pacific race migratory, generally in Chukchi Sea off ne Siberia in summer, Bering Sea off sw Alaska in winter.

Walrus are sociable animals, gathering in mixed herds of up to 2,000 bulls,

cows, and calves when feeding and migrating, as well as when hauled out on ice floes. The sexes segregate only during the breeding season. If a Walrus is attacked, neighboring animals will come to its defense, and injured herd mates are also helped from the water onto ice. Excellent swimmers, Walrus use hind flippers alternately for propulsion and can travel about 15 mph. They can dive to 300' and remain submerged about half an hour. During deep dives, blood goes from the skin to the internal organs, leaving internal skin pale; after surfacing, the heartbeat is unusually rapid at first and skin gradually resumes its usual color. The Pacific Walrus is migratory, riding pack ice whenever possible, though it will swim if its chunk of ice begins going in the wrong direction. Although ungainly on land, Walrus spend more time out of the water than other aquatic carnivores, resting and sunbathing on ice and beaches for long periods, but they will dive immediately if they scent man. When asleep at sea, they hang vertically in the water, with head held up by a pair of inflatable air sacs in the neck.

The size of tusks is important in helping bulls establish dominance, and all Walrus use tusks to defend themselves against predators, including Eskimoes in kayaks. Tusks are also used like grappling hooks to help animals haul out onto ice. Walrus generally feed in early morning. In the fall they frequent shallow water, keeping air holes open by butting ice with their heads. They forage along the sandy sea bottom, using their tusks like sled runners and the highly sensitive bristles on their faces to search for prey. Mollusks, especially clams, and crustaceans are chief foods, but Walrus do not swallow shell fragments. Rather they use their dome-shaped mouths like vacuum cleaners to suck flesh from shells, which are discarded. Adults require about 100 lb. of food daily but during good weather may go without food for a week. Individual bulls may prey on seals, grabbing them with fore flippers and stabbing with the tusks. Small whales, probably already dead, are also eaten. Vocalizations include bellows, grunts, and a sound like pealing churchbells given by bulls during courtship. Courting and mating occur at sea April–May. Bulls do not form harems but may engage in courtship battles in which tusks are sometimes broken. Unlike the seal, the female Walrus does not mate in the same year she gives birth. Every other year she has a single calf, weighing 100–150 lb. The young remains with its mother almost 2 years, nursing most of the time until tusks sprout and it can forage for itself. Holding on with its flippers, it often rides on its mother's back while she swims. A cow is fiercely protective and will charge a Polar Bear to defend her calf. Females are sexually mature at 4–5 years, males at 5–6 years. Life span is up to 40 years. The Walrus is about as important to the Eskimo as the Bison was to the Indian. Almost every part is used: flesh provides food for Eskimoes and their dogs; skins are used for boat covers and leather, intestines for rain gear, and bones for tools; blubber is rendered for the oil, which is burned as fuel; the ivory tusks, previously used for sled runners, are now mainly used for carvings (scrimshaw), a source of considerable revenue; and even the bristles serve as toothpicks. The Polar Bear, Killer Whale, and man are its sole enemies. The Marine Mammal Protection Act of 1972 fully protects the Walrus from commercial hunting except by Eskimoes.

HAIR SEALS
(Family Phocidae)

The phocids, sometimes called earless seals or true seals, are the most abundant and widespread of the aquatic carnivores, with representatives found throughout most of the world's seas and in some freshwater lakes. Hind flippers are permanently turned backward and thus are almost exclusively for aquatic use, and fore flippers are smaller than those of eared seals or the Walrus. There is no external ear, only a small orifice. The fur is stiff and in several genera distinctly marked, but there is little soft underfur. In most species, newborn have a woolly coat, often white, called the lanugo; it is usually shed within a month and replaced with adult pelage better adapted to a cold climate. Hair seals move on land in a slow (1 mph), clumsy fashion, propelled solely by muscular contraction of the body; whenever possible they roll or slide on ice. In water they swim easily, moving hind flippers up and down and using fore flippers for steering. They often appear upright at sea, treading water with fore flippers. Most species are gregarious but form small groups only; and most are monogamous, pairing up during breeding season. Members of this family are believed to have evolved from otter-like mustelid ancestors.

---

308 Harbor Seal
"Hair Seal" "Leopard Seal"
(*Phoca vitulina*)
Related species: Spotted

Description: Usually *yellowish-gray or brownish with dark spots* above, but highly variable from cream to dark brown; spotted creamy white below. Males and females about same size. L 4'–5'7" (120–170 cm); T 3⅜–4½" (87–115 mm); Wt to 300 lb. (136 kg).

Similar Species: Elephant and Gray seals larger, lack spots; Ringed Seal has both streaks in a marbled pattern and spots.

Habitat: Coastal waters, mouths of rivers; some northern populations permanently inland in freshwater lakes.

Range: In West, s Arctic from Yukon and n Alaska south along California coast; in East, s Greenland and Hudson Bay coasts south to Carolinas.

Harbor Seals spend much time basking on beaches and rocky shores in groups of several individuals to 500. At the first sign of danger, they give an alarm bark and dive into the water. They can dive to 300' and remain submerged up to 28 minutes. They feed when the tide comes in, sometimes ascending rivers with the tide, and haul out at low tide, sleeping high and dry until the next rising tide unless disturbed. In the spring they may follow fish runs upriver for hundreds of miles, returning to coastal waters in the fall. Feeding mostly on fish, including rockfish, herring, cod, mackerel, flounder and salmon, they eat some mollusks (about 5% of their diet), including squid, clams, and octopus; and sometimes crayfish, crab, and shrimp. Some learn to steal fish from nets, which are often damaged, incurring the wrath of commercial fishermen. Populations vary in their breeding season, and pupping may occur from March to August. Coastal forms are promiscuous and may breed with several females, except in the northern parts of their range. Pups are usually born with adult pelage, having shed the lanugo before birth, and may enter the water within a few days. These seals mate after weaning the young. For many years bounties were paid on Harbor Seals. Polar Bears, Killer Whales, and sharks are their main predators aside from man; Golden Eagles sometimes prey on pups.

Closely related is the similar Spotted Seal (*Phoca largha*), which breeds on ice floes in the northern Pacific. It is monogamous, forming pairs in March, pupping March–April, and mating a month later after the pup is weaned, by which time the pup has shed its white lanugo.

310 Ribbon Seal
(*Phoca fasciata*)

Description: Males dark brown with *creamy-white rings around neck, rump, and base of front flippers*. Females gray with rings indistinct. Males slightly larger than females. L to 6' (180 cm); Wt males to 200 lb. (90 kg), females to 176 lb. (80 kg).

Similar Species: Harbor Seal lacks rings, has spots; Harp Seal is light with harp-shaped black saddle on back.

Habitat: Open sea and Arctic ice floes.

Range: Bering Sea from Alaska to Aleutian Islands; 1 taken near Morro Bay, California, in 1962.

As it seldom occurs near shore, this rare seal seems even less common than it is. Usually solitary, it molts, rests, and gives birth on pack ice and swims in the open waters of the Bering Sea when the ice is gone. It can remain submerged almost half an hour. Various fish, including pollack, capelin, eelpouts, sculpin, and polar cod, along with shrimp and octopus, compose its diet. Among seals its way of moving on ice is unique: it slithers along, alternating front flippers and throwing its head and body from side to side to stretch its flippers forward. It breeds in late April–mid-May; gestation is 11 months, including delayed implantation of 3½ months; a single calf is born April—early May with eyes open and body covered with white fur (lanugo); weaned at 1 month when weighing about 65 lb. (30 kg). During the reproductive and molting season in spring, the adults fast, losing 40—50 lb. Ribbon Seals often live more than 20 years.

309 Ringed Seal
(*Phoca hispida*)

Description: *Smallest aquatic carnivore.* Coloration highly variable, often brownish to bluish-black above, streaked and marbled with black on back, often with irregular light rings on sides; whitish to yellowish below with scattered dark spots. Males slightly larger than females. L 4′3″–5′3″ (130–160 cm); Wt to 222 lb. (101 kg).

Similar Species: Harbor Seal lacks marbled pattern.

Habitat: Land-fast ice; seldom on shifting ice of open sea.

Range: Arctic seas from Point Barrow, Alaska, east to Labrador and Newfoundland.

Ringed Seals spend most of the year under thick ice, using the strong claws on their fore flippers to dig and maintain breathing holes; juveniles often move to open water near the edge of ice. Females also use their claws to dig a pupping den 10′ long by 2′ high in the snow by their breathing hole, although sometimes they use natural snow caves. In late March—early April, a single calf is born weighing 8–10 lb. and covered with lanugo; helpless at birth, it is nursed 2 months. Mating occurs the following month (April—early May); during this period the monogamous bulls have a strong odor, similar to gasoline, and both sexes fast. At this time they bask frequently on the ice by their air holes, raising their heads every minute or so to scan the horizon for the Polar Bears that prey upon them. Implantation is delayed about 3½ months, making apparent gestation about 11½ months. Females breed at 6–8 years. Life span is up to 40 years. Ringed Seals are solitary, and females maintain territories around their dens. The Ringed Seal dives to 300' and can stay submerged up to 20 minutes but usually surfaces in about 3 minutes. Feeding mostly on crustaceans and small fish, in deep water it eats the larger zooplankton. Besides the Polar Bear, Killer Whales and sharks prey upon it, and Arctic Foxes take pups in the den. Coastal Eskimoes take great numbers, which they use for food, clothing, tools, and oil (burned for light and heat).

---

311 **Harp Seal**
"Saddleback Seal"
(*Phoca groenlandica*)

Description: Males yellowish-white to grayish above, with *harp-shaped black saddle on back;* silvery with scattered small spots below. Females less distinctly marked or markings broken up into irregular spots. Black or dark brown face. Juveniles blue-gray with darker gray markings. Males slightly larger than females. L 4'7"–6'7" (140–200 cm); Wt to 400 lb. (181.5 kg).

Habitat: Drifting pack ice; occasionally up streams.

Range: Arctic seas from n Hudson Bay and w coast of Greenland south along Labrador into Gulf of St. Lawrence, west to mouth of Mackenzie River.

Annual oceanic migrations of this seal cover 6,000 miles. Harp Seals can dive to 900' and remain submerged up to 15 minutes. Small fish, especially such schooling kinds as capelin and herring, are chief foods along with some crustaceans, including prawns; young pups feed on still smaller items, especially krill, various shrimp-size invertebrates. In April seals begin an annual molt, lasting about a month, which has been termed catastrophic, as the coat and even large pieces of skin peel off. After the molt, seals in our range—the western Atlantic population—move north via the Davis Strait to Baffin Bay and thence to Thule and the Canadian Archipelago. In late September, when the Arctic bays begin to freeze, they move along the eastern coast of Baffin Island, from Hudson Bay eastward through the Hudson Strait, with the first seals reaching northern Labrador in late October. In November and December they travel south along the Labrador coast to the Gulf of St. Lawrence, eastern coast of Newfoundland, or the Grand Banks. In February adults move to the edge of the ice pack, where cows give birth to a single pup, weighing about 12 lb. and covered with white fur (lanugo). After being nursed only 2 weeks, the baby seal has grown to 90–100 lb. and is then abandoned. For the next couple of weeks it does not feed; its weight drops to about 50 lb., and the lanugo is molted. Many pups perish, but the rest learn to gather food for themselves and will migrate north with the herd. Meanwhile, the bulls, which have a musky odor during breeding season, have congregated in the water between ice floes, where they court cows by swimming about furiously and perhaps even battling among themselves. Mating occurs in the water; breeding peaks in early March. Females are sexually mature at 5–8 years, males at 8 years. The Harp Seal's life span may be up to 30 years, but animals more than 20 are rare. The annual fast, observed by both sexes during the breeding period, causes the formation of rings on the canine teeth, which can be examined to determine a seal's age. This seal is the mainstay of Newfoundland sealing, bringing in $9.5 million in 1979. In the early 1960's, kills of more than 300,000 caused a dramatic decline in populations. The harvest quota for 1979, set at 180,000, should allow the herd to increase.

---

312 Bearded Seal
(*Erignathus barbatus*)

Description: *Large.* Uniformly grayish to yellowish. *Bearded with tufts of long, flat bristles* at sides of snout. Fore flippers squared off, with third digit longer than others. Males larger than females. L 8−11' (240−340 cm); Wt to 902 lb. (410 kg).

Habitat: Arctic and subarctic continental shelf, in relatively shallow water up to 500' deep; moves seasonally with drift ice.

Range: Northern coastal waters and shallow seas from Alaska to Labrador, including Hudson Bay.

The nonmigratory Bearded Seal is generally solitary but during breeding season may congregate in groups of up to 50. At this time, although bulls do not form harems, they may fight each other; they give a long warble to woo cows. Mating is in May, but implantation is delayed until August, making apparent gestation just under a year. In April−May a single pup is born, eyes open, with a brown woolly coat and weighing about 70 lb. After nursing for 12−18 days, it weighs about 200 lb., most of it blubber; its mother then abandons it. Cows that give birth late may not breed and so are barren the following year. Females are sexually mature at 6 years, males at 7, but this slow-growing species does not attain full size until 10 years old. Life span may exceed 25 years. They occasionally eat bottom-dwelling fish, but mainly feed upon whelks, clams, crabs, and octopus, which they use their sensitive bristles and strong claws to help locate and dig out. The Polar Bear, man, and an occasional Walrus are their chief predators. Bearded Seals have little commercial value, but 2,000–4,000 are taken annually by Eskimoes for their flesh, and their rough hides are used for nonskid boot soles. Meat should be cooked thoroughly to prevent trichinosis.

313 Gray Seal
(*Halichoerus grypus*)

Description: Large. *Grayish to almost black* above, usually with lighter splotches; somewhat paler below. Head squarish, *snout long.* Males larger than females and have wrinkled necks. L males to 9′10″ (300 cm), females 7′6″ (230 cm); Wt males to 638 lb. (290 kg), females to 548 lb. (249 kg).

Similar Species: Bearded Seal has prominent beard; Harbor Seal smaller, has rounder head; Hooded Seal has pouch above nose.

Habitat: Waters along rocky coasts and islands.

Range: Labrador south to New England, including Gulf of St. Lawrence.

This relatively rare seal has a world population of 50,000–70,000, with more than 5,000 in North American waters. Quite gregarious, it gathers in groups to feed on such bottom-dwelling fish as pollack, cod, flounder, whiting, and cuttlefish. It dives to 480′ and can remain submerged up to 20 minutes. On land it maneuvers better than other members of its family and may crawl far inland to breed. Breeding season varies with locality; there may be 100–900 seals in a breeding colony. Bulls defend territories with vocal threat and vigorous fighting to form harems of up to 10 cows. Throughout this 4–6 week period both sexes fast. One pup is generally born January–February, weighing about 30 lb. and covered with white lanugo. After this baby fur is shed, in 4–5 weeks, pups enter the water. Pups have a shrill yap, adults a threatening hoot, bark, and hiss. Cows wean pups in about 2 weeks and then mate. Life span in the wild is probably up to 22 years for bulls, 35 for cows. Unlike many other seals, a Gray Seal bull cut off from water will fiercely attack the seal hunter threatening him. Formerly protected, in the past 15 years its population has increased tenfold. In Nova Scotia its damage to fishing gear and excessive consumption of fish has led to a bounty system and a controlled cull.

West Indian Monk Seal
"Caribbean Monk Seal"
(*Monachus tropicalis*)

Description: *Uniformly brownish-gray above; yellow or yellowish-white below.* Hind flippers with first and fifth toes longest, giving V-shaped outline. Nails on front toes well developed, vestigial on hind toes. Males larger than females. L males about 7'6" (230 cm); Wt 150–300 lb. (68–137 kg).

Habitat: Tropical seas off sandy beaches.

Range: Gulf of Mexico.

Quite common when first encountered by Columbus in 1494, this seal was last seen in Jamaican waters in 1952. Living along islands with no terrestrial predators, it had no fear of man, and so groups of them sunning on the beaches were easily approached and slaughtered for meat and oil. This species is probably extinct, but if sighted it

should be reported to conservation
authorities immediately. Pups are born
jet black, with eyes open.

306, 307   Hooded Seal
"Bladdernose Seal"
(*Cystophora cristata*)

Description: Steel gray above, often with irregular
whitish or brownish blotches; paler
below. Females paler, with less distinct
markings. Both sexes have *hood on head,*
larger in males; when inflated, this
elastic nasal sac stretches from nostrils
to forehead; when deflated, appears
wrinkled. *Juveniles bluish-gray above.*
Claws light colored and strong. Males
larger than females. L males 6'7"–8'2"
(200–250 cm), females 6–7' (180–
210 cm); Wt males 660–880 lb.
(300–400 kg), females to 400 lb.
(180 kg).

Habitat: Edge of Arctic pack ice; in deep water.

Range: Gulf of St. Lawrence to Greenland
waters; not in Hudson Bay.

When a bull is angry or threatened, it
inflates its hood, which greatly
increases the apparent size of its head
and may make the seal more formidable
to an enemy. Usually in small groups,
this seal is more gregarious when
breeding, mating, or migrating. On
winter ice northeast of Newfoundland,
in late March–early April, a single pup
is born weighing about 50 lb. It is slate
blue above with a black head and
lighter below; the molt of its first coat,
the white lanugo, occurred before its
birth. When it is about 2 weeks old,
the pup's mother abandons it to mate
again. Bulls are monogamous. After
mating, in groups segregated by sex
seals follow the retreating ice through
Davis Strait to waters east of
Greenland, where they haul out onto
the ice to molt. At this time, late

June–early July, they fast, and their weight drops significantly. Then they slowly migrate south, feeding far out to sea, and finally winter off the Grand Banks of Newfoundland. Hooded and Harp seals often migrate together but do not intermingle. Pups migrate by the same route as adults but a month later. Members of this highly migratory species may stray as far south as Florida. This deep-diving seal probably eats mostly mussels, starfish, squid, octopus, and such fish as herring and cod. The bluish-gray juveniles, known as "blue-backs" or "bluemen," are prized in the fur trade.

304, 305 Northern Elephant Seal
(*Mirounga angustirostris*)

Description: *The largest aquatic carnivore.* Brown or gray above, lighter below. Adult male with *large snout* drooping over muzzle; when inflated during mating season, it curves down and back into mouth. Hind flippers with 2 lobes, reduced claws. L males 14'9"–21'4" (450–650 cm), females 9'10"–11'6" (300–350 cm); Wt males to 7,700 lb. (3,500 kg), females to 1,980 lb. (900 kg).

Similar Species: Sea Lions and Fur Seals much smaller; can rotate hind flippers forward.

Habitat: Temperate seas; subtropical sandy beaches for breeding and molting.

Range: Pacific coastal waters from Gulf of Alaska south to Baja California; breeds on islands from California's Farallon Islands south to San Benito Island off Baja California.

In the 1890's this seal was nearly exterminated by the whaling industry for the oil to be rendered from its great rolls of blubber. In 1892 a tiny colony of fewer than 20 animals was discovered on Guadalupe Island, off Baja

California; they were protected, and the herd now numbers about 65,000 seals, which breed on offshore islands from Baja north to San Francisco. Limited to sandy beaches by its enormous bulk, the Elephant Seal has recently been forced onto mainland beaches owing to the increase in its population. The first birth on the mainland occurred in 1975, and by 1979 almost 100 cows had given birth in a new rookery at Ano Nuevo Point, near Santa Cruz, California.

Polygamous bulls arrive on the beaches first, in early December, and fight for territories in which to establish harems. Inflating their huge snouts, they rear and threaten each other, the distended nasal pouches causing their snorts and bellows to resonate as much as a mile away. If visual and vocal threats fail, they lunge at each other with their large canine teeth. Although at first there is much battling, by the time females arrive, most disputes have been settled. In late December–January a cow gives birth to a single black-furred pup, weighing about 65 lb. After nursing a month, it weighs about 400 lb.; of all mammals, the milk of the Elephant Seal is the richest in fat (54.5%) and lowest in water content (32.8%). After the pup is weaned, by which time it has grown a silver-gray coat, the mother abandons it to mate. The biggest danger to the young is the possibility of being fatally crushed when bulls of 2–3 tons crawl over them, oblivious to their presence. Pups that attempt to suckle at a strange cow may also be killed, though some orphans are adopted by cows that have lost their own pups. Mating season is January–March; bulls fast but cows feed periodically. Females mate at 2 years; bulls are sexually mature at 4 years but rarely gain access to females until 7–8 years old. The weaned young remain on the beach until May, living

off their fat and practicing swimming
nightly. Females haul out onto beaches
to molt in late May, with males
following in July and August; both
sexes fast while they undergo a
"catastrophic" molt, in which hair and
skin fall off in large patches. After the
molt the seals swim out to sea, where
they remain until December, feeding
mostly on ratfish, hagfish, squid, small
sharks, and other deepwater marine
life. They can dive to more than 200'
and remain submerged for up to 40
minutes. Killer Whales prey upon the
young, but healthy adults seem
relatively immune to predation.

Manatees and Sea Cows
(Order Sirenia)

Sirenians are large, cylindrically shaped aquatic mammals that live in coastal waters or rivers in tropical regions of the world. The skeleton is heavy, an adaptation that probably helps them to remain submerged. There is no distinct neck, and a fold of skin separates head from body. Forelegs are rounded flippers; hindlegs are absent. The tail is a horizontally flattened paddle-shaped fluke. Although embryos are well haired, adults are nearly hairless except for thick bristles on the snout. Nostrils are valved, closing when submerged. Incisors and canines are absent in adults; when a front molar wears away, it is replaced by a molar moving forward from the rear. These highly evolved animals have their closest evolutionary ties with the terrestrial hoofed mammals, particularly elephants. Sirenians are herbivorous, and like most herbivorous hoofed mammals, their stomachs have several chambers. The name of the order comes from the supposed resemblance of its members to the mermaids, or sirens, of myth. Actually, the myth was probably inspired by the sight of a female sirenian cradling an infant in her arms and pressing it to 1 of her 2 breasts. There are 4 species in 2 families, the dugong (Dugongidae), found in the Indian Ocean, and 3 manatees (Trichechidae), 1 each in the rivers of Central West Africa, the Amazon basin of South America, and the shores of the Caribbean, including Florida.

Manatee
(*Trichechus manatus*)

Description: *Massive, torpedo-shaped,* nearly hairless aquatic mammal. *Grayish* to blackish when wet. *Tail* broad, flattened, *paddle shaped.* Broad head with *upper lip deeply cleft* and bearing stiff bristles. Front legs like large flippers with 3 nails at end; hindlegs absent. No external ears. L to about 15′ (460 cm); Wt to 1,922 lb. (874 kg).

Similar Species: Whales have a much more fishlike form.

Habitat: Shallow coastal waters, bays, rivers, and lakes.

Range: Gulf and Atlantic coastal waters of se U.S. north to Beaufort, North Carolina. Florida's waters have the largest remaining populations.

The Manatee is primarily nocturnal and moderately social; while not part of a herd, Manatees congregate in warm water in winter. They cavort together when they meet, embracing each other with flippers and even pressing their thick lips together in a "kiss." They spend their days browsing on aquatic vegetation, which they grasp in lips and bristles, with flippers helping to hold loose grass blades; they consume 60–100 lb. per day. Propelling themselves with undulations of the hind ends of their streamlined bodies, they use flippers and tails mainly for steering and stabilization. Flippers are also used to clean their teeth and rub their sides, which they do often and with apparent pleasure, also rubbing against underwater objects like rocks. When at rest, they either hang in the water, partially supporting themselves on submerged vegetation, or lie on the bottom. They can remain submerged for up to 16 minutes, but when sleeping, they surface every few minutes for air. Their sounds include squeals, chirp squeaks, and a high-pitched scream when frightened; females give an alarm call to their young. There is 1 offspring every 2–3 years. Born underwater, the young Manatee is immediately brought to the surface on its mother's back; after about 45 minutes it is gradually immersed again. Nursing takes place underwater and may continue for 1–2 years. Manatees cannot survive water colder than 46° F. (8° C.) and in winter move upriver to warm lakes or to the heated discharge from power plants. In Florida, they perform a valuable service by consuming quantities of water hyacinth, which chokes many waterways. As they are slow and not cautious, many are injured by boat propellers (in some Manatee habitats, boating is now prohibited or speeds regulated). Other dangers include too much human activity, which may drive them from areas of good browse, and the release of warm waters from power plants if it lures them to areas of insufficient browse. Manatees make very good food, which is partly why they are now an endangered species and fully protected. Federal studies of the Manatee's ecological requirements, habits, and reproduction are part of an effort to restore the species.

Even-toed Hoofed Mammals
(Order Artiodactyla)

The name of the order means "even-toed," and most members of the 5 families in our range have either 2 or 4 toes on each foot. Most are medium-size to large mammals and have long, slender legs with the third and fourth toes forming a hoof, so that the animal literally "walks on its toes." The other toes, called "dewclaws," are much smaller and higher on the leg, touching ground only in soft mud or snow. Except for the omnivorous Wild Boar (*Sus scrofa*) and the Collared Peccary (*Dicotyles tajacu*), North American members of this order are herbivorous and have a cartilaginous pad instead of incisors at the front of the upper jaw. Their molariform teeth are adapted for nipping or tearing off and grinding vegetation rather than biting in the manner of carnivores. Most have a 4-chambered stomach and chew their cud, or ruminate. Hastily swallowed food is stored temporarily in the largest compartment, the rumen, or paunch; the food then passes to the second stomach, the reticulum, where it is shaped into pellets—the cud. While the animal is at rest, the cud is returned to the mouth and slowly chewed to pulp. It then passes through the other 2 stomachs where digestion begins. This complex process permits an animal to feed quickly—which reduces its exposure to predators in open country—but chew its cud at leisure in the relative safety of a concealed spot. American artiodactyls are important as game animals, and because of their large size, speed, and stamina, they have relatively few predators apart from man. Some of man's most important domestic animals—cows, goats, sheep, and pigs—are members of this order.

OLD WORLD SWINE
(Family Suidae)

Members of this family are characterized by their long, pointed heads and barrel-like, stocky bodies. The domestic pig is a member of this family and is derived from the wild pig (*Sus*). Some domestic species have escaped and formed feral populations; also, the European Wild Boar (*Sus scrofa*), the same species as the domestic pig, has been introduced in many areas as big game.

---

275 Wild Boar
(Sus scrofa)

Description: *Usually black,* sometimes brown or gray, often with *grizzled or frost-tipped guard hairs.* Pureblooded Wild Boars have coat of long, bristly hairs thickening into erect mane on neck and shoulders, upper spine, sometimes onto jaw; dense undercoat in winter. Hybrids much more variable in color—sometimes spotted black and tan—frequently less hairy. *Tail moderately long,* lightly haired, hangs *straight*—never coiled. Head long, shaggy, with flexible but tough cartilaginous snout disc like that of domestic swine. Upper tusks (modified canines) usually 3–5" but up to 9" long, curl out and up along sides of mouth; lower canines smaller, turn out slightly, rising outside mouth and pointing back toward eyes. Height at shoulder to 3' (91 cm). L 4½–6' (132–182 cm); T to 12" (30 cm); Wt males 165–440 lb. (75–200 kg), females 77–330 lb. (35–150 kg).

Similar Species: Peccary much smaller; more uniformly and thickly coated; grayish, usually with light collar over shoulders; with vestigial tail and upper tusks pointing down. Domestic pig much more variable in color, less shaggy; lacks mane and long curved tusks; has much rounder body, shorter legs, tail usually coiled. Hybrids between Wild Boar and feral hogs have intergrading characteristics.

Sign: Rooted-up earth showing ragged plowing; tree rubs from ground level to 3' high, with hair or mud clinging; muddy wallows.

Bed: Dry, shallow, saucer-shaped depression heaped with twigs or grass, usually in secluded thicket.

Scat: Massed pellets or sausage-like segments, usually found with other sign.

Trail: Narrower than domestic pig's, almost a single line.

Tracks: Cloven but more rounded and splayed than deer tracks, 2½" long; hindprints often half covering foreprints. Front dewclaws low, long, and pointed, in soft earth almost always print as crescents outside and behind main print; hind dewclaws print as dots; stride 18".

Breeding: Mating peaks in December; gestation 16 weeks; litter of 3–14 young, usually 4–5, born April in small, grass-lined depression that sow has hollowed in pile of grass and branches in secluded thicket; piglets at birth 6–8" long, brown, with 9–10 pale longitudinal body stripes that disappear within 6 months; follow sow at 1 week; weaned at 3 months; disperse the following spring; sexually mature at 1½ years; fully grown 5–6 years.

Habitat: Variable: densely forested mountainous terrain, brushlands, dry ridges, swamps.

Range: Chiefly w North Carolina; e Tennessee (especially Nantahala and Cherokee national forests); Santa Cruz Island (off California); Monterey and San Luis Obispo counties, California. Small numbers, primarily in preserves, in New Hampshire, Vermont, Pennsylvania, perhaps other states.

Small feral hogs in Florida; hybrids or feral hogs in Alabama, Arizona, Arkansas, Georgia, Louisiana, Mississippi, Missouri, Oklahoma, Oregon, South Carolina, and Texas.

Native to Europe and Asia, the Wild Boar first appeared in North America in 1893, when a herd of 50 was brought from the Black Forest in Germany to a hunting preserve in the Blue Mountains of New Hampshire. Russian Wild Boars were released in 1910 and 1912 on a North Carolina preserve near the Tennessee border; in 1925 near Monterey, California; and a few years later on Santa Cruz Island, off the California coast. Some of these animals escaped from preserves, and many of their progeny bred with feral descendants of domestic hogs. Although pure-blooded Wild Boars are still found in North Carolina, Tennessee, parts of California, and preserves in other states, America's wild swine elsewhere are hybrids or feral hogs descended from purely domestic stock.

Especially active at dawn and dusk, Wild Boars are fast runners and good swimmers. Sometimes they heap up a mat of grasses and other vegetation, then squirm underneath to bed. Sows and their young forage in family groups, usually of about half a dozen animals, but sometimes join other groups in herds up to 50. Except during breeding season, mature males are solitary or band in small groups. Boars usually trot from one foraging area to another, then slow to a walk. Their wanderings seldom exceed 10 sq. mi. if food is abundant but may be as much as 50 sq. mi. when forage is poor. Where oaks are prevalent, acorns are a staple; beech, hickory, and pecan nuts are also favored. In late fall and winter, when the nuts accumulated on the forest floor have all been eaten, boars leave to forage in swamps and marshes. They rely on a wide variety of vegetation, including roots, tubers, grasses, fruit, and berries, but also eat crayfish, frogs, salamanders, snakes, mice, the eggs and young of ground-nesting birds, the young of rabbits, and any other easy prey or carrion encountered while foraging, and have been known to kill and eat fawns. In America, Wild Boars do not grow as large as those in some parts of Europe, probably because they must compete for ground food—especially nuts—with so many squirrels and deer; while some European boars weigh over 500 lb., few American ones reach 350 lb. Life span is generally 15–25 years. Bears, Bobcats, and feral dogs occasionally kill a baby boar, but predation is light on older individuals because the tusks of a mature boar are as effective for fighting as for rooting; the chief predator is man. In some states there are hunting seasons, and in others, where feral hogs have become agricultural pests, they can be killed at any time. Wild Boar populations are not endangered and are monitored by game departments as a valuable resource. The meat of an old boar may require parboiling with a little baking soda before roasting or frying, but that of a young one well fed on acorns is tender and more delicious than domestic pork; it should be well cooked to ensure against trichinosis.

PECCARIES
(Family Tayassuidae)

Peccaries, related to domestic swine and Wild Boars, are relatively small animals descended from large pigs that lived about 25 million years ago. They are distinguished from wild and domestic swine (Suidae) by their smaller size, straight tusks, single dewclaw, and strong musk gland on the back just forward of the rump. They have fewer teeth than swine, and their stomachs have 2 compartments, features that seem to be transitional toward the suborder of ruminants. Of the 2 living species in this family, 1, the Collared Peccary (*Dicotyles tajacu*), is in our range. The only other living member of this family, the White-lipped Peccary (*Tayassu pecari*), occurs from southern Mexico to Paraguay.

---

276 **Collared Peccary**
"Javelina"
(*Dicotyles tajacu*)

Description: *Piglike.* Grizzled grayish or blackish above and below, with yellowish tinge on cheeks and *whitish to yellowish irregular collar* from shoulder to shoulder. Heavy, bristly hair from head to back can be erected into a mane. Inconspicuous tail; piglike snout; tusks (canines) nearly straight. Four toes on forefeet, 3 on hindfeet; all feet with 2 hooves. Young brownish with a black stripe down back. Height at shoulder 20–22" (50–55 cm); L 34¼–40" (87–102 cm); T ¾–2¼" (19–55 mm); Wt 30–65 lb. (13.6–29.5 kg).

Sign: Rooted-up ground; chewed cactus, especially prickly pear, and other low vegetation. Sometimes a light skunky odor.
Scat: Usually large, irregular segments;

flattened disks when feeding on very succulent vegetation.

Tracks: Similar to pig's but smaller. Cloven hooves are rounded oblongs, generally about 1–1½″ long, with hindprint slightly smaller than foreprint. Stride, short, usually 6–10″ between pairs of overlapping fore and hind prints.

Habitat: Brushy deserts, rocky canyons, wastelands.

Range: Southeastern Arizona, extreme se and sw New Mexico, central and s Texas.

Active mainly in the early morning and late afternoon, the Peccary often beds down in a hole rooted in the earth or takes shelter in a cave during the midday heat. Peccaries travel in herds of 6–30, grunting softly while feeding. As they move about, a musk gland on their back exudes a mild skunky scent, which probably serves as a bonding mechanism, helping to keep members of the group together. The musk gland also serves as an alarm signal: when a Peccary is agitated, the hairs on its back become erect, uncovering the gland, which then involuntarily discharges scent. Their alarm call is a barking cough; they can squeal but do so only if terrified or injured. They prefer to flee danger, galloping away at speeds up to 25 mph and swimming through streams if necessary, but will fight viciously if cornered. Primarily herbivorous, Peccaries prefer cactus, particularly prickly pear, which provides water as well as food; they devour even the spines. Mesquite fruit, sotol, and lechuguilla are among the succulent plants they favor. They also root for tubers and occasionally eat insects, worms, toads, frogs, lizards, mice, and the eggs and young of ground-nesting birds, as well as snakes, which they stomp to death. In parts of New Mexico and Arizona, Peccaries sometimes forage at elevations as high as 6,000', moving along the gentler mountain slopes and eating quantities of scrub-oak acorns. Like many herd animals, Peccaries are polygamous. Breeding may occur at any time of the year, as food is abundant the year round in their mild habitat, but most births occur in summer. After a 4-month gestation, 2–6 young, usually twins, are born with yellowish or reddish hair. Although the Peccary has 4 nipples, only the rear 2 produce milk; and while most young nurse alongside their mother, peccaries stand behind to nurse. Life span is 15–20 years. Once ranging as far north as Arkansas, the peccary was extirpated in the northern part of its range by settlers who wanted it for meat and as a cheap source of pigskin. Now it is hunted as game. The alternate common name, "Javelina," comes from the Spanish *javeline,* referring to the spearlike tusks.

DEER
(Family Cervidae)

All male members of North American deer species and female Caribou are distinguished by having antlers—bony outgrowths of the frontal bone that are normally shed annually. The antlers begin growing in the early summer, at which time they are soft and tender, covered with short fine hairs, the "velvet"—whence the phrase "in velvet"—containing a network of blood vessels that nourishes the growing bone beneath. By late summer antlers have reached full size, and the blood supply diminishes, causing the velvety skin to dry up, loosen, and peel off. The bare horns then serve as sexual ornaments, and rival males may use them as weapons in courtship battles. Antlers are shed after mating season, usually both branches within 2–3 days of each other. An animal's first set of antlers consists of short, straight spikes ("spikehorns"); as long as diet is adequate, antlers become larger and have more points each year until the animal reaches maturity. Inadequate diet may result in stunted antlers. In the temperate zone, winter coats of most deer tend to be darker than summer coats. Does are generally smaller than bucks and more delicately built. Fawns are spotted; when they rest motionless in foliage, the pattern of the coat provides excellent protective coloration. Also enhancing their chance of survival is the fact that the young of many deer give off very little odor during the first few days or weeks of their lives.

287 Elk or Wapiti
(*Cervus elaphus*)

Description: Large deer, with slender legs, thick
neck. Brown or tan above; *darker
underparts.* Rump patch and tail
yellowish-brown. *Males have dark brown
mane on throat* and *large, many-tined
antlers:* 6 tines on each side when
mature, with main beam up to 5' (150
cm) long. *Females lack antlers,* are
approximately 25% smaller than males.
Height at shoulder 4½–5' (137–150
cm). L 6¾–9¾' (2,032–2,972 mm); T
3⅛–8⅜" (80–213 mm); Wt males
600–1,089 lb. (270–495 kg), females
450–650 lb. (203–293 kg).

Sign: During the rut, thrashed saplings and
large shrubs; "rubs" on saplings and
small trees made as the animals polish
their antlers.
Wallows: Depressions dug in ground by
hooves and antlers, where copious urine
and feces give a strong, musky odor.
Scat: When feeding in lush pastures in
summer and early fall, flattened chips
similar to dung of domestic cattle; in
winter, when chief foods are dried
grasses and browse, dark pellets similar
to deer scat but larger, sometimes more
than 1" long.
Tracks: Cloven hearts, much larger and
rounder than those of White-tailed or
Mule deer; somewhat smaller and
rounder than those of Moose; 4–4½"
long. When walking, hindprints
slightly ahead of and partly overlapping
foreprints; stride 30–60". When
running and bounding, fore and hind
prints are separate and stride up to 14'.
In snow or mud, dewclaws often print
behind lobed main prints.

Habitat: Variable; chiefly high, open mountain
pastures in summer; lower wooded
slopes, often dense woods, in winter.

Range: From se British Columbia and central
Alberta, east to s Manitoba and south
to central New Mexico and Arizona;
also along coast from Vancouver Island

to n California; isolated populations elsewhere in California, Nevada, Utah, Arizona, New Mexico, Oklahoma, South Dakota, Minnesota, and Michigan; small numbers in several e states, notably in Pennsylvania and Virginia. Great numbers in Colorado, Wyoming, Montana, and Washington.

The Elk is primarily nocturnal but especially active at dusk and dawn. Unlike the much smaller White-tailed Deer, which is often heard crashing through the brush, the Elk moves through the forest rapidly and almost silently. Bulls can run up to 35 mph, and both bulls and cows are strong swimmers. They feed on many kinds of plants but are primarily grazers; east of the continental divide, they feed more heavily on woody vegetation, owing to the scarcity of grasses and forbs. Lichen is also consumed. The availability of food appears to influence the time of mating, the percentage of cows that become pregnant, and the age of puberty. During the nonbreeding season, cows with their young herd separately from bulls; as they approach maturity, juvenile bulls spend less and less time with the cow-dominated herds. The larger herds occur in open areas; smaller groups are found in woods. Elk·mark the areas they frequent. Seedlings are stripped of bark by cows with their lower incisors or by bulls with the base of their antlers and then rubbed with the sides of chin and muzzle. These posts may serve as territorial markers, warning other Elk to keep out. Young Elk squeal, adults snort and grunt, and cows neigh to their calves. The alarm call is a sharp, barking snort. The "bugle," or "whistle," of rutting bulls is a challenge to other bulls and a call of domination to cows; this vocalization begins as a bellow, changes almost immediately to a loud, shrill whistle or scream, and ends with a series of grunts. Only the whistle carries over long distances. A good imitation of this call, usually made with a commercial or homemade whistle about 1' long, may be answered by a bull, the most vocal of the American cervids. Cows also whistle but not as loudly as bulls and chiefly in spring rather than fall. During the rutting season, late August–November, peaking in October and November, adult bulls join the herd of cows. At this time bulls give their bugling call, roll in wallows of stagnant water and mud, and urinate on vegetation, which they then catch in their antlers and toss over their backs. Bulls clash their racks of antlers in mating jousts, but they are seldom injured, though occasionally there is a major injury or even a death. The most polygamous deer in America and perhaps the world, bull Elk assemble harems of up to 60 cows. After a gestation of about 255–275 days, a cow leaves the herd to give birth usually to 1 calf, sometimes 2, weighing 25–40 lb. After a week the cow rejoins the herd with her calf, which is entirely dependent on milk for 1 month but may suckle for up to 9 months. The Elk's main predator is the Mountain Lion, although bears get some calves. "Elk," the British name for the Moose, was misapplied to the Wapiti by early settlers. "Wapiti," a Shawnee word meaning "white (or pale) deer," alluded to the sides and flanks of the Rocky Mountain subspecies (*C.c. nelsoni*), which are often very pale. Elks once ranged through most of what is now the U.S. and southern Canada, but their number dwindled as settlement and farming took over their habitats and as a result of hunting, both for the market and for subsistence. In the nineteenth century many Elk were primarily plains animals and were shot by cattlemen to reduce grazing

competition with domestic livestock.
Thousands were also killed solely to get
"Elk's teeth," the 2 upper canines,
which were popular as watch-fob
charms. Today Elk herds appear to be
stable. In winter, large numbers can be
observed as they gather at a refuge
outside Jackson Hole, Wyoming, to
receive supplemental feed.

288 Fallow Deer
(*Cervus dama*)

Description: In summer, usually *brown with white spots;* in winter, usually *grayish-brown without spots*. Individuals may also be black, white, pale yellow, cream, silver-gray, and piebald. *White below.* Black stripe down back onto tail. Relatively long tail. Hindlegs slightly longer than forelegs, with rump held high. Short neck with prominent larynx (Adam's apple). Dewclaws reduced; high on legs. *Buck's antlers with terminal flattened palms.* Height at shoulder about 39" (1 m). L 55–71" (140–180 cm); T 6⅜–7½" (16–19 cm); Wt 88–176 lb. (40–80 kg).

Similar Species: Native deer lack spotting in summer; antlers lack flattened palms.

Sign: Browse marks, beds, scat, and tracks similar to those of White-tailed Deer, but tracks never show prints of dewclaw behind main prints.

Habitat: Brushy hills with grassy fields.

Range: First introduced to James Island, British Columbia, and Land Between the Lakes, a 172,000-acre national recreation area in Kentucky. It now occurs also in Maryland, Saint Simon and Jekyll islands off the coast of Georgia, Alabama, Oklahoma, Texas, California.

Native to Asia Minor and the Mediterranean region, Fallow Deer get their common name from the Anglo-

Saxon word *fealo,* meaning "sallow," referring to the pale yellow that is among the deer's colorations. Unusually gregarious, these deer form herds of up to 150–175 members, including bucks, does, and fawns. Grazing on grasses and herbaceous plants in summer, they browse on the woody parts of deciduous trees and conifers in winter. They utter a sound similar to a dog's bark when they are nervous, as when a buck battles or a doe has lost a fawn. They run in a distinctive stiff-legged fashion, bouncing along as if on pogo sticks. During the rutting season, in November at Land Between the Lakes, Kentucky, males make scrapes on the ground, clearing patches about 18–24" by 2–3', onto which they urinate. Does in heat frequent these scrapes, and mating often occurs on pathways between scrapes. Bucks are polygamous and fight among themselves during rutting season. Antlers are shed in late winter. After gestation of 6–7 months, a single spotted fawn (rarely 2) is born in June and weaned during rutting season. If truly wild, Fallow Deer are wary of man, but unlike most other deer species, they easily become semidomesticated and have been established as "park deer" in many parts of the world.

---

289 Mule Deer (includes Black-tailed Deer)
(*Odocoileus hemionus*)

Description: Stocky body with sturdy legs. In summer, reddish- or yellowish-brown above; in winter, grayish above. Throat patch, rump patch, inside of ears, inside of legs white; lower parts cream to tan. *Large ears* 4¾–6" long (12–15 cm). *Bucks' antlers branch equally,* each a separate beam forking into 2 tines.

Antler spread to 4' (120 cm). Two major subspecies: Mule Deer with tail white above, tipped with black; Black-tailed Deer, with tail blackish or brown above. Males larger than females. Height at shoulder 3–3½' (90–105 cm). L 3¾–6½' (116–199 cm); T 4½–9" (114–229 mm); Wt males 110–475 lb. (50–215 kg), females 70–160 lb. (31.5–72 kg).

Similar Species: White-tailed Deer has antlers with 1 main beam, tail not tipped with black.

Sign: Browse marks, buck rubs, scrapes, beds, and droppings similar to those of White-tailed Deer. Examination of a bed often reveals the sex. Both bucks and does urinate when they rise, but doe first steps to one side; a buck urinates in the middle of the bed. *Tracks:* Fore and hind prints 3¼" long (males), 2⅜" long (females); walking stride 22–24". Distinctive bounding gait ("stotting"), with all 4 feet coming down together, forefeet printing ahead of hindfeet.

Habitat: Mixed habitats, forest edges, mountains, and foothills.

Range: Southern Yukon and Mackenzie south through w U.S. to Wisconsin and w Texas.

These deer have large ears that move independently and almost constantly and account for the common name. Primarily active in mornings, evenings, and on moonlit nights, deer may also be active at midday in winter. Summer forage is chiefly herbaceous plants but also blackberry, huckleberry, salal, and thimbleberry; winter browse includes twigs of Douglas fir, cedar, yew, aspen, willow, dogwood, serviceberry, juniper, and sage. Acorns and apples are also eaten. Mule Deer have a stiff-legged bounding gait, with back legs then front legs moving together. They are also good swimmers. Deer in mountainous areas migrate up and down seasonally to avoid heavy snows.

They seldom form large herds. The usual groups consist of a doe with her fawn or a doe with twin fawns and a pair of yearlings. When does encounter each other they often fight, so family groups space themselves widely, thereby helping to ensure food and cover for all. Many bucks are solitary, but some band together before and after rutting season. Deer often "yard up," or herd, in winter. Bucks are polygamous and have larger home ranges than does, but during the rutting season both bucks and does may leave their home range. Displays and threats often prevent actual conflict between bucks, but vigorous fights do occur when, with antlers enmeshed, each tries to force down the other's head. Even in such battles injuries are rare; usually the loser withdraws. But if antlers become locked, both perish through starvation. After a gestation of 6–7 months, a single fawn is produced by a once-bred doe, while the older does usually have twins. Newborns weigh about 8 lb. For their first month they are kept concealed; their mother visits them regularly to nurse. All Mule Deer have glands on the hindlegs above the hooves. A fawn seems able to recognize its mother by these glands, and when deer are in groups, the glands are frequently sniffed. The long hairs around these glands are usually erected when aggressive confrontations between bucks begin. Mule Deer can cause a great deal of damage to crops and growing timber. Prized as trophies and for their flesh, they are hunted by man. Cougars, wolves, and Coyotes are their major natural predators; Bobcats and bears take a few; and others are killed by trains and automobiles.

285, 286 White-tailed Deer
"Whitetail" "Virginia Deer"
(*Odocoileus virginianus*)
Subspecies: Coues, Key

Description: Tan or reddish-brown above in summer; grayish-brown in winter. Belly, throat, nose band, eye ring, and inside of ears white. *Tail brown, edged with white above,* often with dark stripe down center, *white below.* Black spots on sides of chin. *Bucks' antlers with main beam forward and several unbranched tines* behind; a small brow tine. Antler spread to 3' (90 cm). Does normally lack antlers. Fawns spotted. Height at shoulder 3–3½' (90–105 cm). L 4½–6¾' (134–206 cm); T 6–13" (15–33 cm); Wt males 200–300 lb. (90–135 kg), females 150–250 lb. (67.5–112.5 kg).

Similar Species: Mule Deer has antlers with both main beams branching, tail tipped with black.

Sign: *Bed:* Shallow, oval, body-size depression in leaves or snow.
"Buck rubs": Polished scars or oblong sections where bark removed from bushes, saplings, or small trees, usually close to ground; made when a buck lowers its head and rubs antlers against a tree to mark territory; trees chosen to fit antlers (for example, a rub on a tree 4–5" in diameter indicates the rub was made by a very large buck).
Raggedly browsed vegetation: Lacking upper incisors, deer rip away vegetation instead of snipping it neatly like rabbits.
Scat: When browsing, almost always hard, dark pellets, usually slightly oblong or acorn-shaped, about ¾" long; sometimes round. When grazing on succulent vegetation, cylindrical and segmented, even massed.
Tracks: Like narrow split hearts, pointed end forward, about 2–3" long; dewclaws may print twin dots behind main prints in snow or soft mud. In

shallow snow (1" deep), buck may drag its feet, leaving drag marks ahead of prints; in deeper snow, both bucks and does drag feet. Straddle 5–6" wide. Stride, when walking, 1'; when running, 6' or more, and hindprints sometimes register ahead of foreprints; when leaping, 20'.

Habitat: Farmlands, brushy areas, woods.

Range: Southern half of s tier of Canadian provinces; most of U.S. except most of California, Nevada, Utah, n Arizona, sw Colorado, and nw New Mexico.

If alarmed, the Whitetail raises, or "flags," its tail, exhibiting a large, bright flash of white; this "hightailing" communicates danger to other deer or helps a fawn follow its mother in flight. Although primarily nocturnal, deer may be active at any time, grazing on green plants, including aquatic ones in the summer; eating acorns, beechnuts, and other nuts and corn in the fall; and in winter, browsing on woody vegetation, including the twigs and buds of viburnum, birch, maple, and many conifers. Deer usually bed down near dawn, seeking concealing cover. They are good swimmers and graceful runners, with top speeds to 35 mph, though in flight they do not run great distances but flee to the nearest cover. When nervous, Whitetails snort through their noses and stamp their hooves, a telegraphic signal that alerts other deer nearby to danger. Bucks and does herd separately most of the year, but in winter gather together, or "yard up." Whitetails are less polygamous than other deer, and a few bucks mate with only 1 doe. Gestation is 7 months; a young doe bred for the first time usually produces 1 fawn but thereafter has twins and occasionally triplets if food is abundant. A Whitetail's age is determined not by the number of tines on its horns but the wear on its teeth. Once nearly exterminated in much of the Northeast and Midwest, Whitetails are now more abundant than ever, owing to hunting restrictions and the decline in numbers of their predators. They have become the most plentiful game animal in eastern North America. There are two dwarf subspecies: the Coues Deer (*O. v. covesi*) of the Arizona desert and the Key Deer (*O. v. clavium*) of the Big Pine Key area in the Florida Keys. Although still considered an endangered species, the tiny, dog-size Key Deer, weighing 50 lb. or less, is now fully protected and making a comeback thanks to the establishment of the National Key Deer Refuge, Florida, in 1961.

291 Moose
(*Alces alces*)

Description: *Largest deer in the world.* Horse-size. Long, dark brown hair. High, *humped shoulders;* long, pale legs; stubby tail. Huge *pendulous muzzle; large dewlap under chin;* large ears. Males much larger than females, with *massive palmate antlers,* broadly flattened. Antler spread usually 4–5′ (120–150 cm); record of 81″ (206 cm). Height at shoulder 6½–7½′ (195–225 cm). L 6¾–9′ (206–279 cm); T 6¾″ (17 cm); Wt males 900–1,400 lb. (405–630 kg), females 700–1,100 lb. (315–495 kg).

Sign: Browse raggedly torn. Thrashed shrubs and barked trees.

Wallows: Cleared depressions in ground, 4′ wide, 4′ long, 3–4″ deep, muddy, smelling of urine, marked with tracks. During the rut bulls urinate and then roll in wallow; cows also roll in it.
Bed: Similar to that of other deer; marked by tracks and droppings.
Scat: Chips or masses when feeding on aquatic plants, lush grasses. Pellets, more oblong than Elk's, 1½–1¾″ long, sometimes round, when feeding

on woody browse. Pale, resembling compressed sawdust, when feeding on woody winter browse.

Trail: Wider and deeper than that of smaller deer; more likely to detour around obstructions or entanglements.

Tracks: Cloven prints similar to those of Elk but larger, more pointed; usually more than 5" long; 6" long and 4½" wide in large bull. Lobes somewhat splayed in snow, mud, or when running. Dewclaws often print behind main prints in snow, mud, or when running, lengthening print to 10". Stride 3½–5½' when walking, more than 8' when trotting or running.

Habitat: Spruce forest, swamps, aspen and willow thickets.

Range: Most of Canada; in the East south to Maine, Minnesota, and Isle Royale in Lake Superior; in the West, Alaska, n British Columbia and southeast through Rocky Mountains to ne Utah and nw Colorado.

Moose are solitary in summer, but several may gather near streams and lakes to feed on willows and aquatic vegetation, including the leaves of water lilies. When black flies and mosquitoes torment them, Moose may nearly submerge themselves or roll in a wallow to acquire a protective coating of mud. Good swimmers, they can move at speeds of 6 mph for up to 2 hours at a time. Migrating up and down mountain slopes seasonally, they may herd in winter, packing down snow, which facilitates movement; then they browse on woody plants, including the twigs, buds, and bark of willow, balsam, aspen, dogwood, birch, cherry maple, and viburnum. Despite their ungainly appearance, they can run through the forest quietly at speeds up to 35 mph. Vocalizations include a bull's tremendous bellow and the cow's call, which ends in a coughlike *moo-agh*. During mating season, mid-

September–late October, bulls do not gather a harem but stay with one cow for about a week and then with another. Bulls thrash brush with antlers, probably to mark territory. Occasionally they battle, but generally threat displays prompt one to withdraw; if horns interlock, both may perish. After a gestation of 8 months, 1–2 calves are born, light colored but not spotted. Within a couple of weeks they can swim; at about 6 months they are weaned; and just before the birth of new calves they are driven off. Life span is up to 20 years. A bull's antlers begin growing in April, attain full growth by August, and are shed between December and February. Moose are unpredictable and dangerous. They are normally retiring animals and avoid human contact, but cows with calves are irritable and fiercely protective, and rutting bulls occasionally have charged people, horses, cars, and locomotives.

---

290 Caribou
(*Rangifer tarandus*)

Description: Coloration variable; generally *brown shaggy fur with whitish neck and mane;* belly, rump, underside of tail white. Nearly white on Arctic islands; more brownish on tundra, taiga, and forest. *Fawns unspotted.* Large snout; short, furry ears; short, well-furred tail. Foot pads large and soft in summer, shrunken in winter; rounded hooves. *Males and most females with antlers.* Bulls' antlers are branched, semipalmated, and have flattened brow tines, 20–62″ (52–158 cm) long. Cows' antlers relatively small and spindly, 9–20″ (23–50 cm) long. Antler spread to 60″ (153 cm). Height at shoulder 3–3½′ (90–105 cm). L 4½–6¾′ (137–210 cm); T 4–8¾″ (102–218 mm); Wt males 275–600 lb. (124–270 kg), females 150–300 lb. (67.5–135 kg).

Similar Species: Elk lack flattened brow tines, white throat; have large yellowish-brown rump patch. Deer smaller, lack brow tines.

Sign: Deeply worn trails made during migrations. Rubs on saplings, thrashed bushes, bedding depressions similar to those of other cervids; distinguishable mainly by tracks and locale. Audible clicking sounds when long ankle tendons slide over bones.

Scat: Usually small, bell-shaped pellets similar to Whitetail's; occasionally massed when feeding on succulent summer vegetation.

Tracks: Widely separated crescents, 5″ wide, slightly shorter, almost always followed by dewclaw marks; on thin, crusted snow, only round outlines of hooves may print; hindprints usually overlap foreprints, leaving double impressions 8″ long.

Habitat: Tundra, taiga; farther south where lichens abound in coniferous forests in mountains.

Range: Alaska and much of Canada south through British Columbia to e Washington and n Idaho; also n Alberta and n two thirds of Saskatchewan and Manitoba; in the East, south to Lake Superior and east to Newfoundland.

The Caribou of North America, now considered to be the same species as the Reindeer of Europe and Asia, is among the most migratory of all mammals. These gregarious animals usually form homogeneous bands of bulls, cows with calves, or yearlings, but may gather in groups of 10–100,000 of both sexes and all ages in late winter before the spring migration, after calving, and before the fall migration and rutting. Especially active in mornings and evenings, in summer Caribou feed on lichens, mushrooms, grasses, sedges, and many other green plants, twigs of birches and willows, and fruit; dropped antlers are avidly eaten by Caribou and rodents. In winter, lichens are the chief food, but horsetails, sedges, and willow and birch twigs are also eaten. Usually quiet, Caribou may give a loud snort, and herds of snorting animals may sound like pigs. Good swimmers, Caribou swim with nearly a third of their body above water; the air-filled hollow hairs of their coat give them great buoyancy. They can run at speeds of nearly 50 mph but cannot maintain such a pace for very long. In summer, to avoid heat and insects, they often lie on snowbanks on the north side of hills; in winter they sun on frozen lakes. Their spongy foot pads provide traction and good weight distribution on boggy summer tundra; in winter, when the pads have shrunk, hardened, and are covered with tufts of hair, the hoof rim bites into ice or crusted snow to prevent slipping. In the fall, bulls fatten up to sustain themselves through the rigors of the rut, when they seldom eat. In October and November, the polygamous bulls try to establish harems of 12–15 cows and rush about, thrashing bushes with their antlers and battling other bulls. After gestation of 7½–8 months, usually 1 calf, sometimes 2, is born mid-May–early July. It weighs about 11 lb. and is well developed, able to stand in about 30 minutes, run some distance after 90 minutes, and keep up with the herd within 24 hours. It begins to eat solid foods at 2 weeks but may continue to nurse into the winter. Chief predators are man and wolf, though Grizzly Bears, Wolverines, Lynx, and the Golden Eagle may take a few Caribou, particularly the young. Caribou have traditionally been a major source of food for natives of the far North.

PRONGHORN
(Family Antilocapridae)

This family consists of a single species, which occurs only in western North America. Until fairly recently, all ruminants with horns that were not sheep, goats, or oxen were called antelopes; but despite its generic name, *Antilocapra,* meaning "antelope goat," the Pronghorn is neither goat, antelope, nor even closely related to either, but instead is the sole remnant of an ancient family dating back 20 million years. Horns, unlike antlers, are not branched and grow throughout an animal's life; the unique horn that gives this animal its common name is pronged, and its sheath of keratin (the same substance as in human fingernails) is shed each year.

---

284 **Pronghorn**
"American Antelope"
(*Antilocapra americana*)

Description: Medium-size; long-legged; deerlike. Upper body and outside of legs pale tan or reddish-tan; *sides, chest, belly, inner legs, and rump patch white.* Two broad white blazes across tan throat. Cheeks and lower jaw usually white. Buck has broad, black band from eyes down snout to black nose and black neck patch. *Horns black:* bucks' 12–20" (30–50 cm) long when full grown, lyre shaped, curving back and slightly inward near conical tips, each with *1 broad, short prong* jutting forward and slightly upward usually about halfway from base; does' seldom more than 3–4" (7.5–10 cm) long, usually without prongs. Short erectile mane, about 2¾–4" (7–10 cm) long. Height at shoulder 35–41" (88–103 cm). L 49¼–57⅛" (125–145 cm); T 2⅜–6¾" (6–17 cm); HF 15⅜–16⅞" (39–43 cm); Wt males 90–140 lb. (40.5–63 kg), females 75–105 lb. (34–48 kg).

Similar Species: Deer larger, lack large white rump patch, and have antlers rather than pronghorns.

Sign: *Scat:* Similar to Mule Deer's; segmented masses when grazing on succulent grasses; small pellets when browsing; pellet shape variable, bluntly oval or elongate, bell or acorn-shaped.
Tracks: Shaped like split hearts about 3″ long; hindprints slightly shorter than foreprints. Tracking usually relatively unimportant for field observer since Pronghorn inhabits open terrain and can often be seen at a great distance.

Habitat: Grasslands; grassland-brushlands; bunch grass-sagebrush areas.

Range: Southeastern Oregon, s Idaho, s Alberta, s Saskatchewan, and w North Dakota south to Arizona, and w Texas.

The fastest animal in the Western Hemisphere and among the fastest in the world, the Pronghorn, making 20′ bounds, has been clocked at 70 mph for 3–4 minutes at a time. Speeds of 45 mph are not unusual, and 30 mph is an easy cruising speed, which it can maintain for about 15 miles. It runs with its mouth open, not from exhaustion but to gasp extra oxygen. Active night and day, it alternates snatches of sleep with watchful feeding. Because it inhabits open terrain, it relies for safety on seeing enemies at a distance and on its speedy flight. Its large protruding eyes have a wide arc of vision and can detect movement 4 miles away. If alarmed, the rump hairs, which are about twice as long as other body hairs, become erect, almost doubling the size of the white rump rosette and producing a "flash" visible for great distances. When a herd flees, a buck usually serves as rear guard. If the terrain, presence of young, or a surprise attack forces a Pronghorn to fight rather than flee, it uses as weapons only its sharp hooves, which are effective enough to drive off a Coyote. The Pronghorn avoids muddy ground but is a good swimmer. In summer, it grazes on a number of plants, including grasses, various forbs, and cacti, and drinks little water when moist green vegetation is available; in winter, it browses on many different plants, favoring sagebrush. Pronghorns roam in scattered bands in summer, with does and fawns gathering in groups of a dozen or fewer, yearling and two-year-old males forming bachelor herds of about the same size, and older males establishing territories. In the fall, older males attempt to form harems of up to 20 does. During breeding season —in September or October in the North, earlier in the South—males defend territories by staring down rivals, giving loud snorts, chasing them away, and fighting if necessary, battling fiercely with their horns. About a month after breeding, horns are shed. In winter, herds may include 100 animals or more. Migration from summer to winter range is variable, depending on altitude, latitude, and range conditions. Cold is no deterrent in itself, for Pronghorns' coats keep them warm even in severe weather; the air that fills the long, hollow outer hairs provides insulation, and the hairs themselves flatten against the body to seal in warmth. (In summer these hairs ruffle up to provide cooling ventilation.) While a Pronghorn can scratch through light snow for food, deep snow forces it to areas where browse is uncovered, including higher elevations where winds have swept away expanses of snow. After delayed implantation of 1 month and gestation of 7 months, the young are born in May or June, with unspotted coats and weighing 2¼–13 lb. A doe's first breeding usually produces 1 fawn;

subsequent breedings bring twins,
rarely triplets. The doe spaces births
several hundred feet apart. Nearly
odorless for their first few days of life,
fawns lie quietly in high grass or brush
while their mother grazes at some
distance to avoid attracting predators.
For about 1 week she frequently returns
to nurse, and then doe and fawns join
the herd. Life span is 7–10 years.
Pronghorns, once abundant in their
range, declined in numbers almost as
precipitously as the Buffalo; in 1924,
owing to the fencing of rangeland,
which hampered migration and
foraging (Pronghorns cannot leap fences
like deer), and the enmity of stockmen,
there were fewer than 20,000 animals.
Now, owing to efforts at
transplantation and management of
herds by game departments, their range
is expanding and their numbers have
increased to about half a million.

BISON, GOATS, MUSKOX, AND SHEEP
(Family Bovidae)

Unlike deer, bovids have true horns, which are permanent bony outgrowths of the frontal bone. Always present in males, sometimes in females, the horns are hollow—never branched—and grow throughout the life of the animal. Males use them as weapons when competing for females, and both males and females may use them as defensive weapons against predators. Most bovids favor grasslands or open areas and depend on size and speed, as well as horns and hooves, for protection. The domestication of bovids began in Asia about 8,000 years ago, and today the domestic cow and goat are of great economic importance.

---

278 Bison
"Buffalo"
(*Bison bison*)

Description: *Largest terrestrial animal in North America.* Dark brown, with shaggy mane and beard. Long tail with tuft at tip. Broad, massive head; *humped shoulders;* short legs clothed with shaggy hair; large hooves. *In both sexes, short black horns* curving out, then up, and in at pointed tips. Horn spread to 3' (90 cm). Males: height at shoulder to 6' (180 cm). L 10–12½' (304–380 cm); T 16⅞–18⅞" (43–48 cm); Wt 991–2,000 lb. (460–900 kg). Females: height at shoulder to 5' (150 cm). L 7–8' (210–240 cm); T 12–18" (30–45 cm); Wt 793–1,013 lb. (360–460 kg).

Sign: In wooded habitat, trees ringed with pale "horn rubs" or "head rubs" where bark is worn away; trampled ground underneath such trees or around rubbed boulders.
Wallows: Especially in plains habitat,

are dusty saucer-like depressions, 8–10'
wide, 1' deep, where Bison have rolled
and rubbed repeatedly, dust-bathing to
relieve itching and rid coats of insects.
Bulls may urinate in dry wallows and
then cake themselves with mud as
protection against insect pests.
Scat: Similar to that of domestic cow.
Tracks: Similar to those of domestic
cow but rounder and somewhat larger,
about 5' wide for a mature bull. On
hard ground, cleft between facing
crescent lobes may not show, and tracks
may then resemble horses' hoofprints.

Habitat: Varied; primarily plains, prairies, river
valleys, sometimes forests.

Range: Free ranging Bison occur only at Wood
Buffalo National Park, Northwest
Territories, Canada, and in Yellowstone
National Park, Wyoming.

Bison are most active in early morning
and late afternoon but sometimes also
on moonlit nights. In the midday heat,
they rest, chewing their cuds, or dust-
bathing. Usually 4–20 Bison herd
together, with sexes separate except
during breeding season; occasionally
herds gather into bands of several
thousand. They will stampede if
frightened, galloping at speeds up to
32 mph. Good swimmers, Bison are so
buoyant that head, hump, and tail
remain above water. Vocalizations
include the bull's bellow during
rutting, the cow's snort, and the calf's
bawl. Bison feed on many grasses,
sedges, and forbs, and sometimes on
berries, lichens, and horsetails; in
winter, they clear snow from vegetation
with their hooves and head. Formerly
undertaking annual migrations of 200
miles or more between winter and
summer ranges, some Canadian Bison
still travel up to 150 miles between
wooded hills and valleys. In July, bulls
rejoin the herd and battle other
contenders in their attempts to form
harems of 10–70 cows. They walk to

within 20' of each other, lower heads, raise tails, and charge. Their massive foreheads, not their horns, collide without apparent injury. They charge repeatedly until one gives up. During the 24-hour period that a cow is in heat, a bull mates with her repeatedly. After a gestation period of 270–285 days, a single calf is born in May; occasionally there are twins. The reddish newborn stands to nurse in 30 minutes, walks within hours, and in 1 or 2 days joins the herd with its mother. At 2 months, hump and horns start to develop. Most are weaned by late summer; some nurse up to 7 months. Life span in the wild averages 25 years. In the fifteenth century some 60 million Bison grazed from the Atlantic almost to the Pacific and from Mexico and Florida into Canada. Probably no other animal has been as central to a people's way of life as was the Bison to the American Indian, who ate the meat, used the skins for clothing and shelter, made thread and rope from sinew, and glue and tools from hooves and bones, and burned the droppings as fuel. Although Indians occasionally killed more Bison than they could use, stampeding thousands over cliffs, they had no significant effect on Bison populations. The destruction of the Bison began about 1830 when government policy advocated their extermination to subdue hostile tribes through starvation, equating Bison carcasses with "discouraged Indians." Railroad construction crews often subsisted on Buffalo meat, as did some Army posts, and the railroad provided a means of shipping hides to eastern markets. Ultimately, millions of pounds of Bison bones were ground into fertilizer or used for the manufacture of bone china. By 1900 fewer than 1,000 Bison remained, and a crusade of rescue and restoration was begun. Today more than 30,000 Bison roam national parks, national Bison ranges, Canadian Buffalo parks, and privately owned rangelands.

---

280 Mountain Goat
(*Oreamnos americanus*)

Description: Compact, short-legged body. *Yellowish-white fur,* long and shaggy in winter, shorter in summer; "beard" about 5" long retained year round. Eyes, nose, hooves, and horns black. Both sexes have backward-curving, *dagger-like horns,* up to 12" long in males, 9" in females. Females approximately 15% smaller than males. Height at shoulder 3–3½' (90–105 cm). L 4–5¾' (1,245–1,787 mm); T 3¼–8" (84–203 mm); HF 11¾–14½" (300–368 mm); Wt 102–300 lb. (46–136 kg).

Sign: *Bed:* Shallow depression scraped out in shale or dirt on ledge at base of cliff. White hair snagged on vegetation and rock, or blown to ground.
Scat: Similar to that of sheep and deer; massed when feeding on lush grasses; separate, compacted pellets, usually bell shaped, sometimes oblong or nearly round, when feeding on drier, brushier foods.
Tracks: Double-lobed, squarish, widely splayed at front; 2½–3½" long.

Habitat: Rocky mountainous areas above timberline.

Range: Extreme se Alaska, s Yukon, British Columbia, sw Alberta, parts of Washington, n Idaho, nw Montana.

The Mountain Goat is not a true goat but belongs to a group known as goat-antelopes, which includes the Chamois (*Rupicapra rupicapra*) of Europe and Asia Minor. Whereas the horns of true goats sweep up and back and are transversely ridged or tightly spiraled like a corkscrew, the Mountain Goat's horns curve back only slightly and are nearly smooth. Its "beard" is not the true chin beard of male goats, but an extension of a throat mane. Active in morning and evening and sometimes during moonlit nights, it feeds on grasses, sedges, and other green plants in summer, woody plants in winter, and mosses and lichens year round, migrating up and down mountains with the season. On warm days it will bed on a patch of snow, in a shady spot, or on a mountain ledge. The sexes herd apart until rutting season, usually in November or December but even into January. During rut, a male often marks a female with a musky oil from glands at the base of his horns by rubbing his head against her body. Breeding battles between rival males are uncommon, their skulls and horns being relatively fragile; but they frequently threaten each other. During rutting season, males dig pits from which they paw dirt onto their flanks and bellies. A single kid (sometimes 2–3) is born in May or June, usually on a mountain ledge. It can stand shortly after birth, weighs about 6½ lb., and remains with its mother until the next year's young is born. The Mountain Goat's hooves are well adapted for the rocky peaks, with a sharp outer rim that grips and a rubbery sole that provides traction on steep or smooth surfaces. Traversing razorbacks and hairline ledges at a stately walk or trot, a Mountain Goat may seem to move across the face of an almost sheer cliff. It has, however, been known to lose or miss its footing and fall to its death. Avalanches and rock slides are the greatest killers, accounting for many more deaths than predation. Among the peaks, only the Golden Eagle can attack a Mountain Goat; it may try to drive a kid over a cliff. Carnivores like the Cougar may attack Mountain Goats as they descend into valleys, but their sharp hooves make them dangerous prey.

277 **Muskox**
(*Ovibos moschatus*)

Description: Large. Dark brown *shaggy hair hanging nearly to feet;* lighter "saddle" on back; lower legs whitish. Broad head; slightly humped shoulders. Both males and females have *massive horns,* light or dark brown, *curving down close to sides of head,* then out and up near pointed tips. Female's horns shorter, more slender, and more curved than male's. Horn spread to 30" (75 cm). Males considerably larger than females. Height at shoulder 3–5' (91–152 cm). L 6¼–8' (194–246 cm); T 2⅜–6¾" (6–17 cm); Wt males 579–900 lb. (263–405 kg); females 370–670 lb. (167–302 kg).

Sign: *Scat:* Similar to cow manure but often drier, harder.

Tracks: Pair of facing crescents, about 5" long; front and rear contours so similar that direction of travel may be difficult to ascertain, but front usually prints deeper than rear; similar to tracks of domestic cattle and Bison. On very hard ground, cleft may not print clearly and then may look similar to those of horses.

Habitat: Arctic tundras; in summer, grassy river valleys, lakeshores, and meadows with willows and heath plants; in winter, windswept hilltops and slopes where vegetation is exposed.

Range: Northern part of Northwest Territories and islands to, but not including, Greenland.

The genus name combines sheep (*ovis*) and oxen (*bos*). The Muskox is more or less intermediate between the 2 groups, being oxlike in size, while its profile, hairy muzzle, thin lips, and relatively small, pointed ears might belong to a giant, long-haired ram. Muskoxen form herds of 3–100. The basic social ties are between a cow, her newborn calf, and her yearling; breeding-age bulls are

solitary except when they join the herd
in summer during rutting season.
When threatened, adults form a
fortress-like ring or a line with the
young inside. If a wolf, its chief
predator, approaches too close, it is
thrown into the air on a bull's horns,
then crushed with its hooves;
occasionally a bull will leave the ring to
attack. Muskoxen have good sight and
hearing and can run rapidly when
necessary, usually moving in a closely
packed herd. Both sexes snort and
stamp their feet, and excited males give
a deep, throaty bellow. Undertaking no
major migrations, they travel only
about 50 miles between summer and
winter ranges. In summer, they feed on
green vegetation, such as sedges,
grasses, and willows; in winter,
primarily woody plants. In July, bulls
join the herd and charge and clash
heads when jousting for cows.
Muskoxen give off a stronger odor than
Bison or domestic cattle, and during
breeding season, which peaks in
September, bulls exude an especially
strong scent; both the animal's common
and scientific names refer to this musky
odor, which, however, is from urine,
not musk, as these animals have no
musk glands.
After an 8-month gestation, usually 1
calf is born every other year in late
April or May. It is able to stand shortly
after birth, and horns begin to appear
at 6 months. Life span is about 20
years. In the past century, Muskoxen
were hunted for meat and hides, and for
a time herds were reduced to 500 on
the mainland. Recently their
population was estimated at about
25,000. Small, semidomesticated herds
can be found in Alaska; a herd of about
170 has been maintained at Unalakleet
for their valuable underwool, called
quiviut, which is used by Eskimo
village weavers to fashion luxury
garments.

283 Bighorn Sheep
"Mountain Sheep"
"Rocky Mountain Bighorn Sheep"
(*Ovis canadensis*)

Description: Muscular body with thick neck. Color
varying from *dark brown above* in
northern mountains to pale tan in
deserts; belly, rump patch, back of
legs, muzzle, and eye patch white.
Short, dark brown tail. Coat shed in
patches June–July. *Rams have massive
brown horns* that curve up and back over
ears, then down, around, and up past
cheeks in a C shape called a "curl." A
7- or 8-year-old may have a full curl,
with tips level with horn bases; a few
old rams exceed a full curl, but often
horns are "broomed"—broken off near
tips or deliberately rubbed off on rocks
when they begin to block ram's
peripheral vision. Ewes' horns are short,
slender, never forming more than a half
curl. Horn spread to 33″ (83 cm). Ewes
much smaller than rams. Rams: height
at shoulder 3–3½′ (90–105 cm). L
5¼–6′ (160–185 cm); T 3⅞–5⅞″
(10–15 cm); Wt 127–316 lb. (57–142
kg). Ewes: height at shoulder 2½–3′
(75–90 cm). L 4¼–5¼′ (128–158
cm); T 3½–5″ (9–13 cm); Wt 74–200
lb. (33–90 kg).

Similar Species: Dall Sheep is white, gray, or blackish
and found farther north.

Sign: *Bed:* A depression about 4′ wide, up to
1′ deep, usually smelling of urine,
almost always edged with droppings.
Scat: Dark pellets, usually bell shaped,
sometimes massed if vegetation is
succulent.

Trail: Similar to that of Mountain Goat
or deer, but at elevations higher than
deer trails and on slopes less precipitous
than Mountain Goat trails. Shed or
snagged hair, longer and darker than
deer hair, may help identify trail (goats
have white hair).
Tracks: Double-lobed prints, 3–3½″
long, with hindprints slightly smaller

than foreprints; similar to deer's but with straighter edges—less pointed and often more splayed at front, less heart shaped. When walking downhill on soft ground, dewclaws may print 2 dots behind hoofprint. Walking gait about 18″; bounding gait on level ground, 15′, down steep incline, 30′.

Habitat: Alpine meadows and foothills near rocky cliffs.

Range: South British Columbia, sw Alberta, Idaho, and Montana south to se California, Arizona, and New Mexico.

Bighorns inhabit areas rarely disturbed by man; they are active by day, feeding in early morning, midday, and evening, lying down and chewing their cud at other times, and retiring to bedding spots for the night. These may be used for years; other hoofed mammals in our range bed down in different spots each night. A good swimmer and an excellent rock climber and jumper, the Bighorn has hooves hard at the outer edge and spongy in the center, providing good traction even on sheer rock. Highly gregarious, it lives in herds usually of about 10 animals, including ewes, lambs, yearlings, and 2-year-olds; in winter, when rams also join the herd, there may be as many as 100 animals, all led by an old ewe. In spring, rams band together and move to separate higher summer ranges, but all Bighorns migrate between high slopes in the summer and valleys in winter. In summer, they feed mainly on grasses and sedges; in winter, on woody plants. As the fall rutting season approaches, rams have butting contests, which increase in frequency as the season progresses. They charge each other at speeds of more than 20 mph, their foreheads crashing with a crack that can be heard for more than a mile, often prompting other rams to similar contests. Butting battles may continue as long as 20 hours. Horn size determines status; fights occur only between rams with horns of similar size. With nose elevated, head cocked to one side, and upper lip curled, rutting males follow any female in heat, stopping occasionally for butting jousts if more than one follows the same ewe. Depending on latitude, the mating season occurs between August and early January. After a gestation of 180 days, usually in spring or early summer, a single well-developed lamb is born with a soft, woolly, light-colored coat and small horn buds. It remains hidden the first week, then follows its mother about, feeding on grasses, and is weaned at 5–6 months. Life span is about 15 years. Predators include Cougars, Golden Eagles, wolves, Coyotes, bears, Bobcats, and Lynx; but on cliffs, Bighorns easily escape all but the first 2, and the eagles only attack lambs. Bighorns have always been prized for their meat; the horns were used by Shoshone and Gros Ventre Indians to make powerful bows and are still prized by hunters as trophies.

281, 282 **Dall Sheep**
(*Ovis dalli*)

Description: *White above and below,* often with *yellowish or brownish cast;* hooves yellowish-brown. Horns on ram massive (but more slender than those on Bighorn Sheep), light yellow, with well-defined growth rings flaring out and away from head. Ram's horns about 35½" (90 cm) long, with 48½" (125 cm) largest recorded size; ewe's slender spikes less than 15" (38 cm) long. Horn spread to 3' (90 cm). In southernmost part of range, *black phase* known as Stone Sheep, varying from charcoal gray verging on black to light gray or gray-brown; in Yukon, where Dall and Stone

phases intergrade, *gray phase,* called
Fannin Sheep or Saddleback Sheep,
usually darker on back and occasionally
forming dark "saddle." Stone and
Fannin sheep have belly, rump patch,
back of legs, blaze on face white,
hooves dark, and are often slightly
bigger with slightly heavier horns than
Dall Sheep. Ewes much smaller than
rams. Ram: height at shoulder 33–42"
(83–105 cm). L 52¾–60¼" (134–153
cm); T 3½–4½" (89–115 mm); Wt
174–200 lb. (79–90 kg). Ewes: height
at shoulder 2½–3' (75–90 cm). L 3½–
4½' (105–135 cm); T 3–3½" (75–90
mm); Wt 100–125 lb. (45–56 kg).

Similar Species: Bighorn Sheep is brown and occurs to
the south.

Sign: Tufts of white hair, snagged or shed,
sometimes left on bushes, rocks.
Tracks, beds, and droppings similar to
those of Bighorn Sheep, but when Dall
Sheep have been licking a salt lick, scat
forms pellets, which are round like
marbles.

Habitat: Rocky mountainous areas.

Range: Alaska, Yukon, w Mackenzie, n British
Columbia.

Its habits are similar to those of the
Bighorn, but it seems more wary and
agile. In winter, the entire herd feeds
together on such woody plants as
willow, sage, crowberry, and cranberry.
In spring, the herd splits into 2 groups,
with ewes, lambs, and yearling rams in
1 group, older rams in the other,
though older rams sometimes remain
solitary; the oldest member in each
group is its leader. In summer, they
graze on grasses, sedges, and forbs. In
late fall, when rams try to gather a
harem of ewes, butting contests are
common. After walking apart 15–20
yards, rams turn, rise up on hindfeet,
then drop to all 4s and race toward each
other. The clash of their horns can be
heard more than a mile away. Collisions
may be repeated, but ultimately the

contest becomes a matter of pushing and shoving in which the stronger, heavier ram drives off the weaker. Both sexes mate promiscuously. After a gestation of slightly less than 6 months, 1 lamb, rarely 2, is born in mid-May, walks when 3–4 hours old, and begins eating grasses at about 10 days. Life span is up to 15 years. The wolf is its chief predator; occasionally a Lynx, Wolverine, Cougar, or bear takes a sheep, and the Golden Eagle sometimes seizes a lamb.

---

279 Barbary Sheep
(*Ammotragus lervia*)

Description: Coat uniformly tawny, except chin, insides of ears, and line on underparts white. A *long mane* hangs from throat, chest, and upper forelegs. Heavy, wrinkled, *goatlike horns* bend outward, then backward and in; measure to 33½" (84 cm) long. Height at shoulder 3–3½' (90–105 cm). L 4¼–6¼' (130–190 cm); T 9¾" (25 cm); Wt 110–253 lb. (50–115 kg).

Sign: Tracks and droppings similar to those of Bighorn Sheep.

Habitat: Rocky mountainous terrain in arid or semiarid areas.

Range: Southwestern U.S.

The single species in this genus is native to North Africa, where it is hunted for meat. It was introduced as a game animal in the southwestern U.S. in 1950. The Barbary Sheep gets its water primarily from dew and the green vegetation upon which it chiefly feeds. A gland beneath the tail gives it a goatlike odor. In behavior it is sheeplike, following its leader, usually an adult female. Families of male, female, and young remain together. During breeding season males stand apart, run toward each other, and clash horns. They also stand side by side, lock horns, and try to pull each other down in a display of strength similar to Indian arm wrestling. There are usually 1–3 young, which are nursed about 6 months.

Part III
Appendices

GLOSSARY

Buff Dull brownish-yellow.

Cache A place in which food stores are hidden; food hidden in such a place.

Calcar In bats a small bone or cartilage that projects from the inner side of the hindfoot into the interfemoral membrane.

Carnivorous Flesh-eating.

Colonial Living in a colony or group, in which individuals usually maintain close associations (e.g., prairie dogs).

Crepuscular Appearing or becoming active at twilight or just before sunrise.

Cross phase A color phase between summer and winter pelage in certain mammals, such as the Red Fox.

Dewclaw A functionless digit or "toe," usually on the upper part of a mammal's foot; on deer, it is located above the true hoof.

Dewlap Loose folds of skin hanging from the throat of cattle and certain other animals, such as the Elk and the Moose.

Digitigrade Walking on the toes with the heels not touching the ground; hoofed mammals, cats, and canids are digitigrade (*see* plantigrade).

Diurnal Active by day.

Dusky Dull grayish-brown.

Echolocation The way in which certain animals orient themselves by emitting high-frequency sounds and interpreting the reflected sound waves; bats navigate and locate prey by this means.

Estivation Dormancy during hot or dry periods rather than cold ones.

Estrus The period during which female mammals are sexually receptive to males (*see* heat).

Extirpation Extinction of a species in a particular geographical area.

Forb An herb other than grass; weed.

Fossorial Adapted for a burrowing existence (e.g., moles).

Gregarious Living harmoniously with other individuals of the same species; sociable.

Grizzled Gray or streaked with gray.

Guard hairs Long coarse hairs that form a protective coating over the underfur of a mammal.

Habitat The environment in which an organism lives.

Heat The period during which a female mammal is sexually receptive to males (*see* estrus).

Herbivorous Plant-eating.

Hibernation Dormancy during the winter;

temperature and all bodily processes are greatly reduced, thereby conserving energy and enabling certain mammals to sleep through the winter.

Interfemoral membrane The thin skin that stretches between the hindlegs of bats.

Keeled calcar In bats the calcar is said to be keeled when there is a flat projection of bone protruding from the calcar into the interfemoral membrane.

Keratin A fibrous protein that forms the principal matter of horn, hairs, and nails in mammals; human fingernails are composed of keratin.

Marsupium A fold of skin in the abdomen of marsupial mammals that forms a pouch in which the young complete their development, feeding from the mammary glands which the marsupium encloses. The only North American mammal to have a marsupium is the Virginia Opossum

Melanism A dark color in animals that is the result of an increased development of black pigment in the skin, hair, feathers, etc.

Midden A dung hill or refuse heap; when squirrels eat nuts at a regular feeding post, the discarded nutshells may form a midden.

Molariform teeth Teeth adapted for grinding; all teeth behind the canines, including premolars and molars.

Montane Pertaining to or inhabiting mountainous country.

Nocturnal Active by night.

Omnivorous Feeding on both plant and animal material.

Plantigrade Walking on the soles of the feet; men and bears are plantigrade (*see* digitigrade).

Roadkill Animal killed on a road or highway by a passing automobile or truck.

Ruminant An even-toed hoofed mammal, such as a sheep or a deer, having a complex 3- or 4-chambered stomach from which stored food, the "cud," is regurgitated into the mouth for chewing to aid more complete digestion.

Rut The periodic sexual excitement of male deer, sheep, and goats (corresponding to estrus or heat in females); also the period when this occurs.

Scat Fecal pellet or dropping; feces.

Semicolonial Living in loose association with other individuals, usually without very close contact.

Semifossorial Partially adapted for a burrowing existence but spending some time aboveground (e.g., pocket gophers, prairie dogs).

Straddle The width of a set of animal tracks.

Stride The distance between sets of animal tracks.

Subalpine Mountain regions below timberline.

Tawny Brownish-yellow.

Torpor Temporary loss of all or part of the power of sensation or motion, resulting from the reduction of body temperature and the slowing of bodily processes.

Tragus In bats, the lobe that projects upward from the base of the ear.

Unicuspid In shrews, any of the small teeth

between the single large front tooth and the large molariform teeth.

Velvet The soft furry covering on a deer's growing antlers that contains a network of capillaries to supply nourishment to growing bone; when antlers are so covered, the deer is said to be "in velvet."

Vibrissae Long, stiff facial hairs or whiskers around the nose or mouth of certain mammals; often serving as organs of touch, as in cats and the Walrus.

Yard A place where hoofed mammals, such as wild deer or Moose, herd together to feed during the winter; when they so gather, they are said to "yard up."

RANGE CHARTS

Many of the smaller mammals, such as shrews, are so similar in appearance and so reclusive in their habits that often one gets only a glimpse of them in the field. However, since most species occupy a specific geographical area, it is often possible to distinguish between species simply on the basis of where the animal is seen. For example, if you are in Delaware and see a shrew darting across a clearing in the open country, you will find, on consulting the range charts, that only one species of shrew occurs in Delaware—the Masked Shrew (*Sorex cinereus*). Reading the habitat section of the species account confirms your identification.

Groups   Range charts are provided for the following groups of smaller mammals:

Shrews
Bats
Rabbits and Hares
Chipmunks
Ground Squirrels
Pocket Gophers
Pocket Mice
Kangaroo Rats
Harvest Mice
White-footed Mice
Woodrats
Voles

Regions   The range charts for each group are
divided into the following geographical
regions:

Eastern
Northeast
Southeast
Midwest
Western
North Central
South Central
West
Northwest

Each region is further divided into
states and provinces. Because of space
restrictions we have combined North
and South Dakota as one area with the
abbreviation NSD. The range for North
Dakota appears at top; the range for
South Dakota at bottom.

Key   ◯ = throughout
(N) = north
(S) = south
(E) = east
(W) = west
(C) = central

Abbreviations   The following abbreviations of states
and provinces are used in the charts:

Northeast   NB   New Brunswick
NE   New England
NJ   New Jersey
NY   New York
NF   Newfoundland
NS   Nova Scotia
PA   Pennsylvania
QU   Quebec

Southeast   DE   Delaware
FL   Florida
GA   Georgia
MD   Maryland
NC   North Carolina
SC   South Carolina
VA   Virginia
WV   West Virginia

Midwest	IL	Illinois
	IN	Indiana
	IA	Iowa
	KS	Kansas
	MI	Michigan
	MN	Minnesota
	MO	Missouri
	NE	Nebraska
	OH	Ohio
	ON	Ontario
	WI	Wisconsin
North Central	AB	Alberta
	MB	Manitoba
	MT	Montana
	ND	North Dakota
	NSD	North and South Dakota
	SK	Saskatchewan
	SD	South Dakota
	WY	Wyoming
South Central	AL	Alabama
	AR	Arkansas
	KY	Kentucky
	LA	Louisiana
	MS	Mississippi
	OK	Oklahoma
	TN	Tennessee
	TX	Texas
West	AZ	Arizona
	BC	British Columbia
	CA	California
	CO	Colorado
	ID	Idaho
	NV	Nevada
	NM	New Mexico
	OR	Oregon
	UT	Utah
	WA	Washington
Northwest	AK	Alaska
	NW	Northwest Territories
	YK	Yukon

BERING SEA

BEAUFORT SEA

AK

YK

GULF OF ALASKA

NW

BC

AB

SK

WA

MT

N

OR

ID

S.

WY

N

NV

CA

UT

CO

K

PACIFIC OCEAN

AZ

NM

TX

MEXICO

	Northeast								Southeast		
	NB	NE	NJ	NY	NF	NS	PA	QU	DE	FL	GA
SHREWS											
Masked or Cinereous Shrew (*Sorex cinereus*)	O	O	O	O	(E)	O	O	O	O		
Southeastern Shrew (*S. longirostris*)										(N)	C
Water Shrew (*S. palustris*)	O	O		(E)	(S)	O	(NE)	(S)			
Smoky Shrew (*S. fumeus*)	O	O	(NW)	O		O	O	(S)			(NE)
Arctic Shrew (*S. arcticus*)	O					O		(S)			
Gaspé Shrew (*S. gaspensis*)								(SE)			
Long-tailed or Rock Shrew (*S. dispar*)		O	(NW)	(E)			O				
Pygmy Shrew (*Microsorex hoyi*)	O	O			O	(E)	O	(NW)	O		
Short-tailed Shrew (*Blarina brevicauda*)	O	O	O	O		O	O	(S)		(WC)	(N)
Southern Short-tailed Shrew (*B. carolinensis*)										O	(S)
Swamp Short-tailed Shrew (*B. telmalestes*)											
Least Shrew (*Cryptotis parva*)		(SW)	O	(S)			O		O	O	O
Desert Shrew (*Notiosorex crawfordi*)											
BATS											
Little Brown Myotis (*Myotis lucifugus*)	O	O	O	O	O	O	O	(S)	O		(N)(C)
Southeastern Myotis (*M. austroriparius*)										(N)	(S)(C)
Gray Myotis (*M. grisescens*)											
Cave Myotis (*M. velifer*)											
Keen's Myotis (*M. keenii*)	O	O	O	O	O	O	O	(S)		(NC)	(W)

Midwest

MD	NC	SC	VA	WV	IL	IN	IA	KS	MI	MN	MO	NE	OH	ON	WI
○	W		W	E	N/E	○	N		○	○		○	○	○	○
S	○	○	E	S/C	S	S/C					SW				
	W		W	○					N	N/C				W/S	N
	W	NW	W	○									E	S	
									N	○				○	○
W	W		W	E											
	W		○		N		N		○	○			E	○	○
○	W	W	W/N	○	○	○	○	○	○	○	NE	○	○	S	○
	○	○	E				SW	○				○	S		
			SE												
○	○	○	○	○	○	○	○	○	S	S	○	○	○	S	S
								S							
○	○	○	○	○	○	○	○	○	○	○	○	○	○	○	○
				S	S										
				S	S					○					
								SC							
○	W	W	W	○	○	○	○	E	○	○	○	N/E	○	S	○

	Northeast									Southeast	
	NB	NE	NJ	NY	NF	NS	PA	QU	DE	FL	GA
BATS (continued)											
Indiana or Social Myotis (*Myotis sodalis*)		ⓢ	ⓝⓦ	ⓢⒺ			◯			ⓝⓒ	ⓝⓦ
Long-legged Myotis (*M. volans*)											
Small-footed Myotis (*M. leibii*)		ⓢ ⓒ		◯			◯	ⓢ			Ⓝ
RABBITS AND HARES											
Marsh Rabbit (*Sylvilagus palustris*)										◯	ⓢ
Eastern Cottontail (*S. floridanus*)		ⓢ	◯	ⓢ ⓒ			◯	ⓢ		◯	◯
New England Cottontail (*S. transitionalis*)		ⓢ	◯	Ⓔ			Ⓔ ⓒ				Ⓝ
Desert Cottontail (*S. audubonii*)											
Swamp Rabbit (*S. aquaticus*)											Ⓝ ⓦ
European Rabbit (*Oryctolagus cuniculus*)	◯	◯	◯	◯	◯	◯	◯	◯	◯	◯	◯
Snowshoe Hare (*Lepus americanus*)	◯	◯	◯	◯	◯	◯	◯	◯			
White-tailed Jack Rabbit (*L. townsendii*)											
Black-tailed Jack Rabbit (*L. californicus*)											
Cape or European Hare (*L. capensis*)		ⓦ	ⓦ	◯			Ⓔ	ⓢ			
CHIPMUNKS											
Eastern Chipmunk (*Tamias striatus*)	◯	◯	◯	◯	◯	◯	◯	ⓢ	◯		
Least Chipmunk (*Eutamias minimus*)								ⓦ			
GROUND SQUIRRELS											
Richardson's Ground Squirrel (*Spermophilis richardsonii*)											

Midwest

MD	NC	SC	VA	WV	IL	IN	IA	KS	MI	MN	MO	NE	OH	ON	WI
(N)	(W)		(W)	◯	◯	◯	(E)		(S)		◯		◯		(S)
												(W)			
◯	(W)		(W)	◯				(NW)			(S)	(W)		(SE)	
	(E)	(E/C)	(SE)												
◯	◯	◯	◯	◯	◯	◯	◯	◯	◯	◯	◯	◯	◯	(SE)	◯
◯	(W)		(W)	(E)											
									(W)			(W)			
		(W)			(S)	(SW)		(SE)			(S)				
◯	◯	◯	◯	◯	◯	◯	◯	◯	◯	◯	◯	◯	◯	◯	◯
(W)	(W)		(W)	(E)					◯	(N)				◯	(N)
					(WC)		(•l/C)	(W/C)		(W/S)		◯			(SW)
								◯			(W)	◯			
									(N/E)	(NE)				(S)	(N)
◯	◯	(NW)	◯	◯	◯	◯	◯	◯	◯	◯	◯	(E)	◯	(S)	◯
									(N)	(N)		(W)		◯	(N/C)
										(W)					

	Northeast								Southeast		
	NB	NE	NJ	NY	NF	NS	PA	QU	DE	FL	GA
GROUND SQUIRRELS (continued)											
Thirteen-lined Ground Squirrel (*Spermophilus tridecemlineatus*)											
Spotted Ground Squirrel (*S. spilosoma*)											
Franklin's Ground Squirrel (*S. franklinii*)											
POCKET GOPHERS											
Northern Pocket Gopher (*Thomomys talpoides*)											
Plains Pocket Gopher (*Geomys bursarius*)											
Southeastern Pocket Gopher (*G. pinetis*)										ⓃN	Ⓢ
Colonial Pocket Gopher (*G. colonus*)											ⓈE
Sherman's Pocket Gopher (*G. fontanelus*)											Ⓔ
Cumberland Island Pocket Gopher (*G. cumberlandius*)											ⓈE
POCKET MICE											
Olive-backed Pocket Mouse (*Perognathus fasciatus*)											
Plains Pocket Mouse (*P. flavescens*)											
Silky Pocket Mouse (*P. flavus*)											
Hispid Pocket Mouse (*P. hispidus*)											
KANGAROO RATS											
Ord's Kangaroo Rat (*Dipodomys ordii*)											

Midwest

MD	NC	SC	VA	WV	IL	IN	IA	KS	MI	MN	MO	NE	OH	ON	WI
					N/C	N/C	○	○	○	○	N/W	○	W		○
								W				W/C			
					N/C	NW	○	N/E		○	N/C	○		SW	SW
										NW		W			
					C	NW	○	○		○	N/E	○			W
												NW			
							N/W	W/C		S		○			S/W
								W				W			
								○				○			
								W/C				W/C			

	Northeast								Southeast		
	NB	NE	NJ	NY	NF	NS	PA	QU	DE	FL	GA
HARVEST MICE											
Plains Harvest Mouse (*Reithrodontomys montanus*)											
Eastern Harvest Mouse (*R. humulis*)										◯	◯
Western Harvest Mouse (*R. megalotis*)											
Fulvous Harvest Mouse (*R. fulvescens*)											
WHITE-FOOTED MICE											
Deer Mouse (*Peromyscus maniculatus*)	◯	◯		◯	Ⓔ	◯	◯	◯			Ⓝᴱ
Oldfield Mouse (*P. polionotus*)										Ⓝ Ⓔ	◯
White-footed Mouse (*P. leucopus*)	Ⓢᴱ	◯	◯	◯		◯	◯				Ⓝ Ⓒ
Cotton Mouse (*P. gossypinus*)										◯	Ⓢ Ⓒ
Brush Mouse (*P. boylii*)											
Texas Mouse (*P. pectoralis*)											
Florida Mouse (*P. floridanus*)										Ⓢ Ⓒ	
WOODRATS											
Eastern Woodrat (*Neotoma floridana*)		Ⓢᵂ	Ⓝ	Ⓢᴱ			◯			Ⓝ Ⓒ	◯
Southern Plains Woodrat (*N. micropus*)											
Bushy-tailed Woodrat (*N. cinerea*)											
VOLES											
Southern Red-backed Vole (*Clethrionomys gapperi*)	◯	◯	◯	◯	◯	◯	◯	◯	◯		
Heather Vole (*Phenacomys intermedius*)	◯				◯	◯		◯			

MD	NC	SC	VA	WV	IL	IN	IA	KS	MI	MN	MO	NE	OH	ON	WI
								○				○			
Ⓦ	○	○	○	○										Ⓢ	
					Ⓝ	ⓃⓌ	○	○		Ⓢ	○	○			ⓈⓌ
								ⓈⒺ			ⓈⓌ				
Ⓦ	Ⓦ	ⓃⓌ	Ⓦ	○	○	○	○	○	○	○	○	○	○	○	○
		Ⓦ													
○	Ⓦ/Ⓒ	Ⓦ/Ⓒ	○	○	○	○	○	○	Ⓢ	○	○	○	○	ⓈⒺ	○
	Ⓔ	Ⓔ/Ⓒ	ⓈⒺ			Ⓢ					ⓈⒺ				
								ⓈⒺ			ⓈⓌ				
								ⓈⒺ			ⓈⓌ				
Ⓦ	ⓈⒺ/Ⓦ	Ⓔ/Ⓦ	Ⓦ	○	Ⓢ	Ⓢ		Ⓝ/Ⓔ			Ⓢ/Ⓒ		Ⓒ	Ⓢ	
								ⓈⓌ							
													Ⓦ		
○	○		○	○					Ⓝ	Ⓝ				○	○
										ⓃⒺ				○	

| | Northeast | | | | | | | | Southeast | | |
	NB	NE	NJ	NY	NF	NS	PA	QU	DE	FL	GA
VOLES (continued)											
Meadow Vole (*Microtus pennsylvanicus*)	◯	◯	◯	◯	Ⓔ	◯	◯	◯	◯		ⓃⒺ
Rock Vole (*M. chrotorrhinus*)	Ⓦ	Ⓝ		Ⓔ	Ⓔ		Ⓝ Ⓔ Ⓒ	Ⓢ			
Prairie Vole (*M. ochrogaster*)											
Woodland Vole (*M. pinetorum*)		◯	◯	◯			◯		◯	Ⓝ Ⓒ	◯

Midwest

MD	NC	SC	VA	WV	IL	IN	IA	KS	MI	MN	MO	NE	OH	ON	WI
○	W/C	○	○	○	N	○	○		○	○	N	NE/SW	○	○	○
NE	W		W	E						NE				SE	
				W	○	○	○	○	SW	S/W	○	○	SW		SW
○	○	○	○	○	○	○	S/E	E	S/C	SE	○	SE	○	SE	S

SHREWS	North Central						South Central				
	AB	MB	MT	NSD	SK	WY	AL	AR	KY	LA	MS
Masked or Cinereous Shrew (*Sorex cinereus*)	○	○	○	○○	○	○			○(N)/○(E)		
Mt. Lyell Shrew (*S. lyelli*)											
Preble's Shrew (*S. preblei*)											
Pribilof Shrew (*S. pribilofensis*)											
St. Lawrence Island Shrew (*S. jacksoni*)											
Southeastern Shrew (*S. longirostris*)							○	○(N)	○(W)/○(E)	○(NE)	○
Vagrant Shrew (*S. vagrans*)			○(W)	○(WC)		○					
Dusky Shrew (*S. monticolus*)	○	○(WC)	○(W)		○	○					
Pacific Shrew (*S. pacificus*)											
Ornate Shrew (*S. ornatus*)											
Inyo Shrew (*S. tenellus*)											
Ashland Shrew (*S. trigonirostris*)											
Dwarf Shrew (*S. nanus*)				○(SW)		○					
Suisun Shrew (*S. sinuosus*)											
Water Shrew (*S. palustris*)	○	○	○(W)/○(C)	○(NE)/○(NE)	○	○					
Glacier Bay Water Shrew (*S. alaskanus*)											
Pacific Water Shrew (*S. bendirii*)											
Smoky Shrew (*S. fumeus*)									○(E)		
Arctic Shrew (*S. arcticus*)	○	○		○(N-E)/○(NE)	○						

OK	TN	TX	AZ	BC	CA	CO	ID	NV	NM	OR	UT	WA	AK	NW	YK
	(E)			(○)		(○)	(○)		(NC)		(○)	(○)	(○)	(○)	(○)
					(EC)										
							(SW)			(E)		(SE)			
													(W)		
													(NW)		
	(○)														
			(E)(N)	(SW)	(N)	(W)	(○)	(N)	(W)	(○)	(NW)	(○)			
				(○)	(E)	(W)(C)	(○)	(WC)	(C)(NC)	(W)	(○)	(○)	(○)	(SW)	(○)
					(NW)					(SW)					
					(○)										
					(EC)			(WC)							
										(SW)					
			(NE)			(W)(C)	(SE)		(NW)		(E)				
					(N)										
	(E)		(EC)	(○)	(NE)	(○)	(○)	(○)	(NC)	(○)	(○)	(○)	(SE)	(SC)	(S)
													(SE)		
				(SW)	(NW)					(W)		(W)			
	(E)														
				(NE)									(○)	(W)	(N)

	North Central						South Central				
	AB	MB	MT	NSD	SK	WY	AL	AR	KY	LA	MS
SHREWS (continued)											
Long-tailed or Rock Shrew (*Sorex dispar*)											
Trowbridge's Shrew (*S. trowbridgii*)											
Merriam's Shrew (*S. merriami*)			(E)	(SW)(NW)		○					
Arizona Shrew (*S. arizonae*)											
Pygmy Shrew (*Microsorex hoyi*)	○	○	(W)	(NE)(NE)	○						
Short-tailed Shrew (*Blarina brevicauda*)		(S)		(E-C)(E)	(SE)		(EC)		○		
Southern Short-tailed Shrew (*B. carolinensis*)							○	○	(W)	○	○
Least Shrew (*Cryptotis parva*)							○	○	○	○	○
Desert Shrew (*Notiosorex crawfordi*)								(W)			
BATS											
Little Brown Myotis (*Myotis lucifugus*)	○	○	○	○○	○	○	(N)(C)	(N)	○	(N)	(N)(C)
Yuma Myotis (*M. yumanensis*)			(N)(W)			(NW)					
Southeastern Myotis (*M. austroriparius*)							(S)(NW)	(S)	(W)	○	○
Gray Myotis (*M. grisescens*)							○	(N)	(W)		
Cave Myotis (*M. velifer*)											
Keen's Myotis (*M. keenii*)		(S)	(E)	○○	(S)(C)	(NE)	(E)	(NW)	○		
Long-eared Myotis (*M. evotis*)	(S)		○	(W)(W)	(SW)	○					
Southwestern Myotis (*M. auriculus*)											
Fringed Myotis (*M. thysanodes*)				(SW)		(NE)					

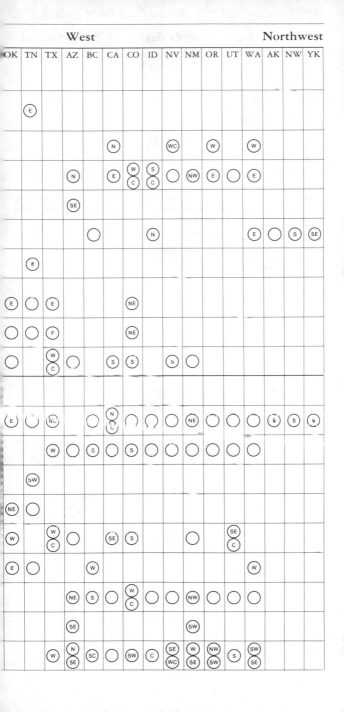

OK	TN	TX	AZ	BC	CA	CO	ID	NV	NM	OR	UT	WA	AK	NW	YK
	E														
					N			WC		W		W			
			N		E	W/C	S/C	○	NW	E	○	E			
			SE												
				○			N					E	○	S	SE
	E														
E	○	E				NE									
○	○	F				NE									
○		W/C	○		S	S		S	○						
E	○	NC		○	N/C	○	○	○	NE	○	○	○	S	S	S
		W	○	S	○	S	○	○	○	○	○	○			
	SW														
NE	○														
W	○	W/C	○		SE	S			○		SE/C				
E	○			W								W			
			NE	S	○	W/C	○	○	NW	○	○	○			
			SE						SW						
		W	N/SE	SC	○	SW	C	SE/WC	W/SE	NW/SW	S	SW/SE			

	North Central						South Central				
	AB	MB	MT	NSD	SK	WY	AL	AR	KY	LA	MS
BATS (continued)											
Indiana or Social Myotis (*Myotis sodalis*)							(E)	(N)	○		
Long-legged Myotis (*M. volans*)	(S)		(W)	(SW)		○					
California Myotis (*M. californicus*)											
Small-footed Myotis (*M. leibii*)	(S)		○	(SW)		○	(N)	(NW)	(NC)		
RABBITS AND HARES											
Pygmy Rabbit (*Sylvilagus idahoensis*)			(SW)								
Brush Rabbit (*S. bachmani*)											
Marsh Rabbit (*S. floridanus*)							(S)				
Eastern Cottontail (*S. floridanus*)		(S)	(SE)	○○		(SE)	○	○	○	○	○
New England Cottontail (*S. transitionalis*)							(NE)		(SE)		
Nuttall's Cottontail (*S. nuttallii*)	(S)		○	(W)(SW)	(S)	○					
Desert Cottontail (*S. audubonii*)			(SE)(C)	(SW)(W)		○					
Swamp Rabbit (*S. aquaticus*)							○	○	(W)	○	○
European Rabbit (*Oryctolagus cuniculus*)	○	○	○	○○	○	○	○	○	○	○	○
Snowshoe Hare (*Lepus americanus*)	○	○	○	○	○	(W)					
Northern Hare (*L. timidus*)											
Arctic Hare (*L. arcticus*)											
White-tailed Jack Rabbit (*L. townsendii*)	(S)	(S)	○	○○	(S)	○					
Black-tailed Jack Rabbit (*L. californicus*)				(S)		(SE)		(NW)			
White-sided Jack Rabbit (*L. callotis*)											

OK	TN	TX	AZ	BC	CA	CO	ID	NV	NM	OR	UT	WA	AK	NW	YK
(NE)	○														
		(W)	(E)	(W/S)	○	(W/C)	○	○	○	○	○	○			
		(W)	○	(W)	○	(W/C)	(N)	(W)	(W)	○	(SE)	○			
(SW)	(E)	(W)	(E/C)	(SC)	○	○	○	○	○	(E)	○	(E/C)			
					(NE)		(S)	(N/C)		(E/C)	(NW)	(SE)			
					(W/C)					(W)					
○	○	○	○			(E)			(NE/C/SW)						
	(E)														
			(N)	(SC)	(E)	(W/C)	○	○	(N)	(E/C)	○	(E)			
(W)		(W/C)	○		(S/C)	○		(S)	○		(?/C)				
(E)	(W)	(E)													
○	○	○	○	○	○	○	○	○	○	○	○	○	○	○	○
	(E)			○	(NE)	(W/C)	○	(W)	(NC)	○	○	○	○	(W/C)	○
													(W/N)		
														(N/C)	
				(SC)	(NE)	○	○	(N/C)	(NC)	(E/C)	○	(E/C)			
○		○	○		○	(E/S)	(S)	○	○	○	○	(W/S)	(SC)		
									(SW)						

	North Central					South Central				
	AB	MB	MT	NSD	SK	WY	AL	AR	KY	LA	MS
RABBITS AND HARES (continued)											
Antelope Jack Rabbit (*Lepus allebi*)											
CHIPMUNKS											
Eastern Chipmunk (*Tamias striatus*)		Ⓢ		○○							
Alpine Chipmunk (*Eutamias alpinus*)											
Least Chipmunk (*E. minimus*)	○	○	○	Ⓦ Ⓦ	○	○					
Yellow-pine Chipmunk (*E. amoenus*)	ⓈⓌ		Ⓦ			ⓃⓌ					
Townsend's Chipmunk (*E. townsendii*)											
Yellow-cheeked Chipmunk (*E. ochrogenys*)											
Allen's Chipmunk (*E. senex*)											
Siskiyou Chipmunk (*E. siskiyou*)											
Sonoma Chipmunk (*E. sonomae*)											
Merriam's Chipmunk (*E. merriami*)											
California Chipmunk (*E. obscurus*)											
Cliff Chipmunk (*E. dorsalis*)						ⓈⓌ					
Colorado Chipmunk (*E. quadrivittatus*)											
Red-tailed Chipmunk (*E. ruficaudus*)	ⓈⓌ		Ⓦ								
Gray-collared Chipmunk (*E. cinereicollis*)											
Gray-footed Chipmunk (*E. canipes*)											
Long-eared Chipmunk (*E. quadrimaculatus*)											

OK	TN	TX	AZ	BC	CA	CO	ID	NV	NM	OR	UT	WA	AK	NW	YK
			SC												
E															
					WC										
			EC/NW	N	NE	W/C	S	○	N/SC	E/C	○	SC		S	S
				S	N			○	N/WC	E/C	NW	○			
				S						W		W			
					NW					SW					
					N			WC		WC					
					NW					SW					
					NW										
					S										
					SC										
			○			NW	SE	E	W		○				
W			NE			W/C			N		SE				
				SE			N					NW			
			E						SW						
		NW													
					E			W							

	North Central					South Central				
	AB	MB	MT	NSD	SK	WY	AL	AR	KY	LA	MS
CHIPMUNKS (continued)											
Lodgepole Chipmunk (*Eutamias speciosus*)											
Panamint Chipmunk (*E. panamintinus*)											
Uinta Chipmunk (*E. umbrinus*)			ⓈC			Ⓦ Ⓢ					
Palmer's Chipmunk (*E. palmeri*)											
GROUND SQUIRRELS											
Townsend's Ground Squirrel (*Spermophilus townsendii*)											
Washington Ground Squirrel (*S. washingtoni*)											
Idaho Ground Squirrel (*S. brunneus*)											
Richardson's Ground Squirrel (*S. richardsonii*)	Ⓢ	Ⓢ	◯	◯ ⓃE	Ⓢ	◯					
Uinta Ground Squirrel (*S. armatus*)			ⓈW			Ⓦ					
Belding's Ground Squirrel (*S. beldingi*)											
Columbian Ground Squirrel (*S. columbianus*)	ⓈW		Ⓦ								
Arctic Ground Squirrel (*S. Darryii*)											
Thirteen-lined Ground Squirrel (*S. tridecemlineatus*)	ⓈE	Ⓢ	Ⓔ Ⓒ	◯	Ⓢ	◯					
Mexican Ground Squirrel (*S. mexicanus*)											
Spotted Ground Squirrel (*S. spilosoma*)				ⓈW		ⓈE					
Franklin's Ground Squirrel (*S. franklinii*)	Ⓔ	Ⓢ		Ⓔ-Ⓒ Ⓔ	Ⓢ						
Rock Squirrel (*S. variegatus*)											

West													Northwest		
OK	TN	TX	AZ	BC	CA	CO	ID	NV	NM	OR	UT	WA	AK	NW	YK
					E, C			W							
					E			W							
			NC		EC	NW	E	E, S			○				
								S							
					NE		S	○		E, C	W	SC			
										NC		SE			
							SW								
						NW	E, SW	NE		SE	NE				
							E				NW				
					[illegible]		[illegible]	N		E	NW				
				SE			N			NE		E			
				NW									○	○	○
○		N, E	EC			○			N, C		NE				
		W, S							SE						
W		S, W	N, SE			E, SW			○		SE				
W		W, C	○		SE	○		S	○		○				

	North Central						South Central				
	AB	MB	MT	NSD	SK	WY	AL	AR	KY	LA	MS
GROUND SQUIRRELS (continued)											
California Ground Squirrel (*Spermophilus beecheyi*)											
Mohave Ground Squirrel (*S. mohavensis*)											
Round-tailed Ground Squirrel (*S. tereticaudus*)											
Golden-mantled Ground Squirrel (*S. lateralis*)	(SW)		(W)			(W)(S)					
Cascade Golden-mantled Ground Squirrel (*S. saturatus*)											
POCKET GOPHERS											
Southern Pocket Gopher (*Thomomys umbrinus*)											
Botta's Pocket Gopher (*T. bottae*)											
Townsend's Pocket Gopher (*T. townsendii*)											
Northern Pocket Gopher (*T. talpoides*)	(SE)	(SW)	(O)	(O)(O)	(S)	(O)					
Wyoming Pocket Gopher (*T. clusius*)						(SW)					
Western Pocket Gopher (*T. mazama*)											
Idaho Pocket Gopher (*T. idahoensis*)											
Mountain Pocket Gopher (*T. monticola*)											
Camas Pocket Gopher (*T. bulbivorus*)											
Plains Pocket Gopher (*Geomys bursarius*)		(SC)		(E)(S-E)		(SE)		(W)(S)		(W)	
Desert Pocket Gopher (*G. arenarius*)											
Texas Pocket Gopher (*G. personatus*)											

OK	TN	TX	AZ	BC	CA	CO	ID	NV	NM	OR	UT	WA	AK	NW	YK
					○			WC		W		SC			
					S										
			SW		SE			S							
			NE	SE / SC	○	W / C	○	○	N	○	○	NC / SC			
												○			
			SE						SW						
		W	○		○	SW		S / C	○	SW	○				
					NE		N			SE					
			N	SE	NE	○	○	N	N	E / C	○	E / C			
					NC					NW		W			
							○								
					NE			WC							
										NW					
○		N / E				E			EC						
									SC						
		S													

	North Central						South Central				
	AB	MB	MT	NSD	SK	WY	AL	AR	KY	LA	MS

POCKET GOPHERS
(continued)

Southeastern Pocket
Gopher
(*Geomys pinetis*)
— AL: (S)

Yellow-faced Pocket
Gopher
(*Pappogeomys castanops*)

POCKET MICE

Olive-backed Pocket
Mouse
(*Perognathus fasciatus*)
— AB: (SE), MB: (SW), MT: (E), NSD: ◯ (E-C), SK: (S), WY: ◯

Plains Pocket Mouse
(*P. flavescens*)
— NSD: (SE) (E-C)

Silky Pocket Mouse
(*P. flavus*)
— WY: (SE)

Little Pocket Mouse
(*P. longimembris*)

Arizona Pocket Mouse
(*P. amplus*)

San Joaquin Pocket Mouse
(*P. inornatus*)

Great Basin Pocket Mouse
(*P. parvus*)
— WY: (SW)

White-eared Pocket
Mouse
(*P. alticola*)

Yellow-eared Pocket
Mouse
(*P. xanthonotus*)

Long-tailed Pocket Mouse
(*P. formosus*)

Bailey's Pocket Mouse
(*P. baileyi*)

Hispid Pocket Mouse
(*P. hispidus*)
— NSD: (SC) (WC), WY: (E), LA: (W)

Desert Pocket Mouse
(*P. penicillatus*)

Rock Pocket Mouse
(*P. intermedius*)

Nelson's Pocket Mouse
(*P. nelsoni*)

OK	TN	TX	AZ	BC	CA	CO	ID	NV	NM	OR	UT	WA	AK	NW	YK
(W)		(W)				(SE)			(E)						
						(N)					(NE)				
(W)		(N)				(E)									
(W)		(W)	(E)(C)			(E)(SC)			○		(SE)				
			(N)(S)		(S)(C)			○		(SE)	(W)(S)				
			○												
					(C)										
			(NW)	(SC)	(NE)		(S)	○		(E)(C)	○	(E)(C)			
					(S)										
					(S)										
			(NC)		(S)			(S)(C)				(W)			
			(S)		(SE)				(SW)						
○		○	(SE)			(E)			(E)(S)						
		(W)	(S)(NC)		(S)			(S)	(S)						
		(W)	○						(SW)		(SC)				
		(W)							(SE)						

	North Central						South Central				
	AB	MB	MT	NSD	SK	WY	AL	AR	KY	LA	MS
POCKET MICE (continued)											
San Diego Pocket Mouse (*Perognathus fallax*)											
California Pocket Mouse (*P. californicus*)											
Spiny Pocket Mouse (*P. spinatus*)											
Mexican Spiny Pocket Mouse (*Liomys striatus*)											
KANGAROO RATS											
Ord's Kangaroo Rat (*Dipodomys ordii*)	(SE)		(E)	(SW)(C)	(SW)	( )					
Chisel-toothed Kangaroo Rat (*D. microps*)											
Big-eared Kangaroo Rat (*D. elephantinus*)											
Narrow-faced Kangaroo Rat (*D. venustus*)											
Agile Kangaroo Rat (*D. agilis*)											
Heermann's Kangaroo Rat (*D. heermanni*)											
California Kangaroo Rat (*D. californicus*)											
Giant Kangaroo Rat (*D. ingens*)											
Panamint Kangaroo Rat (*D. panamintinus*)											
Stephens' Kangaroo Rat (*D. stephensi*)											
Banner-tailed Kangaroo Rat (*D. spectabilis*)											
Texas Kangaroo Rat (*D. elator*)											
Desert Kangaroo Rat (*D. deserti*)											

OK	TN	TX	AZ	BC	CA	CO	ID	NV	NM	OR	UT	WA	AK	NW	YK
					SW										
					SW C										
					S										
		S													
W		W S	N E		NE	○	S	○	○	E C	○	SC			
			NW		E		WC	○		SE	W				
					W										
					W										
					SW										
					WC										
					N					SC					
					SW										
					C E			WC S							
					S										
		W	SE NE						○						
SW		NC													
			SW		S			SW			SW				

	North Central						South Central				
	AB	MB	MT	NSD	SK	WY	AL	AR	KY	LA	MS
KANGAROO RATS (continued)											
Merriam's Kangaroo Rat (*Dipodomys merriami*)											
Fresno Kangaroo Rat (*D. nitratoides*)											
HARVEST MICE											
Plains Harvest Mouse (*Reithrodontomys montanus*)				SW		E					
Eastern Harvest Mouse (*R. humulis*)							●	N	●	S	●
Western Harvest Mouse (*R. megalotis*)	SE		E	S / ●		E / C		NE			
Salt-marsh Harvest Mouse (*R. raviventris*)											
Fulvous Harvest Mouse (*R. fulvescens*)								W / C		●	SW
WHITE-FOOTED MICE											
Cactus Mouse (*Peromyscus eremicus*)											
Merriam's Mouse (*P. merriami*)											
California Mouse (*P. californicus*)											
Deer Mouse (*P. maniculatus*)	●	S / C	●	● / ●	●	●		●	●		
Sitka Mouse (*P. sitkensis*)											
Oldfield Mouse (*P. polionotus*)							E / C				
White-footed Mouse (*P. leucopus*)	SE		E	● / ●	E	NE	N / C	●	●	●	●
Cotton Mouse (*P. gossypinus*)							●	S / C	SW	●	●
Canyon Mouse (*P. crinitus*)						SW					
Brush Mouse (*P. boylii*)								NW			
Texas Mouse (*P. attwateri*)								NW			

OK	TN	TX	AZ	BC	CA	CO	ID	NV	NM	OR	UT	WA	AK	NW	YK
		(W)	(S)(NW)		(S)			(W)(S)	(S)		(SW)				
					(C)										
		(W)(C)	(SE)			(E)			○						
	○	(SE)													
		○	○	(SC)	○	○	(S)	○	○	(S)(C)(E)	○	(E)			
					(WC)										
(E)		(E)(C)	(SE)						(SW)						
		(SW)	○		(S)			(S)	(S)		(SW)				
			(SC)												
					(▦)										
○	(N)	(W)(C)	○	○	○	○	○	○	(W)(C)	○	○	○		(SW)	○
				(W)									(W)		
○	○	○	(SE)(C)			(SE)			○						
(SE)	(W)(C)	(E)													
			(N)(W)		(E)	(W)	(SW)	○	(NW)	(SE)	○				
○		(W)(C)	○		○	(S)(W)		(S)(W)	○		○				
(E)(C)		(NC)													

	North Central						South Central				
	AB	MB	MT	NSD	SK	WY	AL	AR	KY	LA	M
WHITE-FOOTED MICE (continued)											
White-ankled Mouse (*Peromyscus pectoralis*)											
Pinon Mouse (*P. truei*)						(sw)					
Rock Mouse (*P. difficilus*)											
Palo Duro Mouse (*P. comanche*)											
WOODRATS											
Eastern Woodrat (*Neotoma floridana*)				(sw)			◯	◯	◯	◯	◯
Southern Plains Woodrat (*N. micropus*)											
White-throated Woodrat (*N. albigula*)											
Desert Woodrat (*N. lepida*)											
Arizona Woodrat (*N. devia*)											
Stephens' Woodrat (*N. stephensi*)											
Mexican Woodrat (*N. mexicana*)											
Dusky-footed Woodrat (*N. fuscipes*)											
Bushy-tailed Woodrat (*N. cinerea*)	(sw)		◯	(sw)(w)	(sw)	◯					
VOLES											
Northern Red-backed Vole (*Clethrionomys rutilus*)											
Southern Red-backed Vole (*C. gapperi*)	(s)	(s)	◯	◯◯	(s)	◯					
Western Red-backed Vole (*C. occidentalis*)											
Heather Vole (*Phenacomys intermedius*)	◯	◯	(w)		◯	◯					

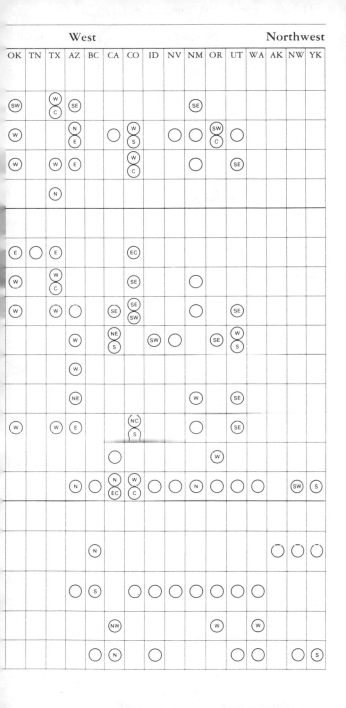

OK	TN	TX	AZ	BC	CA	CO	ID	NV	NM	OR	UT	WA	AK	NW	YK
(SW)		(W)(C)	(SE)						(SE)						
(W)			(N)(E)		○	(W)(S)		○	○	(SW)(C)	○				
(W)		(W)	(E)			(W)(C)			○		(SE)				
		(N)													
(E)	○	(E)				(EC)									
(W)		(W)(C)				(SE)			○						
(W)		(W)	○		(SE)	(SE)(SW)			○		(SE)				
			(W)		(NE)(S)		(SW)	○		(SE)	(W)(S)				
			(W)												
			(NE)						(W)		(SE)				
(W)		(W)	(E)			(NC)(S)			○		(SE)				
					○					(W)					
			(N)	○	(N)(EC)	(W)(C)	○	○	(N)	○	○	○		(SW)	(S)
				(N)									○	○	○
			○	(S)	.	○	○	○	○	○	○	○			
					(NW)					(W)		(W)			
				○	(N)		○				○	○		○	(S)

	North Central						South Central				
	AB	MB	MT	NSD	SK	WY	AL	AR	KY	LA	MS
VOLES (continued)											
White-footed Vole (*Phenacomys albipes*)											
Dusky Tree Vole (*P. silvicola*)											
Red Tree Vole (*P. longicaudus*)											
Meadow Vole (*Microtus pennsylvanicus*)	○	○	○	○	○	E / W			E / C		
Montane Vole (*M. montanus*)			SW			W / C					
California Vole (*M. californicus*)											
Townsend's Vole (*M. townsendii*)											
Tundra Vole (*M. oeconomus*)											
Long-tailed Vole (*M. longicaudus*)	SW		W / C	SW		○					
Coronation Island Vole (*M. coronarius*)											
Mexican Vole (*M. mexicanus*)											
Rock Vole (*M. chrotorrhinus*)											
Yellow-cheeked Vole (*M. xanthognathus*)	N	N			N						
Creeping Vole (*M. oregoni*)											
Singing Vole (*M. gregalis*)											
Insular Vole (*M. abbreviatus*)											
Prairie Vole (*M. ochrogaster*)	SE	SW	E	○	S	E / C			○	SW	
Woodland Vole (*M. pinetorum*)							N / C	○	○	N / C	○
Water Vole (*Arvicola richardsoni*)	SW		W			W					
Sagebrush Vole (*Lagurus curtatus*)	S	SW									

OK	TN	TX	AZ	BC	CA	CO	ID	NV	NM	OR	UT	WA	AK	NW	YK
					NW					W					
										NW					
					NW					W					
	E			○		C	N/E		NW		N	NE	C/S	○	○
			EC	SC	NE	W	○	○	NW	○	○	E/C			
					○					SW					
				SW	NW					W		W			
				NW									○	N	○
			E/NC	○	N/SC	W/C	○	○	W/C	○	○	○	SE	SW	S
				W											
		W	E/WC			SW			W/S		SC				
	F														
				NE									EC	W	N/C
				S	NW					W		W			
				NW									○	W	○
													W		
N	NW/C	SE				E									
E/C	○	NE													
				SE/SW			N			C/E	NC	C/E			
					NE			○		E	○	E			

PICTURE CREDITS

The numbers in parentheses are plate numbers. Some photographers have pictures under agency names as well as their own. Agency names appear in boldface. Photographers hold copyrights to their works.

Ronn Altig (25, 31, 50, 53, 66, 84, 103, 130, 191, 246)

Amwest
Joseph J. Branney (271) Charles G. Summers, Jr. (263)

Animals Animals
Z. Leszczynski (313) Alan G. Nelson (35) Mark Newman (280) John C. Stevenson (205) Stouffer Productions, Ltd. (55, 231, 256, 269)

Ardea Photographics
Ake Lindau (234) Tom Willock (232)

Roger W. Barbour (26, 32, 33, 36, 38, 39, 44, 54, 57, 58, 59, 65, 67, 68, 71, 77, 83, 94, 95, 98, 99, 104, 105, 112, 113, 114, 115, 116, 117, 126, 135, 138, 139, 141, 142, 143, 148, 149, 150, 151, 153, 154, 155, 156, 158, 160, 161, 162, 164, 170, 171, 172, 173, 174)
Erwin A. Bauer (254, 270)
Craig Blacklock (80)
Reagan Bradshaw (196)
Tom Brakefield (88, 124, 201, 209, 224)
Harold E. Broadbooks (13, 108)
Edmund Brodie (42, 64, 72, 75)

Fred Bruemmer (255, 277, 298, 306, 307, 311)
Sonja Bullaty & Angelo Lomeo (194)
James H. Carmichael, Jr. (248)
Stewart Cassidy (219, 284, 289)
Glenn D. Chambers (258, 260)
Herbert Clarke (119)

Bruce Coleman, Inc.
Jen & Des Bartlett (304) Alan Blank (49) Bob & Clara Calhoun (259) Jack Couffer (189) Dr. E. R. Degginger (301) Francisco Erize (233, 236) M. P. L. Fogden (10) J. Markham (73) Hans Reinhard (244, 275) Leonard Lee Rue III (288) Stouffer Productions, Ltd. (181)

Lois & George Cox (198)
Thase Daniel (18, 285)
Kent & Donna Dannen (193, 226)
Dr. E. R. Degginger (9, 37, 43, 268)
Jack Dermid (24)
John Ebeling (220)
John F. Eisenberg/Smithsonian Institution Photographic Services (89, 90, 96)
Harry Engels (241, 291)
William E. Ferguson (40)
Kenneth W. Fink (1, 16, 17, 21, 27, 91, 187, 237, 238, 239, 261, 262, 279, 282, 287)
J. Perley Fitzgerald (20)
Jeffrey Foott (122, 210, 216, 286, 295)
Kathryn Frost (310)
David A. Gill (78, 265)
Gilbert Grant and Patricia Brown (147, 152)
David J. Hafner (12)
Douglas C. Heard (230)
G. C. Kelley (69)
Walter J. Kenner (132)
Stephen J. Krasemann (22, 195, 235, 251, 281, 290, 297)
Thomas H. Kunz (168)
Wayne Lankinen (204)
John R. MacGregor (62, 76, 92, 136, 144, 169 left, 176, 197)
Joe McDonald (48, 60)

Anthony Mercieca (109, 110, 111, 133, 134, 267, 273)
Tom Myers (137)

National Audubon Society Collection/Photo Researchers, Inc.
C. C. Allen/Wildlife Color Photography (14) William Bacon III (206) Cosmos Blank (140) Ken Brate (188, 217) Ed Cesar (211) Stephen Collins (207) Helen Cruickshank (15) Phil A. Dotson (202, 249) Harry Engels (81) Kenneth W. Fink (292, 302) Robert W. Hernandez (299, 300, 303) George Holton (312) Verna R. Johnston (70) G. C. Kelley (28, 294) Russ Kinne (203, 245) Stephen J. Krasemann (184) Calvin Larsen (2, 185) Alexander Lowry (6, 305) Karl H. Maslowski (30, 51, 63, 93, 214, 247) Karl & Stephen Maslowski (41) Tom McHugh (229, 240, 250, 264, 266, 274) Sturgis McKeever (56, 121, 183) Charlie Ott (11, 61, 74, 79, 190) Leonard Lee Rue III (46, 215) James Simon (293, 309) Helen Williams (213) Lovett Williams (221)

Charles F. Peck (85, 87, 100, 101, 102, 107, 118, 120, 125)
Bill Ratcliffe (213)
Len Rue, Jr. (5)
Leonard Lee Rue III (4, 23, 29, 182, 218, 222, 223, 242, 243)
Victor B. Scheffer (52)
Perry Shankle, Jr. (199)
Robert Burr Smith (47, 145 right)

Tom Stack & Associates
Joe Branney (283) John D. Luke (225) C. Summers (208)

Alvin E. Staffan (8, 123, 129, 131, 186, 253, 257)
D. E. Stevenson (165)
Ian Stirling (252, 296)
Lynn M. Stone (278)
Arthur Swoger (127)
William E. Townsend, Jr. (308)

INDEX

Numbers in boldface type refer to color
plates. Numbers in italics refer to pages.
Circles preceding English names of
mammals make it easy for you to keep a
record of the mammals you have seen.

NOTES

NOTES

STAFF

Prepared and produced by
Chanticleer Press, Inc.
Founding Publisher: Paul Steiner
Publisher: Andrew Stewart
Managing Editor: Edie Locke
Art Director: Amanda Wilson
Production: Deirdre Duggan Ventry
Photo Editor: Giema Tsakuginow
Publishing Assistant: Kelly Beekman

Staff for this book:

Editor-in-Chief: Gudrun Buettner
Executive Editor: Susan Costello
Managing Editor: Jane Opper
Guides Editor: Susan Rayfield
Text Editor: Anne Knight
Production: Helga Lose
Art Director: Carol Nehring
Picture Library: Edward Douglas
Maps and Silhouettes: Paul Singer
Drawings: Sy Barlowe
Tracks: Dot Barlowe
Series Design: Massimo Vignelli

All editorial inquiries should be
addressed to:
Chanticleer Press
568 Broadway, Suite #1005A
New York, NY 10012
(212) 941-1522

To purchase this book, or other
National Audubon Society illustrated
nature books, please contact:
Alfred A. Knopf
201 East 50th Street
New York, NY 10022
(800) 733-3000

NATIONAL AUDUBON SOCIETY FIELD GUIDE SERIES

Also available in this unique all-color, all-photographic format:

Birds *(Eastern Region)*

Birds *(Western Region)*

Butterflies

Fishes, Whales, and Dolphins

Fossils

Insects and Spiders

Mushrooms

Night Sky

Reptiles and Amphibians

Rocks and Minerals

Seashells

Seashore Creatures

Trees *(Eastern Region)*

Trees *(Western Region)*

Weather

Wildflowers *(Eastern Region)*

Wildflowers *(Western Region)*